More Advance Praise for *Bind Us Apart*

"Nicholas Guyatt brilliantly captures the tragically unintended consequences of liberal reformers' efforts to create a just and enlightened multiracial society in the new United States. Dedication to the principles of the Declaration of Independence ultimately led reformers to embrace both the colonization of former slaves and the removal of Native Americans. Sympathetically engaging with his well-intentioned subjects, Guyatt compels us to engage with what it has meant—and still means—to be American. Powerfully argued and beautifully written, *Bind Us Apart* is essential reading."

—Peter S. Onuf, author of *Jefferson's Empire:*
The Language of American Nationhood

"Connecting Indian removal and the African colonization movement to early US liberalism, Nicholas Guyatt offers a new origins story for American segregation. Brilliant and engrossing, *Bind Us Apart* reinterprets a formative era, while identifying legacies that continue to shape the present."

—Christina Snyder, author of *Slavery in Indian Country:*
The Changing Face of Captivity in Early America

"In colorful and lively prose, Nicholas Guyatt recovers the history of white Americans who agonized over slavery and the treatment of Native Americans. Some were famous presidents and generals; others were obscure figures. Almost all rejected the nation's founding credo of 'all men are created equal' to promote racial separation instead. A fascinating and little known history."

—Margaret Jacobs, author of *White Mother to a Dark Race*

BIND US
APART

How Enlightened Americans
Invented Racial Segregation

Nicholas Guyatt

BASIC BOOKS
A MEMBER OF THE PERSEUS BOOKS GROUP
NEW YORK

Books published by Basic Books are available at special discounts for bulk purchases in the United States by corporations, institutions, and other organizations. For more information, please contact the Special Markets Department at the Perseus Books Group, 2300 Chestnut Street, Suite 200, Philadelphia, PA 19103, or call (800) 810-4145, ext. 5000, or e-mail special.markets@perseus books.com.

Designed by Jack Lenzo

Library of Congress Cataloging-in-Publication Data
Names: Guyatt, Nicholas, 1973–
Title: Bind us apart : how enlightened Americans invented racial
   segregation / Nicholas Guyatt.
Description: New York, NY : Basic Books, 2016. | Includes bibliographical
   references and index.
Identifiers: LCCN 2015041451 (print) | LCCN 2015045766 (ebook) | ISBN
   9780465018413 (hardback) | ISBN 9780465065615 (ebook)
Subjects: LCSH: Racism—United States—History. | United States—Race
   relations—History—18th century. | United States—Race
   relations—History—19th century. | Indians of North
   America—Colonization—United States. | African
   Americans—Colonization—Africa. | BISAC: HISTORY / United States / 19th
   Century.
Classification: LCC E184.A1 G985 2016 (print) | LCC E184.A1 (ebook) | DDC
   305.800973—dc23
LC record available at http://lccn.loc.gov/2015041451

10 9 8 7 6 5 4 3 2 1

For Tess, Sid, and Kate

When you are persecuted in one city, flee unto another.

—Edward Coles, "Notes on Slavery"
(after Matthew 10:23)

We often congratulate ourselves more on getting rid of a problem than on solving it.

—W. E. B. Du Bois, *The Suppression of the African Slave Trade*

Contents

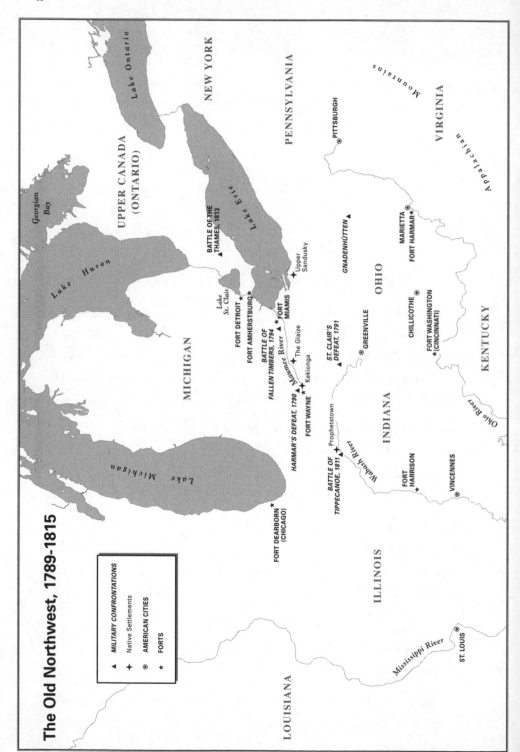

The Old Northwest, 1789-1815

MILITARY CONFRONTATIONS

▲ Native Settlements

⊛ AMERICAN CITIES

★ FORTS

Georgian Bay

Lake Huron

Lake Michigan

Lake Ontario

Lake Erie

NEW YORK

PENNSYLVANIA

⊛ PITTSBURGH

UPPER CANADA (ONTARIO)

Appalachian Mountains

VIRGINIA

MICHIGAN

Lake St. Clair

BATTLE OF THE THAMES, 1813 ▲

FORT DETROIT ★

FORT AMHERSTBURG ★

★ FORT MIAMIS

✛ Upper Sandusky

BATTLE OF FALLEN TIMBERS, 1794

Maumee River

The Glaize

GNADENHÜTTEN ▲

OHIO

MARIETTA ⊛
FORT HARMAR ★

HARMAR'S DEFEAT, 1790 ▲
Kekionga

FORT WAYNE ★

ST. CLAIR'S DEFEAT, 1791 ▲

⊛ GREENVILLE
GREENVILLE

CHILLICOTHE ⊛

FORT WASHINGTON ★ (CINCINNATI)

KENTUCKY

INDIANA

Prophetstown

BATTLE OF TIPPECANOE, 1811 ▲

Wabash River

FORT HARRISON ★

VINCENNES ⊛

Ohio River

FORT DEARBORN ★ (CHICAGO)

ILLINOIS

LOUISIANA

Mississippi River

ST. LOUIS ⊛

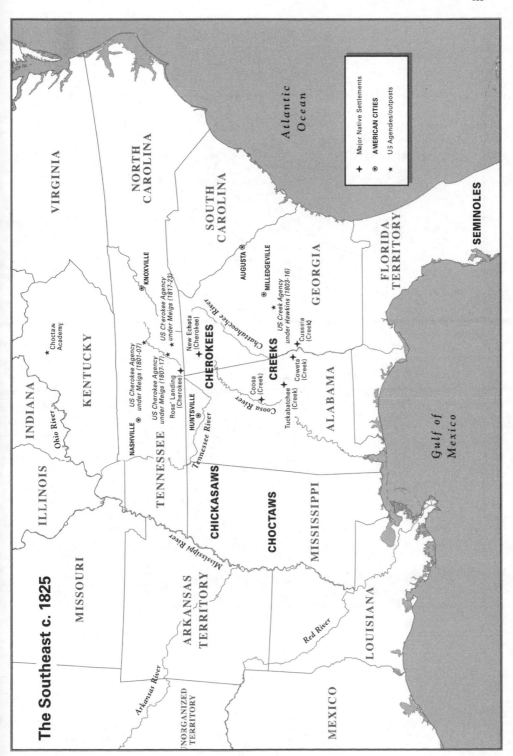

The Southeast c. 1825

Legend:
- Major Native Settlements
- AMERICAN CITIES
- US Agencies/outposts

Atlantic Ocean

Gulf of Mexico

VIRGINIA

NORTH CAROLINA

SOUTH CAROLINA

GEORGIA

FLORIDA TERRITORY

SEMINOLES

KENTUCKY

TENNESSEE

ALABAMA

MISSISSIPPI

LOUISIANA

MEXICO

ARKANSAS TERRITORY

MISSOURI

ILLINOIS

INDIANA

UNORGANIZED TERRITORY

CHEROKEES

CREEKS

CHICKASAWS

CHOCTAWS

KNOXVILLE

AUGUSTA

MILLEDGEVILLE

NASHVILLE

HUNTSVILLE

Choctaw Academy

US Cherokee Agency under Meigs (1801-07)

US Cherokee Agency under Meigs (1807-17)

US Cherokee Agency under Meigs (1817-23)

New Echota (Cherokee)

Ross' Landing (Cherokee)

US Creek Agency under Hawkins (1803-16)

Cussata (Creek)

Coweta (Creek)

Coosa (Creek)

Tuckabatchee (Creek)

Ohio River

Mississippi River

Tennessee River

Chattahoochee River

Coosa River

Arkansas River

Red River

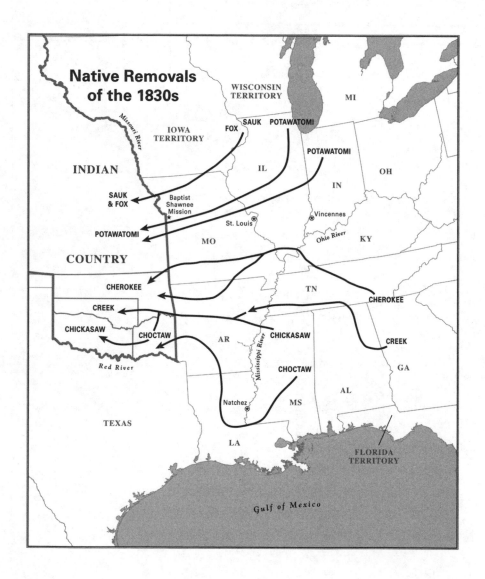

INTRODUCTION
THE PREHISTORY OF "SEPARATE BUT EQUAL"

E DWARD COLES HAD A LOT on his mind. In July 1814 he was private secretary to James Madison and spent his days managing the president's business at a time of war. The United States had been fighting Britain and its Native American allies for nearly three years. Coles and Madison would be forced to flee the White House just a few weeks later, when British troops invaded and razed Washington. Coles still made time during that anxious month to write to Thomas Jefferson about the nation's founding dilemma. "I never took up my pen with more hesitation, or felt more embarrassment than I now do in addressing you on the subject of this letter," wrote Coles. But given the leisure now afforded by his well-deserved retirement, might Jefferson be able to devise "some plan for the gradual emancipation of slavery?"[1]

Coles was twenty-seven years old. He came from a wealthy Virginia family, and had inherited twenty slaves from his father in 1808. The year before, as a student at the College of William and Mary, he had decided that he "would not and could not hold my fellow man as a slave." The insight came to him in class one day, when he was listening to the president of the college "lecturing and explaining the rights of man." Coles asked his professor ("in the simplicity of youth") how it was possible to reconcile human rights and the equality of mankind with slaveholding. "I can never forget his peculiarly embarrassed manner," Coles later recalled. "He frankly admitted it could not rightfully be done, and that slavery was a state of things that could not be

1

justified on principle." The only excuse for failing to end slavery was "the difficulty of getting rid of it," his professor suggested. Coles continued to harass him when the class was over, insisting that the practical problems of emancipation were no excuse for apathy or inaction. In 1814, he was making the same point to Thomas Jefferson.[2]

Jefferson had been retired for five years at Monticello. He spent his days reading, entertaining, and corresponding with an extraordinary range of people. Sally Hemings, with whom he had been in a sexual relationship for more than a quarter of a century, was living in the servants' quarters in the south wing. Four of Hemings's six children had survived past infancy and were still on the mountain. (All enslaved, like their mother.) Jefferson was sixty-seven years old. He had criticized the institution of slavery since his time in the Virginia governor's mansion in the 1770s, and as president of the United States he'd signed the bill that ended American participation in the international slave trade. And yet the nation's slave population was still creeping upward. Edward Coles badgered anyone who would listen on this topic. When he and James Madison strolled through the nation's capital and encountered "gangs of negroes, some in irons," Coles upbraided the president for doing nothing to secure "the rights of man." But Coles felt that Jefferson had a special responsibility to lead the nation's struggle against slavery. He was, after all, the "immortal author" of "all men are created equal," the nation's founding creed. The time had arrived "to put into complete practice those hallowed principles contained in that renowned Declaration."[3]

In his reply, Jefferson conceded that "the love of justice and the love of country plead equally the cause of these people." But what would happen to them (and their white neighbors) if slaves were suddenly set free? For decades, Jefferson's anxieties about integration had weakened his antislavery convictions. Coles had his own solution: he would take his freed slaves to the western states and forge a new life with them there. Jefferson was alarmed by this plan to "abandon" them in the midst of white people. He urged a different solution: slaves should be freed gradually and on condition that they leave the United

States. Coles should temper his radicalism until he found a way to reconcile "all men are created equal" with the need for racial separation. The former president would offer his best hopes to this effort, but no more. "I have overlived the generation with which mutual labors and perils begat mutual confidence and influence." Antislavery, Jefferson declared, was an "enterprise for the young."[4]

Coles was unimpressed. He wrote again, rejecting Jefferson's view that "the difficult work of cleansing the escutcheon of Virginia" should fall solely upon young men like himself. Elder statesmen were, in fact, "the only persons who have it in their power effectually to arouse and enlighten the public sentiment." Hadn't Benjamin Franklin become a convert to emancipation "after he had passed your age?" Coles dismissed Jefferson's suggestion that his slaves would benefit more from a kindly master than from a liberator, or that their survival depended upon their exile from the United States. When he had completed his work for Madison, he vowed, he would take his slaves out of Virginia, free them, and live alongside them in "the country northwest of the River Ohio." That letter went into a drawer at Monticello and remained unanswered. It would be another five years before the impetuous Edward Coles made good on his promise.[5]

WHILE COLES MAY HAVE BEEN an outlier, his correspondence with Jefferson reveals a broader truth about the evolution of slavery in America. Even slaveholders were aware of a contradiction between the nation's founding principles and the practice of holding human beings in bondage. Abolition, the most obvious way to resolve that contradiction, would convert slaves into citizens at a stroke. But the vast majority of white Americans were nervous about what freed people might do next. Slavery had denied African Americans an education and an opportunity to better themselves, and it had given them ample reason to resent the people who had benefited from their bondage. These anxieties crowded the minds of slaveholders and reformers alike and encouraged a third way of thinking: if slavery was immoral and multiracial citizenship was beset with difficulties, perhaps black people could be freed and resettled away from whites. This plan was usually known as "colonization," and Jefferson was one of the first people in North America to endorse it. In the decades between the Revolution and the Civil War, the idea that the races might be separated became a mainstay of the movement against slavery in North and South alike. It was promoted by reformers across the country, but was especially popular in the northern states. St. George Tucker, perhaps the most influential legal mind in the South, wrote a long colonization proposal in 1796 and presented it to the Virginia assembly. In 1816, a group of politicians, clergymen, and antislavery activists from across the United States founded the American Colonization Society (ACS), a charity to encourage the resettlement of African Americans in West Africa. In 1821, the society founded its own settlement, Liberia, with the support of President James Monroe. In 1833, James Madison, the last of the Founding Fathers, assumed the presidency of the ACS. Racial separation had become the most popular means of imagining a world after slavery.

Its appeal hardly faded in the decades before the Civil War, even as the slave population climbed inexorably. Henry Clay of Kentucky, perhaps the most influential nineteenth-century politician never to occupy the White House, succeeded James Madison to the presidency of the Colonization Society instead. Daniel Webster, the great Massachusetts statesman who had helped to found the ACS in 1816, lobbied for federal assistance to the society in the 1850s. Harriet Beecher Stowe, in the final pages of *Uncle Tom's Cabin*, dispatched her hero George Harris to Liberia. And Abraham Lincoln, in the first years of his presidency, did more to secure government support for black emigration than any politician since James Monroe. When he addressed a group of free blacks in Washington in the summer of 1862, with the war's outcome uncertain, Lincoln insisted that they had a duty to leave the country and build a separate nation for African Americans. "You may believe you can live in Washington or elsewhere in the

United States," he told them. "This is (I speak in no unkind sense) an extremely selfish view of the case."[6]

If so many of the most iconic figures in American life before 1865 were committed to the idea of colonization, why has it played such a muted role in our stories of slavery, abolition, and citizenship? For many historians, the idea that the entire black population of the United States could be resettled beyond the nation's borders seems outlandish. Between the American Revolution and the Civil War, perhaps 20,000 African Americans left for Africa or the Caribbean. The black population remaining in America increased across the same period by around 3.5 million. Given the negligible number of black emigrants before 1863, and the transcendent achievement of the Emancipation Proclamation and the Thirteenth Amendment, historians have often consigned colonization to a footnote in America's struggle against slavery.

In fact, racial separation served as a rallying point for slavery's opponents for more than seventy years, from the publication of Jefferson's *Notes on the State of Virginia* in 1785 to the first years of the Civil War—perhaps even later. For much of the nineteenth century, the most respectable way to express one's loathing for slavery was to endorse the logic of colonization. Free blacks came to see this logic as the biggest threat to their future in the United States. In 1829, the Boston-based writer David Walker, in his *Appeal to the Colored Citizens of the World*, warned his fellow blacks to resist the "colonizing trick" and stand firm against the offer to relocate to Africa. "This country is as much ours as it is the whites'," he wrote. "Whether they will admit it now or not, they will see and believe it by and by." Although Walker's ideas broke through to a small group of white radicals—most notably to the Boston reformer William Lloyd Garrison, who had previously supported the Colonization Society—the mainstream of public opinion in both the North and the Upper South remained firmly committed to colonization. The radical abolitionists who clustered around Garrison and his newspaper, *The Liberator*, were a tiny minority in the three decades before the Civil War. Most critics of slavery believed that the only way to break its grip on America was to move black people somewhere else.[7]

THE STORY OF BLACK COLONIZATION has played a peripheral role in our understanding of the struggle against slavery. It has almost never featured in our analysis of another pivotal episode in nineteenth-century American history: the removal of Native Americans. In the earliest years of the republic, successive presidents committed themselves to a policy of "civilizing" the Indian nations living east of the Mississippi River. Federal officials, missionaries, and reformers promoted the idea that Native Americans could be incorporated into the United States: white settlers on the frontier would live alongside Indians and eventually intermarry with them, producing a single people in the West. After the War of 1812, and the suppression of a massive Native uprising led by the Shawnee warrior Tecumseh, the rhetoric of politicians and reformers changed. The anticipated marriage (figurative and literal) between Indians and white settlers had failed to materialize. As western settlers continued to disrupt Native communities with alcohol, land seizures, and violence, eastern reformers concluded that the original "civilizing" model was doing more harm than good. In 1824, President James Monroe told Congress that Indian nations should move west of the Mississippi, where the federal government might more easily manage their journey toward "civilization." The same policy was adopted by the administration of John Quincy Adams in 1826 and enthusiastically endorsed by Andrew Jackson through the passage of the Removal Act of 1830.

The parallels between black colonization and Indian removal are striking. Both came to dominate the national conversation in the two decades following the War of 1812. Both were premised on the idea that contact between non-whites and whites tended to "degrade" the former, preventing them from achieving their natural potential and making equal citizenship all but impossible. Both promised a happier future for non-whites beyond the borders of the United States in self-governing and prosperous offshoots of the American republic. Crucially, both were couched in terms of benevolence. Missionaries and religious reformers took the lead, anchoring their good intentions with a simple promise: colonization should be voluntary. When African Americans and Native Americans expressed wariness or outright opposition, the white architects of colonization insisted that blacks and Indians would eventually realize the benefits of resettlement and willingly leave the United States.

Most high school history students know that things didn't turn out this way. Andrew Jackson was so determined to remove Native peoples from the southeastern states that he abandoned the pretense of consent, exchanging colonization for expulsion. The Trail of Tears in 1838–1839, when thousands of Cherokees were forcibly marched by the US Army across a thousand miles to Oklahoma, has become our most enduring image of Indian removal. But this profoundly illiberal outcome took root in the same soil that had nourished black colonization: the insistence that racial segregation was a benevolent and far-sighted measure that would allow non-white people to thrive. If we place these efforts to resettle black people and Indians in a single frame, an unsettling but inescapable truth emerges. White reformers, politicians, and churchmen believed that non-whites could only realize their innate potential as human beings—and perhaps even their equality with whites—by separating themselves from the American republic.

In accounting for these removal initiatives, it's tempting to conclude that the early United States was a blindly racist society, worlds apart from the refined morality of today. This is, I think, a mistaken assumption. One of the arguments of this book is that educated Americans in the early republic found it far harder to be outright racists than we usually imagine. When they consulted the authorities of scripture or science, early Americans couldn't easily conclude that non-white people were different from or permanently inferior to themselves. Colonization proposals were crafted by intellectuals, reformers, and politicians—men (and occasionally women) who saw themselves as "liberal" in their sentiments. To be liberal in the early United States involved specific beliefs and actions: it meant that you embraced the rational thought of the Enlightenment, that you manifested a Christian benevolence to others, and, most importantly, that you were determined to reject the temptations of "prejudice." With few exceptions, the architects of racial separation in the early republic emphatically denied that blacks or Indians were permanently inferior to whites. Instead, they spoke of their duty to help non-white people complete their journey toward "civilized" status.[8]

Liberal whites in the early United States faced two distinct challenges that set them apart from European reformers. First, the American republic encompassed very large numbers of non-white people. In the 1780s, when reformers William Wilberforce and Thomas Clarkson launched their celebrated assault on slavery in the British Empire, they could promote abolition without owning its social consequences. The British sugar islands of the Caribbean were overwhelmingly populated by black slaves who were ruled by a tiny white minority. Emancipation there would produce a black society, and would likely displace the tiny knot of white planters who had ruled those islands with the lash. In the United States, the demography of slavery was very different. In 1800, black people made up just a fraction of the population in New England, and were a small but significant minority in New York and Pennsylvania. But in Virginia, home to the greatest number of slaves in the Union from the Revolution to the Civil War, blacks were nearly 40 percent of the total population. Farther south, the Lowcountry of South Carolina and Georgia had a black majority, and looked more like the Caribbean than New England. When we factor in the significant numbers of Native Americans who lived east of the Mississippi—perhaps 200,000 at the opening of the nineteenth century, with twice that number living in areas that would later become part of the United States—we can see that the challenge of integrating non-white people in the American republic was enormous. The abolition of slavery and the extension of "civilization" to Native American nations would create a genuinely multiracial republic. Reformers would need to acknowledge this reality as they plotted their strategies for freeing slaves or incorporating Indians.[9]

The second challenge was more abstract, but no less profound. In 1776, the United States declared independence from Britain with a devastatingly simple phrase: "All men are created equal." While Thomas Jefferson may not have originally intended those words to encompass non-white people, they had leaked into the struggle for black and Indian rights long before Edward Coles threw them at their author in 1814. In Massachusetts, enslaved people drew upon the state constitution's claim that "all men are born free and equal" to demand their freedom. The state's judges found in their favor in 1783, and slavery in Massachusetts was outlawed. Over the following decades, anti-slavery societies founded by black and white activists employed the Declaration's most sonorous line relentlessly. "That a people who have declared 'that all men are by nature equally free and independent,'" wrote the Virginia judge St. George Tucker in 1796, "should in defiance of so sacred a truth . . . tolerate a practice incompatible therewith, is such an evidence of the weakness and inconsistency of human nature, as every man who hath a spark of patriotic fire in his bosom must wish to see removed from his own country." While the Spanish and the British had organized their colonial possessions around hierarchies of wealth or title, the new United States had declared itself a horizontal society. But this meant that the end of slavery or the incorporation of Native Americans would commit the new republic to becoming something without precedent in the modern world: a multiracial society dedicated to equal rights and potential.[10]

THIS IS THE STORY OF how "liberal" whites—men and women who thought themselves enlightened and benevolent—struggled to realize this multiracial society in the formative decades of the United States. It takes seriously the idea that blacks and Indians claimed a share in the Declaration of Independence, and it traces the efforts of white reformers to end slavery and incorporate Native Americans. The first part of the book examines early attempts to free slaves and "civilize" Indians alongside the nation's expanding white population. The second explains why white Americans found it so hard to accept interracial marriage, an outcome that seemed like the logical extension of "all men are created equal," but which became anathema to even radical reformers. The third part presents colonization as a compromise that became a life raft for liberal whites, who were caught between the unambiguous promises of 1776 and the practical difficulties of creating a mixed-race republic. To say that racial separation was a racist idea is to misunderstand its allure: in the soaring rhetoric of its (mostly) white proponents, colonization would allow the races to become "separate but equal."

That phrase first entered the American lexicon decades later in the nation's history, during the Supreme Court's deliberations over *Plessy v. Ferguson* in 1893. The case was a test of the segregationist Jim Crow laws that had swept through southern legislatures after the collapse of Reconstruction in 1877. The Court, by a majority of 7 to 1, decided that segregated washrooms, railroad cars, or lunch counters were constitutional, provided that they were of comparable quality. We usually see "separate but equal" as the capstone of a white southern counterrevolution: The Supreme Court had given a green light to white racists to invalidate the black political gains of the Reconstruction period, and had capsized the egalitarian efforts of Abraham Lincoln and the Radical Republicans of the 1860s. This book argues instead that "separate but equal" lies at the heart of American history. It was a mental and political compromise forged in the era of the Founding Fathers, and applied to Native Americans as well as to black people a century before the cynical reasoning of the *Plessy* decision.

If the essential principle of colonization—that African Americans and Native Americans should leave the United States—seems unambiguously racist to our eyes, is there anything to be gained by studying its rhetoric of benevolence and equality? Absolutely, for three reasons. First, the fact that the proponents of colonization imagined that they were *not* racists was fundamental to their belief that blacks and Indians could be settled elsewhere. Liberal whites consoled themselves that colonization would not damage the founding ideals of the United States, and might even help to secure them. This belief persisted despite the widespread refusal of blacks and Indians to consent to their own removal. Modern commentators, especially those who defend the Founding Fathers on the issues of slaveholding or Indian removal, often remark that it's bad history to apply the morals of the present to a different time. While that is generally good advice, it should not deter us from recognizing that, on the question of race, early Americans juggled moral and political challenges that are disconcertingly familiar to us.

Second, the rhetoric of "separate but equal" helps to explain why the antislavery struggle produced such a limited commitment among whites to genuine equality for African Americans. We sometimes imagine the struggle against slavery as a gradual expansion of abolitionist sentiment, as if the ideas of William Lloyd Garrison and *The Liberator* metastasized into the Emancipation Proclamation and the Thirteenth Amendment. In fact, colonization enabled "moderate" opponents of slavery to denounce human bondage without accepting black citizenship, to believe that they were upholding their principles while denying non-whites a place in the expanding republic. That Liberia recruited only a tiny minority of African Americans or that Lincoln ultimately embraced emancipation without colonization are beside the point: generations of white reformers in the early United States had detached the cause of antislavery from a commitment to accept black people as citizens, neighbors, family. When the circumstances of the Civil War made emancipation all but inevitable, 4 million freed slaves entered a republic that had spent decades imagining that they would end up somewhere else. Colonization had a profound effect on the long exile of blacks and Indians from "all men are created equal."

Third, it's important that we recognize that, alongside its episodes of vicious and open racism, the nation has always incubated a form of racial "improvement" that sees space as a solution to the problem of race. Segregation was never limited to the South, and it took such a firm grip there after the Civil War only because so many African Americans lived below the Mason-Dixon Line. The United States bears the scars of its segregated past, of course. It also retains an instinct for racial separation that manifests itself even among those who forswear racist beliefs. You can see it in the beating or killing of African Americans who end up in the "wrong" neighborhood, or in the chronic problem of housing discrimination in major cities, or in the struggles against poverty facing Native and African American communities across the country. Our segregated present isn't solely the legacy of a regional racism that gripped the South after the Civil War. Racial separation was a national preoccupation in the nation's first decades, and it was presented as impeccably liberal in its intentions and effects. If we are ever to unravel the legacy of this thinking, we have to start by acknowledging its origins and its attractiveness to people who imagined themselves to be both enlightened and benevolent. We have, in other words, to take "separate but equal" for what it was: a founding principle of the United States.

THE TITLE OF THIS BOOK comes from Nina Simone's song "I Wish I Knew How It Would Feel to Be Free"; or, to be more precise, a performance of the song she gave in Montreux, Switzerland, in 1976. Simone had spent the previous two years living in Monrovia, the capital of Liberia, a place she had found exhilarating and bewildering in equal measure. Her appearance in Montreux was a comeback after years of relative obscurity. In the middle of her set, she sat at the piano and performed the song she had famously recorded in 1967. "I wish I could share all the love that's in my heart," goes the original version. "Remove all the bars that keep us apart." That night in Switzerland, she wished instead to "break all the things that bind us apart." She finished the line with a stabbing chord in the right hand, and the song climbed toward its ecstatic conclusion.

"Bind us apart" stayed with me as I wrote this book because it seemed to encapsulate the contradiction driving my subjects. The proponents of colonization frequently recognized black and Indian humanity and potential, envisaging a moment at which non-whites could emulate the political achievement of the United States. But they directed Native Americans and African Americans to vindicate their freedom somewhere else. Black and Indian colonies were attempts at what we would now call "ethnic cleansing," and yet they promised that non-whites could resemble white people more closely by being removed from their midst. An Indian state might emerge in the West, mirroring the established states of the Union. Liberia might spread "civilization" into the interior and produce a United States of Africa, a facsimile of the American republic. These powerful visions had a formative influence on the social and political landscape, from the Founding Fathers through Abraham Lincoln and beyond. And yet we haven't properly acknowledged their origins, development, and persistence in American history. By doing so, we can better understand not only the histories of slavery and dispossession that link whites, Native Americans, and African Americans, but the reasons why racial justice in the United States has remained such an elusive goal.

PART I
DEGRADATION

ONE

BECOMING GOOD CITIZENS

IN THE LAST DECADE OF the eighteenth century, Virginia was home to around 300,000 slaves: a third of the total number in the United States. What would happen if they were set free? A number of Virginians had raised this question—including, most famously, Thomas Jefferson—but in 1795 one resolved to answer it with a concrete plan for emancipation. St. George Tucker was a slaveholder and one of the state's most prominent judges, but he was also an outsider. He had been born and raised in Bermuda, more than eight hundred miles north of the harsh plantation slavery of the West Indies, and had acquired his slaves through marriage. Tucker thought slavery a curse upon the state and the nation: it made a nonsense of the Declaration of Independence, and it brought the danger of a mass rebellion that might overwhelm the South. Like many Americans, Tucker had been watching the bloody slave uprising in the French Caribbean colony of Saint-Domingue, which would culminate in the death or expulsion of slaveholders and the establishment of the world's first independent black republic, Haiti. Tucker was careful not to embarrass his white neighbors: slavery was an unfortunate condition which Virginians "could no more have avoided, than an hereditary gout or leprosy." The state had taken its first steps toward abolition back in 1778, when the legislature had banned the importation of slaves from overseas. Tucker wanted to go further. Although he had never been to

17

New England, he knew that slavery had been abolished there. So he wrote to a friend of a friend in Boston with a series of questions. Had black people been happily integrated after slavery? Were they hard working and intellectually curious? All things being equal, was emancipation a success?[1]

The recipient of Tucker's letter was Jeremy Belknap, a Congregationalist minister from Boston. Belknap knew everyone: he wrote for magazines, supported numerous charities, and founded the Massachusetts Historical Society in 1791. His views on slavery were typical of his class and moment. He had been a strong supporter of abolition in Massachusetts, citing the language of the Declaration of Independence. He deplored the tendency of unscrupulous slave traders to prey upon Boston's free black population, and in 1788 he organized a petition in support of the local free black community as it protested the kidnapping of free blacks by Caribbean slave traders. (The state responded by outlawing the practice, and three men who had been taken from Boston to the Swedish island of St. Barts were restored to the city.) Belknap knew Prince Hall, the free black artisan who had founded North America's first black Masonic Lodge in 1784, and he was publicly upbeat about black ability. In private, though, he was snobbish and condescending about free blacks—and about the enthusiasm for liberty that prevailed among the poorer residents of Boston, regardless of race.[2]

For Belknap, an ardent nationalist, even a worthy cause such as antislavery could not be allowed to threaten American unity. When Benjamin Franklin and the Pennsylvania Abolition Society (PAS) petitioned the House of Representatives for immediate abolition in 1790, Belknap bemoaned the "contemptible politicians" among the PAS leadership who threatened the delicate compromises that had brought the federal government into existence. What if South Carolina were to say "we will keep our slaves, and you may keep your Quakers? What a contemptible figure will America make in the eyes of the world!" If abolition were to make headway in the South, it would require men like St. George Tucker to domesticate the idea. Belknap was delighted, then, to help his new friend. He prepared copies of Tucker's questions and sent them to forty of his associates, including James Sullivan, the attorney general of Massachusetts; Prince Hall; and John Adams, who was enduring the final months of his unhappy vice-presidency in Philadelphia.[3]

The responses were revealingly inconsistent. Some of Belknap's friends assumed that blacks couldn't vote or hold office in Massachusetts; others insisted that they did both. Most respondents thought abolition a success, though a few wondered if a more gradual transition would have provided slaves with a better foundation for freedom. Two points of consensus among Belknap's circle revealed the paradox at the heart of emancipation: nearly everyone accepted that abolition was an inevitable consequence of the Declaration of Independence, and nearly everyone agreed that abolition had failed to level the playing field for blacks and whites.

The problem seemed to stem from the experience of slavery itself. To be enslaved was to suffer an assault on one's morals and outlook. John Eliot, another Boston clergyman, told Belknap that while free-born blacks were just as capable as whites, those who had been enslaved and denied an education displayed a "palpable difference" in their morals. This difference was entirely the product of "habits of life"—the travails of slavery—rather than of race. Unquestionably, though, it had strengthened prejudices among whites toward black people generally. "There is here a great number of worthy good men and good citizens that are not ashamed to take an African by the hand," reported Prince Hall, the black Mason. "But yet there are to be seen the weeds of pride, envy, tyranny, and scorn, in this garden of peace, liberty and equality."[4]

In his report to Tucker, Belknap wondered whether blacks had been so "oppressed with poverty and its attendant miseries" since emancipation that they might have been better off had they remained slaves. He wouldn't attribute their problems to race, noting that there was no difference in "general, moral, or social conduct" between Boston's free black population and poorer whites with the same levels of education. He praised the hundreds of free blacks who had volunteered in 1786 to help put down Shays' Rebellion in western Massachusetts. But the findings of his survey suggested that emancipation had not produced social harmony between races. Even if blacks were entitled to the promises of the Declaration of Independence, and race offered no grounds for discrimination, the abolition of slavery would not in itself create an equal society. Tucker thanked Belknap for his help and acknowledged his cautious conclusions. Some of his neighbors in Virginia had already assured him that slavery was "infinitely preferable to that degraded freedom [blacks] would enjoy, if emancipated."[5]

To Belknap's surprise, Tucker didn't see the survey as an excuse to mothball his plans for emancipation. Instead, the Virginian marked out three alternatives to slavery, all deeply problematic in their own way. First, slaves could be freed on condition that they be exiled beyond the Mississippi River, an option that Thomas Jefferson had floated in his *Notes on the State of Virginia*. This would be expensive, probably impractical, and possibly cruel: "If humanity plead for their emancipation," Tucker suggested, "it pleads more strongly against colonization." Second, they could be freed but denied civil and political rights. This would take care of slavery, but would make blacks reluctant to work, perhaps even restive. If freed blacks saw second-class citizenship as a reason to "procure by force what you have refused to grant them," white Virginians would gain little release from the anxieties that haunted the slave system. Finally, slaves might be freed and given the same rights as white people, regardless of the ways in which slavery had "depraved their faculties," and despite the preponderance of "prejudices too deeply rooted to be eradicated" among white Virginians. The race war that was currently raging in Saint-Domingue made Tucker especially wary of this third path. But it was hard to hedge moral imperatives, or to rank the perils of emancipation against the dangers of doing nothing. Sometimes, Tucker confessed to Belknap, he felt "prompted to exclaim, *Fiat Justitia ruat coelum*." Let justice be done, though the heavens fall.[6]

When Belknap circulated Tucker's reply to his Massachusetts friends, their eyes caught on that alarming phrase. John Adams challenged Tucker's premise directly: "What is justice? Justice to the negroes would require that they should not be abandoned by their masters and turned loose upon a world in which they have no capacity to procure even a subsistence." Slavery had stripped blacks of skills and industry, perhaps even of virtue: if they were to be emancipated, this should happen gradually, for their sake as much as for the good of society in general. The Massachusetts attorney general, James Sullivan, had a similar reaction. Belknap handed him Tucker's letter at dinner one night, and Sullivan promised to write a few lines in response at work. The next day, as his clerks and clients buzzed around him, Sullivan wrestled furiously with Tucker's problem. "All the morning surrounded by people on business," Sullivan wrote, "I have kept the pen in motion." Sullivan noted Tucker's anguish and suggested that the Virginian's sensitivity "in some degree atones for the violation of human rights which his fellow citizens have been guilty of." But could the black population be freed? Sullivan believed slavery had always corrupted its victims. Even the Israelites had been prone to "rebellions and insurrections" on their way to Canaan; their defiance of God's word—the result of slavery's corroding effects on human virtue—meant "that it was necessary to waste them all in the wilderness." Sullivan had a better idea: slave children should be educated at the public expense. The only way to eliminate white prejudice was "by raising the blacks, by means of mental improvements, nearly to the same grade with the whites." This was not a short-term fix; it would take decades, though eventually it would fit both blacks and whites for equal citizenship. In the meantime, while Tucker enjoyed the admiration of New England's most distinguished citizens, Sullivan was clear on what should happen next: in his abolitionist thinking, St. George Tucker should "make haste slowly."[7]

BANISHING BLACKS FROM THE DECLARATION of Independence was an awkward maneuver for educated Americans in the early republic. Science and religion offered little support for the idea of a permanent racial hierarchy. Instead, the most influential thinkers of the Enlightenment era emphasized that appearance and achievement were conditioned by one's surroundings and experiences. This was the settled view of the Comte de Buffon, perhaps the most important naturalist before Charles Darwin. Between 1748 and his death in 1793, Buffon published dozens of volumes of his *Natural History*, a massive work that attempted to describe and explain virtually everything: geology, mineralogy, plants, birds, horses, the weather, and, in the midst of all this, human beings. Buffon believed that differences in human skin color, facial features, and behavior were circumstantial rather than innate. Humanity had a common origin. People looked or behaved differently from each other solely because of their social and physical environment.[8]

Buffon isolated three factors as the cause of physical and behavioral differences: climate, diet, and what he called the "manner of living." Peoples with darker skin lived in warmer climates; the features of European women were more attractive than the features of, say, aboriginal or Native American women because Europeans had the benefits of a better climate and more advanced civilization. "Race" was not an essential category but a consequence of experience. If a group of Europeans reverted to the life of primitive hunters, Buffon suggested, they would soon begin to resemble those "savage" peoples who populated the frontiers of the empire. To test this hypothesis, Buffon suggested a simple experiment: a group of people from Senegal should swap places with a group from Denmark. Within a few generations, he predicted, the appearance and habits of the two groups would become perfectly inverted.[9]

To say that Buffon rejected the idea of racial hierarchies—or that he doubted the utility of "race" more generally—is not to say that his thinking was free from cultural superiority. Buffon clearly believed that the best civilizations, as well as the most handsome men and

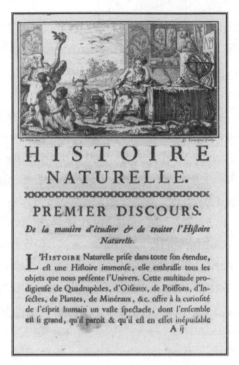

Buffon's enormous *Natural History* (1749) offered the most influential account of human physical difference in the eighteenth century. COURTESY OF THE LIBRARY OF CONGRESS.

women, were European. But he didn't think that there was anything special about the human beings who currently lived in Europe, beyond their good fortune in being born in this optimal environment. People born in other parts of the world could achieve precisely the same things, if placed in the right circumstances. Buffon was decidedly not a cultural relativist—he occasionally marveled at other cultures, but didn't question the superiority of European society. In the strict sense of the term, however, he was not a racist. He even suggested that human ingenuity might hedge against the effects of the harshest climates. Those living in the world's torrid or frozen zones might emulate European civilization if given the tools and encouragement to do so. Even the most terrible experiences—including enslavement—could not crush the "seeds of virtue" that were every human being's birthright.[10]

Although Buffon's theories were extraordinarily influential, he had his critics. In the 1770s and after, during a backlash against the rise of antislavery sentiment in Britain and France, a series of British authors speculated that black people were in fact permanently inferior to whites. A more subtle challenge came from other scientists who proposed grouping human beings into fixed categories. The Swedish naturalist Carl Linnaeus thought that all of humanity could be placed within one of four races; the German theorist Johann Friedrich Blumenbach proposed five. But neither Linnaeus nor Blumenbach suggested that their racial groups had been separately created. Nor did they dissent from Buffon's belief that physical differences were created by environment and circumstance. Blumenbach was at pains to insist that his racial groups were fluid, and that "races" had permeable boundaries: "You see that all do so run into one another, and that one variety of mankind does so sensibly pass into the other, that you cannot mark out the limits between them." Even the Enlightenment's architects of "race" refused to depart from Buffon's view that human beings shared both a common origin and an innate plasticity.[11]

In the young United States, Buffon's *Natural History* was broadly applauded, save for one telling detail. In one of his twelve (!) volumes on quadrupeds, he had casually asserted that the animals of North America seemed a little smaller than their counterparts in Europe and Asia. He even claimed, improbably, that American mutton was "less succulent and tender" than its European equivalent. The suspicion that the North American climate was somehow enfeebling was taken up with gusto by Buffon's compatriot, the Abbé Raynal, who insisted that the hardiest Europeans would "degenerate" in the New World. Buffon's cautious speculation became clumsily chauvinistic in the hands of Raynal, who already had a complicated relationship with the United States. Although France became a vital ally to the Patriot cause in 1778, Raynal and other French intellectuals were snobbish about American claims that the Revolution had global significance. Degeneration was a tool for mocking American exceptionalism, but Benjamin Franklin—who spent much of the Revolutionary War in

Paris as US envoy to France—had the best riposte. At a dinner one evening that brought Raynal and Franklin together, the Frenchman could not resist taunting the American. Franklin and his aides were seated on one side of the table, Raynal and the French guests on the other. "Let both parties rise," Franklin ordered, "and we will see on which side nature has degenerated." At five ten, Franklin was the shortest American at the table, but still comfortably taller than his "remarkably diminutive" hosts. Raynal, Franklin later told Thomas Jefferson, was "a mere shrimp." Franklin could easily have tossed one of the French guests out of the window. ("Or perhaps two.")[12]

The degeneration thesis fired Jefferson's interest in natural history. This was why he never tired of the search for giant moose heads, mastodon skeletons, and other examples of American fecundity, many of which ended up in the entrance hall at Monticello. More seriously, it prompted him to defend the ability and potential of Native Americans. In his *Notes on the State of Virginia*, which made a sustained assault on degeneration, Jefferson insisted that the "vivacity and activity of mind" among the Indians "is equal to ours in the same situation." Perhaps Jefferson would have become fascinated by Native Americans regardless of the French challenge, but Buffon and Raynal made the defense of Indian ability a patriotic imperative. The notion that Europeans looked down on America spread widely across the new nation: in the 1790s and 1800s, it was not unusual to find local newspapers from New England to Georgia trumpeting a giant radish or an "inimitable hog" to disprove the view that "nature degenerates in America."[13]

In his emphasis on Native American ability, Jefferson was merely following the environmental theories of Buffon himself. In the *Notes*, however, Jefferson departed from the Frenchman in one crucial respect. "I advance it as a suspicion only," he wrote carefully, "that the blacks, whether originally a distinct race, or made distinct by time and circumstances, are inferior to the whites in the endowments both of body and mind." Jefferson hedged this in countless ways: he warned that one could only speculate about black inferiority "with great diffidence"; that it would be a terrible thing to "degrade a whole race of men from the rank in the scale of beings which their creator may perhaps have given them." Nonetheless, in Jefferson's most sustained engagement with the issue of racial hierarchy, he had offered an unambiguous judgment: Native Americans had the same capacity as white people, but African Americans did not.[14]

This short passage has had an outsized influence on historians, who are accustomed to placing Jefferson in the vanguard of American thought. We'll return later to the question of why he departed so dramatically from Buffon's theory in the case of African Americans. For now, though, we need to place Jefferson's jarring conclusions in context. First, his arguments about black inferiority drew plenty of criticism, especially from those who knew most about the orthodoxies of the Enlightenment. From South Carolina, the doctor and historian David Ramsay praised Jefferson for his "merited correction" to Buffon on degeneration, but chided him for his racism: "You have depressed the negroes too low," Ramsay wrote. "I believe all mankind to be originally the same and only diversified by accidental circumstances." The surveyor and land speculator Gilbert Imlay declared himself "ashamed, in reading Mr. Jefferson's book, to see, from one of the most enlightened and benevolent of my countrymen, the disgraceful prejudices he entertains against the unfortunate negroes." When the antislavery sections of the *Notes* were invoked by newspapers and reformers in the 1790s and 1800s, the section on black inferiority was usually omitted—unsurprisingly, perhaps, since it seemed to undermine the case for freeing blacks in the first place.[15]

The notorious passage on black ability even became a political issue in 1800, when Jefferson's Federalist opponents seized on his remark about blacks being a "distinct race" to accuse him of blasphemy. One of Jefferson's supporters supplied the newspapers with a letter he'd written in 1791 to the free black mathematician Benjamin Banneker, in which Jefferson declared that "nature has given to our black brethren talents equal to those of other colors." If appearance didn't always bear out this truth, Jefferson continued, this "is owing merely to the degraded condition of their existence both in Africa and America." At other moments in his private correspondence, Jefferson incubated his earlier view on black inferiority. But he seems to have persuaded very few of his compatriots to accept his unorthodox position. The vast majority of writers and thinkers on race preferred Buffon's emphasis on human adaptability, and Jefferson learned to couch his own views with more "diffidence" across the rest of his public life.[16]

The controversy over Jefferson's *Notes* illuminates two further aspects of the debate over race in the early United States. First, by invoking the possibility that blacks were permanently inferior to whites, Jefferson had opened himself to the charge of religious infidelity. The same problem faced any proslavery writer in the southern states or the West Indies who denied the common origins of humanity. A separate creation for black people could not be squared with the descent of humanity from Adam and Eve; racism, put simply, was a rejection of the Bible's authority. Ingenious proslavery theorists would eventually propose workarounds that might relieve some of this pressure, but the inconvenient truth of Genesis acted as a brake on racist theory throughout the antebellum years.[17]

If religious infidelity presented one threat to the budding race theorist, the accusation of prejudice was another. One of the core objectives of the Enlightenment had been to free people from irrationality and parochialism: to aggregate and disseminate knowledge in ways that would open up people's minds and transcend their baser instincts. The word "prejudice" was an important part of this intellectual liberation. As we'll see, the liberal white thinkers who confronted race in the early United States distinguished clearly between rational views about human difference and the knee-jerk reactions of the untrained mind. Human beings might easily recoil from people who looked different or who behaved in different ways; it was the duty of the liberal mind to see past this initial reaction and to bring knowledge and reason to bear on every situation.[18]

Many of the characters we will meet in this book discussed the dangers of prejudice; the most candid admitted that they themselves were vulnerable to its operation, though the task of the liberal mind was to free itself from the snare. "There is something exceedingly curious in the constitution and operation of prejudice," wrote Thomas Paine in 1782. Unlike other vices and passions, it didn't seem to limit itself to a particular people or personality; instead, "like the spider, it makes everywhere its home." Even if one made one's mind "as naked as the walls of an empty and forsaken tenement" or as "gloomy as a dungeon," the spider would crawl back in, "fill it with cobwebs, and live where there seems nothing to live on." The remedy was to keep thinking, to avoid complacency, to subject one's instincts and passions to the closest scrutiny. Only in this way could one keep prejudice in check.[19]

One aspect of this battle against the "spider of the mind," which will become increasingly important to our story, relates to another kind of hierarchy. Most of the actors in this book were middling and elite Americans: churchmen, writers, scientists, politicians, slaveholders. Although they typically defined themselves against prejudice—and pledged to remain alert for the first sign of cobwebs—these better-off Americans referred easily and often to the prejudices of the people at large: the poorer whites who lived alongside black people in the East, or were rushing toward the Indian lands of the West. In crafting national policies to address slavery or the future of Native Americans, liberal thinkers not only had to conquer their own prejudices, but also had to manage and account for those of poorer whites. In the process, they faced a terrible temptation: it would be easy to invoke the hostility of their less enlightened compatriots to mask their own reluctance to accept blacks and Indians as equals.

FOR JAMES SULLIVAN, THE BOSTON judge who corresponded with St. George Tucker, the evidence from black people in slavery—and even those who had briefly enjoyed freedom in New England—provided "great reason" to think blacks might be inferior to whites.

But how could anyone know for sure, given the terrible damage done to their character by enslavement and prejudice? The only way to test the theory would be to give freed people the "same prospects" as white people, and "confer upon them the same advantages for the space of time in which three or four generations shall rise and fall." This might "so mend the race, and so increase their powers of perception," that they would eventually "exceed the white people." The problem was getting blacks from the damaged state of slavery to a position in which their natural talents and potential could vindicate their equality. The nation would need to address the issue of "degradation."

From the 1780s, liberal thinkers insisted that both black people and Indians would require an active process of education before they were ready for meaningful membership in American society. Although it was blacks, rather than Indians, who were initially described as "degraded," by the 1810s the term was used to refer to Indians as well—and it had mutated considerably from its roots in the debilitating experience of slavery. There were important differences between the efforts to educate free blacks and to "civilize" Native Americans, but degradation eventually provided a comforting way to confront the apparent failure of both.[20]

When antislavery campaigners described slaves and free blacks as degraded, they did so in defiance of any fixed conception of race: what distinguished black people from whites was the searing experience of slavery, rather than the color of their skin. The idea that slavery permanently damages its victims dated back to antiquity. Romans fretted about *macula servitutis*, the "servile traits" that dulled the moral character of slaves. Roman slavery, as Thomas Jefferson wrote in his *Notes on the State of Virginia*, was not founded on racial lines. Nonetheless, its debilitating effects took on a biological dimension for some classical writers. The philosopher Favorinus warned Roman women against using slaves (or even freedpeople) as wet nurses, for fear that servile traits could be transmitted through milk to freeborn children. Most Roman theorists of slavery, however, opted for a more conventional family metaphor: slaves were perpetual children, whose passage to freedom could only be secured through a process of growth and maturation directed by a sympathetic master.[21]

In the seventeenth and eighteenth centuries, one could find numerous societies around the world that discriminated against or excluded people without reference to either race or slavery. Latrine-cleaners in India and butchers in Japan were viewed by their neighbors as spiritually defiled—untouchables, in the Indian case. Even excepting the persistence of serfdom in Europe—to which we will return later—certain occupations were classed as degrading or dishonorable, a label that adhered not only to the person actually doing a particular job but to his family and descendants. One effect of the Enlightenment was to draw attention to this problem, in Europe at least. Metropolitan commentators lamented the hereditary exclusion of certain professions; a German imperial decree of 1772 insisted both that executioners were now honorable and that the children of skinners should not be subject to discrimination. Motivated by the same ideas about natural rights and innate human equality, American reformers in the late eighteenth and early nineteenth centuries insisted that abolition and education could reverse slavery's effects. Human beings were so sensitive to their environment, and so thoroughly adaptable, that a change in circumstances could be expected to transform a person: savages might become civilized, criminals might become moral exemplars, slaves could become citizens.[22]

But although these ideas offered blacks (and Indians) a measure of protection from the harsher certainties of racial hierarchy, they created another set of problems. In the case of blacks, the idea of degradation encouraged white thinkers—and even some blacks—to accept the idea that freed slaves were damaged people: that degradation was not simply the product of prejudice, or an unfortunate consequence of social rituals, but a moral injury with lasting effects. That slavery could mark people in this way was another powerful argument against the institution. But if emancipation did not in itself cure the debility, how was the gap between degradation and equality to be closed? Was this to be the responsibility of private individuals and charities, or of government? And if blacks remained degraded until this process of education was complete, how could philanthropists and politicians prevent whites from fearing or shunning freed people in the meantime?

WRITERS IN THE EARLY UNITED States invoked the term "degradation" all the time, usually in contexts that had nothing to do with race. It often described a demotion or punishment: the laws of Harvard College reminded students on a dozen occasions that, for the commission of various infractions, they could expect to be "admonished, degraded, suspended, or rusticated." In the early days of the republic, "degradation" was regularly used by patriotic speakers to describe the fate of peoples in Europe suffering under monarchical government. For some, it was a synonym for "degeneration": the word crept into the many bruised responses to the Abbé Raynal's slur on America's potential. (In the first editions of his dictionary, Noah Webster defined degradation as "a degeneracy.") In the hands of different writers, degradation described the condition of Europe during the Napoleonic Wars; the fate of Scots-Irish Protestants who had been forced out of Ulster by an ungrateful British Crown throughout the eighteenth century; and the sad state of the Jewish people, who had been "long since forsaken of God," but "not forgotten." By the War of 1812, the Federalists who dominated New England politics openly entertained secession from a nation ruled by Virginians, and lamented the nation's political course under Thomas Jefferson and James Madison: "How speedy has been the decline to meanness and degradation," Noah Webster told a Massachusetts crowd in 1814.[23]

The term was also well known in Europe. It appeared dozens of times in Edward Gibbon's *Decline and Fall of the Roman Empire*, usually to describe the corruption of a public official by his or her vices (or those of the public). Numerous people were degraded (*dégradé*) in the Abbé Raynal's pioneering critique of European imperialism, the *Histoire des deux Indes* (*A History of the Two Indies*), but the term had a special association with slavery. Raynal noted with sadness that enslaved people were subjected to a double debility: slavery depressed their spirits and morals; and, even when slaves were emancipated, the prejudices of white people made it impossible for them to enjoy their freedom. Raynal's history, which made its way into the libraries of the American Founders, was especially harsh on the spurious arguments used to defend slavery. It would be "degrading reason" to take seriously the claims of proslavery theorists. "Whoever justifies so odious a system deserves the utmost contempt from a philosopher," concluded Raynal, "and from the negro a stab with his dagger."[24]

A similar focus on reason informed Mary Wollstonecraft's pioneering works on the place of women in society. "When a man makes his spirit bend to any power but reason," she wrote in 1790, "his character is soon degraded, and his mind shackled by the very prejudices to which he submits with reluctance." In *A Vindication of the Rights of Women*, she exhaustively cataloged the "false system of education" that fitted women to become "alluring mistresses" rather than "affectionate wives and rational mothers." Men not only treated women like children, but persuaded them to style themselves as needy and fitted only for pleasure. The challenge, thought Wollstonecraft, was to convince these women "that the illegitimate power which they obtain by degrading themselves is a curse, and that they must return to nature and equality." She slipped a familiar metaphor from antislavery tracts into the debate about sexual equality. If men continued to prevent women from obeying the dictates of reason, they might succeed in creating "convenient slaves," but they would ultimately corrupt themselves: "Slavery will have its constant effect, degrading the master and the abject dependent."[25]

Degradation also played a role in European debates about crime and punishment, especially given the growing interest in rehabilitation in the eighteenth century. Since 1500, Portugal had banished tens of thousands of criminals and other unwanted people to the farthest reaches of its empire: to India, Angola, São Tomé, and Brazil.

Portuguese officials imagined that these exiles, who were known as *degredados*, would find a productive way to contribute to colonial society without the supervision of the state. British officials sent their criminals to the North American colonies, mostly, until the American Revolution intervened. After a frantic search for a new destination, the British government dispatched the First Fleet to Australia in 1787, carrying those who were "by their crimes degraded to a level with the basest of mankind." The quiet ambition of the Australian effort was to reverse this degradation in a new environment, albeit under closer supervision than the Portuguese *degredados* had experienced.[26]

For antislavery writers in the United States, degradation could be presented as a lamentable effect of slavery and a powerful argument against the idea of racial hierarchies. It could also be used to concede or reinforce white prejudices about the supposedly sorry state of the black population at present. Crucially, it was reversible. Samuel Hopkins, a Rhode Island minister, insisted in 1776 that black people had "as good a right as any of their fellow men" to liberty. He proposed that slaves be freed and invited to serve in the American cause during the war with Britain, then integrated into the United States. "Let them be subject to the same restraints and laws, with other freemen," Hopkins urged, "and have the same care taken of them by the public." Slavery had "a mighty tendency to sink and contract the minds of men," and it clearly prevented black people from reaching their potential. But emancipation and "proper encouragement to labor" would eventually set things right. Hopkins's assault on slavery drew momentum from the benighted condition of black people, but his sharp observations—that blacks were "destitute of prudence and sagacity to act for themselves," or prone "to vices of all kinds"—reinforced the view that merely freeing slaves would not fit them for citizenship.[27]

The idea that black people had been relegated from a rightful equality—that they had been "degraded into a perpetual bondage," as Benjamin Franklin and the Pennsylvania Abolition Society put it in their incendiary petition to Congress in 1790—became an antislavery standard in the years after the American Revolution. It also provided a simple way to refute Thomas Jefferson's arguments about permanent inferiority in the *Notes on the State of Virginia*. Noah Webster, who was editing a newspaper in New York during the 1790s, attacked Jefferson's ideas directly in his 1793 essay on the *Effects of Slavery on Morals and Industry*. Webster didn't deny that slaves seemed "remarkable for their inaction, their want of foresight and their disinclination to improvement," and he allowed that these characteristics had created "very great doubts in the minds of some men of a philosophical cast, whether they are not a distinct and inferior race of beings." But a proper attention to Enlightenment principles would yield a different conclusion: "All the peculiar features in the character of the African race in America, may justly be ascribed to their depressed condition." Slavery, not race, was to blame.[28]

Webster looked to Europe to prove his point. Weren't serfs in Russia and Poland just as idle as black slaves in America? How could race explain the apparent decline of the "debased" inhabitants of modern Greece, who seemed nothing like their classical ancestors? Everything was circumstantial. Ireland was full of thieves only because the British ruled with an iron hand. Jews lent at "exorbitant" rates because they experienced the barbs of prejudice wherever they lived. As he both indulged in and made allowances for national stereotypes across and beyond Europe, Webster seems not to have considered whether they were false—or worried that he himself had succumbed to prejudice in recycling them. Behind his judgments and clichés was an Enlightenment confidence that any form of degradation could be overcome.[29]

Webster thought that blacks who had lived in freedom before their enslavement would retain their "early virtues" more or less indefinitely. They would chafe against the denial of their liberty, launch "bold and manly" rebellions against their masters, and, if restored to freedom, make the most of emancipation. By contrast, those born into slavery would "sink into a state of sullen apathy," more likely to perpetrate "petty frauds" than daring uprisings. Like many of his contemporaries, Webster viewed free blacks as disproportionately responsible for "burglaries, rapes or murders"; this supposedly proved that granting freedom to lifelong slaves would not "correct the depravity of their hearts." If blacks were degraded, wasn't this likely to deter, rather than encourage, white people to advocate their emancipation? Webster conceded that "a bare emancipation of them is not an act of adequate justice." White citizens could and should do much more "towards correcting their ill habits and rendering them valuable members of the community."[30]

The same ideas guided antislavery activists in the South and West. In the spring of 1792, as delegates gathered in Lexington to draft a constitution for the proposed state of Kentucky, the Presbyterian minister David Rice urged them to outlaw slavery. Rice had been born in Virginia in 1733, and he had studied at the College of New Jersey in Princeton before becoming a preacher in western Virginia and North Carolina. He ministered to black and white congregations and often felt that he had more success with the former than with the latter. When the residents of Kentucky were numerous enough to petition the federal government for statehood, Rice was elected to the constitutional convention and given a platform for his antislavery views. Like Webster, he argued that blacks and whites were "creatures of God" who were equally entitled to liberty. Moreover, slavery was "a degradation to our own nature" as well as a crime against blacks, and it had ruined generations of young people in Virginia and in the rest of the slaveholding South. In his *Notes on the State of Virginia*, Thomas Jefferson had captured this dynamic with ghastly concision: To be "nursed, educated, and daily exercised in tyranny" was hardly the proper upbringing for a republican. From his years in Virginia, David Rice, too, had learned to loathe that genteel laziness that shadowed slavery's cruelties. "What—must young master saddle his own horse?—Must pretty little miss sweep the house and wash the dishes?—and these black devils be free!—No heart can bear it!"[31]

Rice knew the excuses of slaveholders better than anyone, and he was ready to expose their fallacies at the convention. Even if slavery had originally been the fate of captives of war, and a more humane alternative to genocide, relying on this outdated logic in the modern age was "unreasonable and cruel" (a point that Benjamin Franklin, among others, had already made). True, African leaders and merchants were complicit in the slave trade, but it was Europeans who "furnish the sinews, add the strength, and receive the gain." Rice doubted that the inhumanity that fueled the slave system could be contained within racial boundaries: "If I have been long accustomed to think a black man was made for me, I may easily take it into my head to think so a white man." Those poorer whites who were temporarily protected from rapacious masters by the color line could not sleep easily. "Will straight hair defend me against the blow that falls so heavy on the woolly head?" If slavery's place in Kentucky was consolidated, Rice feared the worst: the state's poor white population would be "spew[ed] out" into other states, treated "with contempt" by a new class of masters, or actually subjugated.[32]

Like Noah Webster, Rice agreed that abolition should be gradual. Slaves had a just claim to immediate freedom, but "by our bad conduct we have rendered them incapable of enjoying . . . their birth-right." The institution, then, had to be dismantled carefully, "the trunk gradually hewn down, and the stump and roots left to rot in the ground." No more slaves should be brought into Kentucky, but those currently enslaved would have to live out their lives in the service of their owners. Their children would be free from birth, though bound to a trade or schooled at the public expense "until actually freed at a proper age." If given a decent education, they would quickly escape the degradation of their parents and could even grow "to become useful citizens." Rice hoped the constitutional convention would have the courage and foresight to embrace his plan before Kentucky went the way of Virginia.[33]

Rice realized that this would be strong medicine for many slaveholders, though he knew that a great many of them were already struggling with their consciences. Rice himself owned four slaves, and he imagined that this gave credibility to his crusade. Perhaps it did: the delegates who eventually voted for a ban held nearly fifty slaves between them. But Rice's arguments ran against slavery's rising tide. Kentucky's black population had roughly tripled between the end of the Revolutionary War and 1790; it would triple again before 1800, when slaves constituted nearly 20 percent of the new state's population. At the 1792 convention, the defenders of slavery countered Rice by pleading the rights of property and warning against government intrusion. Their counterproposal co-opted Rice's language of conscience while placing slavery beyond the reach of even an enlightened majority: masters should be free to manumit their slaves in a personal capacity, but the new state legislature should be barred from imposing abolition without the consent of slaveholders. The convention voted 26 to 16 to entrench slavery, and the dream of a free Kentucky was lost.[34]

Rice's defeat, like the rejection of the 1790 Quaker petition by the US Congress, can make the early abolitionist effort seem hopelessly naïve. But the continuing interest of Virginians like St. George Tucker in a general emancipation, along with the growing antislavery movement in New York and Philadelphia, left reformers feeling anything but dejected. In 1798, a young Henry Clay wrote a newspaper article urging the state's voters to remedy "defects" in the Kentucky constitution. Although the state was flourishing, "can any man be happy and contented when he sees near thirty thousand of his fellow beings around him, deprived of all the rights which make life desirable?" In fact, "all America acknowledges the existence of slavery to be an evil." Clay, like Rice, thought that slavery should not be abolished immediately, and he attacked the scare tactics of slaveholders who had warned of "an immediate and unqualified liberation of slaves." The challenge for Rice and Clay, in "the present enlightened age," was to find a gradual plan that would cushion the social upheaval of abolition.[35]

David Rice's ideas continued to circulate in Kentucky, and they were also published in Philadelphia as a new national antislavery movement began to take shape. In 1794, delegates from Connecticut to Maryland converged on the city for the first Convention for Promoting the Abolition of Slavery. The attendees pledged to help local abolition societies in their efforts to free black people wherever they were still enslaved, and to encourage the education of free blacks, "thereby to prepare them for becoming good citizens of the United

States." Abolition conventions met every year or so during the 1790s, recruiting delegates from as far south as Baltimore and Richmond. When New York and New Jersey passed gradual abolition legislation in 1799 and 1804, delegates confidently predicted that the march of emancipation would continue.[36]

Degradation had quickly become a powerful argument against slavery. It emphasized the corrosive effects of the institution on human beings whose subjugation had no scientific or religious justification. But if the language of degradation was rooted in the idea that African Americans had retained their innate human potential and ability, it also affirmed the view that slaves and freed people were *currently* inferior to whites. Temporarily and reversibly inferior, perhaps, and degraded through no fault of their own, but inferior nonetheless. "In vain do you liberate the African," warned the 1800 Abolition Convention, "while you neglect to furnish him with the means of properly providing for himself, and of becoming a useful member of the community." The new antislavery movement now had to make good on its boast that degradation could be overcome as convincingly as it could be defined, and that benevolence and enlightened government could turn slaves into citizens.

TWO

A FEW BAD MEN

V IRTUALLY EVERYONE AGREED THAT THE denial of liberty
would have a terrible effect on human beings, causing them to
stagnate or regress in their moral development. But how could liberal
reformers explain the apparently primitive state of Native Americans?
Thomas Jefferson wondered if the Indians had declined from a more
civilized group of ancestors that had built ancient cities in the Mississippi Valley. The antislavery congressman Elias Boudinot of New Jersey suggested that Native Americans were originally Jews: they were
"perfect republicans," "exceedingly intoxicated with religious pride,"
and "the conduct of the women seems perfectly agreeable (as far as
circumstances will permit) to the law of Moses." Most liberal whites
accepted a more prosaic explanation for the rougher edges of indigenous culture: Native Americans had never been exposed to the stimuli
that would encourage civilized society. They hadn't been degraded—
at least, no more than any other primitive people who had fallen from
the settled societies of the biblical era. Instead, they had to be brought
for the first time through the stages of civilization, in accordance with
Enlightenment theories about human progress.[1]

As we'll see, Native Americans became caught up in the debate
about degradation along with African Americans. To understand
how this happened, we need to explore how white reformers understood and responded to Indians in the first decades of the republic. In

particular, we need to confront the extraordinary and ultimately cata-
strophic policy of "civilizing" Native peoples that was launched during
George Washington's first administration and remained an obsession
of the federal government for decades. If it was hard for liberal whites
to deny that African Americans were capable of improvement, it was
no easier to reject the humanity and potential of Native Americans.
(In 1785, Noah Webster declared the morals of the Indians "as perfect . . . as in more enlightened nations," and their laws on a par with
"the most civilized.") The challenge was to devise a process by which
the innate human potential of Native peoples could be nurtured amid
the political turmoil of the nation's first decades.

During the colonial era, Britain had shown little interest in promoting "civilization." Colonial merchants and British importers happily encouraged Indians to furnish the European market with furs
and pelts, but gave them little thought beyond commerce and military
strategy. Britain and France were the predominant powers in North
America before the French defeat in the Seven Years' War (1756–1763).
In the first half of the eighteenth century, these European powers
competed to build and protect their Indian alliances without making
serious efforts to impose their way of life on Native people. Given that
the British North American colonies had a much larger population of
settlers than New France, government officials in London (and colonial assemblies in America) had to balance the Indian trade against a
temptation to expand westward. By the mid-eighteenth century, with
American settlers rushing toward the Appalachians, imperial managers found themselves juggling two different visions of empire: one
based on Indian trade, the other on white settlement.

With the French conclusively defeated in North America by 1761,
British commanders and imperial bureaucrats assumed they could
dictate terms to indigenous people. Settlers on the ground in the British colonies saw an opportunity to seize Indian land in the West without fear of reprisal. Native Americans, however, refused to recognize
British hegemony over the American interior. In 1763, a pan-Indian
rebellion in the Great Lakes led by the Ottawa warrior Pontiac forced

Britain to readjust its Indian policy. George III proclaimed that the Appalachian Mountains should mark the dividing line between British America and Indian country. Any future cessions of Indian land would be secured not by colonial governors or ambitious white settlers, but by British officials reporting directly to London.[2]

If the new Proclamation Line offered reassurance to Indians, it enraged poorer whites who sought land and opportunity beyond the mountains. Benjamin Franklin did little to disguise his contempt for these renegades: "Our frontier people are yet greater barbarians than the Indians," he wrote the British superintendent for Indian affairs in 1766. The unmanaged expansion they desired would tear the commercial web that connected businessmen in Philadelphia, New York, and London to the Native peoples of the American interior. Franklin knew that westward expansion wasn't just a sop to white settlers. Merchants and political insiders could make a lot of money from land speculation, and Europeans could not be contained forever by the Appalachians. But he shared the British view that land cessions should be secured from the Indians with patience and precision. When British negotiators reached a new treaty agreement in 1768 that would push the border of white settlement to the Ohio River, Franklin and his merchant friends in Philadelphia greeted the news with excitement. The Ohio stretched for a thousand miles to the Mississippi, and it linked the interior to the distant Atlantic. (Spain still controlled the river and its entrepôt, New Orleans, but this was an investment in the future.) The only problem was that Britain had agreed upon this boundary with the wrong group of Indians.[3]

The 1768 treaty was signed by the Six Nations of the Iroquois Confederacy, whose power was centered on the vast region between what is now Pittsburgh and the Hudson River. But the lands south of the Ohio, roughly corresponding to West Virginia and Kentucky, belonged mostly to Indians who were not invited to (or even informed of) the 1768 negotiations. The powerful Shawnee were the most notable absentees, and their resentment led eventually to war with the colony of Virginia. In 1774, the British governor Lord Dunmore sent troops

to the backcountry to defend the cessions of 1768, adding to the antag-
onism between the Indians and Britain. But the onset of the American Revolution changed the political calculus. Dunmore, barely a year
into his efforts to consolidate western land for white Virginians, was
ignominiously forced back across the Atlantic by militant Patriots.
The settlers rushing onto Indian lands in the West now proclaimed
loyalty to George Washington rather than George III. To complete the
reversal, the Indians who had been betrayed by Britain in 1768 now
chose to ally with the Crown against the new United States.[4]

The Revolution went badly for Native peoples in the Ohio Valley.
The Shawnees and their allies inflicted heavy casualties on white frontier communities, but they were fighting a rearguard action. By 1783,
under the pressure of American armies and multiplying settlers, the
Indian presence south of the Ohio had become almost impossible to
sustain. Worse, the British neglected to defend their Indian allies at
the peace negotiations in Paris, ceding territorial rights in the West to
the new United States. At best, this left Native peoples clinging to the
onerous terms of the 1768 treaty, exiled from their lands south of the
river. But American politicians immediately tested a more ambitious
argument: if Britain had ceded all its claims, the United States had a
right to any Indian land east of the Mississippi. Between 1783 and 1787,
the Confederation Congress imposed treaties on Native Americans
encompassing vast areas. As delegates gathered in Philadelphia in the
summer of 1787 to draft the new federal Constitution, the old Congress passed its most important piece of legislation. The Northwest
Ordinance divided Indian land between Pennsylvania and the Mississippi into neat parcels ready for absorption into the United States.

That summer, Congress reminded Arthur St. Clair, the new governor of the Northwest Territory, that he should "not neglect any
opportunity that may offer, of extinguishing the Indian rights to the
westward, as far as the river Mississippi." General St. Clair sympathized with the land grab, but he knew that phony treaties could not
secure the evacuation of northwestern Indian nations. Sooner or later,
the United States would have to either negotiate equitable agreements

or meet Native Americans on the battlefield. The extension of white settlement forced the issue of whether Indians would be assimilated, removed, or even exterminated. This question would become a central concern for the United States in the three decades from 1785 to 1815. The testing ground for its resolution was the territory that now encompasses Ohio, Indiana, and Illinois.[5]

DURING THE CONFEDERATION ERA AND the first years of the federal government, Arthur St. Clair reported to Henry Knox, secretary of war. Before the Revolution, Knox had run a bookstore in Boston supplying the latest military tracts to British officers. After Lexington and Concord, Knox slipped through the British blockade and brought his knowledge of artillery to George Washington and the Continental Army. During the Confederation period, his job entailed managing Indian frustrations with fraudulent treaties and addressing the intransigence of white settlers who pushed beyond even the disputed borders. In a report to Congress in July 1787, Knox insisted that, if the Indians near the Wabash River continued to prey upon American settlers and forts, US troops should "expel them from their towns or extirpate them." Knox was, after all, no ordinary bookseller; even before 1775, he had gravitated to the shelves of his store that explained the trigonometry of modern warfare. But he fancied himself both amiable and humane. As he laid out the prospect of extirpation, he insisted that any war should be "founded on the immutable principles of Justice." In 1789, Knox became the only senior official in the Confederation government to retain his post during Washington's first administration, and he was given the difficult task of squaring the nation's commitment to Enlightenment ideals with its boundless western ambitions.[6]

Like other federal officials, Knox juggled fear about the immediate dangers of a frontier war with an expansive complacency about the long-term prospects of American domination. In the summer of

1789, as he lobbied Washington and Congress for a new direction in Indian policy, Knox claimed that the United States could overrun the Indians north of the Ohio River as easily as it had done the original inhabitants of the thirteen states. He wondered, though, if there was a better way forward. "How different would be the sensation of the philosophic mind," Knox told the president, "to reflect that instead of exterminating a part of the human race by our modes of popula-tion, that we had persevered through all difficulties and had at least imparted our knowledge of cultivation, and the arts, to the Aborig-inals of the country." In 1790 and 1791, it was far from obvious that the United States could destroy the Indians, and Knox admitted in his more candid moments that an alliance of indigenous peoples with Britain or Spain could easily result in the extirpation of the American republic. But Knox wanted to present Washington with an alterna-tive to the saber-rattling of General St. Clair and his supporters in Congress. He was also conscious that the public—both in the United States and in Europe—might not share the enthusiasm of frontier sol-diers and settlers for a campaign of annihilation. This broader audi-ence might even "consider the Indians as oppressed," a conclusion that would damage the republic's reputation at home and abroad.[7]

The idea that Indians were impervious to civilized ways was "more convenient than just," Knox admitted in 1790. The vast major-ity of Indian nations had already discovered the benefits of settled agriculture, but their societies would have to be reengineered to fit the expansionist blueprint of the Northwest Ordinance. This meant concentrating their settlements in a much smaller area, selling their "excess" land to the federal government, using the proceeds to procure the equipment and skills to grow crops for the market, and embracing Christianity. Above all, Native people would need to accept that land and possessions should be held privately, rather than communally. To the exasperation of federal officials, this key principle seemed any-thing but obvious to Native Americans.[8]

What was the best way to introduce the program to the Indians? Before 1789, a small number of Native Americans had been educated in eastern colleges in the hope that they would become emissaries of "civilization." The results were disappointing. In 1779, Congress voted to send George Morgan White Eyes to Princeton. George was the son of a Delaware leader who had allied with the United States, but who had been killed by a Virginia militiaman in 1778. Congressional members hoped to conciliate the angry Delawares by giving White Eyes's son the same educational opportunity they might wish for their own children. (The tuition bills were to be settled later, with land cessions.) But the curriculum hardly fitted George for a role as cultural ambassador. His tutors were skilled in moral philosophy, divinity, and mathematics rather than practical matters like husbandry, and George felt nervous about returning to his people. Like the two other Delaware students who matriculated at Princeton in the eighteenth century, George did not complete his degree. Henry Knox concluded that these ad-hoc attempts at civilizing were inadequate. The United States had to find a way to penetrate Native American societies directly in order to root its ideals and practices among Indians at the frontier.[9]

Knox's alternative plan was to revive the old British practice of giving gifts to the Indians during treaty-making, with the goal of providing Indian elders with a personal stake in the concept of private property. With this method, he told Washington, the United States could win the friendship of the troublesome Wabash Indians for only $11,000 per year. This was a bargain. A military expedition of 1,600 men would cost $200,000 annually, and an army that could win a full-blown Indian war in the Northwest—5,000 men, say—would cost $1.1 million or more. (Excepting interest payments on its debts, the federal government's annual budget at this moment was less than $2 million.) To complement his plan of buying off Indian leaders, Knox proposed Christian missionaries as "the instruments to work on the Indians." These men would live alongside Native Americans, promise not to become involved in any form of land speculation, and take up agriculture. With their new indigenous neighbors by turns rapt and envious, the missionaries would find it easy to transmit civilized principles and to reform Native American societies from within.[10]

Knox is usually credited by historians as the architect of the federal civilizing policy, but that role should really be shared with his collaborator and successor, Timothy Pickering. Both were veterans of the Continental Army and unusually tall. In all other respects, however, they were opposites. Knox, who weighed more than 250 pounds, was as fat-faced and red-cheeked as a James Gillray caricature. Pickering was thin, with a long jaw and a look of pinched seriousness. Knox came from humble origins, acquiring his bookstore only after serving ten years as the apprentice of its previous owner, and he viewed the Revolution with a hungry ambition. He eventually succeeded Washington as commander-in-chief in 1783, becoming secretary of war two years later. Pickering, a Harvard graduate and the son of a clergyman, sat out the first two years of fighting, suspicious of the Patriot hotheads who had plunged the colonies into war. He joined up with the army in 1777 and rose to become its quartermaster, but this was an unforgiving and thankless reward for his service. He could hardly conceal his annoyance at being blamed for the army's problems even as Washington seemed beyond reproach. (Like John Adams and the eminent physician Benjamin Rush, Pickering was an early critic of Washington's numerous "idolaters.") After the war, Pickering became a merchant in Philadelphia, then a land speculator. Following a ruinous struggle between competing land companies, he was reduced to a small farm in the Pennsylvania countryside and the charity of his wealthier siblings. Finally, in September 1790, a group of old friends in Congress came to his rescue: Although he had no relevant experience, would the colonel like to become the federal representative to the Six Nations Indians?[11]

Pickering had found his calling. "I was an utter stranger to the manners of the Indians and to the proper mode of treating with them," he wrote Washington on his return from Seneca country. "But, Sir, I have found that they are not difficult to please. A man must be destitute of humanity, of honesty, or of common sense, who should send them away disgusted." Pickering's mission was to keep the Six Nations from allying with the western Indians, even though the two groups shared many of the same grievances about the treaty-making of the 1780s. In the short term, their quiescence might be purchased. But if the United States wanted a lasting peace, it had to replace its piecemeal civilizing efforts with concerted and well-funded programs of engagement and instruction.

Pickering told Washington that it was pointless to "take a few young Indians and educate them in the style of the children of men of fortune." The president knew this only too well. After George Morgan White Eyes had left Princeton, the young Delaware Indian had struggled to support himself in New York. In 1789, he wrote Washington for money and advice. Without the assistance of the federal government, he would have to "steer my Course towards my native [country] let the Consequence be what it will." But he still hoped the United States would find him "some kind of Employment . . . agreeable to the Education they have been pleased to bestow upon me." Without Washington's permission, George ran up a tab for clothing and provisions from a New York merchant, which resulted in another plaintive letter to the president. (And one from the merchant's wife, begging Washington to honor the bills and keep her struggling husband from "a loathsome Prison.") Recalling this episode in his correspondence with Timothy Pickering, Washington concluded in 1791 that the plan of sending the Indian elite to America's most prestigious schools had been misguided. It was "not such as can be productive of any good to their nations. . . . It is, perhaps, productive of evil."[12]

Pickering thought it more sensible to teach Native students in colleges of "plain learning and husbandry" to be established on their lands. Enrollment would be voluntary, and the federal government would supply buildings, tutors, and supplies. (These expenses might eventually be recouped through land sales.) The plan was a bargain when compared with the alternative: "A single campaign would cost more than the entire establishment of these schools of humanity among all the Indian nations within their limits," Pickering noted. Washington liked the idea so much that he asked Pickering to become Indian superintendent for the entire Northwest. The pay was lousy, and Pickering thought he'd be happier balancing his life as a farmer with occasional diplomatic missions to the Six Nations. But he was thrilled to have persuaded Washington that "husbandry, and consequently civilization, should be introduced among the Indians." Between Knox and Pickering, the outlines of a federal civilizing program seemed to be taking shape.[13]

GEORGE WASHINGTON AND TIMOTHY PICKERING concluded that the students at Princeton—the "children of men of fortune"—had been poor role models for George Morgan White Eyes during his unhappy college tenure. Were the white inhabitants of the frontier more likely to exert a civilizing influence on Native Americans? This was initially the hope of Arthur St. Clair, the Revolutionary veteran and former president of the Continental Congress, who reluctantly agreed to become governor of the new Northwest Territory in 1787. Despite the strategic importance of the West to the republic's future, it wasn't immediately clear to St. Clair that he would feel at the center of things in his new role. He was, he told Alexander Hamilton, "a poor Devil banished to another Planet." Having traveled by boat down the Ohio River to take up his new appointment in the summer of 1788, St. Clair arrived in the administrative capital of the Northwest Territory, Marietta, Ohio, in time for Independence Day. The town was still very small, but its settlers knew it had become the gateway to the vast Ohio country. Accepting their invitation to deliver a July Fourth address, St. Clair told the residents that they could bring Native Americans into the circle of civilization simply by setting a good example. But the journals and letters of the first residents of Marietta hardly suggest that they were fitted to become emissaries of Enlightenment. Indians regularly came into the town to trade, but mistrust on both sides ran high.[14]

"I cannot say I am fond of them," wrote John May, a Revolutionary veteran from Massachusetts who had moved to Marietta to make his fortune. "These Indians are of an evil nature," he told his journal.

May's wariness was nourished by the western landscape itself. On his way to Ohio from New England, he had stopped near Pittsburgh at the site of the famous defeat of General Edward Braddock in 1755—an Indian victory over Virginia militiamen that had very nearly taken the life of a young colonel named George Washington. May could still see bones on the ground; they "did not seem much decayed, although it is above thirty years since the battle." The visceral evidence of white-Indian conflict stirred May's prejudices. Indians, he reminded himself, shot from the shadows and behaved "monstrously" toward anyone who survived their ambushes. Ohio settlers like May harbored a sense of the region's immense promise and a sharp fear for their immediate safety. Despite Arthur St. Clair's hopes, they had very little interest in the civilizing agenda. When May had sailed down the Ohio River in the spring of 1788 in a barge called the *Mayflower*, he could hardly resist recording his hopes for the Northwest in the Puritan style. "What though the heathen rage, and savage natives roar and yell in midnight hellish revels?" he wrote in his journal. "Our feet shall nevertheless stand fast; for our bow is bent in strength, and our arm made strong by the mighty God of Jacob."[15]

It was clear to Knox, Pickering, and Washington that the frontier settlers had, in Knox's words, "imbibed the strongest prejudices against the Indians." How could the government keep them in check? Western settlers already suspected that the federal government would try to limit their advance, perhaps keeping them on the south side of the Ohio River. Arthur St. Clair, when acquainted with his new neighbors, joined forces with the land speculator Rufus Putnam to dissuade government officials from this course. Both men made the same arguments: that western land could help discharge "many millions of National Debt," and that a failure to protect settlers would jeopardize US control of the interior. If the United States should "give up the protection of the Country"—and deny settlers' claims on Native land—the white frontiersmen would take matters into their own hands. National allegiances would dissolve, resulting in an independent republic or a new province for the Spanish Empire. (St. Clair twisted the knife when he warned George Washington that the current settlers were "laying the foundation of the greatness of a rival country.") Since the "private adventurers" of the frontier would "pay little or no regard to the laws of the United States or the rights of the natives," thought St. Clair, the government had a simple choice: it could pursue a proactive expansion policy with a measure of justice toward the Indians; or it could renounce its claims on the West and watch breakaway settlers wage a war of conquest and extermination.[16]

Henry Knox heard these arguments with growing alarm. The United States was "embarrassed with a frontier of immense extent," he told Washington in 1791, and could easily be blackmailed by its most distant inhabitants. But to cave in to settler demands was to invite war with the Indians. As an old friend of Washington's told him in the summer of 1791, "I cannot see much prospect of living in tranquility with them so long as a spirit of land-jobbing prevails—and our frontier-Settlers entertain the opinion that there is not the same crime (or indeed no crime at all) in killing an Indian as in killing a white man." For Knox, the only solution would be to brandish "the sword of the republic": a federal military force that might occupy the frontier, reminding both sides—"the lawless whites as well as Indians"—of their responsibilities. But who would pay for these western peacekeepers? And how could federal officials establish Timothy Pickering's "schools of humanity" in the middle of a war zone? Federal officials edged toward the conclusion that, while the United States could incorporate Native Americans as surely as it could absorb western territory, it might require an army to accomplish the task.[17]

IN 1791, TIMOTHY PICKERING FOUND himself at the center of the great lie that sustained the first major war of the federal era. As Henry Knox had admitted, the treaties of the Confederation period had angered every Indian nation from upstate New York to Lake Michigan. Knox and Arthur St. Clair had attempted to repair some of the damage at the Treaty of Fort Harmar in 1789, but this negotiation had made some Native nations still angrier (especially those who, like the Miami Indians, were not even present). Since 1788, St. Clair and Knox had been talking up the prospect of war in the Northwest: not to coerce the consent of unhappy Native Americans, they insisted, but to punish those Indians whose "wicked and bloodthirsty dispositions" made them impervious to reason. The Indians who had refused to negotiate with the United States, or had been bypassed by federal negotiators, became increasingly belligerent in their defense of their lands. In the summer of 1790, Congress finally approved an expeditionary force of more than 1,400 men to attack the Indian "banditti" of the Maumee River in what is now northeastern Indiana. Most of the soldiers were militiamen from Kentucky and Pennsylvania, and as they marched slowly into Miami country they found that the Indians had vanished. The commander of the force was General Josiah Harmar, who had given his name to the 1789 treaty that had so infuriated the Indians. Frustrated by the lack of targets, and bored with burning abandoned villages, Harmar approved scouting parties to track down the missing locals. The first of these parties was surprised and scattered by waiting Indians; the second left an opening for the Indians to attack the rear of the army, inflicting serious casualties and forcing Harmar into ignominious retreat.[18]

This was a clumsy overture, even for those who viewed force as an alternative to Pickering's civilizing policy. Nearly a quarter of the regular soldiers in Harmar's force were killed; the Indians made off with supplies and equipment, and began to wonder if the United States was as mighty as it had previously seemed. While Harmar puffed that he had reduced the banditti in their "headquarters of iniquity," Knox fretted about the consequences of the US defeat. The Shawnee, Miami, and their allies might become still more intransigent if the United States seemed weak; yet a show of strength would reinforce the Native perception that whites employed violence to advance their expansionist designs. Writing to Washington in December 1790, Knox disavowed any interest in territory: to seize land would "give the expedition an avaricious aspect" and "disgrace the government." Instead, "the motives of the expedition ought to appear as they really are—a clear and uncompounded dictate of Justice to punish a banditti of robbers, and murderers, who have refused to listen to the voice of peace and humanity." While Washington, St. Clair, and Knox continued to blame "banditti" and "bad Indians" for the growing unrest, the true causes of their predicament were hard to conceal.[19]

With the prospects of peace diminishing, Washington and Knox wondered if their old quartermaster, Timothy Pickering, might be drafted into a military effort against the western Indians. Knox advised the president to launch a shock-and-awe campaign against the Western Confederacy of Shawnee, Miami, and Wabash Indians: an expanded US Army would burn crops and houses and target women and children in an attempt to deter Native Americans from raiding white settlements in central and southern Ohio. Washington agreed, but Pickering politely declined a commission. In a letter to a friend, he explained his reasons: "I have heard the Indians against whom Harmar's expedition was formed represented as a banditti," he reported. "But do such opprobrious gangs as the description designates, cultivate extensive fields of corn and fruits? Do they build numerous and large villages?" Pickering thought that the "banditti" were "not very unlike the Indian tribes with which I have some acquaintance." These were men, women, and children who "feel sore of the many injuries they have received of the white people." As soon as white settlers "cease to provoke them," Pickering thought, "they would cease their hostilities." The key to pacifying Indians was civilization, not warfare.[20]

Pickering's insight may have saved his life. The 1791 campaign against the "banditti" of the Northwest was a disaster, partly because the US forces (under the command of Arthur St. Clair) lacked a decent quartermaster. Their saddles were too big to fit western horses; animals wandered away from the encampments because no one had remembered to buy bells; the weather was terrible; soldiers were poorly trained; St. Clair was crippled by gout. When Blue Jacket and Little Turtle—the leaders of the new Western Confederacy of Indians—attacked the American camp before dawn on 4 November, they must have already known that an Indian victory was likely. In the event, the US Army suffered a defeat that, proportionally speaking, remains the worst in its history. Seven hundred Americans in a force of around 2,000 were killed, including 100 women and children who had been following the army. St. Clair escaped, only to face the wrath of Congress.[21]

After this catastrophe, selling the war to eastern audiences became still more difficult. Jeremy Belknap in Boston shared his delight with Benjamin Rush in Philadelphia that "the western war is so unpopular." Americans both famous and obscure wrote the president directly to complain. Washington received a rasping letter from Benjamin Hawkins, US senator from North Carolina, insisting that the root cause of the conflict was the persistent refusal of the United States to respect Indian land rights. "As long as we attempt to go into their country or to remain there," Hawkins warned, "we shall be at war." Washington heard the same argument from the Philadelphia lawmaker and doctor William Stoy, an immigrant from Germany who had arrived in America just before the Seven Years' War. Didn't the Constitution protect ordinary people in their property? And didn't the Indians have "the same right with an alien from Europe to receive American citizenship if he desires it?" Stoy knew that Washington heard this kind of thing all the time from the Quakers, and that the archaic language and mores of the Friends had little impact on hardened politicians. He tailored his message accordingly: "I will not speak from principles of Christianity, which by most people are laughed at nowadays, but from principles of nature, or reason, and morality. God is the common father of the Indian as well as of the white man."[22]

The federal government prepared a typically double-edged response to the defeat of 1791. Washington accepted the need "to restrain the commission of outrages upon the Indians" by white settlers, and he sent Pickering's civilizing plan to the Senate for approval. He approved the creation of a US commission to negotiate with the

Western Confederacy at Sandusky on Lake Erie, while Congress voted to raise 5,000 troops for yet another excursion into the Northwest. Meanwhile, the leaders of the Western Confederacy argued about how much they could extract from a punch-drunk United States. The Miami were willing to cede some territory north of the Ohio River, but the Shawnee, Delaware, and other members of the Confederacy were adamant that the river should remain the boundary. (They may have been encouraged in their inflexible stance by the British, who continued to meddle quietly from Canada.) Pickering had already urged Knox and Washington to return Native land that had been improperly ceded to the United States. At a fraught cabinet meeting in February 1793, Knox, Alexander Hamilton, and attorney general Edmund Randolph agreed that Washington could undo the terms of previous treaties if circumstances required it. (Only Thomas Jefferson dissented.) But in pressing for the restoration of the Ohio River as the boundary with the American republic, the Shawnee and Delaware were placing thousands of white settlers and millions of acres of traded land on the wrong side of the border.[23]

Even Timothy Pickering knew that the Ohio River was a boundary "which we could not admit," but he hoped to prevent another northwestern war at the make-or-break Sandusky negotiations in the summer of 1793. More than a dozen Indian nations sent representatives to meet the commissioners, from the Seneca in the North to the Creek and Cherokee in the South. As they laid out their response to US demands, Pickering must have been astonished by their perceptiveness. "Brothers," the Native negotiators declared, "we know that these settlers are poor, or they would have never ventured to live in a country which has been in continual trouble ever since they crossed the Ohio." Instead of paying federal annuities to Indian nations, why not give the money to the settlers on condition that they return to the East? "You will certainly have more than sufficient [funds] for the purpose of repaying these settlers for all their labor and improvements"— especially if the United States included "the great sums you must expend in raising and paying armies with a view to force us to yield to you our country." Perhaps the Indians already knew that this neat solution was impossible. Then, as now, the United States could more easily raise money to fight wars than to lift people from poverty. And the Northwest was as valuable to the federal government (in land sales) as it was to frontier settlers. Pickering kept up negotiations with the Six Nations in the summer of 1794, but the representatives of the Western Confederacy returned to Indiana to await another American attack.[24]

It had been three years since the US Army had been routed by the western Indians. Anthony Wayne, the latest commander to be sent into the Ohio country, was determined to learn from experience. Wayne could seem intemperate and unpredictable—he was unaffectionately known as "Mad Anthony"—but Washington had picked him for his "active and enterprising" qualities. Basing himself in Pittsburgh in 1792, he began to train an army that could fight with the discipline and skill that had been lacking in the previous campaigns. He was remorseless toward deserters—he shot them, if a court martial would allow it—and proposed to brand the foreheads of those who shied from danger with the word "COWARD." By 1793, Wayne thought he could win a fight against Little Turtle and Blue Jacket, the Miami and Shawnee leaders holding up the US advance in the Northwest. He was less sure he could win a fight with Henry Knox over whether the US Army could be unleashed on the Western Confederacy. Knox agonized over the cost of a war, and whether the public at home and abroad would support it. He warned Wayne that most people would side with the underdog; if the general got the war he was looking for, "the disinterested part of mankind and posterity will be apt to class the effects of our Conduct and that of the Spaniards in Mexico and Peru together." Only when the Sandusky negotiations became deadlocked did Knox decide to release Wayne upon the Indians.[25]

In July 1794, Little Turtle and Blue Jacket encountered a very different US Army from the one they had previously vanquished. Wayne used a new network of forts and his exhaustively drilled troops to lure the Indians into traps and sap their strength. After the first skirmishes between the sides, the Western Confederacy chiefs called a tribal council. Little Turtle suggested they sue for peace, reasoning that their bargaining position would be stronger before a battle than after a defeat. Blue Jacket and the Shawnees persuaded the bulk of the western Indians to press on. With the Miami chief in a subordinate role, the full Indian army finally met Wayne's forces at Fallen Timbers, near present-day Toledo, on 20 August 1794. The ground was strewn with trees that had been leveled in an instant by a tornado a few years earlier. The battle was scarcely more protracted. Within two hours, Wayne's ruthless troops secured the victory. When Blue Jacket and his forces sought refuge in Fort Miamis, a British garrison nearby, the commander refused to open the gate. Britain was at that moment concluding the negotiations that would produce Jay's Treaty, in which it agreed to end its interference in Northwestern affairs. Little Turtle, to his dismay, had been right.[26]

Timothy Pickering, meanwhile, made good on his promise to reverse an injustice of the 1780s: he negotiated the return of 1 million acres of land near Lake Erie to the Six Nations. The effect of his triumph was to make it easier for American officials to strong-arm the western Indians in the separate treaty talks that followed Fallen Timbers. Barely a month after his victory, Anthony Wayne built a road into the Miami country so that his army could penetrate what Josiah Harmar had called "the headquarters of iniquity"—the Miami town of Kekionga, where Little Turtle and his allies had planned their long defiance. Wayne was confronted by extraordinary sights. The "banditti" had cleared five hundred acres for the cultivation of crops. Most of them lived in log houses, neatly arranged in a fashion that would put to shame many white frontier settlements, and used the same utensils and manufactured goods as the soldiers who had defeated them. After years in which Wayne had methodically planned the Indians' extirpation, he found himself among a people who seemed uncomfortably familiar.[27]

WHEN HENRY KNOX ADDRESSED CONGRESS in December 1794 to mark his departure from the War Department, he reviewed the progress of his policies with pride. The treaty-making process had been cleaned up, and American negotiators had worked assiduously to keep the peace with the Six Nations and the southern Indians even during the war with the Western Confederacy. The United States had developed the outlines of a civilizing program, while officials had taken action to curb the intransigence of frontier settlers. And yet Knox could not entirely shut out the fact that "our modes of population have been more destructive to the Indian natives than the conduct of the conquerors of Mexico and Peru." On the face of it, this seemed absurd: the Americans were "powerful" but also "enlightened." But "a future historian may mark the causes of this destruction of the human race in sable colors." Knox struggled to make sense of the contradiction between "benevolent" intentions and malevolent effects; hence his determination to attribute the clash of cultures to a disembodied process ("our modes of population") rather than the conscious actions of the War Department. Even if subsequent generations might dwell upon the tragedy of American expansion, Knox reassured Congress, "the present Government of the United States cannot with propriety be involved in the opprobrium."[28]

Timothy Pickering, who agreed to succeed Knox, was considerably more cautious in his handling of Indian affairs. But the war with the western Indians had generated its own momentum. In 1795 the Western Confederacy was cajoled into signing the Treaty of Greenville, which codified the aggressive American encroachment of the 1780s. Most of Ohio and the southeastern corner of Indiana were signed away by Native leaders who had hoped to halt the American advance at the Ohio River. Pickering did not indulge in triumphalism, but focused instead on the two problems that might yet confound a durable peace with the Indians: the encroachment of white settlers across treaty lines, and the need to "civilize" the Indians so that they might be incorporated into the republic. Without solutions to these, no treaty could hold for long.[29]

A contemporary rendition of the Treaty of Greenville, which marked the end of Native hopes that the United States could be contained to the southeast of the Ohio River. COURTESY OF THE CHICAGO HISTORY MUSEUM, ICHi-64806.

The problems of settler encroachment became especially acute in the Southeast. The Native peoples of the Northwest lived within the boundaries of a new federal territory; tens of thousands of Native Americans in the Southeast, on the other hand, lived within the limits of existing states. North Carolina, South Carolina, and Georgia—as well as Tennessee, which had only achieved statehood in 1796—had substantial Native populations living within their borders. Federal officials were therefore forced to craft southeastern Indian policy alongside state governments that reflexively sided with settlers and squatters over Native people. In 1796, Washington shared with Pickering his exasperation at the tendency of white Georgians to cross into Indian territory and steal Cherokee horses and land. One remedy was to mark the boundary as clearly as possible, as the law and the Indians demanded, but the president doubted this would be sufficient:

"I believe scarcely any thing short of a Chinese wall, or a line of troops, will restrain Land jobbers, and the encroachment of settlers upon the Indian territory." Creek Indians complained directly to Washington that their sons had been led astray in white towns near the border with Indian country. US commissioners to the Creeks conceded the point: "Your young men . . . associated too much with our bad people," they told the leaders of the Creeks, and "from bad examples acquired bad habits." Even after the Treaty of Greenville had brought a measure of calm to the Northwest frontier, Washington continued to confront the fundamental irony of federal Indian policy: for all the boasts that Native Americans could be brought to civilization, the evidence suggested that contact between Indians and frontier whites led only to conflict and, according to federal officials, "bad habits."[30]

In November 1796, Indian representatives from the Great Lakes to the Gulf of Mexico traveled to Philadelphia, which would remain the nation's capital until 1800. These delegates had been invited to meet President Washington before his retirement. Philadelphians were fascinated by the visit, and the city's newspapers reported the Indians' every move. From the Northwest came Blue Jacket, the Shawnee leader who had proved most obdurate in his opposition to the United States, and Little Turtle, who had predicted the calamity of Fallen Timbers. From the Southeast came representatives from the principal nations: Cherokees, Creeks, Choctaws, and Chickasaws. These two delegations from opposite ends of the republic bumped into each other in, of all places, Charles Willson Peale's museum of scientific curiosity. The Indians convened an impromptu council a few days later, and somewhat inadvertently, the capital of the United States played host to a national meeting of indigenous peoples. Later, the southeastern Indians made a deal with a British impresario, John Ricketts, to perform a dance at one of the city's theaters on a Saturday evening. Eighty-five years before Buffalo Bill Cody created his famous Wild West show, Philadelphia audiences were treated to the spectacle of a "young Cherokee Chief" riding between two horses "with Mr. Ricketts on his shoulders."[31]

When Washington formally received the Indian delegations, he reverted to the old understanding of what divided the races: "Bad white men" had invaded Indian land and stolen Indian property, while "bad Indians in like manner will go into the settlement of the whites, and steal their horses." Timothy Pickering had taken the same line on his first visit to the Senecas back in 1790, when trying to explain why so many whites who had killed Indians or stolen their land managed to escape justice. The American population was enormous, Pickering averred, and "among such multitudes a few bad men may pass unknown." Pickering may have believed this back in 1790, but by the end of Washington's presidency it was far from clear that the federal government had the means or the will to curb its most distant citizens.[32]

Worse, the federal government had not implemented Pickering's civilizing plan, and the frontier had forts and trading posts rather than "schools of humanity." Missionaries and federal agents had not coordinated their activities, and many Indian leaders remained unwilling to hitch their future to the United States. The underlying assumption of the civilizing plan was that contact between Native Americans and whites would accelerate their convergence: that when Indians got to see civilization up close, their progress through the stages of human society would accelerate. The evidence from the first decade of federal policy was mixed, at best. In the Northwest, which had been the focal point of the civilizing effort, it was alarming. What if the settlers, traders, and soldiers of the frontier had corrupted the people they were supposed to be improving? This was the question that haunted the eastern advocates of the civilizing program in the 1790s and 1800s, and that eventually brought degradation into the debate over the future of Indians as well as blacks.

THREE

Correcting Ill Habits

For those reformers who took up their pens against slavery, degradation was an established fact—and a problem in urgent need of a solution. One of the most learned and influential of these reformers was Samuel Stanhope Smith, a Pennsylvania clergyman who spent much of his life lecturing at Princeton. Smith's most famous work—*An Essay upon the Varieties of the Human Complexion* (1787)— was a classic piece of Enlightenment science. Smith dismissed Thomas Jefferson's arguments about black inferiority and sent his readers back to Buffon: human beings were shaped by climate, diet, and the circumstances in which they lived. Smith amplified the Frenchman's assumptions that Euro-American civilization and white skin were at the summit of human development, but he insisted that an ascending path was open to non-whites. Like many other American writers in the late eighteenth century, he was fascinated by the story of Henry Moss, the Maryland slave whose skin had transformed "from a deep black to a clear and healthy white" over twenty years. Closer to home, he watched the Delaware student George Morgan White Eyes with special interest and convinced himself that the differences in skin tone between George and his fellow students were "sensibly diminishing." Princeton gave Smith an unusual platform for his ideas about the unity of the human race. Many of his students were southerners who had brought their "servants" with them to New Jersey. Smith taught them that human differences were a product of environment and circumstances. Before long, he began telling them that American slavery should be "entirely extinguished."[1]

In the 1790s and 1800s, Smith sparred with challengers who claimed that the races had been created separately or had permanently lost an original unity. Some of the most toxic of these writers—such as the British doctor Charles White—denied that their arguments justified slavery. "Laws ought not to allow greater freedom to a Shakespeare or a Milton," wrote White, "than to men of inferior capacities." Smith refused to let this pass. It was the "miserable habits of living" endured by slaves that explained the differences between them and their white masters. As long as they were denied the opportunities open to white people, and reminded of their "degraded state" by the contempt of free whites, African Americans would suffer a "perpetual sterility of genius." To mistake this condition for innate inferiority was a fundamental error. In the same vein, Smith had no patience for the self-serving arguments of the *Notes on the State of Virginia*. When Jefferson suggested that even those blacks who had been exposed to "the conversation of their masters" had failed to make progress in learning, Smith wondered if southern slaveholders were fit mentors to the men and women they owned.[2]

Would white people change their views of blacks if a general emancipation took place? Smith thought this unlikely, not least because he believed that the damage done by slavery to the character of African Americans was real. Freedom, then, was necessary but not sufficient. Smith told his students that the nation should "deliver this humiliated race of men from the bondage which at present degrades them," and "raise them in time to the true dignity of human nature, in a state of liberty, and self-government." But slaves could not be freed without a proper plan for their education: "No event can be more dangerous to a community than the sudden introduction into it of vast multitudes of persons, free in their condition, but without property, and possessing only the habits and vices of slavery." The dilemma would have been familiar to many of his students, who were witnesses to the slow progress of voluntary manumission in the South.[3]

Smith proposed that slaveholders tackle the problem of degradation before blacks were given their freedom. Drawing on Spanish and even Roman examples, he proposed giving slaves ownership of a small area of land that they could work in their free time. The sale of crops from this "peculium" could fund the manumission of its owner, and slaves would at last have an incentive structure that might build good character: the harder they worked, the closer they would get to freedom. It is hard to know what Smith's students made of their professor's earnest experimentalism. The Virginia abolitionist George Bourne, who read a published version of this lecture in 1815, thought it hopelessly naïve. Bourne had little patience for the notion of the conscientious slaveholder. He imagined that Smith's southern students, "when they heard the Lecturer thus gravely delineate their Negro-quarters, must certainly have been convulsed with laughter." The logic of Smith's plan, though, closely fitted his understanding of degradation. Slaves would have cause to demonstrate "good moral and industrious habits" while still enslaved; and white southerners would feel reassured that freed people had overcome a significant portion of their degradation before being granted their freedom.[4]

A similar idea had occurred to Noah Webster in New York, who in the 1790s wanted to destroy slavery "without essentially injuring the slave, the master and the public." Webster was aware that some slaveholders, who doubted that blacks would work without compulsion, feared the collapse of the South's economy after emancipation. The introduction of a feudal system, with blacks obliged to provide labor and rent to a landlord in return for access to land, might soothe their fears. But feudalism had become a hated relic in most of western Europe, and Webster thought it might offend "the spirit of our governments" almost as much as slavery did. Instead, he suggested that masters scan their slave quarters for individuals "whose habits are not firmly riveted." These would become guinea pigs in a bold attempt to prove that degradation was reversible. First, slaves would be encouraged to buy and sell goods at local markets to "accustom themselves to make bargains." Having passed this test, they would be given land to work as tenant farmers, along the lines of Smith's peculium. The premise underlying all of this, which Webster doesn't seem to have interrogated, was that slaves would enjoy the help and guidance of a benevolent master.[5]

For evidence that a scheme of this kind could work, Webster turned to Poland, where serfdom retained its grip into the late eighteenth century. The Polish nobleman Andrzej Zamoyski had resolved in 1760 to turn the workers on one of his village estates into tenant farmers. The serfs had been an ugly bunch: they were hopelessly addicted to alcohol, and they would commit outrages on each other and on passersby. But when Zamoyski raised them to the status of tenant farmers, a "glorious" change took place: the bad habits and immoral behavior ceased, and the degraded serfs became successful freemen overnight. Zamoyski's scheme caught the eye of Prince Stanislaus, the nephew of the Polish king, who pledged to implement it throughout the country. Although Polish serfs were white rather than black, Webster was convinced that "the precedent is important" for the United States. Perhaps southern slaveholders would permit an experiment that had been pioneered so successfully in Poland, and thereby raise the black population "from their degraded condition." Or had "false pride, deep-rooted prejudices, contempt of the African race and unconquerable indolence" turned slaveholders into the "dupes" of those phony philosophers who insisted on racial hierarchies? Webster hoped for the best: "Is there no Zamoyski, no Stanislaus in the southern departments of our free Republic, who will hazard one effective experiment?"[6]

In fact, these ideas had been less popular in Poland than Webster let on. The government there rejected the Zamoyski plan in 1763. A hundred years later, when Abraham Lincoln signed the Emancipation Proclamation, there were still serfs in many Polish regions. (Abolition finally came to Poland the following year.) But Webster believed that the task of abolitionists was to build alliances with slaveholders as well as government, and encourage them to think more like Zamoyski. If the men and women who held slaves could be persuaded to own the emancipation challenge, reformers could circumvent the vexing questions of property rights and government interference. The Constitution allowed that slaves were a distinct and protected kind of property, which placed the institution beyond the reach of federal legislators. The task of freeing black people would become much easier, then, if masters, rather than governments, took the lead. The key to everything was to outline the collective benefits of freedom, for whites as well as blacks, in the face of the prejudices and fears of white southerners. In this enterprise, Webster and other reformers were not limited to Europe for examples of abolition. Between 1777 and 1804, immediate or gradual emancipation was secured in Vermont, Pennsylvania, Massachusetts, Rhode Island, Connecticut, New York, Ohio, and New Jersey. Although the southern slave system looked very different from its northern analogue, the debate about emancipation and degradation in America was increasingly influenced by the experiences of freed people in the North.[7]

IN THE FIRST DECADES OF the republic, the opponents of slavery in the northern states hoped that their emancipation achievements would supply a roadmap for the South to follow. Northern legislatures voted for immediate or gradual emancipation; volunteers (usually affluent, religiously inspired, or both) formed antislavery organizations and societies that promoted black improvement; and free blacks themselves took an increasingly strident role in the fight against slavery and degradation. The resulting antislavery coalition had diverse motives, but its members agreed that education was a prerequisite if blacks were to fully capitalize on their freedom. The Pennsylvania and New York legislatures approved funds for black education. Very occasionally, black children went to school alongside whites, though

Reversing "degradation": the African Episcopal Church (*top*) in Philadelphia, and the New York African Free School (*bottom*). Courtesy of the Historical Society of Pennsylvania (top) and New York Public Library (bottom).

separate schools soon became the norm. Free blacks themselves shuttled between discomfort and anger as segregation replaced slavery in northern cities. The more optimistic among them hoped that the new status quo might be rolled back once black students demonstrated that they were no longer "degraded."[8]

That free blacks themselves employed the language of degradation should not surprise us. Many recognized the term's centrality to the white-led antislavery movement, and realized that it provided a lingua franca for conservative opponents of slavery and more radical voices. Consider the example of Absalom Jones, a Methodist minister and former slave who would become one of the most important members of the Philadelphia free black community. In the fall of 1787, not long after the Constitutional Convention had completed its work, Jones was literally dragged from his seat in the gallery of St. George's Methodist Episcopal Church. He and the other black churchgoers had been told to move further back to accommodate white worshipers. Since blacks had already been exiled to the gallery, and church officials refused even to wait for the conclusion of the service before turning them from their seats, Jones and his friends resolved never to return to St. George's. Their breakaway African Church became the central religious institution for Philadelphia's growing free black population. Even Jones, who was better acquainted with white prejudice than anyone, recognized degradation as a rhetorical necessity. He signed a 1799 free black petition to Congress demanding the end of the slave trade and of the terrible practice of kidnapping northern free blacks into slavery. But the petitioners stopped short of demanding "the immediate emancipation of the whole, knowing that the degraded state of many and want of education would greatly disqualify for such a change."[9]

Free blacks developed a complicated relationship with white antislavery campaigners. The annual abolition conventions organized by white reformers insisted that blacks were being fitted for citizenship, and yet most antislavery societies did not extend equal membership across the color line. It was much easier for slaveholders to join the first wave of abolition societies than free blacks—a position that betrayed not only white paternalism, but the emphasis placed by reformers on recruiting masters into the fight against degradation. Many prominent free blacks decided nonetheless to make use of white "benevolence" even if it came with an acceptance of their own degradation. In his speech at the American Convention for Promoting the Abolition of Slavery in 1806, Peter Williams Jr., a young black abolitionist from New York, thanked his white audience for helping blacks to emerge from their "complicated misery to the full enjoyments of civilized life." He conceded that the "ignorance" fostered by slavery often produced vice in freed people, and hoped the efforts of abolitionists to fight degradation would create a society in which "all distinctions between the inalienable rights of black men, and white" were "set at nought."[10]

As blacks were freed from slavery in the North, they looked for a place in the growing economies of the major cities. By 1800, nearly half of Philadelphia's black population continued to live and work within white households. Given the unreliable labor market for free blacks, many opted for the dismal certainties of domestic or indentured service over the risks of unemployment (and the almshouse). Others struck out on their own, becoming skilled laborers, shopkeepers, or sailors. Perhaps the most successful black person in Philadelphia was James Forten, who had been born free in 1766 and educated at a school directed by Anthony Benezet, the storied abolitionist. During the American Revolution, many black Americans had concluded that Britain was a more dependable source of liberty than the new United States. Lord Dunmore, the last colonial governor of Virginia, had offered freedom in 1775 to slaves who crossed the lines to fight for the king. George Washington and Congress, meanwhile, had dithered for years over whether to allow blacks to enlist in the Continental Army. James Forten, however, had seen enough promise in the Philadelphia of his youth to take the Patriot side during the fighting, serving with distinction on an American privateer. After the war, he proved such a good apprentice in the sail-making trade (his father's profession) that his boss eventually agreed to sell him the firm. By 1800, Forten employed more than thirty men—black and white—to cut sails for the biggest ships in the harbor. Though Forten had never been a slave, the story of his success was used by abolitionists to demonstrate the potential of black people more generally.[11]

Were Forten and other free blacks citizens? This was a surprisingly difficult question to answer. The emancipation laws that destroyed slavery in northern states usually did little to clarify the status of the freed population. An effort to pass a gradual abolition bill in New York in 1785 failed precisely because it excluded any "negro, mulatto or mustee" from holding office or voting. The Council of Revision, consisting of the governor and the state's leading judges, noted that blacks should be given all the privileges of citizens; this commitment could not be diluted "without shocking those principles of equal liberty, which every page in the constitution labors to enforce." The exclusion of "mustees"—a term that usually referred to a person with any kind of non-white ancestry—raised the specter of "an aristocracy of the most dangerous and malignant kind, rendering power permanent and hereditary in the hands of those persons who deduce their origin through white ancestors only." The council members didn't assume that racial mixing would be rife in the new republic, but if even one in a thousand black New Yorkers married a white spouse, the vagueness of the word "mustee" would place a terrible shadow over future generations. By 1985, they predicted, perhaps only a fiftieth of the population would qualify as purely white, and race-proud aristocrats would become tyrants over the masses.[12]

Citizenship itself was a slippery concept in the early republic. Authorities at the local, state, and federal levels made citizenship and suffrage laws, but there was no coordination between them and little shared logic. Hence the confusion of Jeremy Belknap's correspondents in 1795, when they tried to answer St. George Tucker's question about black suffrage. The original draft of the Massachusetts state constitution contained a raft of conservative measures—including an explicit provision barring blacks and Indians from voting—and was soundly rejected by the electorate. When the constitution was finally approved in 1780, it restricted the franchise on the basis of property, sex, and age—but not race. The property requirement easily excluded many free blacks in the state, but blacks were never explicitly barred from the franchise in Massachusetts on account of their color. Other states began to restrict suffrage only after large numbers of black people began exercising their right to vote. In New York, blacks were initially subject to the same laws on suffrage as whites. But when delegates at the state constitutional convention of 1821 opted to relax property qualifications for white men, they insisted on retaining those restrictions on African Americans. (Less than 1 percent of the state's black population was allowed to vote under the new rules.) In Rhode Island, blacks could vote until 1822, after which the state began a decades-long process of flip-flopping on the question of race and suffrage. Black Pennsylvanians were barred from the vote only in 1836, though many, including the sailmaker James Forten, had avoided the polls before this date to keep from inflaming their white neighbors. (Forten did, however, escort his white employees to vote for Federalist candidates.) And New Jersey restricted the franchise to free white men in 1807, disenfranchising not only black people but also a number of women who had been voting in previous elections.[13]

If the trend in individual states was toward the gradual disenfranchisement of free blacks, the federal picture was opaque. Black people were not formally excluded from citizenship until the Supreme Court ruling in the Dred Scott case of 1856, but black rights were curtailed in numerous ways before then. The delegates at the Philadelphia Convention in 1787 had zealously kept the word "white" from the Constitution, but in 1790, Congress restricted the new naturalization provisions to "free white" immigrants. For black sailors, who faced special dangers as they served on American ships, the State Department was unusually proactive: a "seaman's protection certificate" was widely issued to African Americans, affirming that the holder was "a citizen of the United States of America." (Given the continuing plague of the British press gang in the Atlantic world, the document was cherished by white sailors as well as black.) More generally, federal legislators tended either to restrict black rights or to fudge the question of citizenship status. Black people were excluded from militias, but could serve in the regular armed forces. They were barred from working as mail carriers in 1810, but were eligible for land grants in the West if they fought in the War of 1812. The system, with its loopholes and trap doors, was hopelessly and designedly inconsistent.[14]

The epic congressional battle in 1819–1821 over the admission of Missouri to the Union should have settled the question definitively, but it only highlighted the confusion. When the slaveholding supporters of Missouri's admission to the Union insisted on barring "free negroes and mulattoes" from settling in (or even visiting) the would-be state, northern congressmen complained that the Union would collapse if any one state tried to curb the free movement of "citizens" from elsewhere in the United States. The eventual compromise that secured a slave Missouri stipulated that the new state could not exclude "any citizen" from the "privileges and immunities" supplied by the Constitution. The wording offered no specific protection to free blacks, did not explicitly recognize their citizenship, and offered no guidance on how they might hold Missouri to account if it barred their entry. Instead, it offered a wink to both sides: the House of Representatives recognized the tension between Missouri's targeting of "free blacks and mulattoes" and the rudiments of black citizenship elsewhere in America, but it wouldn't resolve the contradiction.[15]

The saga only confirmed something free blacks and abolitionists already knew: the federal government was a poor guarantor of citizenship in the United States. Until ratification of the Fourteenth Amendment in 1868, the Constitution envisaged that Americans would become citizens through the laws of the state in which they were born or naturalized. This fact stymied even the most tentative efforts to enlist the federal government in overcoming degradation. White and black abolitionists petitioned the US Congress on a regular basis in the 1790s and 1800s for measures that might ameliorate slavery and improve the condition of free blacks, but with very little success.

While northern states could supply blueprints for emancipation to the South, there was no prospect of a truly coordinated national strategy under federal auspices. The effective abdication of the federal government from the management of US citizenship made the task of dismantling slavery still harder.[16]

IT WAS DURING THE HIGH-WATER moment of congressional action against slavery that the limits of federal power were most clearly visible. The Constitutional Convention in 1787 had explicitly prevented Congress from abolishing the slave trade for twenty years. In the winter of 1806–1807, as that deadline approached, congressmen debated the terms by which the external slave trade could be brought to an end. In the process they encountered an uncomfortable problem: When that trade became illegal, what would happen to ships that tried to smuggle human beings into the United States? Legislators discussed the punishments that might be imposed on captains or merchants, but it was the fate of their slaves that proved most divisive. James Sloan of New Jersey thought the solution obvious: every person illegally carried to the United States should go free. Sloan recalled the memories of his childhood: the specter of slave ships offloading their desperate cargo at New Jersey ports, and the strange experience of befriending and playing with slave children before their fate diverged from his.[17]

Yet it seemed equally obvious to Sloan's southern colleagues that illegally imported Africans should remain in slavery after their arrival. The Speaker of the House, Nathaniel Macon of North Carolina, reminded members that rescued slaves would be penniless and probably uneducated: "By what means are they, understanding nothing about the country, to be supported?" Joseph Clay of Pennsylvania seconded Macon's claim that these Africans would be "ignorant and unacquainted with our language or habits," and suggested they would create havoc if they were given freedom. The alternative—that they would be auctioned on the wharves of Charleston or New Orleans, as if there had been no ban on the external slave trade—struck northern legislators as obscene. "The United States ought to retain the control of them," insisted Josiah Quincy of Massachusetts, though "what is to be done with them, is another question." Another Massachusetts member thought that rescued slaves should be "taken care of by the Government, and comfortably provided for." But it was difficult to conceive of a mechanism for such a program. Lawmakers spoke of rescued Africans in exactly the same terms that were used to describe freed slaves: they were morally entitled to freedom, but uneducated and likely to be a nuisance without a coordinated effort to fit them for citizenship. If Congress accepted responsibility for their fate, it would confront the same problems that had stymied the effort to counter degradation at a local level.[18]

The most obvious precedent for rescuing smuggled slaves pointed away from government altogether, and toward the kindness of strangers. In July 1800, the US Navy schooner *Ganges* intercepted two slaving vessels off the coast of Cuba that had been outfitted in Philadelphia. Although the external slave trade was still legal, Congress in 1794 had banned the construction of slaving vessels in US ports. The captain of the *Ganges* brought the ships to Philadelphia and unloaded around 140 Africans at the city's quarantine station. While the local authorities fretted over what to do with them, a group of concerned residents (including members of the Pennsylvania Abolition Society) took up their cause. Newspapers across the northern states shared the affecting story of a husband and wife who had been put on the separate ships, destined for "the lash of different task-masters," before their reunion at the confluence of the Delaware and the Schuylkill. "The feelings of the female were too powerful for her emaciated frame," noted one paper, "and she was prematurely a mother." The PAS arranged for the rescued Africans to be indentured to local farmers, artisans, and merchants. When their terms were complete, they melted into Pennsylvania's free black population, distinguishable only by the fact that their surname was "Ganges." In this isolated example, it was civil society rather than government that solved the problem of black belonging.[19]

For northern radicals in the 1806–1807 congressional debate, anything short of immediate freedom was an unconscionable encroachment on the rights of contraband Africans. Josiah Quincy thought that no jury in New England would side with the government if it tried to indenture the slaves it had rescued at sea. Conservative northern legislators were nervous about where this might lead, and clutched at straws: Weren't children and other "incompetent" people placed in indentured service without great harm to the "rights of man"? Southern lawmakers were delighted by this argument among northerners. "You have got, gentlemen, into a great difficulty," said a South Carolina member. "It is so bad that you cannot go on, and must stick where you are." The debate stretched into January 1807, and the proponents of freeing contraband Africans put that principle to the vote. But when the proposal for emancipation with apprenticeship gathered speed, Speaker Macon became nervous. It was important, he said, to realign the debate around "commercial principles" rather than the supposed moral obligations of the United States. Pennsylvania congressman James Smilie, an opponent of slavery, seized upon Macon's crudely material logic. The debate should be about "principles of a higher order than those merely commercial," Smilie told the House. He and his antislavery colleagues were trying to uphold "the principles of 1776," which, though "laughed at" by slavery's apologists, were "now beginning, I hope, to be held in universal estimation."[20]

In early January 1807, the proponents of freeing rescued slaves— either immediately or after indenture—felt confident enough to call a vote on the motion that "no person shall be sold as a slave by virtue of this act." The House split perfectly, sixty members for each side, until Nathaniel Macon exercised his privilege as Speaker and voted down the resolution. The issue moved to a House committee, whose northern members were willing to compromise by diluting the punishments to captains in exchange for defending Africans. It was imperative to protect illegally trafficked people from "conversion into slaves, and so to save the United States from the humiliation and disgrace of sanctioning a principle at which the strongest feelings of humanity, as well as the plainest dictates of reason, revolted." The committee spent a month drafting a new plan in which the president himself would have the power to seize rescued slaves and send them to "such place or places in the United States, as the President thereof may direct, and there be indentured as apprentices or servants, as the President may judge most beneficial for them." Crucially, the law would restrict the choice of possible destinations to those states which had already abolished slavery, or which had passed gradual abolition laws. "The Southern gentlemen had said if we would take away the negroes from them, they would be satisfied," James Sloan reminded the House. "We have exerted every stretch of our genius to do this; we have agreed to take them ourselves."[21]

Sloan thought this clever plan would force his southern antagonists to cut a deal. In fact, they promised open rebellion if the bill passed the House. Peter Early of Georgia calmly declared that "the inhabitants of the Southern States would resist this provision with their lives." When a Pennsylvania member rose to object—"This opens a scene as I never expected to witness in this House. Are we to be threatened with civil war?"—Early demurred that he had simply "communicated the idea that military force would be necessary to carry the law into execution." Sloan and his allies dropped their proposal. The prospect that freed slaves would be indentured or apprenticed under presidential authority vanished, and the bill's final version upheld a familiar concession: the states, and not the federal government, would decide the fate of rescued Africans. The US government had been spared the embarrassment of auctioning contraband slaves on its own authority, but had missed another opportunity to take ownership of the problem of educating and integrating black people. Many illegal slaving vessels made it to southern ports undetected in the aftermath of the 1807 act, their cargoes spirited into the growing slave population of the region. Those that were apprehended by the navy or coast guard became the responsibility of southern legislatures, which quickly passed laws directing the new arrivals toward the auction block. This grimly ironic outcome had a typically perverse coda: the proceeds from the sale of "rescued" Africans would benefit the local workhouse. For the contrabands themselves, it mattered little if they were smuggled into the United States undetected or intercepted by US authorities. There was, it seemed, no escape from American slavery.[22]

FROM THE PERSPECTIVE OF NORTHERN antislavery reformers, the most unsettling element of the debate about contraband slaves was the intransigence of the Deep South representatives. When James Smilie of Pennsylvania invoked the Declaration of Independence on the House floor to argue for the rights of rescued slaves, he knew that the document had resonance in the South as surely as in the North. The Georgia congressman Peter Early pushed back. At best, he explained, Georgians thought slavery a "political evil" rather than a moral one. Even this might overstate the case: "A large majority of people in the Southern States do not consider slavery as even an evil." This may have been true of the white population in the Deep South. It had been the narrow alliance of South Carolina and Georgia that had prevented the House of Representatives from considering Benjamin Franklin's petition for immediate emancipation back in 1790. More alarming to abolitionists was the fear that this calloused view of slavery might be creeping northward into Virginia, the state that had previously sustained the hope that abolition could be national rather than sectional.[23]

In 1800, Virginia had nearly twice as many slaves as the combined total for Georgia and South Carolina, along with a growing population of free blacks. African Americans had been excluded from the vote since 1723, and the House of Delegates passed a series of social restrictions on free blacks during the 1790s in response to their growing numbers. The state's 1782 manumission law had encouraged masters to free their slaves without consulting state authorities. Many did so in the years after the Revolution, and free people made up around 10 percent of the state's black population by the turn of the century. Washington, who died a few weeks before the turn of the nineteenth century, stipulated in his will that his slaves at Mount Vernon should be set free (though not those belonging to his wife, Martha). In acknowledgment of the lively debate about degradation and the difficult transition to freedom, he provided apprenticeships for his younger slaves and pensions for the elderly. Washington encapsulated the achievements and limits of the early antislavery movement in Virginia. The most powerful man in the republic had freed his slaves and provided for their future, but he had done so without the aid of either the state or the federal government.[24]

If Washington managed (posthumously, at least) to vindicate Noah Webster's hope of American Zamoyskis, the antislavery landscape of Virginia was turned upside down less than a year later. The nation had been gripped by political turmoil during the final years of John Adams's presidency. Federalists and Republicans in Philadelphia had waged an increasingly toxic battle over domestic affairs; each side accused the other of trying to drag America into the Napoleonic Wars. As the summer of 1800 drew to a close, and the election struggle between John Adams and Thomas Jefferson entered its final, acrid phase, a slave named Pharaoh, who worked on a farm just north of Richmond, told his master, Mosby Sheppard, of a plot to overthrow the Virginia government. The plot had been masterminded by another slave named Gabriel, a blacksmith who was owned by one of Sheppard's neighbors, Thomas Prosser. The news that a slave revolt was imminent reached Richmond the next day, where Governor James Monroe took quiet steps to thwart the conspirators. The conspiracy had been discovered in time to avoid bloodshed, at least until the courts sent a train of supposed plotters to the gallows. But its psychological impact on white Virginians was considerable.[25]

As they picked over the details, Virginia's ruling class told themselves that they had reaped the consequences of unchecked emancipation. Gabriel himself was a discomfiting figure. Although he lived with Thomas Prosser on the rural outskirts of Richmond, his skills at metalwork allowed him to spend most of his time in the workshops of the state capital, earning wages that he shared with his master. Unlike

Philadelphia or New York in the 1790s and 1800s, where free blacks struggled to find a place for themselves among white-dominated trades, Richmond had a black majority and a lively artisanal culture that put free blacks and skilled slaves in close proximity. Gabriel was hardly a model of degradation: he could read and write, and he had been encouraged by Thomas Prosser to hire out his labor in the city. But Gabriel's leadership of a widespread insurrection suggested the damage that a little education might do, especially atop Virginia's precarious demography. Here, surely, was the rebuke to the gradualism of Noah Webster or Samuel Stanhope Smith: if you gave slaves freedom and learning to ameliorate the iniquity of their situation, they were less likely to thank you for the remedy than to kill you for the cause.[26]

The authorities in Virginia were desperate to extract a confession from Gabriel, but he told them virtually nothing. From that febrile summer to the present day, the work of establishing his intentions has fallen to other people: to Gabriel's co-conspirators at his original trial, who offered competing testimonies in the hope of saving their skins; to the Federalist opponents of Thomas Jefferson, who delighted in associating Gabriel with the excesses of the French Revolution; and to modern historians, who have reconstructed the conspiracy of 1800 from a variety of perspectives. Some have suggested that Gabriel's real fight was with the wealthy merchants of Richmond, who seemed determined to cheat white artisans and black slaves alike. Others have placed the events in a broader tradition of black resistance to slavery. (African Americans in Virginia kept the memory of Gabriel alive through the state's next major slave revolt, Nat Turner's rebellion, in 1831.) In reviewing the trial documents, it is hard not to snag on the extraordinary claim of one witness: "If the white people agreed to their freedom," Gabriel supposedly told his associates, "they would then hoist a white flag" and "dine and drink with the merchants of the city." Did Gabriel imagine reconciliation rather than race war on the other side of his victory? Another witness remembered the plan differently: "None were to be spared of the whites, except Quakers, Methodists and French people."[27]

The events of 1800—and a smaller, though no less alarming plot in 1802—badly damaged the abolitionist cause in Virginia. A few months before Gabriel's Rebellion, members of the state's antislavery society had proudly informed the national abolition convention in Philadelphia of their efforts to promote black education: Virginia stood ready "to prepare the minds of our unfortunate African brethren for that condition of freedom and rank in society to which, we believe, they will sooner or later arrive." At the 1801 convention, a much bleaker dispatch arrived from Richmond: "Many who were once hearty in the cause of emancipation" had reconsidered their position after Gabriel's Rebellion. The antislavery society at Alexandria confirmed that the events of the previous summer had "renovated persecution against the helpless Africans," though at least in Alexandria, abolitionists had managed to reopen their Sunday school for local blacks. The delegates in Philadelphia approved sending funds to help the cause of abolition in Virginia, and in their "Address to the Citizens of the United States," they looked for an upside in the recent, unfortunate events. Gabriel's Rebellion was a deplorable development, of course, but it should serve as a reminder that black people could not be oppressed without consequences: "There is a certain state of degradation and misery to which they may be reduced, a certain point of desperation to which the human mind may be brought, and beyond which it cannot be driven." The lesson of 1800, the convention insisted, was that emancipation and education were the only "effectual security against revolt."[28]

The rulers of Virginia saw things differently. Within three years, the Sunday school in Alexandria—"the brightest ornament that ever attracted our attention," in the words of one local abolitionist—had been forced to close. "We are in fact dead," wrote an unnamed Virginian to the convention in 1805, "and I may say, I have no hope of reanimation." It was more than twenty years before Virginia sent another delegation to the abolition convention in Philadelphia—and then it was to promote the cause of black removal to Haiti and Africa. In the meantime, the Virginia House of Delegates made a renewed effort to monitor and restrict Virginia's free black population, encouraging many to leave the state and head for the cities north of the Mason-Dixon Line. In 1806, Virginia legislators finally addressed the 1782 manumission act and its encouragement of black freedom in the state. Henceforth, every freed slave would be compelled to leave Virginia within a year of his or her emancipation, on penalty of re-enslavement. If blacks were to be redeemed from degradation and fashioned into "useful members of society," this would have to happen beyond state lines.[29]

ALTHOUGH JAMES SLOAN AND HIS northern colleagues in Congress had offered to save contraband slaves from the auction blocks of Charleston and Savannah, no antislavery writer had yet promoted the idea that the North could become a refuge for the existing slave population of the South. Instead, the political logic of abolitionism was rooted in the power of example. Southern states were supposed to witness the success of emancipation and education in New York or Philadelphia and follow suit. This logic was vulnerable in two ways that would become mutually reinforcing. If northern emancipation did not produce a harmonious society, the progress of southern manumissions would stall. Similarly, if the South failed to own the social consequences of emancipation—refusing to educate blacks or to employ them as free laborers—the North could unwittingly become a magnet for southern blacks seeking meaningful freedom. This flood of refugees would in turn threaten the precarious racial and social equilibrium in the North.

In the first decade of the nineteenth century, the Pennsylvania Abolition Society felt the pressure of black migration to the northern states. In 1806, the society bemoaned the "constant influx" of blacks from the South into Philadelphia, warning that uneducated and degraded migrants would threaten the progress made by the city's long-established free black population. Three years later, the society urged Pennsylvanians to take pride in the fact that their state was seen by free blacks as "an asylum where the repetition of the wrongs they

had endured was not to be feared." The dilemma of northern reformers on the migration question was best captured in the career of the
maverick antislavery campaigner Thomas Branagan. Born in Dublin
in 1774, Branagan spent his early years in the bowels of the slave system: working on slave ships initially, then as an overseer on an Anti-
gua plantation. He later claimed that his four years in the Caribbean
had made him an abolitionist. Certainly by the time he emigrated
from Ireland in 1798, he was ready to bear witness against the system
he had previously served. His arrival in the United States was inaus-
picious: the ship containing his luggage was wrecked off the coast of
Delaware, and he suffered the unusual indignity of being robbed of his
remaining possessions by a Quaker. But with an antislavery sentiment
honed by experience—and a yearning to become a writer—he found
many friends in Philadelphia. In the first years of the nineteenth century, supported by black and white reformers, he put his pen at the
service of abolition.[30]

Branagan's 1804 *Preliminary Essay on the Oppression of the Exiled
Sons of Africa* made much of the author's inside knowledge of the slave
system. Branagan offered a careful refutation of the argument that
black people were "an inferior order of beings," dismantling Jefferson's
arguments in the *Notes on the State of Virginia* with patience and precision. The claim that blacks were mentally impaired was "supported
by no shadow of evidence" and had been "ably refuted by writers
who had the best opportunities of information." Branagan's travels
had confirmed the wisdom of Buffon and Samuel Stanhope Smith:
the societies of the African interior, which he had visited many times,
were "as sensible, ingenious, hospitable and generous as any people,
placed in such circumstances." One of Jefferson's strategies in the
Notes had been to dismiss the literary value of black writers such as
the Boston poet Phillis Wheatley and the British sailor Olaudah Equi-
ano. Branagan, who had just published his own epic poem attacking
slavery, reprinted one of Wheatley's verses and invited readers to judge
its merits for themselves. Could any "young white female" produce "a
just comparative estimate?" With so much evidence of racial equality

now in the public domain, resorting to charges of inferiority betrayed the predicament in which slaveholders found themselves: "When our opponents bring [the inferiority argument] forward, they proclaim to all the world that their cause is desperate, and that they are reduced to their last shift." Branagan's plan to end slavery was careful and confident: Congress should abolish the external slave trade; local officials in the South should begin a gradual emancipation program "with all convenient speed"; and schools for slaves should be established immediately and funded from the public purse.[31]

But when Thomas Branagan published a sequel to the *Essay* in 1805, his tone had changed beyond recognition. In his *Serious Remonstrances, Addressed to the Citizens of the Northern States*, Branagan concluded that the model of educating and incorporating freed slaves within the southern states had not taken root. Instead, a terrible alternative seemed to be emerging: slaves would be freed in the South, but the work of educating and improving them for citizenship would be outsourced to the northern states. This was "big with very unpleasant effects, and exceedingly injurious to the citizens of the North." After insisting on racial equality in his 1804 *Essay*, Branagan now launched an astonishing attack on the character of southern freed people who had trekked to Philadelphia. They were "sunk into the lowest state of debasement," and a nuisance to their new neighbors. If the slaves of the South should eventually revolt against their masters, every black resident of Philadelphia would become more dangerous than "a thousand Indians on our frontiers."[32]

What had produced this astonishing turnaround? A number of factors seem to have warped Branagan's idealism. In 1804, the Pennsylvania Abolition Society had been forced to close one of its schools, as poorer blacks couldn't afford to keep their children in education rather than indenture. That summer, news reached Philadelphia that the new black emperor of Haiti, Jean-Jacques Dessalines, had killed thousands of white colonists at the successful conclusion of the Haitian Revolution. While Branagan was hardly alone in being unnerved by this alarming outcome, Haiti may help to explain the lurid spiral of his thinking. Then there were his financial problems. While writing his *Remonstrances*, Branagan fell out with Richard Allen, the free black clergyman and educator, over the arrangements they had made for publication of Branagan's antislavery poetry. As his finances suffered, Branagan felt bruised by the failure of Philadelphia's free black community to recognize him as their Moses. (Branagan complained of "haughty" blacks who "begin to feel themselves consequential.") In November 1805, Branagan begged even Thomas Jefferson for money, informing the president that he was "not above doing any thing for an honest living." Branagan's munificence toward free blacks seems to have shriveled as his fortunes worsened. This decline would explain another especially bleak passage in the *Remonstrances*: Branagan complained that Philadelphia's "poor reputable whites" were being forced "to seek employ in the back woods," because the city's do-gooding elites preferred to hire blacks. In the city's almshouses that year, Irish immigrants outnumbered free blacks by almost two to one. That fact must have been the more troubling to Branagan as he himself became an object of charity.[33]

The difficulties of uplifting Philadelphia's existing black population were compounded in Branagan's mind with the prospect of tens of thousands—perhaps hundreds of thousands—of new arrivals from the southern heartlands of degradation. Slaves who had been "ruined" by the "injustice of others" were "exported to the North, where we have to provide for, and support them, with all their vices upon them." Barely a year after he had published his upbeat program for gradual emancipation, Branagan had changed course entirely. If the South had been a pupil of northern benevolence in 1804, it was now a prostitute forcing its "virtuous neighbor to maintain her spurious offspring." The Pennsylvania Abolition Society, in its boldest moments, wanted Philadelphians to feel flattered by black migration and what it said about the city's benevolent reputation. Thomas Branagan's work suggested that public opinion was moving in the opposite direction.[34]

BRANAGAN'S DIRE WARNINGS OF A free black invasion did not materialize. Although the population in Philadelphia was considerably increased by arrivals from neighboring states and the Upper South, the proportion of black people in the city barely kept pace with the influx of whites from the countryside, from other parts of the Union, and from Europe. Nonetheless, the perception that free blacks from the South had not been fully redeemed from the degradation of slavery fed the prejudice that blacks would never be equal to whites. It became harder for white and black reformers to maintain schools and other services for the overwhelmingly impoverished black populace.

Even though Branagan surrendered to prejudice in 1805, he still wasn't able to follow Jefferson's lead and ground the impossibility of racial integration in black inferiority. In his *Remonstrances*, he reprinted the section from the *Notes on the State of Virginia* on the obstacles to a mixed-race society, but deleted Jefferson's long paragraphs of pseudo-science about "scarf skin," the secretions of the kidneys, and the other physical manifestations of black debility. (He also cut the section on the supposedly mediocre poetry of Phillis Wheatley.) There was nothing accidental about Branagan's surgery: between the redactions, he preserved Jefferson's self-serving claim that black people could never forget or forgive the evils they had suffered, and that the prejudices of blacks against whites—grounded in "ten thousand recollections of the injuries they have received"—would be just as intractable as the prejudices of whites against blacks. Even in his despair about integration, however, Branagan wouldn't accept Jefferson's invitation to fix black people on a lower rung of humanity.[35]

The efforts to combat degradation among northern reformers always had a dual aim: to remove the real debilities forced upon blacks by slavery, and to lift the fog of prejudice that prevented whites from recognizing human brotherhood. The Boston judge James Sullivan had told Jeremy Belknap and St. George Tucker that the only way "to eradicate the prejudice which education has fixed in the minds of the white against the black people" would be "by raising the blacks, by means of mental improvements, nearly to the same grade as the whites." But Tucker's other correspondents noted that prejudice itself had a withering effect on black improvement. John Adams thought that prejudice might have played a greater role in corrupting the characters of black people in Massachusetts than the mild forms of slavery they had endured. The "scoffs," "insults," and "continual insinuations" of the "common white people" had made black people "lazy, idle, proud, vicious, and at length wholly useless to their masters." Tucker thought that prejudices in Virginia would be "almost innate," and wondered if their eradication might be "beyond the power of human nature to accomplish."[36]

The free black community of Philadelphia was well placed to chronicle the ways in which white prejudice became its own source of degradation. In 1813, the Pennsylvania legislature agreed to debate a bill that would sell any black person into slavery if he or she failed to produce a valid registration document. In a series of essays, James Forten protested the "degrading tendency" this law would have on ordinary blacks who were already struggling to improve themselves. "Are not men of colour sufficiently degraded?" Forten asked. "Why then increase their degradation!" Forten imagined a scene in which a black man was stopped by a constable demanding to see his papers, with a crowd of white children "delighting in the sport" of repeating the constable's question: "Negro, where is your certificate?" The question would be shouted "from a hundred tongues," shaming even the most distinguished and upstanding black resident of the city. "Can any thing be conceived more degrading to humanity?" If only Philadelphians could approach the question with an "unprejudiced mind," they would recognize the iniquities involved. Forten's pleas were not in vain: the state senate rejected the bill. But blacks continued to experience prejudice in the city's streets and workplaces, despite Forten's insistence that blacks could be "useful members of Society."[37]

In the 1810s and 1820s, abolitionists increasingly came to recognize white prejudice as a potent source of black degradation. Even as free blacks tried to overcome the debilitating effects of slavery, they were sideswiped by abuse that ignored the root causes of black poverty or illiteracy. "We believe it is not the *color*, correctly considered, which causes this prejudice," declared George Newbold of the New York Manumission Society in 1828, "but the condition in which we have been accustomed to view the unfortunate subjects of a degrading thraldom." White people failed to recognize their double injury of blacks: "We adopt a system towards them which is directly calculated to debase and brutalize the human character," Newbold told the national abolition convention, "and then condemn them for the moral and intellectual desolation which this system has produced." The solution was the same in 1828 as it had been forty years earlier. The "first and most important requisite" for the total abolition of slavery, Newbold said, was education. "What the second? and the third— our answer would still be as before—education. It is the philosopher's stone, which will turn the baser metals into gold." But with few American Zamoyskis emerging in the South, little appetite for the promotion of black education among city and state legislators in the North, and condescension and exhaustion among the veterans of antislavery societies, it seemed as if the engines of "degradation"—slavery, limited black opportunity, and white prejudice—were running out of control.[38]

FOUR

One Nation Only

ON INDEPENDENCE DAY IN 1795, General "Mad Anthony"
Wayne and 1,500 of his troops gathered at Fort Greenville to hear
an oration from a Welshman. Wayne was preparing for treaty talks
with the Western Confederacy, which he had defeated on the battlefield at Fallen Timbers. To the preacher that day, thirty-four-year-old
Morgan John Rhys, the Indians were a source of endless fascination.
Rhys's journey to the front line of the republic's first Indian war was
an improbable one. He had landed in New York in October 1794 with
plans to establish a colony of Welsh Baptists somewhere in the South.
A few weeks later, he was in Philadelphia to see George Washington
deliver his Annual Message to Congress. Rhys lamented in his diary
that Americans had "stumbled, as it regards the poor Africans, at the
threshold of equal rights," though he took comfort from Philadelphia's "zealous" abolition societies and from his visit to a black school
in the city. "They have certainly equal abilities with the whites," he
observed of the pupils, though it remained to be seen if their potential
would be blocked by "the prejudice of the age." Further south, Rhys
walked excitedly through the foundations of the new Federal City on
the Potomac, only to feel deflated by the slave cabins on the grounds
of Washington's Mount Vernon estate. "Thou great man Washington,"
he wrote in his diary. "What meaneth the bleating of these black sheep
and the lowing of these Negro oxen that till thy ground?" Rhys was

already aware of one of the president's excuses: "Say not, they belong to thy wife. Such paltry excuses are beneath thy character."[1]

Rhys eventually ended up in the Northwest, where he befriended the chaplain of Anthony Wayne's victorious army. He made his way to Greenville in June 1795 just as the defeated Indians were gathering there to learn how much land they would lose. Rhys's view of Native Americans may have been colored by his suspicion that they were originally from Wales—a long story for another time—but his encounters with Arthur St. Clair and other western officials made him wary of a new triumphalism on the frontier. When Wayne's chaplain became indisposed on Independence Day, Rhys took over as orator and told the army that "the love of conquest and enlargement of territory should be sacrificed" to promote harmony with Native people. Rhys would not accept that Native people were incapable of "civilization." The problem, he thought, was that the frontier contained "a great number of white as well as red savages." It was unfortunate, he told his audience of mostly frontiersmen, that "the frontiers of America have been peopled in many places by men of bad morals." The federal government would have to double down on its civilizing policy, and the "many virtuous characters" who lived in the West would need to commit themselves to a vision of coexistence between whites and Indians.[2]

Anthony Wayne, who must have listened to this speech with a pinched smile, had staked out a different view in his recent correspondence with Secretary of War Timothy Pickering. "I have examined your instructions to me relative to the General boundary line between the United States and the Western Indian Nations with the most serious attention," Wayne wrote in the spring of 1795, "and I much fear that it will make the White & Red people too near neighbors." In close proximity, Indians and whites would feel a "constant and mutual distrust." Instead, he recommended a neutral zone between the races—"a kind of consecrated ground"—which would be zealously maintained by Congress. Wayne gestured vaguely toward future reconciliation. Perhaps on "some distant & future day," the buffer zone might no longer be necessary. But in the short term, Congress should "neither sell nor suffer it to be settled upon any occasion or pretext whatever." After consulting with Washington, Pickering declined the general's request. A neutral zone would cost a fortune to police, and it would almost certainly be violated by frontier whites, who were "nearly as eager in the pursuit of game, as the Indians." Pickering urged Wayne to focus on the positive, however. Now that a "certain boundary" was being negotiated between whites and Indians, the prospects for conflict would be greatly reduced.[3]

Pickering wasn't alone in his opposition to Wayne's plan. In the aftermath of the war with the Western Confederacy, missionaries, philanthropists, and federal officials continued to argue that proximity—not separation—was the key to the civilizing program. During his speech at Greenville, Morgan Rhys promised that if "interchanges of persons" could be arranged, with whites and indigenous people living in each other's towns, "the Americans and Indians would become one people." A similar proposal came from the Philadelphia reformer Charles Crawford, who called for a group of Indian pioneers to move east to the cities and observe white people in their settled surroundings. Crawford respected the efforts of missionaries who had worked in Indian country, but he had more faith in the potential of civil society to transform the fortunes of Native people. He and his fellow philanthropists would happily "invite the Indians now and then to [our] houses," paying for bed, board, and instruction until the civilizing work was done.[4]

The Princeton lecturer Silas Wood, who later became a US congressman, identified three factors that were holding the Indians back: the lack of a proper civilizing effort on the part of whites; population decline caused by warfare and disease; and the Indians' physical separation from white people. Like Rhys and Crawford, Wood imagined that greater contact between the races would result in a happy convergence. If the United States could offer "the neighborhood of an improved and social people" to the Indians, the races would be linked by commerce, friendship, and marriage. Like many reformers, Wood prescribed close contact between the races without personal involvement: he expected "suitable persons" to come forward among the white population and act as civilizational emissaries to Native people. (Unlike Charles Crawford, he didn't plan to invite Indians to his house for dinner.) But Wood recognized that the process would not be straightforward. There was, after all, an "amazing difference between the savage and civilized state." The example of unlicensed conduct between Indians and "bad" whites in the Northwest suggested that an "immediate coalition" between the races was "impracticable." It would be the responsibility of the federal government—which had been "languid and steady," at best, in its Indian policy—to create the circumstances in which Native people and whites could happily converge. At the opening of the nineteenth century, federal officials seemed ready to accept Wood's challenge.[5]

ONE OF THE PRINCIPAL FIGURES in this effort was Benjamin Hawkins, the North Carolina senator who in 1792 had criticized George Washington for the federal land-grab in the Northwest. Hawkins, a wealthy Princeton graduate, had served on the Committee on Indian Affairs and had acted as a negotiator with the southern tribes in the 1780s. A decade later, he helped George Washington mediate between the Creeks and land-hungry state officials in Georgia. In 1796, he accepted Washington's invitation to become the agent of the United States to the southern Indians. He was forty-two years old, and he would spend his remaining years, almost two decades, living among the Creeks in central Georgia. In the early years of his agency, Hawkins moved regularly among the Creek towns of the region, sleeping in the houses of the people he sought to "civilize." In 1803, he took up a plantation on the Flint River, hoping to woo Indians with his own prosperity and refinement.[6]

During the early 1790s, as the Western Confederacy embarrassed the US Army in the Northwest, federal Indian policy in the Southeast blended urgent diplomacy with Enlightenment optimism. "It is of high

importance that the Southern Indians should be prevented [from] joining the Indians north of the Ohio," read the orders issued by the War
Department to its new agent to the Cherokees in 1792. Then, without
a beat: "The difference between civilized and savage modes of life is
so great, as, upon a first view, almost leads to the conclusion that the
earth is peopled with races of men possessing distinct primary qualities; but, upon a closer inspection, this will appear fallacious, and that
the immense difference arises from education and habits." The biggest challenge in the Southeast was the location of the major Indian
nations within the boundaries of existing states. From North Carolina
to Georgia, as disputes between white settlers and Native nations multiplied, state governments had done little or nothing to keep squatters
and other intruders from Indian land. In 1793, a federal Indian agent
in Georgia complained angrily to Edward Telfair, the state's governor,
that the government's work of pacifying the tribes had been rendered
"a nullity" by the mischief of white settlers and state militiamen. The
nightmare scenario for the federal government was a pan-Indian alliance that would link the Northwest and the Southeast. In October 1792,
hundreds of warriors from the Cherokee and Creek nations joined up
in Tennessee with a visiting delegation of Shawnees, debating whether
to attack a local white town in retaliation for settler encroachments
and injuries. When an eyewitness account of this parley reached federal officials in Philadelphia—Indians from Ohio to Alabama had performed a war dance around an American flag, before riddling it with
bullets—they could be forgiven for fearing the worst.[7]

But an Indian alliance of continental proportions never quite
materialized in the 1790s. Partly this was because the federal government worked desperately to deny the premise that unlawful American
land-grabs had given Native peoples a reason to unite. In August 1792,
William Blount, the federal official responsible for the unorganized
territory south of the Ohio River, nervously explained to the Chickasaw leader Piamingo that the war with the Western Confederacy had
been caused by renegade Indians rather than territorial ambition. (The
Confederacy had already sent emissaries to seek Piamingo's support.)

"If these people would give proof of their wishes for peace," assured Blount, "the United States would forget and forgive what is past." The federal charm offensive in the Southeast was only one obstacle to a southern Indian alliance with the Confederacy. On the other side of the Atlantic, the French Revolution had shaken the capitals of Europe, placing limits on the ingenuity of British and Spanish officials who had previously plotted Indian intrigues from Florida. In 1793, an illness claimed the life of the preeminent Creek leader, the canny and experienced Alexander McGillivray. The following year, militant Cherokees suffered heavy defeats at the hands of state militiamen. With white settlers pouring into Kentucky (which had become a state in 1792) and Tennessee (1796), well-trodden routes between Indians in the Southeast and Northwest were closed off. Most of the southern nations found themselves enclosed by state sovereignty, and it was in these cramped circumstances that Benjamin Hawkins looked for converts to "civilization."[8]

By 1802, Agent Hawkins had exciting news for the US Congress. The Creeks were raising cattle, horses, and sheep. They were making "slowly progressive" improvements in agriculture. They had accepted the need to fence their fields, and they had happily adopted plows and spinning wheels. While the debate over "civilization" created considerable conflict within Indian nations—and lasting divisions in some—Hawkins relayed evidence of similar "progress" among the Cherokees, Chickasaws, and Choctaws. Indian delegates made formal requests to Congress for agricultural equipment and supplies; instead of "rum and geegaws," reported Hawkins, the Creeks had spent $1,000 on axes, hoes, and salt at the government store. These bright reports encouraged northern religious denominations to launch a new wave of Indian missions.[9]

Gideon Blackburn, a Presbyterian missionary, founded a school for Cherokee children in southeastern Tennessee in 1804. The progress of his pupils convinced him that the Cherokees would "become American citizens, and a valuable part of the Union." Within a year, he was able to show off his achievements to the state's governor, John

Sevier, who was visiting the area to press the Indians for another land cession. Blackburn's twenty-five "little savages of the forest" sat "neatly dressed in homespun cotton." They spelled words aloud, shared their writing with Governor Sevier and his aides, and sang "a hymn or two, committed to memory," with an affecting simplicity. Sevier was an unlikely sentimentalist: he had fought the British, the Cherokees, and even the government of North Carolina, leading a breakaway movement of disgruntled settlers in the mid-1780s. Confronted with Blackburn's charges, Sevier wept uncontrollably. "I have often stood unmoved amidst showers of bullets from the Indian rifles," he said, "but this effectually unmans me. I see civilization taking the ground of barbarism, and the praises of Jesus succeeding to the war whoop of the savage." By the early 1800s, federal officials in the Northwest were pointing to the success of these "civilizing" efforts to argue that, if the experiment was "fairly tried," the United States might happily absorb its Indian population.[10]

When Thomas Jefferson took office in 1801, most frontier whites thought him a cheerleader of unbridled expansion. (Benjamin Hawkins wrote nervously to Henry Dearborn, the new secretary of war, to ask if this was true.) In fact, Jefferson proved unwilling to abandon the integrationist rhetoric of Henry Knox and Timothy Pickering. In February 1803, Jefferson shared his convictions directly with Hawkins. The Indians should be encouraged to "do better on less land" with a combination of territorial cessions and federal support for agriculture. Their reward would be prosperity (from the proceeds of land sales and farming) and incorporation into the expanding American family. "In truth," wrote the president, "the ultimate point of rest and happiness for them is to let our settlements and theirs meet and blend together, to intermix, and become one people." Jefferson accepted that some whites might find this odd; the idea was "so novel that it might shock the Indians," too. But the "natural progress of things" pointed toward Native Americans becoming "citizens of the U.S." This was a privilege that would bring them many more advantages than continued existence as "a separate people."[11]

Land sales, "civilization," citizenship: the president presented these outcomes as beneficial not only to the Indians, but to Hawkins's reputation among his compatriots. There were, after all, "unreasonable suspicions" from white Georgians that "you are more attached to the interests of the Indians than of the U.S." Jefferson was offering Hawkins a way to secure the best interests of all parties: if Hawkins could deliver land cessions and civilization, his loyalties would be placed beyond question. Jefferson, meanwhile, would supply the citizenship.

THIS WAS THE PLAN PURSUED more or less rigidly by Hawkins for the next dozen years. He adroitly managed rivalries within and between Indian nations, and he leveraged geography to advance the civilizing cause. With the southeastern nations hemmed in by white settlement and state sovereignty, Hawkins offered protection from their inhospitable surroundings. In the Northwest, however, the situation was very different. Even after the Treaty of Greenville transferred vast tracts of land to the United States, Native peoples controlled northwestern Ohio, most of Indiana, and most of Illinois. This difference in circumstances between the Southeast and Northwest had little impact, initially, on Jefferson's civilizing calculus. In February 1803, he sent William Henry Harrison, the governor of the vast Indiana Territory, the same advice he'd given Benjamin Hawkins in the Southeast: he should "cultivate an affectionate attachment" with the Indians, and prepare them for the opportunity to "incorporate with us as citizens of the United States."[12]

Elected to the White House in 1840, Harrison remains one of the nation's least memorable presidents; though trivia buffs will recall that he gave the longest Inaugural Address (nearly two hours) and served the shortest period in office (one month). The two facts were unfortunately related: he caught pneumonia during his speech and never recovered. He deserves to be much better known for his crucial contribution to the fate of the "civilizing" program in the Old Northwest.

Harrison, like Jefferson, was schooled in Enlightenment thinking. According to one source, he joined an abolition society in his late teens before moving to Philadelphia to study medicine with Benjamin Rush. His contemporaries later claimed that his father, a former governor of Virginia who had no truck with abolition, sent Harrison to Philadelphia to remove him from the orbit of Richmond's antislavery activists—though, as Harrison's most recent biographer put it, this would be akin to "sending an addicted gambler to Las Vegas." He soon tired of his studies, however, and decided to seek his fortune as a soldier. Harrison arrived in the Northwest just a few weeks too late to join the ill-starred 1791 campaign against the Western Confederacy. He became aide-de-camp to Anthony Wayne, served in the Battle of Fallen Timbers, and was at Greenville in 1795 to hear Morgan John Rhys's oration—and to witness Wayne's pitiless demands for Indian land. After this brief apprenticeship, Harrison was well prepared for a move into territorial administration.

In 1800, during the final months of John Adams's administration, Harrison was given the most important job in the region: territorial governor of Indiana. Harrison also became US superintendent for the Indians north of the Ohio, Benjamin Hawkins's counterpart in the Northwest. To our eyes, this might seem a conflict of interest. Hawkins was responsible only for Indian relations, and left the concerns of white settlers to the state authorities within whose borders he operated. Harrison, by contrast, was supposed to promote the smooth transition of Indians from savagery to civilization while also protecting the interests of settlers, who had limited patience for Enlightenment idealism. In theory, the civilizing policy admitted no contradiction between these roles: a territorial governor should persuade both sides of their common interest in becoming one people. In reality, federal officials already knew that opposition on both sides to "blending together" was considerable. But if the premise of the "civilizing" program was true, and proximity could bring Indians and whites together, William Henry Harrison was now well placed to prove it. It was up to the governor to "best promote the interests of the

Indians and of ourselves," Jefferson insisted, "and finally consolidate our whole country into one nation only."[13]

In his orders to Harrison, Jefferson offered a new strategy for realizing the goals of the civilization program. The president lamented the role of private individuals in controlling trade with the Indians; he wanted these "pests" to "retire from the competition." But in freeing Native people from the wiles of private credit, Jefferson envisioned a federal replacement that would leverage Indian debts for loftier ends. A new system of federal "factories" or trading houses in Indian territory would protect Native Americans from price gouging and goods of inferior quality. It would not, however, shield them from the burden of debt. Jefferson told Harrison to "push our trading houses" onto the Indians, encourage them to run up accounts, and then, "when the debts get beyond what the individuals can pay," encourage them to "lop them off by a cession of land." In our own historical moment, we would call this predatory lending. But Jefferson eased into the suggestion without breaking his benevolent stride. If it was a good thing for Indians to exchange land for civilization, he saw no contradiction in a trading system that hastened this outcome. On the issue of Indian intransigence, though, Jefferson was coldly inflexible. While Harrison should "cultivate their love," he should remind the northwestern Indians that they were now in the palm of the United States, and "we have only to shut our hand to crush them." This blunt assessment ought to win their affection, Jefferson suggested, since it proved that "all our liberalities to them proceed from motives of pure humanity only." If Native people chose to resist the overtures of pure humanity, the federal government would have no compunction about "driving them across the Mississippi."[14]

In the 1790s, missionaries, politicians, and generals—not to mention the Indians themselves—complained incessantly about "bad whites" and their deleterious impact on relations between the races. Harrison inherited the same problem after 1800. Writing to the new secretary of war, Henry Dearborn, shortly after Jefferson's inauguration, Harrison insisted that most Indians felt "a friendship for the United States," but made "heavy complaints of ill treatment on the part of our Citizens." Whites routinely murdered Indians, squatted on their land, killed their game, and cheated them at business. "All these injuries the Indians have hitherto borne with astonishing patience," Harrison told Dearborn, although eventually, "nine tenths of the Northern Tribes" would likely rise up against the United States, perhaps with the help of a European power. Of all of the crimes committed by whites, the most terrible involved the peddling of alcohol to Native peoples. Strong liquor allowed settlers a way to turn wheat into a product that would not spoil, hedging against the vast distances and slender infrastructure of the American interior. It also offered a way to turn Indians into repeat customers. Native people were irritatingly frugal in their purchasing habits, making guns, kettles, and clothing last many years. Alcohol kept them hooked on American commerce. It disrupted the hierarchies and social functioning of Indian nations, and it frequently led to violence. But it delivered solid and expanding business to the frontier whites who controlled the trade.[15]

Little Turtle, the Miami leader who had urged the Western Confederacy to sue for peace in 1794, agreed after the Treaty of Greenville to promote Timothy Pickering's civilizing plans among the northwestern tribes. On his visits to the East to see Washington (1796), John Adams (1797), and Thomas Jefferson (1802), he struck a consistent note: alcohol was "not an evil of our own making," he told eastern audiences, but it would likely "destroy" the Indians. Little Turtle's track record in this area was not spotless: he had himself once acted as a middleman for alcohol sales in Indian country, encouraged by the government system of annual payments and privileges attached to treaty-making with the Indians. In 1802, Congress passed a law to restrict alcohol sales, but the patchwork of authority on the frontier made the measure ineffective. Congress could legislate for Indian country—but what if Indians crossed into Kentucky (or the white towns of Georgia) to buy alcohol? Even in Vincennes, the capital of Indiana Territory, traders were selling liquor in open defiance of the federal ban.[16]

William Henry Harrison agreed that alcohol posed a terrible threat to the proximity theory of civilization. "You have seen our towns crowded with furious and drunken savages, our streets flowing with their blood, their arms and clothing bartered for the liquor that destroys them," the governor told the Indiana assembly in 1805. "Is it then to be admitted as a political axiom that the neighborhood of a civilized nation is incompatible with the existence of savages? Are the blessings of our republican government only to be felt by ourselves?" Harrison felt the same shiver of historical opprobrium that had chilled Henry Knox's blood during the early 1790s. Were Native Americans to meet the same fate as the victims of the Spanish conquest? It was up to the assembly members to "divert from those children of nature the ruin which hangs over them." His words seemed to get through: the assembly soon prohibited alcohol sales to Indians within forty miles of Vincennes. But traders continued to glide past the law, and the liquor trade—both legal and illegal—persisted among northwestern and southeastern Indians over the coming decades.[17]

GREENVILLE HAD BEEN A TREATY of conquest: Blue Jacket, Little Turtle, and the other veterans of the Western Confederacy signed away their land only after a painful defeat in the field. After 1795, however, Little Turtle wasn't the only Indian leader to hope for a fresh start between whites and Indians. The Miami, under Little Turtle's leadership, embraced the civilizing agenda; other Native nations viewed the Greenville boundary, which left most of the territory beyond southern Ohio in Native hands, as an opportunity to continue their ways of life without further interference from the United States. For eight years, the new status quo prevailed. Then, between 1803 and 1809, more than a dozen treaties were signed in the Northwest, most at the instigation of William Henry Harrison. Greenville had ceded only a sliver of Indiana's southeastern corner to the United States. By 1809, however, Harrison had acquired all of the future state's southern region, along with a strip of territory that ran from the Ohio River to Fort Wayne. Little Turtle had been willing to accept the Jeffersonian argument

William Henry Harrison (1773–1841), territorial governor and architect of the US land-grab in the Old Northwest. Courtesy of the Library of Congress.

Tecumseh (1768–1813), Shawnee leader and organizer of the pan-Indian confederacy. Courtesy of the Indiana Historical Society.

that Indians could do better with less land, but the speed and extent of Harrison's land-grab was without precedent. Little Turtle's standing with his own people was undermined, and Harrison became estranged from his Native allies.[18]

Those Indian nations that had remained aloof from the civilizing program responded by building a new alliance that could roll back the white advance. They were led by two Shawnee brothers, Tenskwatawa and Tecumseh. Both had fought at Fallen Timbers. Although Tenskwatawa was probably at the Greenville negotiations, neither he nor Tecumseh had embraced the argument that whites and Indians would happily intermix. From the spring of 1805, Tenskwatawa experienced a series of religious visions that served as the mythology of a new pan-Indian movement: white Americans had been created by the Great Serpent, and they were an evil force that had to be repelled. If Native people rejected European goods and practices—manufactures, alcohol, Christianity—the Great Spirit would drive whites back across the Ohio, perhaps even across the Atlantic. Religious revivals had structured Native resistance throughout the eighteenth century, but the combination of Jefferson's civilizing rhetoric and Harrison's land hunger made Tenskwatawa's preaching almost irresistible. Within two years of the first of these visions, Jefferson was writing nervously to his secretary of war about the power and extent of the Shawnee Prophet's movement. What had seemed a "transient enthusiasm" could become a serious threat to the United States. Jefferson activated the usual protocol: "prepare for war" and "redouble our efforts for peace."[19]

It is tempting to see this religious revivalism as the ironic opposite of Jefferson's civilizing rhetoric: the president insisted that the races could blend into a single people, whereas Tenskwatawa preached that all men were *not* created equal, and that whites were the progeny of the devil. In reality, Native views of race and creation were diverse and complex. One of the Shawnee Prophet's chief missionaries to other Native nations, the Michigan Indian known as Trout, insisted that the Great Spirit was "the father of the English, of the French, of the

Spaniards, and of the Indians." Only the Americans fell outside this single creation. "They are not my children," the Spirit had told Trout. "They are numerous, but I hate them." While this version of humanity's origins hardly flattered Americans, nor did it mark out a hierarchy in which Indians held the entire white race to be outcasts. Sensing that he might still head off a race war, Harrison invited the Prophet to Vincennes in August 1808, and he was pleasantly surprised to find common ground. Tenskwatawa abjured alcohol, but asked for needles and hoes from the town's store (also flints and powder). In a move that might have seemed emollient or provocative, Tenskwatawa moved his followers from Ohio to the village of Prophetstown, about 150 miles up the Wabash River from Vincennes. He and his brother were now within striking distance of Harrison's benevolence.[20]

"He is rather possessed of considerable talents," Harrison wrote Secretary of War Dearborn after their meeting, "and the art and address with which he manages the Indians is really astonishing." Tenskwatawa had had more success than anyone—perhaps even the governor of Indiana Territory—in fostering temperance among Native peoples, and his brand of separatism initially seemed milder than Harrison had feared. There was every reason to hope that the civilizing agenda—that "wise, humane, and beneficent policy which has been adopted by our government"—could still come to fruition in the Northwest; perhaps even that "the influence which the Prophet has acquired will prove rather advantageous than otherwise to the United States." During the winter of 1808–1809, which was unusually cruel, Harrison sent food from the government store at Vincennes to Tenskwatawa's hungry followers. The Miami Indians, who were alarmed by the rise of their rival Shawnee, urged Harrison to "starve all those who appertained to the Prophet." But the governor stuck stubbornly to his administration's higher principles: "I did not believe that that was the philosophy of the President."[21]

PERHAPS IT WAS OVERCONFIDENCE THAT drove Harrison toward yet another treaty in 1809, seizing a triangle of land stretching 100 miles up the Wabash River from Vincennes toward Prophetstown. The governor had honed his negotiating tactics, combining familiar tricks (buying land from the wrong Indians) with some new ones (threatening to stop annuity payments from previous treaties if Indians refused to cooperate). Even his hardiest Indian allies were shocked, but Harrison exploited their rivalries and their hunger to force the outcome. Tenskwatawa and Tecumseh, whose new hunting grounds were encompassed in the 1809 treaty cession, were not even invited to the negotiations. This insult confirmed their skepticism about Harrison's intentions, and they readied their allies for war.[22]

When he later defended his provocative treaty-making during this period, Harrison insisted that the pressure from settlers had forced his hand. In fact, there were fewer than 25,000 whites in the Indiana Territory in 1809, and the idea of a settlement rush was largely chimeric. If his aggressive treaties were destabilizing the region, why would the governor risk a war with the Indians to secure territory that wasn't even needed? One answer was the persistence of British troops and settlers north of the Great Lakes and in a chain of disputed outposts in the Northwest Territory. Although Canada's population remained small, American policymakers routinely expected Britain to make a play for the great Mississippi Valley. Using its forts and agile indigenous proxies, Britain might still check the republic's westward advance—or so American legislators feared. If the United States could close up the Great Lakes region, stranding the Indians within a sea of American settlers and sovereignty, the British would be unable to skim Native commerce or recruit indigenous allies. In December 1808, as Jefferson prepared to hand over the presidency to James Madison, he reminded Governor Harrison that Britain's treaties with the United States allowed for navigation rights in areas controlled by Native people. "Their treaty can only operate on the country so long as it is Indian," Jefferson wrote. "In proportion as it becomes ours exclusively, their ground is narrowed." What the president had failed to anticipate was that aggressive treaty-making might force Indians into the arms of the British: that the remedy would create the disease.[23]

And then there was the key tenet of the civilizing program, that concentrating Indians on narrower stretches of land would hasten their march toward civilization. The idea received fresh impetus in 1807 from one of Harrison's best-informed experts on Indian policy: William Wells, the US agent at Fort Wayne. In a letter to Secretary Dearborn, Wells reported that "the Indians of this country are too much scattered for the United States to civilize them." He recommended the resettlement of the region's Indian nations into twelve compact communities. Within this narrower geography, the inducements to hunt would be vastly reduced, Indians might happily sell their land, and the government could more easily deliver education and agricultural expertise to the entire population. (Wells proposed that the teaching be subcontracted to "civilized" Indians from Massachusetts.) Wells even offered to implement this plan personally: having married Little Turtle's daughter years earlier, Wells had chosen to live his life between the white and Indian worlds of the Northwest. If nothing else, he urged the federal government to recognize that the current civilizing model had little chance of success: "It might as well be said that corn would grow in the woods without clearing the ground."[24]

Perhaps Harrison hoped that the logic of concentrating the Indian population would overwhelm the immediate challenge of the Shawnee-led insurgency. In a letter to Tenskwatawa in July 1810, he blamed "bad white men" for the differences between them, hinting that a new war in the region would end badly for the Indians. Would the Prophet like to visit the new Federal City at Washington, he wondered, to receive assurances of the government's intentions from the president himself? Harrison hoped that the Shawnee troublemakers would be so awed by a journey to the heart of US power that they would recognize the futility of resistance. Tenskwatawa declined the invitation, sending his brother instead to visit the governor at Vincennes. The

Shawnees had done their homework. Their scouts had surveyed the lands ceded since 1803, and Tecumseh asked Harrison why so much of the territory remained devoid of settlers. In a brilliant inversion, the Shawnee styled the American as a provincial figure, perhaps even a renegade. Tecumseh had heard that the citizens of Vincennes were "equally divided" on Harrison's handling of the Indians, with a strong faction opposed to further land cessions that would endanger peace. Perhaps the governor had "purchased the lands against the consent of the Government and one half of the people?" After all, "you were placed here by Government to buy land when it was offer'd to you, but not to use persuasion and threats to obtain it." Tecumseh had touched a nerve. In response to his implication that the federal government might undo Harrison's treaties if it knew about their fraudulent premises, the governor nervously wrote to William Eustis, who had succeeded Dearborn as secretary of war in March 1809, a few days after James Madison's presidential inauguration. Might Harrison be given a note "signed by the President or yourself informing him that the land would not be given up?" Tecumseh, meanwhile, left Harrison with an ultimatum. If the governor refused to return this land to its rightful owners, the gathering Indian alliance under the Shawnee brothers would track down the chiefs who had signed the treaties and kill them all.[25]

The movement led by Tecumseh and Tenskwatawa could never truly cleanse itself of European influence. From technology to culture, from religion to bloodlines, centuries of contact between whites and Indians had created a syncretic world. Authentic "Indian" values carried traces of the collisions and collaborations that had marked North American history since the sixteenth century. Tecumseh made ironic use of the parallels and analogies between the two cultures to bolster his view that they should live apart. In 1811, when Tecumseh informed Harrison that his pan-Indian alliance was nearly complete, he confessed that "the U. States had set him the example of forming a strict union amongst all the fires that compose their confederacy." To the idea that the Indians should place their faith in Harrison's good intentions, meanwhile, Tecumseh had a sharp retort: "How can we have confidence in the white people? When Jesus Christ came upon the earth, you killed him and nailed him on a cross." Even this point betrayed the ultimate weakness of the whites—their perennial over-confidence: "You thought he was dead, but you were mistaken."[26]

The effect of the Shawnees' elegant intimidation was to shake Harrison loose from his Jeffersonian moorings. A few days after Tecumseh left Vincennes in August 1810, Harrison sent an extraordinary break-up note to Secretary Eustis. "There is no man who has a greater respect than I have for the political talents of Mr. Jefferson," he wrote, "but I think it my duty to observe that the integrity of his principles seduced him to commit a political error." It had been wrong to imagine that "concord and friendship" could prevail on the frontier. "The mind of a savage is so constructed that he cannot be at rest, he cannot be happy unless it is acted upon by some strong stimulus." Indians would have to hunt, to kill each other, or to turn on the United States. This didn't stop Harrison from admiring Tecumseh. If anything, it made him more likely to compare the "astonishing" Shawnee warrior with the Aztec and Incan emperors who had dazzled the first Spanish conquistadors. And yet it also made him more determined to kill his bewildering opponent. Although Harrison continued to blame "bad whites" or the British for inflaming the situation, by 1811 he was ready to march up the Wabash River and attack Prophetstown. Secretary Eustis urged him to take enough men to achieve overwhelming victory. Harrison, the veteran of Fallen Timbers, reassured Eustis that his men were as "perfect as Genl. Wayne's army was on the day of his victory over the Indians."[27]

The story of Harrison's attack on Prophetstown was the propellant for his successful shot at the White House nearly three decades later. In reality, the fighting at Tippecanoe Creek on 6 November 1811 represented Harrison's second major stroke of good fortune, twenty years after he had just missed the routing of Arthur St. Clair's army. Harrison's forces marched up to Prophetstown on 5 November and were persuaded by Tenskwatawa and his advisers to camp overnight before beginning negotiations. Just before dawn the following morning, after two Indians had been shot by confused US sentries, the Shawnees and their allies infiltrated the American camp. Harrison always rode a gray horse, but it was his aide-de-camp who leapt onto it that morning and caught the eye of an Indian marksman who had been sent to kill the American commander. Harrison's hapless subordinate was shot in the head, and Tenskwatawa's followers briefly thought that they had won the battle. After sustaining heavy losses, Harrison regained the initiative and forced the Indians to flee Prophetstown. War had finally broken out with the new pan-Indian confederacy, and Harrison's abandonment of the civilizing policy was complete.[28]

When this Indian war bled into the broader War of 1812 with Britain, Harrison began to target even those Native Americans who had previously embraced the civilizing plan. (He burned the villages and crops of the Miami Indians, in particular, including the town where Little Turtle was buried.) The British and Indians enjoyed sweeping victories around the Great Lakes and easily turned back the American invasion of Canada. But the Indian confederacy found itself allied with a particularly feckless British general, Henry Procter, and ultimately they were cornered by Harrison's forces at the Thames River in Ontario. Tecumseh was furious with the British: he told Procter (to his face) that the British were "like a fat animal, that carries its tail upon its back, but when affrighted, drops it between his legs and runs off." Outnumbered by the Americans, Tecumseh was shot through the heart on 5 October 1813. With the US Navy seizing control of the lakes, and the failure of the bold British effort to destroy Baltimore (alongside Washington) in the summer of 1814, the prospect of an Indian victory—and a Native homeland in the Northwest—slipped away.[29]

THE REACTIONS IN THE EAST to the Battle of Tippecanoe in 1811 were not promising for the Indians. Andrew Jackson, at this moment still a militia commander in Tennessee, had been following Harrison's standoff with Tecumseh and Tenskwatawa. Jackson would make his name in the War of 1812 as the principal antagonist of the Red Stick Creeks, the only southern Indians who threw in their lot with the Shawnee brothers during the war. Already in 1811, his views of Indians were narrowing ominously. It would be his pleasure to supply "five hundred or one thousand brave Tennesseans" to aid in Harrison's cause, he told the governor, for the Indians "ought to be swept from the face of the earth." In Massachusetts, meanwhile, John Adams asked his friend Thomas Jefferson to explain the Prophet's significance. Jefferson replied that Tenskwatawa was "more rogue than fool," though he admitted that he had underestimated the appeal of his revivalist message: "I thought there was little danger of his making many proselytes from the habits and comfort they had learned from the whites, to the hardships and privations of savagism," Jefferson wrote, "and no great harm if he did." The two former presidents reminisced about their early years, when local Indians would visit their family homes on business, and bemoaned the changes that meant, in Adams's words, "we scarcely see an Indian in a year." Some of the southern Indians had embraced the civilizing program, Jefferson noted. For the rest, the jaws of history were closing fast. If the Indians "relapse[d] into barbarism and misery," the United States would have only one option remaining: "We shall be obliged to drive them with the beasts of the forest into the stony mountains."³⁰

William Henry Harrison proved adept at blaming external factors for the failure of his Indian policy—bad whites, alcohol, the British, recalcitrant Natives, Jeffersonian idealism. His erstwhile mentor, though, had always been a master of deflected responsibility. In his original draft of the Declaration of Independence, Jefferson had charged the British not only with creating and protecting American slavery, but also with fomenting the Indian wars that had blazed through the backcountry of the infant republic. In December 1813, soon after the death of Tecumseh, Jefferson wrote a requiem for his Indian policy in a letter to the celebrated German scientist Alexander von Humboldt: "You know, my friend, the benevolent plan we were pursuing here for the happiness of the aboriginal inhabitants in our vicinities," he said. The US government had "spared nothing to keep them at peace with one another," and to teach them agriculture, private property, commerce, and the other rudiments of civilization. If the Indians had been allowed to sell their land and embrace their new neighbors, "they would have mixed their blood with ours, and been amalgamated and identified with us within no distant period of time." But instead, the "unprincipled policy of England has defeated all our labors for the salvation of these unfortunate people." The British had "seduced the greater part of the tribes within our neighborhood," leaving the United States with a heartbreaking choice: "to pursue them to extermination, or drive them to new seats beyond our reach."[31]

Jefferson and Harrison found it hard to blame themselves for the failures of the civilizing policy, but the War of 1812 prompted a wave of recognition among liberal Americans that the United States itself had become the obstacle to Indian advancement. This point was made with striking candor by De Witt Clinton, the governor of New York State, in his address to the New York Historical Society in November 1811—days after the news of Harrison's messy engagement with the Prophet had reached the East. Clinton cast an elegiac eye over the history of white engagement with the Indians of North America, noting with particular sadness that New York's own Iroquois Confederacy had become "addicted to idleness and drunkenness." Farther west, Tenskwatawa's revivalist message had at least given a "flattering and consolatory" understanding to Indians who were otherwise fighting to survive. The new Native alliance that had risen in the West was passionately opposed to the American embrace; Clinton thought this perfectly rational. "The causes of their degradation and diminution, are principally to be found in their baneful communication with the man of Europe; which has contaminated their morals, destroyed their population, robbed them of their country, and deprived them of their national spirit." The language of degradation might now explain the failure of the civilizing program.[32]

Just as antislavery reformers began to acknowledge white prejudice as a powerful source of black degradation, the critics of federal Indian policy—missionaries, magazine editors, even politicians—made precisely the same argument about the halting progress of Native people. A pioneer in this regard was the young Washington Irving, whose early writings made repeated reference to the damage done by whites to Native Americans. In his first book, *A History of New York* (1809), Irving used his alter ego—a rasping Dutch historian called Diedrich Knickerbocker—to launch a sardonic attack on the myths surrounding Europe's conquest of America. Clearly, the Indians had been "very unreasonable animals" for living so simply before the Europeans arrived. "No sooner did the benevolent inhabitants of Europe behold their sad condition than they immediately went to work to ameliorate and improve it." The Indians "improved daily and wonderfully by their intercourse with the whites," Knickerbocker recalled. "They took to drinking rum, and making bargains. They learned to cheat, to lie, to swear, to gamble, to quarrel, to cut each other's throats, in short, to excel in all the accomplishments that had originally marked the superiority of their Christian visitors." In a bravura denouement to his satire, Irving asked readers to imagine an invasion of "philosophers from the moon," a spacefaring race as far advanced from the sailing ships of the Europeans as Christopher Columbus had been from the canoes of Native Americans. When these lunar invaders arrived on Earth—"defended with impenetrable armor, armed with concentrated sun beams"—would anything stop them from colonizing the planet, crushing the resistance of the "miserable savages" who inhabited it, and expelling the remnants of humanity to the deserts or the polar regions, "there to enjoy the blessings of civilization and the charms of lunar philosophy?" Irving's Knickerbocker confessed to readers that he often lay awake at night "debating in my mind whether it was most probable we should first discover and civilize the moon, or the moon discover and civilize us."[33]

Washington Irving's conviction that Indians had been terribly damaged by their contact with white people was intensified by the War of 1812. In a long magazine essay published in 1814, he presented Native Americans as the victims of a double injustice. They had been slaughtered by invading whites who "found it easier to exterminate them than to civilize," then traduced by historians who found it "easier to abuse than to discriminate." White prejudices about Indian savagery failed to recognize that "the miserable hordes that infest our frontiers . . . are degenerate beings, enfeebled by the vices of society, without being benefited by its arts of living." "Civilized" society had "advanced upon them like a many-headed monster, breathing every variety of misery." When he revised this essay for publication in his *Sketch Book of Geoffrey Crayon* in 1820—the collection that also included "The Legend of Sleepy Hollow"—Irving rewrote the clash between whites and Indians as a heartbreaking mismatch, including a footnote reassuring readers that "the American government has been indefatigable in its exertions to ameliorate the situation of the Indians." But in its original version, written as Tecumseh's confederacy was collapsing, Irving's critique was cold and pure: the Indians "cannot but be sensible that we are the usurpers of their ancient dominion, the cause of their degradation, and the gradual destroyers of their race."[34]

The years after the War of 1812 saw a shift in the debate about Native peoples and an increasing willingness on the part of liberal whites to acknowledge the failures of the proximity model of civilization. Elias Boudinot, the veteran congressman who had been arguing for decades that the Indians were Jews, reprinted "The Traits of Indian Character" in his 1816 book on the need for fresh missionary overtures to the Indians. (Washington Irving, noted Boudinot, had "rejoiced to know that such despised sufferers, however degraded, had found compassion in other breasts besides his own.") Boudinot had just become the founding president of the American Bible Society, and he helped to introduce the theory of Indian degradation to the missionary community. Some clergymen viewed the fate of the northwestern Indians with a resigned fatalism: Was there any point in trying to convert Native people when it was "poisonous for an Indian to breathe the same air as a white man"? asked one. The vast majority of reformers thought that Native Americans might still be brought to Christ and "civilization," but they now believed that the Indians would need protection from the effects of degradation. This shifted the terms of the debate fundamentally: from an emphasis on how whites and Indians could be brought together, to a suspicion that both sides might fare better if kept apart.[35]

PART II
AMALGAMATION

FIVE

To the Middle Ground

I N JUNE 1798, THOMAS JEFFERSON was in the middle of his unhappy tenure as vice-president to John Adams. Just as he was preparing to exchange the heat and political intrigues of Philadelphia for the seclusion of Monticello, he received an extraordinary letter from his friend William Short. The two had become close more than a decade earlier in Paris, where Short had been Jefferson's personal secretary, but the roots of their friendship ran deeper. Both came from slaveholding Virginia families, both had been educated at the College of William and Mary, and both had imbibed strong sentiments against slavery before entering public life. Short had stayed on in Europe after Jefferson's return to the United States in 1789, filling a number of diplomatic positions and eventually becoming a private businessman in France. Their close correspondence in the 1790s was underpinned by a shared experience, and perhaps by a secret: Short had lived in Jefferson's Paris home during those key years of the 1780s in which France edged toward revolution and Jefferson drew closer to Sally Hemings.[1]

With his usual directness on the slavery question, Short looked to the "restoration of the rights of citizenship of those blacks who inhabit the U.S.," and he wondered how this goal could be achieved. The British experiment of Sierra Leone offered one avenue, though Short wasn't yet convinced that colonizing black people on the other side of the Atlantic would be viable or benevolent. Perhaps it was time instead to reexamine the "evils to be apprehended from the mixture of the two colors." Even "the most enlightened and virtuous minds" might balk at amalgamation, given the degrading effects of slavery upon black people in the United States. But Short thought that more could be done "to remove the aversion to the mixture of the two colors." It was possible that an improvement in the American climate would lighten black skin, which might narrow the gulf between the races. But why not embrace amalgamation, "even admitting that this mixture should change our hue?" What did it matter if white southerners "should advance to the middle ground between their present color & the black?" This mixed race would be no darker than the population of Spain, where Short had served as a diplomat earlier in the decade. In fact, "even in our own country there are some people darker than the gradual mixture of the blacks can ever make us, and yet I do not know that they suffer from thence."[2]

It's hard to know how Jefferson read all this, since he never replied to Short's letter. Instead, he acknowledged its arrival in his neat journal of correspondence and said no more of it to anyone. Short had named a mutual acquaintance of theirs in Virginia, "a Mrs Randolph, afterwards Mrs Tucker," as a fine example that darker skin was no obstacle to beauty. (The preponderance of illicit sex between masters and slaves in the South makes Short's name-dropping seem almost as daring as his prescriptions.) A darker complexion, he concluded, was "capable of inspiring equally" with "the perfect mixture of the rose & the lily." But Jefferson's thoughts must have turned with alarm to a more immediate example: Sally Hemings, the half-sister of Jefferson's late wife, who had already borne three of Jefferson's children while remaining his slave. Short had spent enough time in Jefferson's Paris household to develop suspicions about his boss's relationship with Sally Hemings. What Short could not have known is that, in the spring of 1798, Hemings had given birth to a boy, Beverley Hemings, who was yet to meet his illustrious father. Did Jefferson take Short's letter with him to Monticello that July? Did it lie on the desk of his study as he looked into the eyes of his son for the first time? Perhaps Short imagined that Jefferson's personal life would allow his friend to pierce the veil of prejudice that distorted the American racial landscape. But Short's efforts to press the logic of amalgamation came to nothing. Jefferson's criticisms of slavery remained maddeningly theoretical, his liaisons with Hemings a forbidden topic. Even after a follow-up letter inquiring about the fate of his proposal, Short received no reply.[3]

Given what we know about white Americans' aversion to racial mixing in this period, we might account for this curious letter with a simple observation: Short had been in France for too long. Most historians agree that proponents of amalgamation in the early republic were virtually nonexistent. But discussion of race mixing was not as uncommon as we might think. The prospect of amalgamation produced a lively debate among white intellectuals who valued enlightened thinking over base prejudice. Americans took notice of the interracial marriages and relationships that accompanied the global expansion of European empires and wondered if "all men are created equal" obligated white people to cultivate intimate relationships with blacks and Indians. Might marriage even offer a shortcut to the conquest of degradation or the promotion of "civilization" among America's substantial non-white minority? To answer this question, liberal whites drew not only on the experience of other nations, but on the realization that racial mixing had been going on in America for decades—albeit in contexts that were neither initiated nor sanctioned by government. Slavery itself had become a major driver of amalgamation, with masters regularly impregnating their slaves. In similar vein, white traders working in Indian country took Native wives and fathered mixed-race children. Those intellectuals and reformers who floated intermarriage schemes had to reckon with real-world examples of racial mixing that diverged from the liberal script. Over time, the tension between the theory and the practice of amalgamation persuaded even William Short to revise his views.

WHEN EUROPEAN POWERS BEGAN TO develop their Atlantic empires, racial mixing was central to their strategy of consolidation and control. During the first phases of Spanish rule in Mexico, conquistadors found wives among the most prominent indigenous families. On the west coast of Africa in the sixteenth and seventeenth centuries, Portuguese traders forged commercial and political connections through racial mixing. As part of his "Francisation" policy toward indigenous people in Canada, Louis XIV encouraged intermarriages between settlers and Indians in New France in the middle decades of the seventeenth century. When the French proved reluctant to move in large numbers to North America, amalgamation morphed into a method of extending commercial influence into the distant interior. Beyond a narrow strip of settlement between Quebec and Montreal, France relied on *voyageurs*—French traders who blended with Native peoples and took European trade into the vast Great Lakes region. On the other side of the world in South Asia, intermarriage played a role in bolstering imperial control. Many of the highest officials of the East India Company took Indian wives in the early eighteenth century, as did lower-ranking administrators and soldiers. In 1778, the company offered five rupees for every child of a British soldier born to an Indian mother, on the assumption that this new mixed-race generation would eventually fill the ranks of the army. Although this policy was rapidly reversed in India in the 1790s and 1800s, British imperial officials continued to experiment with amalgamation policies across the world in the nineteenth century, especially in the newly acquired Cape Colony (present-day South Africa and Namibia) and in New Zealand.[4]

While the eventual reversal of intermarriage policies in India and Mexico suggests that European enthusiasm for race mixing was short-lived, Enlightenment thinkers continued to defend amalgamation. In the *Histoire des Deux Indes*, the Abbé Raynal lamented the failure of French colonists to realize the fabulous commercial potential of Madagascar during the mid-seventeenth century. "Nothing was more easy than to have made this island of considerable utility," Raynal insisted, had French settlers only taken the opportunity to marry into the local population. "This tie, so endearing, and of so tender a nature, would have extinguished those odious distinctions, which cherish perpetual hatred and everlasting division, between people who inhabit the same region, and live under the same laws." Instead, the French had oppressed the indigenous population and squabbled with each other before being forced off the island by a Native revolt in 1674. British North America offered a more successful example of colonization without amalgamation, but the British colonies struggled with the same lasting tensions between Europeans and Native people. In 1763, after the sweeping victories of the Seven Years' War, the geographers William Roberts and Thomas Jefferys proposed that Britain should build its new colony of Florida with "the cement of intermarriage." This had, after all, been the preferred method of "civilizing barbarous nations" of "almost every polity, especially the more refined ones." Yet intermarriage never became widespread either in Florida or elsewhere in British North America.[5]

The notion that Britain had missed a trick in its colonizing had been amplified by William Robertson, the celebrated Scottish writer, in the posthumously published sequel to his *History of America*. Robertson noted that one of the most stirring episodes in the early history of Virginia had been the marriage of the Powhatan princess Pocahontas to the English planter John Rolfe. But "notwithstanding the visible good effects of that alliance, none of Rolfe's countrymen seem to have imitated the example which he set them, of intermarrying with the natives." Robertson bemoaned the fact that "of all the Europeans who have settled in America, the English have availed themselves least of the most obvious method of conciliating the affection of its original inhabitants." British aloofness in this respect struck a double blow: it cut off an obvious way of increasing the colonial population, and it earned the enmity of the Indians, who assumed that the white invaders thought them "an inferior order of beings."[6]

The successful conclusion of the American Revolution altered the imperial context of amalgamation. For Europeans, intermarriage was something that took place on the periphery, far from London, Paris, or Madrid. Nobody in France or Britain expected that the consequence of incorporating non-white populations overseas would be a mixed-race population at home. (The same logic had guided the British and French efforts to abolish slavery in the late eighteenth and early nineteenth centuries.) In the United States, on the other hand, independence had erased the distinction between colony and nation. By 1783, white Americans east of the Mississippi River lived among a population that was perhaps 25 percent non-white. If the United States wanted to expand into Indian country without waging a war of extirpation, or free itself from the moral burdens of slavery, it would need to find new models of coexistence. It was in this context that William Short's letter to Jefferson might seem both obvious and incendiary.[7]

Race mixing in the early United States was shaped by the local and the global. States and territories were free to make their own laws about intermarriage and amalgamation that built upon the presumptions and practices of the colonial era. After the Louisiana Purchase of 1803, ideas about race mixing were stretched across an extraordinary variety of cultures and histories: from the Puritan and British colonial settings of New England, through the Dutch beginnings of New York, to the French and Spanish influences of the Mississippi Valley. Each region had its own experiences of black, white, and Indian relations. The US Constitution provided no help in organizing intimate relations between the races, but the dynamics of the Atlantic slave trade worked their own influence. The Caribbean loomed especially large, both as an example of various (usually illicit) forms of black-white sexual relations and as a reminder that Enlightenment thinking and black resistance could react in combustible ways. From the mid-1790s, thousands of refugees—white and black—fled the Haitian Revolution for Philadelphia and New Orleans, creating a panic among those white observers who had already defined color as a social Rubicon.[8]

The legal status of intermarriage and interracial sex in the early republic was messy and inconsistent. A seventeenth-century statute banning marriage between Christians and non-Christians in Virginia eventually morphed into a ban on black-white marriage in 1753. Sex across the color line was legal in Virginia—a fact appreciated by many generations of white slaveholders—though marriage was not. In Georgia, interracial marriage and sex had been illegal since the 1750s, but in South Carolina there were no statutes preventing either (though the state did make provisions to enslave the children of white-black unions). Kentucky, after David Rice's fruitless effort to ban slavery in 1792, adopted the Virginia laws preventing white-black intermarriage in 1799, but marriage between whites and Indians remained legal. Louisiana drew on French and Spanish laws deterring intermarriage until it drafted its own (territorial) law in 1808. Massachusetts passed a ban on intermarriage between blacks and whites in 1786, despite its self-styled position in the vanguard of northern antislavery. And yet New York, which contained many more black people than Massachusetts, never passed a law prohibiting sex or marriage across the color line. Even Pennsylvania, with the largest free black population in the early republic, declined to retreat from its 1780 decision to abolish the colonial-era ban on intermarriage. Despite many appeals from white legislators to reintroduce this ban, and a significant increase in the free black population of Philadelphia during the first two decades of the 1800s, the state would not revive the prohibition on black-white marriage until 1872. That ban survived only nine years before it was withdrawn, this time for good.[9]

Peering through this legal gauze the situation seems untenably confusing. A white person could have sex with a black person without breaking the law in Virginia or South Carolina, but not in Georgia. Whites could marry Indians in most states (though not in North Carolina after 1837), but couldn't marry black people except in New York, Pennsylvania, Connecticut, Tennessee (before 1857), and Massachusetts (after 1843). The law wasn't always a reliable guide to what took place on the ground. In South Carolina, for example, intermarriage was so hard to imagine that the planter-dominated assembly felt no need to prohibit it by statute. When the Massachusetts assembly revoked its ban on black-white marriage in 1843, legislators assured their constituents that this was a symbolic rather than substantial measure: many condemned interracial marriage even as they voted to decriminalize it (a topic we'll return to later). The inconsistencies of the legal landscape provided an opening for liberal reformers, not least because so many of the statutes on sex and marriage were inheritances from the colonial era. While Maryland, to give the most extreme example, retained its 1728 legislation until 1859, liberal thinkers in the first few decades of the republic saw the achievement of national independence as a moment of possibility. Perhaps the United States might free itself from colonial convention and prejudice in the most intimate of settings.

VIRGINIA HAD PLAYED A CENTRAL role in the Patriot campaigns against Native Americans during the American Revolution. "The same world will scarcely do for them and us," declared state governor Patrick Henry in 1779 when endorsing a war of extermination against the Shawnees and the Wyandots. After the war, however, Henry—now serving in the state assembly—became one of the first politicians in the United States to promote intermarriage as a strategy for incorporating Native peoples. In 1784 he introduced a bill that offered £10 to any white man who married a Native woman, and £5 for each child they produced. Strikingly, Henry proposed incentives for white women as well: they would receive £10 for marrying Indian men, in the form of a credit that could be spent on agricultural equipment to propel their husbands toward "civilization." These couples would be exempted from taxes, and their children entitled "to the same rights and privileges, as if they had proceeded from intermarriages among free white inhabitants thereof." (They would also be educated at the state's expense.) While the bill gained two readings from the assembly, Henry was promoted back to the governor's chair before its final approval. In his absence from the legislature, it failed to become law. Henry could only rue the missed opportunity, as whites encroached onto Indian territory in subsequent years without the disarming promises of marriage.[10]

When Henry returned to the governor's mansion in December 1784, one of the first letters he received outlined another plan for intermarriage between Indians and whites. Selina, the Countess of Huntingdon, was an English noblewoman who had been a close supporter of John and Charles Wesley as they established Methodism throughout the British Atlantic. Having previously invested in the cause of evangelism in Georgia, Selina now wrote to state governors along the eastern seaboard with a new scheme. She had followed the limited progress of white missionaries to the Indians, and she doubted that a few isolated schools or churches in Indian country would bring Native people to Christ and "civilization." But what if a new group of white settlers could be established "among the Indians, where they and the Indians may have a free and easy intercourse?" The settlers themselves could serve "as so many Missionaries and School-Masters among them." The countess did not expect this would instantly convert Native Americans, or that the new arrivals should rush to impose their beliefs on the locals. But perhaps Indian women and children would "be induced to mix more in society with the settlers, to join with them occasionally in some little work of agriculture," even if this was only "to amuse themselves and pass away time." The children of Indians and whites might even be schooled alongside each other. Civilization would creep up on Native Americans, enveloping them in its mores and benefits almost imperceptibly.[11]

The scheme appealed to Patrick Henry, who enthusiastically referred the idea to Congress as "the means of forming a good frontier." The countess, in the meantime, had secured the support of an even more famous Virginian. In January 1785, George Washington sent her a message of encouragement: if the countess wanted to buy land for the scheme beyond the Appalachians, she should petition Congress rather than the individual states and emphasize the "great good which may result" from it. The only snag was the countess's insistence that new settlers would be drawn from Britain rather than from the existing states. While Selina had promised that her volunteers would be "good religious people" who had "all along been the friends, and would be glad to become Citizens of America," the memory of the war against Britain was still fresh. When Washington sent the plan to Richard Henry Lee, president of the Congress under the Articles of Confederation, in February 1785, he worried that their compatriots would view a large influx of British settlers as a fifth column, especially since the British were still refusing to abandon their network of forts beyond the Ohio River. Washington urged Lee to focus on the plan's benefits: the countess's emigrants would bring useful skills, consolidate the frontier, and "attempt the conversion of the Savages without any expense to the Union." Lee replied that he could hardly welcome 10,000 settlers who "were remarkable in the late war for an unanimous and bitter enmity to the American cause," especially if the new arrivals were to plug the borderlands between the United States and Canada. Washington sent a letter of apology to England, and the countess returned to her religious efforts closer to home.[12]

Having given up on the idea of importing a fresh settler population that could be combined with the Indians, Washington continued to endorse—both publicly and privately—a process of "civilization" that would culminate in the merging of Indians and whites as a single people. John Adams and Thomas Jefferson did the same. When Morgan Rhys, the Welsh Baptist preacher, found himself addressing General Anthony Wayne's army in 1795 after the defeat of the northwestern Indians, his prescription for peace was amalgamation: "interchanges of persons" would bring Native people into white towns, and whites into Indian country, "and the Americans and Indians would become one people." Despite continuing tensions between Indians and whites in the Northwest and the Southeast, intermarriage was the stated goal of federal Indian policy throughout the first decades of the republic.[13]

COULD INTERMARRIAGE BE APPLIED TO the other major non-white population living in the United States? There were, after all, important differences between Indians and blacks both in their respective situations and in the perception of whites. Despite the bloody battles in the West during the American Revolution, Indians retained an allure of authenticity and innocence in the eyes of many white intellectuals after 1783. The United States had a responsibility, as Secretary of War Henry Knox noted, to ensure that the history of North American colonization avoided the "Black Legend" that still clung to the Spanish conquests of Mexico and Peru. While many frontier inhabitants (and politicians) rejected this paternalism, federal officials usually styled themselves as the Indians' national protectors. In the case of African Americans, it was unthinkable that the federal government could play this role. After Georgia and South Carolina threatened to leave the Union during the 1790 debate in the House of Representatives over the abolition of slavery, federal officials steered away from any position that might endanger the Union. While northern states exercised their power to limit or abolish slavery within their own limits, the institution retained a fierce support base in the South. Successive presidents—Washington, Adams, Jefferson, Madison—fretted about slavery's effects on the republic, but did little to strike at its roots.[14]

Yet for those enlightened thinkers who expected the imminent demise of slavery in the United States, amalgamation was strangely difficult to dismiss. To argue that slavery contradicted "all men are created equal" was to acknowledge the unity of mankind and the premise of human universalism. Was there any reason to think that black people could not become perfectly equal with whites after abolition? And wouldn't this mean that, in the future, one could expect the races to fuse? One way to duck this question was to imagine a very long apprenticeship for black people after the degradation of slavery. Northern and southern theorists outlined a process of education and self-help that could begin during slavery (under the gaze of enlightened masters) but stretch for years, perhaps even decades. This view pushed the issue of amalgamation into a comfortably distant future.

Another answer was to posit physiological arguments for keeping the races separate, though it was hard to make these without confirming the central logic of slavery: that blacks were permanently inferior to whites and fitted to serve them.

Perhaps the most interesting contortionist on this issue was the physician Benjamin Rush, a central figure in the intellectual life of the early republic. Rush was closely involved with the Pennsylvania Abolition Society and the free black community of Philadelphia. Unlike some of his famous friends—Thomas Jefferson, for example—Rush married his abstract opposition to the institution with practical discussions of how black people might be integrated into American society after slavery. He was not immune to the logic of degradation. In 1782, he wrote to a South Carolina correspondent that the immediate emancipation of that state's slaves would "injure them and society," given the "habits of vice" they had developed during their years of servitude. But the free black community of Philadelphia was Rush's laboratory for testing black potential. He shared the Abolition Society's commitment to fostering education for free blacks, and hoped that the new African churches in the city would underpin black civil society. Writing to the famed British abolitionist Granville Sharp in 1791, he praised Sharp's efforts to resettle black people in Sierra Leone, but rejected the idea that colonization was the only viable form of benevolence. "The globe is the native country, and the whole human race the fellow citizens of a Christian," Rush wrote. He wanted to give black people not only freedom, but also the tools they required to "make their freedom a blessing to them."[15]

In his most extensive commitment to black equality, Rush addressed the Pennsylvania Abolition Society in 1795 and confirmed that the "great work of justice and benevolence" could not be secured merely through the abolition of slavery: "The newborn citizen must receive that instruction and those powerful impressions of moral and religious truth which will render him capable and desirous of fulfilling the various duties he owes to himself and to his country."

Eventually, "the unhappy sons of Africa" would prove that, despite the experience of slavery, they were "in no wise inferior to the more fortunate inhabitants of Europe and America." But would black people eventually realize their equality through intermarriage? This thought clearly troubled Rush. Maybe it stirred his own prejudices about racial mixing; or perhaps Rush realized that conservative slaveholders were already invoking the specter of a mixed-race society to deter even the most modest forms of antislavery.

His solution to the problem, which he outlined in a paper delivered to the American Philosophical Society, was as ingenious as it was unhinged. Black skin was "a modification of that disease which is known by the name of Leprosy," he said. While "all the claims of the superiority of the whites over the blacks, on account of their color, are founded alike in ignorance and inhumanity," the strong possibility that blackness was a disease "should teach white people the necessity of keeping up that prejudice against such connections with them, as would tend to infect posterity with any portion of their disorder." Rush's belief that one could code blackness as an ailment "without offering violence to humanity, or calling in[to] question the sameness of descent, or natural equality of mankind," seems extraordinarily naïve. Perhaps he pressed ahead in the hope that his eccentric theory would patch an otherwise fatal tear in the fabric of antislavery. "The inferences from it will be in favor of treating them with humanity and justice," Rush told Thomas Jefferson in 1797, "and of keeping up the existing prejudices against matrimonial connections with them."[16]

When conservative slaveholders developed a proslavery argument in the nineteenth century, they placed at its heart a kind of domino theory: to challenge slavery in any way, especially with arguments based on natural rights and human universalism, would ultimately produce a mixed-race population in America. Why did this prospect unnerve liberal intellectuals who proudly stated their belief in the unity of mankind? Abigail Adams, another critic of slavery, felt the force of this aversion while watching a performance of *Othello* in 1785:

"Whether it arises from the prejudices of education or from a real natural antipathy I cannot determine, but my whole soul shuddered whenever I saw the sooty Moor touch the fair Desdemona." Adams confessed that her disgust was not "natural" but the offshoot of prejudice, and she struggled to contain its effects. (In the manuscript copy of the letter, she crossed out her initial confession that "so powerful was prejudice that I could not separate the color from the Man.") There was a lively literature in the late eighteenth century on the dangers of prejudice, which was taken to be antithetical to the spirit of both enlightened religion and science. The ubiquity of racial prejudices did not make them legitimate; hence Benjamin Rush's need to find some kind of scientific rationale, however spurious, to explain why blacks could join with whites in freedom and even citizenship, but not in matrimony.[17]

Among the many liberal thinkers grappling with the questions of slavery, prejudice, and amalgamation in this period, few were as rigorous in their reasoning as David Rice. When the Virginia-born Rice spoke before the Kentucky constitutional convention in 1792, his pro-slavery antagonists insisted that black freedom would lead to racial mixing: that "our posterity at length would all be Mulattoes," as Rice paraphrased their challenge. The Presbyterian preacher stood his ground and accepted the premise of his opponents, saying, "This effect, I grant, it would produce." And while a mixed-race republic would "appear very unnatural to persons laboring under our prejudices of education," that simply confirmed the importance of confronting and overcoming prejudice. Rice presented himself as being no more enthusiastic about racial mixing than the conservatives at the convention. "My own pride remonstrates against it," he conceded. But that pride "does not influence my judgment, nor affect my conscience." Like any prejudice, the widespread aversion to amalgamation might be overcome in time. The "reasonable man who can divest himself of his prejudices" could already foresee the republic's mixed-race future. For everyone else, the fusion of the races would be "an evil only in its approach; as it drew near, it would decrease; when fully come, it would cease to exist." Like Benjamin Rush, David Rice recognized the need not only to free black people from slavery, but to realize their potential to become "useful citizens." Unlike Rush, Rice was willing to allow that equal citizenship after slavery might eventually produce a mixed-race America.[18]

THOMAS JEFFERSON FAILED TO ADDRESS William Short's amalgamation letter in 1798, but he had already shared his views on racial mixing in *Notes on the State of Virginia*. Blacks were improved "in body and mind" by racial mixing with whites, he concluded, but the reverse did not appear to be true. We saw earlier that Jefferson's tentative speculations about racial inferiority in the *Notes* earned him brickbats and lampoons from his contemporaries. One of his most exacting critics was the writer and land speculator Gilbert Imlay, who unspooled Jefferson's racial hierarchies to reveal their necessary opposite: the amalgamation of the races in America. Imlay acknowledged that the "prejudices of the times" were considerable, but he pointed his readers toward the inevitability of a mixed-race future. "It will doubtless require a length of time to generalize marriages between the whites and blacks," he admitted, but that day would come. Initially, white men would marry the daughters of wealthy blacks. Later, "when prejudices are worn away," relationships would develop "from more tender and delicate sentiments." Like William Short, Imlay dismissed any correlation between beauty and skin color. Jefferson's failure to do the same was both curious and backward, his "paltry sophistry and nonsense" on the subject betraying the triumph of prejudice over reason.[19]

Thomas Jefferson might easily have missed Imlay's suggestions and slights. After publishing his book in London in 1792, Imlay's principal claim to celebrity was his ill-fated relationship with Mary Wollstonecraft, who may have been responsible for some of his more progressive views. (Her *Vindication of the Rights of Women* appeared in the same year as Imlay's endorsement of intermarriage.) Jefferson found it harder to dodge the views of his friend François-Jean de Beauvoir, the Marquis de Chastellux. Like Lafayette, Chastellux fought on the Patriot side in the Battle of Yorktown. Visiting Jefferson at Monticello in April 1782, he found a kindred spirit: "Before I had been two hours with him," the marquis later wrote, "we were as intimate as if we had passed our whole lives together." Chastellux shared many of his host's worries about slavery and the problem of emancipation. His *Travels in North America* (1787) seems so similar to Jefferson's *Notes* on these matters that one wonders which author borrowed from the other. But the Frenchman departed from the Virginian on the crucial question of racial mixing. Male slaves probably couldn't be integrated into American society, thought Chastellux; they would have to be "very gradually" sent beyond the borders of the United States. But black women belonged in a different category. Chastellux had spent enough time in the South to know about the "illicit, but already well established commerce between the white men and negresses." If this practice could be brought into the light, perhaps even "encouraged" by government, black mothers "could not fail of giving birth to a race of mulattoes, which would produce another of Quarterons, and so on until the colour should be totally effaced."[20]

Chastellux and Jefferson exchanged their respective manuscripts in 1785, and the Frenchman was candid about the deficiencies of Jefferson's *Notes on the State of Virginia*. He balked at the suggestion that blacks were inferior to whites and urged Jefferson to read a book by a Spanish writer who praised the strength and industry of the mulatto populations of Latin America. Jefferson made a partial defense of his views, suggesting that Native Americans were "in body and mind equal to the white man," while African Americans at present "might not be so." But he conceded that "it would be hazardous to affirm that, equally cultivated for a few generations, [they] would not become so." The radical proposals for amalgamation in Chastellux's book failed to lure Jefferson into a response; instead, he offered blandly warm regards to the Frenchman, reassuring him that there was nothing in the book that would make Virginians "uneasy." While Chastellux's proposals for amalgamation appeared in an American edition in 1787, and were excerpted by the antislavery publisher Mathew Carey in his

Columbian Magazine that summer, they weren't widely discussed by reviewers. As we'll see, liberal reformers in the ensuing decades had their own hang-ups about the interracial sex that was already taking place in America.[21]

Chastellux assumed that the secret of the South—its "well-established commerce" between masters and their female slaves—was common knowledge. His breezy recommendations were far removed from the formal speculations of Samuel Stanhope Smith on the same topic. We encountered Smith earlier as a theorist of degradation and an advocate of the (scrupulously gradual) abolition of slavery. In his Princeton lectures, he called upon masters to encourage "good moral and industrious habits" by giving blacks their own land to cultivate before emancipation. The obstacle to the gradual plan, though, would be the tendency of freed blacks to lapse back into the company or morals of those who were still enslaved, a declension that seemed certain if whites maintained a "supercilious contempt" toward freed people. If blacks failed to escape the stigma of slavery even when they had been given their freedom, the delicate machinery of gradualism would be destroyed. An embittered class of freed people not only would assume a hostile stance toward their white neighbors, but would alert those who were still enslaved to the emptiness of their liberal deliverance.[22]

The first part of Smith's solution to the problem would have been familiar to Jefferson and many other antislavery theorists: freed blacks should be relocated in "a large district out of the unappropriated lands of the United States," and given land and opportunity to better themselves. But while Jefferson in the *Notes* had recommended that blacks be "removed beyond the reach of mixture," Smith saw removal as the precursor to amalgamation. "In order to bring the two races nearer together," he wrote, and "to obliterate those wide distinctions which are now created by diversity of complexion, and which might be improved by prejudice," the United States should induce white people to leave the eastern states voluntarily and attach themselves to the new black colonists. "Every white man who should marry a black woman, and every white woman who should marry a black man, and reside within the territory, might be entitled to a double portion of land." There were echoes of Patrick Henry's state-sponsored Indian marriage plan in this purported solution to the problem of integration. But Smith recognized, with considerable understatement, that the politics of the day might be inimical to such a sweeping project of racial engineering: "I fear that neither the general government, nor the governments of the individual states, will feel themselves under any obligation to make great sacrifices in order to deliver this humiliated race of men from the bondage which at present degrades them." Smith sensed that he had the building blocks of a solution, and he knew that the abolition of slavery was a cause "of high public concern." The challenge was to imagine a political process by which the difficult work of abolition—let alone amalgamation—might be carried forward.[23]

These plans for intermarriage with Indians and blacks shared some common characteristics. They were rooted in ideas of human universalism and in the conviction that there was no compelling scientific or religious reason that the races could not be fused. They recognized that interracial marriages faced a number of obstacles, given the sociological factors that separated the races—hence the offer of compensation to those white pioneers who would initiate the process of amalgamation. Finally, and perhaps most importantly, intermarriage proponents thought the delicate work of fusing the races could be carried out by other people: a flood of carefully screened English immigrants, perhaps, or poorer whites who would marry for money rather than love. The tendency of intermarriage proponents to see the frontier as the workshop of racial reconciliation had its own logic: it was a clever appropriation of the emerging notion of the West as a place of opportunity and reinvention. But the refusal of liberal intellectuals to embrace interracial unions for themselves—or, in the case of Thomas Jefferson, their failure to embrace them publicly—left no counterweight to the widespread prejudice against racial mixing among the majority of white Americans. Those liberal reformers who imagined themselves least corrupted by prejudice thought that the work of amalgamation belonged to someone else.

SIX

WE SHALL ALL BE AMERICANS

LONG BEFORE THOMAS JEFFERSON PRESCRIBED white-Indian marriages as the solution to the "civilizing" problem, interracial sex was a defining feature of frontier life. During the seventeenth and eighteenth centuries, French traders became adept at binding themselves to Native peoples through marriage, a strategy later pursued by their British counterparts in the American interior. We can't be sure how many of these marriages were driven by love, but there were clear advantages to the traders: They gained a degree of protection, the opportunity to access land, and an introduction to kinship networks that ranged far beyond a particular family or village. Their children usually remained in Indian country, often rising to positions of power and influence within Indian communities. It's hard to give an accurate estimate of the extent of intermarriage within Native societies: historians have suggested that anywhere between 10 percent and 25 percent of the population of some southeastern Indian nations may have had "mixed blood" by the early nineteenth century. Amalgamation had a significant impact on white-Indian relations regardless of the schemes of Patrick Henry or the Countess of Huntingdon.[1]

Apart from their contact with white people, Native Americans had forged separate relations with African Americans since the colonial era, ranging from intermarriage to enslavement. Sometimes Indians married their slaves, a story memorably recounted in historian

Tiya Miles's book about the relationship between a Cherokee man and his black slave during the first decades of the nineteenth century. While the diversity of black-Indian relationships defies easy general-ization, we can identify two crucial roles played by African Americans in indigenous societies. From the seventeenth century, runaway slaves took refuge in Indian country, often becoming full members of Indian communities. This infuriated southern slaveholders and became the cause of considerable tension on the borders of white settlement. But as southern Indians adopted rudiments of the "civilizing" program around the turn of the nineteenth century, they borrowed one marker of respectability from the white planters rushing toward their lands: Native Americans began to practice forms of captivity that increas-ingly resembled the chattel slavery of the southern United States.[2]

On the question of whether amalgamation had brought Native peoples closer to the United States, the evidence available to white reformers was mixed. In the Old Northwest, where French traders had formed extensive kinship networks with local Indians, US officials complained that the "most detestable and unprincipled wretches" had seized control of the Indian trade. The territorial governor of Illi-nois, Ninian Edwards, concluded that "married men of respectabil-ity" had never ventured into Indian country, leaving the field open to baser individuals (French and English) who were barely civilized themselves. These men were especially likely to have children "with a relish for savage life" who would only add to the civilizing prob-lem at the frontier. In the Southeast, meanwhile, government officials were exasperated by mixed-race Indian leaders like Alexander McGil-livray, the son of a Scottish trader and a Koasati (Creek) mother. McGillivray led the Creeks into an alliance with Britain during the American Revolution. After 1783, he expertly played off Britain, Spain, and the United States in an effort to defend Creek territory. McGilli-vray's statecraft reflected an impressive command of geopolitics and a deep-seated commitment to his people. Some federal officials, unable to see McGillivray in his full complexity, took a different view: he was a "half breed," which made him especially unreliable and dangerous.[3]

Could intermarriage produce happier effects if it were managed closely by the United States? An opportunity to answer this question arose in 1792, when a young Princeton graduate named Leonard Shaw accepted a commission from Henry Knox to become the US agent to the Cherokees. This was a delicate moment in American diplomacy. With the war against the Western Confederacy still unfolding in the Northwest, Knox and Washington were desperate to keep the peace in the Southeast. And yet the Cherokees and other southeastern Indians had been displaced and enraged by a series of treaties since the mid-1780s shifting their settlements from what is now western North Carolina to a broad region encompassing southern Tennessee, northwestern Georgia, and northeastern Alabama. The Chickamauga Indians—the southern part of the Cherokee Nation—were in open revolt against the 1791 Treaty of Holston, which had established new boundaries without their involvement or consent. Knox wanted Shaw to keep the rest of the Cherokees in the US orbit. As he laid out his orders, Knox told Shaw to remember that, appearances notwithstanding, "the difference between civilized and savage modes of life" was not so great. Shaw took Knox at his word. Soon after his arrival in Tennessee, he married the daughter of the Cherokee chief Half Breed. In June 1792, he told the Grand Cherokee National Council that, since the "Great Spirit has called me from amongst my own people to reside amongst you, and has created me for the express purpose of being your friend, I shall forget all my former connexions, and attach myself to you." Shaw saw no contradiction between his responsibilities as a federal agent and his new attachment to the Cherokee leadership. If anything, he concluded that these roles would prove mutually reinforcing.[4]

One of Shaw's first actions after getting married vindicated this optimistic view. John Watts, the leader of the Chickamauga insurgency, plotted in September 1792 to attack the white settlers who were pouring into the areas ceded by the Treaty of Holston. Shaw's wife learned of the plan from her relatives and passed on the report to her husband, who swiftly warned the settlers. The longer Shaw spent in

Cherokee country, though, the less certain he became about his allegiances. The touchstone of his disillusionment was his boss William Blount, the territorial governor of Tennessee. Blount had grown up in North Carolina, and during the 1780s he had dedicated himself to opening the lucrative lands west of the state to white settlement. He had also spent several years in Congress, and in 1790 had been rewarded for his friendship with Washington and Knox with a double appointment: he was made governor of the unorganized territory south of the Ohio River as well as US superintendent for Indian affairs in the southern region. These assignments required him—like William Henry Harrison in the Northwest—to represent the interests of white settlers while acting honestly in his dealings with Native Americans. The job would have been impossible, even if Blount had harbored any intention of doing it properly. Instead, he put himself at the service of the settlers, using every trick available to destabilize Indian leaders and expedite land cessions. Blount paid lip service to the notion that whites and Indians were equal, "not one better than the other," but his commitment to settler expansion was absolute. The Cherokees, in a grudging acknowledgment of his territorial appetite, gave Blount a nickname in their own language: they called him the Dirt Captain.[5]

Blount's tactics were pivotal in the drafting of the Treaty of Holston, and both Washington and Knox felt personally embarrassed by reports of his skullduggery. But neither the president nor the secretary acted to remove Blount from office. Instead, Leonard Shaw, the callow Princeton graduate, had to navigate the wreckage. By January 1793, Shaw was in open rebellion. When asked by John Watts and the Chickamauga for his opinion of Governor Blount, Shaw replied that Blount "had wronged them out of their lands," and that they should petition Congress directly for redress. Federal representatives had no idea what was happening in the Southeast, Shaw insisted, or they would never have allowed Blount to cheat the Indians so brazenly. "You know I was sent here by your father the President to do you justice," he told Watts. "And justice you shall have, as far as in my power."

To the delight of the Chickamauga, Shaw volunteered to return to Philadelphia and plead their case directly to the secretary of war.

The young agent soon realized the limits of his commission. Shaw's interpreter informed Governor Blount of the apparent mutiny, and Blount asked Henry Knox to fire the agent for "inebriety" and "great want of prudence." Shaw was duly dismissed; Blount was appeased by a more compliant replacement. Shaw had seen William Blount for what he was: a regional partisan, a man more focused on the interests of western settlers and speculators than on the honor of the new nation. After overseeing Tennessee's admission to the Union in 1796 and becoming the state's first US senator, Blount began to doubt whether the faltering federal government was the best vehicle for his ambitions. He opened secret negotiations with the British over a possible invasion of Spanish Louisiana and Florida. When the plot was discovered, Blount was expelled by the Senate and forced back to Tennessee—where his admiring constituents elected him to the state senate instead. Shaw, by contrast, disappears from the historical record after his dismissal; he may have returned to Tennessee to live out his life among the Cherokees. Despite Blount's eventual treachery, it was his insistence on the primacy of western settlers over Native Americans that would ultimately prevail. Shaw's belief in a broader union between Native peoples and whites did not survive his brief tenure as a US agent. If he found some version of this union in the final years of his life, he did so beyond the gaze of the federal government.[6]

The eclipse of Leonard Shaw was repeated, in more tragic circumstances, nearly two decades later in the Old Northwest. William Wells had been born in Pennsylvania in 1770, but had moved with his family to what is now Kentucky in 1779. Captured by Native Americans while playing near the Ohio River in 1784, he was renamed "Apekonit" (Wild Carrot) by the Miami Nation on account of his red hair. During his teenage years, Wells helped the Miami launch raids on illegal white settlements along the Ohio. He cemented his place in Native society by marrying Sweet Breeze, the daughter of Miami leader Little Turtle. He fought alongside Little Turtle when his father-in-law assembled the Western Confederacy, but switched sides abruptly in 1792. Serving as a translator to the US armies that slowly rolled back the Confederacy's gains, Wells found himself working for General "Mad Anthony" Wayne during the decisive Battle of Fallen Timbers. Wells later claimed he had shifted allegiances after tiring of the hardships of Indian life. But he recognized that the Miami and their neighbors were living through an unprecedented moment in their history, and that their future might depend on the sincerity of the "civilizing" program. Over the next two decades he shuttled between his Native friends and family and the settlers and officials who were extending the boundaries of US control in the Northwest.[7]

After the Treaty of Greenville, as Little Turtle cautiously embraced the "civilizing" program, Wells served as his translator and adviser. Wells's experience on both sides of the conflict in the Northwest fascinated William Henry Harrison, and the governor moved through a cycle of disenchantment and reconciliation with the agent. (At one point, Harrison had to apologize to federal officials in Washington for his wildly inconsistent assessments of Wells's character and qualities.) Wells might have served as a bridge between Harrison and the Miamis during the years after Fallen Timbers, helping Little Turtle to unite the northwestern Indians behind Henry Knox's "civilizing" program. But Harrison's insistence on accelerating Knox's gradual land cessions diluted Little Turtle's influence, and Wells's along with it. By the time of the Miami chief's death in 1811, Wells had become an isolated figure: he was unwilling to accept the expansionist designs of Harrison, but had become estranged from the militancy of Tecumseh and his followers.[8]

Even before the Battle of Tippecanoe in November 1811, Wells realized that his long career in the Old Northwest was over. He resolved to take his (pregnant) wife and children back to Kentucky, but was persuaded by Harrison to remain at Fort Wayne as the Native uprising caught fire. Wells learned that his niece was living in Fort Dearborn, an isolated military outpost on the site of what is now Chicago. The danger of an Indian attack prompted US officials to order its evacuation, and Wells rushed to Fort Dearborn in August 1812 with a small contingent of Miami warriors to rescue the soldiers and civilians there. Soon after his arrival, hundreds of Potawatomi Indians gathered outside and laid siege to the inhabitants. Wells hoped that the Potawatomis might allow safe passage for the US soldiers and their families, in acknowledgment of his long career as a broker between the United States and its Native neighbors. More than a hundred people left the fort on 12 August, around a third of them civilians. Wells was at their head, his face blackened in the style of an Indian warrior. The Potawatomis attacked the caravan, and Wells was shot and scalped. His assailants paid him the compliment of eating his heart, a testament to his bravery, and killed another fifty-one members of the unfortunate party. Although the rest of the evacuees survived— including Wells's niece Rebekah—the story of the "Fort Dearborn Massacre" became a recruitment tool for the anti-Indian campaigns of the War of 1812 and a foundation myth for the city of Chicago. Wells, who had lived a life between the many cultures of the Great Lakes region, had become an unwitting martyr of a white Midwest.[9]

THE STORIES OF LEONARD SHAW and William Wells suggest that to embrace intermarriage was to invite political marginalization, perhaps worse. The extraordinary career of Benjamin Hawkins, on the other hand, allows us to see a white federal official who initially endorsed amalgamation but then thought better of it. Born into a wealthy and politically influential family in North Carolina, Hawkins studied at Princeton, served briefly as a French interpreter to George Washington during the Revolutionary War, and was elected to Congress in 1781 at the age of twenty-seven. From 1785, he became closely involved in Indian affairs, sitting on congressional committees and even negotiating treaties with Indian nations in the South. Hawkins was a formidable opponent of what he took to be the crassness of federal Indian policy. "As long as we attempt to go into their country

An official, usually identified as Benjamin Hawkins, encouraging "civilization" among the Creeks. COURTESY OF THE GREENVILLE COUNTY MUSEUM OF ART.

or to remain thus," he told Washington in 1792, "we shall be at war."
Hawkins accepted Washington's offer to replace William Blount
as US agent to the southern Indians in 1795, remaining in the post
for twenty years. He was easily the most powerful US official living
among Native Americans during that period, and his priorities initially echoed those of Leonard Shaw. A good US agent to the Indians,
he concluded, should find a Native wife.[10]

Hawkins had been toying with the idea since 1786, when he had
asked the Creek leader Alexander McGillivray to "choose for me a
young damsel, out of one of your most reputable families." The gesture had a geopolitical edge: Hawkins wanted to demonstrate that
the United States was more serious than Spain about binding itself to
the Indians. But he also shared his personal preferences: "Let her be
handsome and agreeable, skilled in the customs of her own Country,
and of a mind that will feel the station I shall support her in." When
Hawkins finally moved to Creek country a decade later, he wasted no
time in telling his Indian neighbors "the objects of my mission, my

love for the red women, and my determination to better, if practicable, their situation." His initial encounters with mixed-race couples left him upbeat about the prospects of intermarriage. Sarah Waters, the Indian wife of a Georgian colonel, had produced two fine children, one of whom had recently traveled to England to complete his education. Sally Hews, the Indian widow of another white American, had proved an excellent interpreter on Hawkins's visit to Cherokee country. Writing about these unions to his friend Elizabeth Trist, a Philadelphia socialite, Hawkins offered to marry off her sons: "I have within my agency some beautiful young queens and I will order a factory to be set in motion, to make two for the boys."[11]

If this "factory" was a tongue-in-cheek suggestion, Hawkins soon proved willing to gratify his own sexual appetite in his new surroundings. But it was his frustrated efforts to link sex, power, and patronage in his Indian agency that reversed his views on the virtues of amalgamation. Initially, Hawkins was delighted at the attention he received from Creek women, and he wrote with lavish candor to Elizabeth Trist about his encounter with "the Queen of Tuckabatchee," a young Indian widow who occupied a position of considerable influence within her Creek community. On a visit to her town, he had invited her and several other women to call on him at his agency. One morning, the young woman appeared "very early" in his bedroom with a proposal of marriage. She was willing to give Hawkins access to her cattle and her body if he took "direction of [her] affairs." Should Hawkins subsequently decide to "take a young girl into the house I shall not like it," she told him, "but I won't say a word; maybe I can't love her, but I won't use her ill." Hawkins found this offer hard to resist: "I immediately rose up in my bed and took her in my arms and hugged her, my hands wandered to certain parts the most attractive and she resisted not. Which were they? The milk pots. She was about 23 years of age, plump built, not tall, of copper colour, full breasted, her face regular, with the appearance of neatness in her dress."

In the afterglow of their encounter, Hawkins made a series of counterproposals. He would look after her cattle and her son, and happily pose as her husband, but he recognized that his occasional visits (and other commitments) might incline her to seek solace in the arms of another. "But you must not forget," he told her, "I have not yet determined to set up a manufactory of babes, in either of the four nations. But you are at liberty as you have one, and know the trade, to carry it on under my name, and to chuse any assistant you may deem suitable. The children will be mine and I will attend to you." The details became painfully specific: "I am not a jealous man. You must be neat and clean when I come to Tuckabatchee, and your assistant must leave the house, if I direct him to do so, on my arrival."[12]

Hawkins's ideal arrangement was subtly subversive of Creek traditions. The Creeks allowed unmarried men and women considerable sexual freedom, and husbands and wives could leave a marriage easily. But his offer to the Tuckabatchee widow suggested that his status as a husband might be of more worth than his value as a mate. Both he and his "wife" could have sex with other partners, but Hawkins would expect to fulfill the role of patriarch when they were together. (He might also ask the Queen's lover to vanish during his conjugal visits.) In pursuing this arrangement, Hawkins imagined himself to be reforming a bankrupt Native social structure that degraded women. He complained to Elizabeth Trist and his other friends about the idleness of Indian men and their tendency to abandon children to the care of their wives and extended family. He failed to understand that these arrangements might actually be the hallmarks of a matrilineal culture in which patriarchal assumptions would have little currency. Lamenting the reluctance of even white men in Indian country to engage with Indian women, Hawkins seems to have sought out the company of the opposite sex at every opportunity. He soon came to realize that he was crossing into a social terrain in which his powers would largely dissipate.[13]

Around the time he struck his bargain with the "Queen of Tuckabatchee," Hawkins received another visit, from the mother of a young widow who had been married to a Scottish trader named Timothy Barnard. When the mother "requested I would accept of her daughter,"

Hawkins lectured her on sexual politics: "The ways of the white people differ much from those of the red people," he told her. "We make companions of our women, the Indians make slaves of theirs. . . . If I take a woman who has sons or daughters, I shall look upon them as my own children. The wife must consent that I shall clothe them, feed them, and bring them up as I please, and no one of her family shall oppose my doing so." Most importantly, "red women should always be proud of their white husbands, should always take part with them and obey them." Evidently, neither Mrs. Barnard nor her mother were impressed by this speech, and the proposed union did not proceed. Meanwhile, Hawkins found himself besieged by demands for assistance from the Creek women (including the "Queen of Tuckabatchee") that he had slept with or otherwise led into his unusual version of marriage.[14]

By 1799, Hawkins had concluded that his understanding of patriarchy simply wouldn't translate to the Creeks. It wasn't hard to receive offers of marriage or sex, but Hawkins found it maddeningly difficult to manage the consequences of his indulgence. With Creek women—only some of whom he recognized—rushing to the agency demanding he attend to their business affairs, Hawkins realized that his efforts to encourage amalgamation had incurred vast obligations running along the most distant of kinship networks. Soon he was telling anyone who would listen that "a man who keeps an Indian woman is the slave of her family and a slave to her whims and caprices." Drowning in the unintended consequences of his vainglorious effort to bestow more male attention on Creek women, Hawkins revised his views on intermarriage. By 1799, having witnessed the same crush of matriarchal entitlement press upon one of the white blacksmiths in his agency who had married a Creek woman, Hawkins issued a new directive: no white employee would be allowed to marry an Indian.[15]

When Thomas Jefferson assumed the presidency, he announced that whites and Native Americans would eventually amalgamate under the happy bower of his Indian policy. Hawkins wrote him a long letter explaining why this was a mistake. Hawkins had come to Creek country "in favour of the idea of forming amorous connexions with the women," and had even determined "to set the example myself." By now, he had learned his lesson. "The husband is a tenant, at will only so far as the occupancy of the *premises* of the woman but permanently bound in his property if he has children." (In other words: women seemed to find it easier to avoid the material ties of marriage than men, especially if children were involved.) Worse, Indian women "invariably [had] the habit of governing absolutely in all cases when connected with a white man." After his ban on intermarriage at the Creek agency, some of the Creek women had promised to "reflect on and form proper ideas on the subject," if Hawkins would only rescind his order. But his gaze had already widened to consider the effects of intermarriage throughout the Southeast. He noticed that some of the tensions between settlers and Indians were caused by "idle" whites who had crossed into Indian territory to marry Native women. The idea that the Indians' openness to intermarriage would lure the wrong kind of husbands dovetailed with Hawkins's personal embarrassments. In the summer of 1803, Hawkins wrote in his notebook of "the remarkable fact" that civilization "takes root every where better among the Indians who have had no white people connected with them than where they have." While officials in the federal capital continued to promote intermarriage as the solution to the Indian question, the most senior US agent in the South took the opposite view: perhaps it was only by separating Indians from whites that the civilizing program could triumph.[16]

IF HAWKINS HAD PLANTED DOUBT in Jefferson's mind about amalgamation, the president didn't let this slip. "You will mix with us by marriage," Jefferson told a delegation of Delawares and Mohicans visiting Washington in December 1808. "Your blood will run in our veins, and will spread with us over this great island." Jefferson's vision of the future was encapsulated in a simple phrase: "We shall all be

Americans." Tecumseh's uprising and the War of 1812 did terrible damage to this prospect without entirely destroying it. In 1816, the new secretary of war, William Crawford, declared in a report on Indian policy that "an enlightened and benevolent nation" should eschew any thought of exterminating the Indians. If previous policies had failed to convert them to "civilization" and the virtues of private property, it was time to try something new. "Let intermarriages between them and the whites, be encouraged by the government," he urged. "This cannot fail to preserve the race, with the modifications necessary to the enjoyment of civil liberty and social happiness." Although Crawford seemed to be echoing Jefferson's policy, the rationale had shifted. He presented intermarriage not as a way of placating restive Indians but of salving the American conscience after a bloody war. In this vein, he made a further, daring observation: it would "redound more to the national honor" to incorporate Native Americans "than to receive with open arms, the fugitives of the old world." In a nation that had already mythologized itself as the refuge of liberty, Crawford was favoring Indians over immigrants.[17]

Crawford's background gave him an unusual vantage on these issues. Born in Virginia, he had grown up in Georgia to become a lawyer and state legislator. He was closely acquainted not only with the tenets of the "civilizing" program, but also with the demands and prejudices of white settlers. Elected to the US Senate in 1807, he served as minister to France during the War of 1812 and was appointed to the War Department in 1815. His fame and popularity made him a front-runner among the candidates to succeed James Madison in the election of 1816, though ultimately he withdrew to allow Madison's friend and fellow Virginian James Monroe to win the nomination. As Madison's secretary of war, Crawford inherited the awkward task of managing Andrew Jackson, who was then rampaging through Georgia and Spanish Florida in pursuit of Britain's Native allies. Crawford stood against Jackson's attempts to make Indian policy by military fiat: he even ordered the renegotiation of treaties that Jackson had imposed upon the Cherokees. (Thanks to this intervention, 2 million acres of land south of the Tennessee River were returned to Indian control.) Crawford's firmness drew the enmity of western settlers, who burned his effigy from Tennessee to the Mississippi Territory. This seems not to have troubled him in the least. Crawford understood that victory in the War of 1812 made the search for a liberal Indian policy more rather than less pressing.[18]

Crawford wasn't the only person talking about amalgamation in 1816. A British tract entitled *Colonial Policy* appeared in London that year and was widely reviewed in the United States. "It now appears, beyond the possibility of contradiction, that American policy is directed towards the total extermination of the Indians," the tract declared. The supposed abandonment of the US "civilizing" policy would give Britain an opportunity to gather Native people in Canada and "blend them, if possible, with our own people, by means of inter-marriages." On the American side of the border, meanwhile, news-papers and magazines were divided on the merits of amalgamation. Given the widely acknowledged belief that all of the "present variet-ies of the human race have originally sprung from the same parent-stock," asked the *Virginia Argus*, "what so great absurdity is there in the intermarrying scheme of Mr. Crawford?"

A less generous view came in a series of articles printed in the Philadelphia-based *Democratic Press* under the pseudonym "Amer-icanus." The author, Thomas Cooper, was a Pennsylvania judge on a lifelong journey from radicalism to conservatism. He had been born in Britain in 1759 and was an ardent supporter of the French Revolution before emigrating to the United States in 1794. When he died in South Carolina in 1838, he was an advocate of slavery and states' rights and a critic of the promiscuous egalitarianism of the Declaration of Inde-pendence. In 1816, Cooper was closer to his destination than he was to his point of departure. How could the government force "blooming, healthy, hard, active and enterprising" young whites to marry "dirty, draggle-tailed, blanketed, half-human Squaws?" To suggest that this policy would be preferable to naturalizing hard-working immigrants from Europe (like himself) was perverse. "You can no more convert an Indian into a civilized man," Cooper concluded, "than you can convert a negro into a white man."[19]

Cooper's articles were reprinted across the country, and many papers rushed to amplify Cooper's views. One influential reader was disgusted at the casual prejudice that ensued. Return J. Meigs, US agent to the Cherokees, was born in Connecticut in 1740, served five years in the Continental Army during the Revolutionary War, and became a land agent and territorial legislator in Ohio after 1783. When Jefferson posted him to the Cherokees in 1801, he was already sixty-one years old; he held the post until his death in 1823. Meigs was a persistent opponent of white squatters on Cherokee land and an architect of US policy toward what became known as the "civilized" tribes of the Southeast—the Indian nations that proved most adept at conforming with the federal government's program for improvement. When Crawford made his report in the spring of 1816, Meigs happened to be in Washington with a delegation of Cherokee chiefs for a meeting with the secretary of war. He read Cooper's essays with horror and wrote an angry letter to the newspapers. Meigs vacillated between refuting Cooper—pointing out, for example, that the southeastern Indians had already proven themselves capable of "every valuable improvement" promoted by the federal government—and ridiculing his prejudice. Of Cooper's description of "dirty, filthy, blanketed squaws," Meigs was wearily contemptuous: "What a tissue of vulgarity, rudeness, cruelty and injustice."[20]

The intervention of Meigs prompted other writers to defend Crawford in the press. A New York paper in July 1816 reminded readers that "some of the most respectable men on the borders have Indian wives," mentioning William Wells, in particular (though failing to mention his unfortunate fate). But the most popular defense of intermarriage reassured delicate readers of an important distinction: "Mr. Crawford does not propose to unite our city beaux with the unpolished, untutored rough Indian squaws," reassured the *Virginia Argus*, "nor our *elegantes* with such fellows as Corn-Stalk, Mad-dog, Little-Turtle, Split-Log, etc. No, there is a hardy, laborious race of woodsmen, forming the intermediate link." And again, in the words of the *Washington City Weekly*: "The most refined and accomplished men and women of our country do not inhabit the borders of the wilderness: They are not in the vicinity of, and, therefore, could not readily intermarry with the Indians." As a policy prescription, these newspapers suggested, Crawford's radicalism was limited to those "intermediate" whites who inhabited the outskirts of the United States. "A mixture of half Indian would very considerably improve the frontier breed from its present state," declared a newspaper in Albany, New York. "The Indians would have much the worst of it—if *they* do not object, the whites ought to hold their tongues."[21]

In these responses to Crawford, Cooper, and Meigs, a gap was opening between the proponents of intermarriage and the Americans who were expected to implement the policy. With the end of the war in the Northwest in 1815, and the acquisition of Florida from Spain four years later, the challenge of incorporating Native peoples became ever more urgent. Crawford had supplied an "enlightened" alternative to "the utter extinction of the Indian race," but not the means by which it could be realized. In 1820, in an essay on the challenge of incorporating Florida, the *National Gazette* of Philadelphia reminded its readers of Crawford's 1816 suggestion. Amalgamation, the paper insisted, was a trusted tool for uniting diverse peoples. More than fifty years before Crawford's report, the British author William Roberts had made the same recommendation of intermarriage in his *History of Florida*. "The tie of marriage is the band of nations," Roberts had written; that sentiment was still true half a century later, thought the *National Gazette*. But if the prescription for becoming a single nation was clear, one problem remained to be solved: "Who will begin?"[22]

CRAWFORD'S POLITICAL CAREER SURVIVED HIS endorsement of amalgamation, to the surprise of his enemies. In 1824, when Crawford became a candidate to succeed James Monroe in the White House,

Thomas Cooper's "Americanus" essays were reprinted in a volume clearly intended to destroy Crawford's prospects. (The brief, toxic preface assured readers that a President Crawford would bar immigrants from entering the United States unless they agreed to "marry a savage woman.") In the event, it was a sudden debilitating stroke rather than his advocacy of intermarriage that forced Crawford out of the running. As far as we can tell, he never changed his mind about the wisdom of his earlier prescriptions. In a letter to a friend in 1822, Crawford admitted that his plan had been "ridiculed" by some, but insisted that marriage had always been the most effective way to introduce "civilization" to "savage nations." Crawford flattered himself into thinking that the nation was beginning to agree with him.[23]

Surprisingly, it was in New England rather than on the frontier that a public squeamishness about white-Native intermarriage came most sharply into focus. In 1817, the American Board of Commissioners for Foreign Missions (ABCFM)—the leading missionary organization in the United States—had founded a Foreign Mission School in Cornwall, Connecticut, for the instruction of young "heathens" from around the world. The premise was straightforward: American missionaries would identify promising young men from among the indigenous nations to which they preached; these chosen few would receive instruction in religion and "civilization" at Cornwall; and the school's graduates would return to their communities to spread the good news. Students came to Connecticut from China, India, Hawaii, and other far-flung places, though the largest number were Native American. They were schooled by a team of young missionaries and teachers and supported by some of the most exalted churchmen in New England— including Lyman Beecher, the celebrated evangelical reformer whose daughter Harriet would later write *Uncle Tom's Cabin*.[24]

The Cornwall school drew its Native American students principally from those nations that had embraced the tenets of "civilization." The Cherokees were in the first rank of this group: their growing enthusiasm for commercial agriculture, literacy, and Christianity after 1815 delighted Return J. Meigs, the long-serving US agent to the Cherokees, and federal authorities channeled funds to Cornwall to hasten the "civilizing" process. The school managed its share of problems with homesickness and indiscipline, though the authorities did their best to keep any indiscretions from the public. Cornwall's principal, David Daggett, was especially keen to police the interaction between his students and the outside world. In 1823, Daggett warned Jeremiah Evarts, the secretary of the ABCFM, that two of the "colored boys" had developed inappropriate feelings for a servant girl working in the school's kitchen. Daggett dealt with the situation easily, by dismissing the girl, but he soon discovered a more serious relationship across the color line. One of the Indian scholars who had excelled during his time at Cornwall—a Cherokee named John Ridge—had asked the parents of a local girl, Sarah Northrop, for their daughter's hand in marriage. The circumstances of this romance were singular. Ridge had become seriously ill during his time at Cornwall, and in 1822 he had been moved to the house of John Northrop, the school steward, to be cared for away from the other students. Northrop's daughter Sarah nursed Ridge as he lay stricken, and the two fell in love. Sarah's parents gave their blessing to the marriage, which took place in their home in January 1824. Almost immediately, all hell broke loose.[25]

Newspapers within and beyond New England leapt into the controversy on both sides of the question. "Mr. Crawford's plan for civilizing the Indians, by intermarrying with the whites and amalgamating their blood with ours, appears to be going into practical operation in this state," declared the *Connecticut Herald*. A Pennsylvania newspaper reminded its readers that "it has been the policy of most colonists to intermarry with the aborigines." The *Washington Whig* noted that John Ridge had been an outstanding student and an exemplar of the school's potential, and that the Northrop family were "pleased with the match." Others expressed their horror through the filters of gender or class. One New England paper declared itself happy for "an army of white men" to marry Indian women, but not for white women to submit to an Indian husband. The *Connecticut Herald* held William

Crawford responsible, with the caveat that he had never anticipated "that the 'cold, unripened beauties of the North' were to be the first to yield their embraces to the half-tamed savage."[26]

The ABCFM, which feared that the Cornwall scandal might damage its wider missionary operations, dispatched an official to the offices of the *Connecticut Herald* to straighten out the story. The school staff had known nothing about the match, and the romance was viewed "with reprehension" by teachers and school administrators. An official report followed, in which the school's board emphasized the extraordinary and singular circumstances of what had taken place: "As for the repetition of the event, which gave occasion to so much slander, there is not, as we believe, any distant prospect." In fact, another interracial romance was already underway at Cornwall, involving a young man with a familiar and illustrious name. Elias Boudinot had been born in Cherokee country with the name of Gallegina; he had studied at a Moravian missionary school before coming to Cornwall in 1817. His mother was half-white, and he had grown up in a Cherokee community in which unions between white traders and Indian women were common. On arriving at Cornwall, Gallegina had taken the name of the school's most generous benefactor: the congressman Elias Boudinot, a vocal proponent of the idea that Indians had been degraded by contact with the "wrong" sort of whites. When he completed his studies in 1822, the Cherokee Boudinot returned to the Southeast with the highest hopes of his teachers. But during his time at Cornwall, he had already fallen in love with Harriett Gold, a local girl whose family had multiple connections to the school. Harriett maintained a secret correspondence with Boudinot after his departure for Cherokee country, and in 1824 Boudinot asked her parents to approve their engagement.[27]

They refused. Cornwall was in turmoil over the Ridge-Northrop affair, and Harriett's father had signed the local petition protesting that marriage. But when a devastated Harriett fell into a dangerous illness, her parents relented. To Harriett's delight, they agreed that the wedding could take place when Boudinot returned to Connecticut from Cherokee country. Harriett knew that her intention would create a renewed clamor in the town, perhaps even in her own household. Having secured her parents' consent, her first task was to break the news to her siblings. She asked one of her brothers, Stephen, to meet her in a room of the house with two doors. She locked one of them, handed Stephen a letter explaining her love for Elias, and quickly left through the other door, locking it behind her. His screams of anger shook the walls for what seemed like hours. Harriett had worried about Stephen's reaction; he was only eighteen months older than her, and they had been particularly close throughout childhood. She could scarcely have predicted the extent of his fury. When Harriett's mother judged that Stephen could be safely released, he resolved to unite the town against his sister. He and his friends formed a group called the "Bachelors of Cornwall Valley" and gathered the town's romantic vigilantes on the village green. Harriett recalled the scene in a letter to a friend. "A painting had before been prepared representing a beautiful young Lady and *an Indian*," she wrote. The "respectable young people, Ladies and Gentlemen," gathered round the image, "and Brother Stephen set fire" to it. "The flames rose high, and the smoke ascended. My heart truly sang with anguish at the dreadful scene." Elias Boudinot had not set foot in Cornwall since 1822, but his feelings for Harriett had unleashed a wave of prejudice that seemed certain to consume the Golds, if not the entire school. "There is a great division of feeling among many, but especially in our family," wrote Harriett. "It appears as though a house divided against itself could not stand."[28]

Not every Cornwall resident joined the mob. When the wife of a local preacher told the church choir to wear black armbands to mourn the betrothal of Elias and Harriett, the singers refused to comply. But Harriett's male relatives were especially hostile. Her brother-in-law, the Reverend Herman Vaill, led the efforts to persuade the Golds to change their minds on the marriage before it was too late. "I love the cause which is operating to raise them from their degraded condition," Vaill wrote of the Indians in a letter to Harriett. But "under existing circumstance," with the public unready to accept intermarriage, the match with Elias would "do far more to *hinder* than to promote the measures which are in operation for their welfare." He accused his sister-in-law of selfishness: if she really cared for the missionary cause, she would sacrifice personal happiness to advance God's work.[29]

Finding Harriett immovable, Vaill badgered her sister instead. "I do assure you I have no objections that sister H. should marry the man of her choice," he wrote, "be he white, or black, or even red, if that is the colour she prefers." But the marriage would inflame popular prejudice and harm the school's prospects. Harriett's father, furious at Vaill's meddling, dismissed him as a hypocrite. "It is through pride and prejudice that all this clamor has been raised against Indians," he wrote. How could Vaill hope to defeat prejudice by indulging it? "I have none," Vaill replied. Harriett "has my own declaration in *black and white* that I do not think a *red* connection to be sinful in itself." If Harriett had married Elias Boudinot before the Northrop-Ridge controversy, "like as not I should have said, 'Let 'em mix.' But the experiment has been tried, and it has been so hazardous that under almost any circumstances, it does now appear to be inexpedient." Vaill, who insisted that he had "always been an advocate of intermarriages," presented the prejudices of the wider public as the real threat to the school's future.[30]

Without consulting the leadership of the ABCFM in Boston, the school's four managers—led by Lyman Beecher—issued a statement in June 1825 declaring their "unqualified disapprobation" of the proposed marriage. Harriett and Elias had committed an "outrage upon public feeling." Any local person who had acted as "accessory to this transaction" should be regarded as a "criminal." The school's efforts to manage the crisis seem only to have exacerbated the public reaction. "No incident more shocking could have taken place," wrote a New London, Connecticut, newspaper of the Gold-Boudinot engagement. "Instead of civilizing and christianizing the *savages*, this school is like to be the means of turning our own civilized and christianized inhabitants into savages." A rare dissent came from Hezekiah Niles, the editor of *Niles' Register*, an influential Baltimore newspaper, who was astonished that Lyman Beecher and his benevolent associates had presented Harriett's actions as criminal. Hadn't William Crawford— "a man thought fit by many thousands of the people for the office of the president"—recommended precisely this course? It was a "strange world" in which such an obviously beneficial connection was presented as "criminal." A Pennsylvania newspaper wondered how the missionaries of the ABCFM could win Indian converts with a credo that suggested that the Native American was "not as good as a white man—that he has a soul to save, but it is inferior to the white man's soul."[31]

This was precisely the question that troubled Jeremiah Evarts, the corresponding secretary of the ABCFM. He had traveled extensively in Cherokee country, and he told the board (and the many readers of its magazine, the *Panoplist*) that the children of mixed-race couples in the Southeast were just as clever and industrious as "the children of civilized people." Evarts had personally helped to recruit Gallegina, the young Cherokee who would become Elias Boudinot, and he had watched with anguish as his colleagues had taken their stand against intermarriage. In his private correspondence, Evarts angrily denounced Beecher and his associates for siding with public prejudice. He feared for the future of Indian missions. Many of the same arguments soon reached a wider audience via a series of articles in the *Western Recorder*, an evangelical newspaper in upstate New York. The articles, published in the summer of 1825, were written under a pen name—inevitably, "Crawford"—but a number of clues suggest that Evarts himself may have been the author. (The articles were written by someone with inside knowledge of the scandal, and some of the language from Evarts's private letters reappeared in the "Crawford" pieces.) In his first essay, "Crawford" warned that the Cherokees would interpret the board's rejection of intermarriage as a charge of racial inferiority. This implication was grossly unfair to Native people, particularly those (like Gallegina/Boudinot) who had been "raised from their present degraded state to a level with ourselves in all respects, except the color of their skin." It was ridiculous to imagine that Indians could be maintained as a "separate distinct people," or that they could be sent to another country: "This continent is their home. It is the land of their fathers. We are foreign intruders." The only conclusion, then, was that "they will, by intermarriage, be amalgamated with the white inhabitants of this continent." To prevent this outcome would be like trying to stop a river from flowing into the sea.[32]

The only reason to reject intermarriage would be that the Indians were incapable of civilization, but this premise would undo the entire logic of Christian missions. Granted, some of the white men who had ventured into Indian country had married Native women solely from "motives of gain." Moreover, some Native communities that had experienced an influx of whites appeared to have become "degraded" in recent decades. But this outcome was an indictment not of intermarriage, but of the wrong kind of intimate contact between races. Before the arrival of Europeans, Native Americans could boast a history that was "more honorable than our own." The unfortunate nature of early white-Indian contact did not constitute an argument for permanent separation. Invoking his namesake's 1816 plan, "Crawford" called on the government to regulate encounters between whites and Indians and promote intermarriage. With the proper direction and encouragement, the United States might yet welcome Indians to Congress, to courts and pulpits, and to the most intimate relationships with whites.[33]

The first "Crawford" essay was reprinted across the country. Within a few days, the editor of the *Western Recorder* published a riposte from another anonymous contributor, "HT," who may also have been part of the missionary community. Like Herman Vaill, HT conceded that Indians "possess[ed] native talent equally with their white neighbors" and that there was no theoretical obstacle to intermarriage. But it would be "manifestly improper" and financially risky to encourage these unions while missionaries still depended upon an unenlightened public for the maintenance of their work. "The existence of prejudice," wrote HT, "is to be lamented; but while it does exist its influence will be felt." The job of a preacher was "to meet our fellow sinners *as they are*." "Crawford's" next essay contained a moving letter from Benjamin Gold, Harriett's father, which mapped the Gold family's difficult course through prejudice toward acceptance of the marriage. Benjamin Gold admitted to being initially appalled at the proposed match between his daughter and a non-white suitor. But he "could find nothing in the laws of God or man, forbidding such connexions with Christians of any nation." Benjamin recognized his aversion as prejudice and would not allow it to cloud his moral judgment. He was left with a simple conclusion: Harriett "has a right to this, her choice."[34]

As for the Cornwall school's managers, "Crawford" asked a simple question: Were they "bound to act in accordance with the public will if that will is *wrong*?" A "tremendous fire" had been created from a "spark of love between two individuals." Popular prejudice had fanned the flames, and now the school's managers (and the ABCFM more generally) seemed happy to "increase the blaze by throwing their inflammable reports into it." This point cut to the heart of the dilemma facing liberal reformers. Should they compromise their values and principles by acknowledging popular prejudices? Or stiffen their resolve and challenge those prejudices? While "Crawford" clearly aligned himself with the second position, across his five essays defending the Gold-Boudinot union he became increasingly exhausted. What was the point of bringing Native Americans into the heartland of liberal whites if they were to be "cloistered up like the inmates of a Popish convent," he asked, or "narrowly watched" whenever they left the school premises? Perhaps it would be better for the missionary board to "establish a school of high literary character in some central spot of Indian territory, on the east or west of the Mississippi?" This might, at least, prop up the notion that whites and Indians were equal, a view that had come under concerted attack in Cornwall.[35]

Here was a proposal on which "Crawford" and the ABCFM authorities could agree. The Cornwall Foreign Mission School was closed within a year, and board officials (including Jeremiah Evarts) moved their focus to missionary outposts in Indian country. If this dispelled some of the embarrassment created by the backlash in Cornwall, it pointed darkly toward the alternatives to amalgamation glimpsed by William Crawford and Jeremiah Evarts: expulsion or extermination. It also delighted southern whites, who had long resented the involvement of northeastern philanthropists in Indian affairs. One Mississippi newspaper observed that Cornwall and its sponsors had "done all in their power to place our olive-colored neighbors on an equality with the whites." The paper had no doubt that amalgamation was a terrible idea: "You might as well join the tomahawk and spade in bands of holy wedlock, as look for good fruit from the union of such a couple." But Cornwall had supplied southern white conservatives with pristine evidence that the "civilizing" policy was mere hypocrisy. If "benevolent" northerners weren't willing to live beside Indians as equals, how could they impose this arrangement on whites in the South?[36]

WHEN JEREMIAH EVARTS CAUGHT UP with Sarah Northrop Ridge on his tour of Cherokee country in the spring of 1826, he found that she had been watching the opponents of the Gold-Boudinot marriage with a rueful eye. Sarah "could not help laughing to think how foolish they act," he told his diary. She had no regrets about her choice, and the malicious rumors in New England that she had been badly treated by the Cherokees were false. Three weeks later, a thousand miles to the northeast, Harriett Gold was married to Elias Boudinot in Cornwall. The young Cherokee had been deeply hurt by the controversy over his love for Harriett, but he resolved to address the skeptical white public before returning to the Southeast. He visited Boston and then Philadelphia, where he made a speech in May 1826 in the First Presbyterian Church. Boudinot listed the progress made by his people, both materially ("10 saw-mills, 31 grist-mills, 62 Blacksmith-shops") and intellectually. "The time has arrived," he announced, "when speculations and conjectures as to the practicability of civilizing the Indians must forever cease." In the southeastern states, at least, this process was already close to completion. But what did the future hold for the "Cherokee Nation," given its parlous location within the states of Georgia and Alabama? Boudinot promised that the Cherokees would be "a faithful ally of the United States," implying that a sovereign Indian nation would continue in the midst of the existing southeastern states. But the logic of separate-but-equal was hardly intuitive for Boudinot and his new wife, so he offered a cryptic alternative: if his people were able to complete their passage to civilization, "then, indeed, may true patriots be encouraged in their efforts to make this world of the West, one continuous abode of enlightened, free and happy people."[37]

As he traveled back to the Southeast, Boudinot's vision remained broad enough to encompass two possible futures for the Cherokees: separate status within the United States, or an equal place in a "continuous abode" alongside whites. The former option was anathema to states like Georgia and Alabama, and it sat uneasily with precedent and the federal Constitution. But after the fiasco at Cornwall, the second scenario looked more far-fetched than ever before. Boudinot returned to the Cherokee Nation in the summer of 1826 to found the first Indian newspaper in America, and he played a key role in the debates about Indian removal that would culminate in the Trail of Tears. While his marriage to Harriett was a happy one, the full extent of damage done by the Cornwall controversy became evident in the coming years. After 1826, it would be William Crawford's dire alternatives to amalgamation—extinction or removal—that took center stage in the Southeast and in Washington.

SEVEN

THE PRACTICAL AMALGAMATOR

O N A BRIGHT OCTOBER DAY in 1813, on the banks of the River
Thames in Ontario, Canada, a Kentucky militiaman named
Richard Mentor Johnson advanced into a hail of bullets. Johnson, a
serving member of the US House of Representatives, had left Washington that year to fight in the northwestern war that William Henry
Harrison had done so much to provoke. Harrison was in command
that day, but he remained in the rear as Colonel Johnson and his
mounted riflemen pursued the retreating British and Indian forces.
Johnson's horse limped forward, already bleeding from multiple gun-
shot wounds. Johnson fared no better: he took four bullets, or perhaps
ten, or perhaps twenty-five, before meeting the gaze of an Indian chief
in the distance. The men drew closer until they were a few feet apart.
According to Johnson's first biographer, the chief smiled at the colonel
and, "with a fierce look of malicious pleasure," raised his tomahawk.
Johnson drew the pistol that he had concealed beneath his coat and,
"discharging its contents into the breast of the Indian chief, laid him
dead upon the spot." Exhausted by his efforts, Johnson collapsed with
his horse and lay lifeless on the ground. He was eventually rescued by
a local settler named Medard Labadie, who noticed that both Johnson
and the Indian were still clutching their weapons, as if already captured in a tableau. In the words of his biographer, the colonel had "put

"The Battle of the Thames." This image, showing Richard Mentor Johnson killing Tecumseh, was produced in 1833 to accompany a puff biography of Johnson ahead of his 1836 vice-presidential candidacy. COURTESY OF THE LIBRARY OF CONGRESS.

a complete period to the war upon the northwestern frontier." Richard Mentor Johnson had killed Tecumseh.[1]

Or so Johnson claimed, more or less consistently across the rest of his extraordinary life. Already a popular figure in Kentucky, Johnson parlayed his Canadian heroics into a long and successful career in national politics. Returning to Washington in 1815, still on crutches, Johnson completed two more terms in the House of Representatives before ascending to the US Senate. Unlike his fellow Kentuckian Henry Clay, Johnson became a loyal supporter of Andrew Jackson and the new Democratic Party. By the early 1830s, he was spoken of as Jackson's likely successor. He ultimately joined the ticket of Martin Van Buren, and in March 1837 he became vice-president of the United States. Johnson's political rise was not surprising: he was closely identified with the frontier populism that defined what historians have called "the Age of Jackson." Harder to account for is that he attained the second-highest office in the United States after living openly with his slave mistress in Kentucky for nearly twenty years. Johnson, unlike Thomas Jefferson, did not deny the accusations about his private life. In fact, he helped his mixed-race daughters to marry white men, in defiance of the laws of the state of Kentucky.

Johnson offered a vivid—some would say lurid—demonstration of the prevalence of racial mixing in the slave South, but his treatment of his unconventional family presented awkward challenges to antislavery reformers. Should Johnson be decried for his licentious behavior? Or had he produced, however inadvertently, a model for the biracial families that would underpin an egalitarian society after slavery? Johnson was reluctant to criticize slavery in public, a fact that eventually supplied his critics with an easy argument about his hypocrisy. But the evidence that Johnson loved his daughters dearly, and lamented the prejudice they encountered, complicated the abolitionist stereotype of the venal and predatory master. Although Johnson's fame was forever tied to his supposed triumph over Tecumseh, his reputation became increasingly bound up with racial amalgamation. If the contradictions of Johnson's own thinking on slavery and race ultimately made his political career untenable, they created a parallel set of challenges for reformers seeking to build a national consensus on the iniquities of slavery.

FREE WHITES AND ENSLAVED BLACKS had engaged in interracial sex since the arrival of slaves in America in the 1620s. It became such a prevalent phenomenon that, within a few decades, southern colonies had changed their laws to ensure that children took on the legal status of their mothers, rather than their fathers—a break from European precedent. This simple, cynical revision ensured that the children of master-slave unions had no claim to the assets or standing of their white fathers, preventing the rise of a mixed-race class with economic power and political aspirations. Still more cynically, some of the colonies, including Virginia, banned interracial marriage rather than interracial sex. Such measures did nothing to deter the amalgamation of the races, but they did help to preserve and perpetuate the disparities of power that structured interracial unions. Masters were able to sell their children, to free them from slavery, or—as Thomas Jefferson did—to preserve them in a kind of privileged upper tier of the slave system: unable to leave the service of their master, devoid of rights, but receiving the limited patronage of a sentimental parent.[2]

The perversities of this system became an open secret in the South—and eventually in the North also. As antislavery campaigners began to attack the institution in the 1780s and 1790s, the preponderance of southern "concubinage"—as many northern observers called it—made interracial sex seem shocking and deviant. David Rice, the Kentucky preacher, recognized in 1792 that the actions of masters had helped to demonize amalgamation among respectable Americans. But since racial mixing was already prevalent in the South, he reasoned, it would be sensible to legitimize the practice. "This evil is coming upon us in a way much more disgraceful, and unnatural, than intermarriages," Rice told the Kentucky constitutional convention. It would be better for the nation, and for the individuals concerned, if black-white unions took place within the framework of love and marriage rather than in the selfish confines of a master's lust. This was strong medicine even for liberal reformers, to whom racial mixing seemed one of slavery's clearest perversities. The fact that black-white amalgamation was already taking place far beyond the pale of morality made it hard for liberal whites to imagine intermarriage on the other side of emancipation.[3]

Take, for example, the detailed plan for gradual abolition outlined in 1819 by Hezekiah Niles, the Baltimore newspaper editor. Niles was one of the most prominent and influential journalists in the early United States. Although he lived in a slave state, he was convinced that the institution was immoral and economically inefficient. "Every man's reason is convicted of its wrong," Niles wrote; the only question was how best to end it. Slavery and white prejudice had inhibited the development of African Americans, preventing even freed people from completing the "march to a respectable rank in society." He out-lined a two-stage approach: southern masters should treat male slaves with humanity and kindness, reforming the institution without actu-ally abolishing it, while slave women should be transferred in huge numbers to the northern states. With slaves segregated along gender lines in separate sections of the Union, the growing white popula-tion could contain and eventually dwarf the black minority. If black women were sent to the North, he surmised, "the natural increase of the white people would soon swallow them up, as it were; and by adventitious mixtures, the effect of common association with the whites, and the operation of climate, the dark complexion might in time be nearly removed if not wholly eradicated."[4]

Niles took heart from the fact that European immigrants, who were "very little, if in any respect, superior in intelligence to a large number of our blacks," had blended into American society within a generation or two. Black people faced the additional barrier of their skin color, and the spur it gave to white prejudice; but if "insulated" from the company of other blacks, Niles thought that his female migrants would "lose a very considerable part of their darkness of complexion." Niles was forced to clarify what he meant by "adven-titious mixtures": he was not recommending intermarriage, or so he claimed, but exposure of female black slaves to the climate and improving society of the North. "The original color of the negroes is the effect of climate," he wrote, while slaves and free blacks "are not one jot or tittle more rude or uncultivated than our own immediate ancestors were, boastful as we appear of our accomplishments." His plan would condemn the male slaves of the South to a slow demise, of course; though Niles hoped that the benevolence of masters would comfort them in their loneliness. For black women, however, and for the nation as a whole, the benefits were clear: Niles's plan would destroy slavery and ensure that, "without sexual intercourse," female slaves gradually became white.[5]

One of the many ironies of this extraordinary proposal was how closely it matched the nightmare scenario that had been sketched by

Thomas Branagan of Philadelphia back in 1805. Niles was casting the North in precisely the role that Branagan had eschewed for Pennsylvania. Branagan, however, would have scoffed at Niles's strangely chaste migration. Branagan's chief fear had been African American masculinity: he wrote luridly about black men who roamed the streets of Philadelphia in search of "white women of easy virtue." Even "women of genteel connections" were in danger, given the ability of black predators to produce "libations" that would render any white woman "completely infatuated." Branagan's broader complaint was that wealthy white families in Philadelphia had proven only too eager to hire black domestics, and had already begun to treat black and white servants without any distinction of color. The "respectable" white poor were driven out of the city in search of rural work, and those working-class whites who remained were thereby encouraged to view blacks as romantic partners. Would a white American be "contented to have a negro for thy daughter's husband, a negress for thy son's wife, and in short have them assimilated into thy family as well as the general and state governments"? Placing African Americans in the midst of white cities would universalize rather than extinguish blackness. Interracial relationships were, in Branagan's desperate vision, both unnatural and inevitable.[6]

On balance, the reaction in 1819 to Hezekiah Niles's proposal bore out Branagan's fears more than Niles's hopes. One Virginia newspaper praised Niles for his benevolence and ingenuity, but dismissed his scheme "not only as wild and visionary, but impracticable." Would northern families welcome black women into their households? Would men and women, even in slavery, consent to a separation of the sexes and a lifetime of celibacy? And, most implausibly, could these transplanted black women be successfully segregated from white men in the North? These were preposterous assumptions. If Niles's scheme were ever to work, the paper suggested, it would be sex between blacks and whites that would eventually lighten the skin of the northern black population. And since even Niles didn't expect "the Yankees to

THE PRACTICAL AMALGAMATOR   ❖   165

take to themselves wives of this swarthy tribe," the Baltimore editor had effectively crafted a giant scheme of "illicit intercourse."[7]

Niles's unusual proposal was lost in the scrum over the admission of Missouri to the Union. But as congressmen debated in 1820 whether Missouri would become a slave state or a free state, the issue of resettling African Americans was never far from their thoughts. Antislavery northerners saw the extension of slavery to the West as a metastasizing cancer; southern "moderates," especially those representing the states of the Upper South, wondered if the diffusion of slavery might actually facilitate its abolition. John Tyler of Virginia, who would succeed William Henry Harrison to the presidency in 1841, borrowed a metaphor from his northern opponents: if slavery had darkened the skies of the United States, threatening a deluge of "horrors" where it was most heavily concentrated, would it not be better to spread blacks across the Union and reduce the threat to "a summer's cloud"? Gradual emancipation in the northern states, after all, had relied upon "the paucity of the numbers of their slaves." If emancipation could only take place where whites were an overwhelming majority, argued Tyler and his associates, the slave states must first reduce their black population before ridding themselves of slavery. The antislavery slaveholders of the South would destroy the institution by extending it across the nation.

Not unreasonably, historians have been cynical about the motives of southerners who promoted this odd theory. Even in 1820, it seemed barely credible. Thomas Jefferson's endorsement of Missouri's admission as a slave state astonished his friend the Marquis de Lafayette. "By spreading them over a larger surface," Jefferson wrote of the black population, the nation could "dilute the evil everywhere, and facilitate the means of getting finally rid of it." Lafayette was baffled: "Are you sure, my dear friend, that extending the principle of slavery to the new raised states is a method to facilitate the means of getting rid of it?" Diffusing the "prejudices, habits and calculations of planters" across the Union would surely make it harder to effect a "final liberation."

Jefferson didn't explain himself to his friend, and we can only speculate on his rationale for diffusion. He seems an unlikely convert to
the kind of proslavery expansionism bemoaned by northern congressmen during the Missouri debate. Was he suggesting instead that, if
given enough space and a lower slave population, the "habits of planters" would produce more racial mixing? Might the tangled world of
Monticello be scaled upward and outward, turning the clouds from
black to white? If there is nothing in Jefferson's writing to corrobo-
rate this suspicion, the fate of his own mixed-race offspring is instruc-
tive. When he died in 1826, the Virginia assembly granted Jefferson's
request that two of his four children be allowed to remain in the state,
despite the 1806 law mandating their removal. The other two, Beverly
and Harriet, had already walked off the mountain to live out their
lives as white people.[8]

DAVID RICE HAD PROVED THAT it was possible to oppose slavery and make peace with amalgamation. His great admirer George
Bourne did not agree. After growing up in England, Bourne had emigrated to Maryland in 1804 at the age of twenty-four. He worked in
Baltimore as a newspaper editor, accepting advertisements for runaway slaves before eventually selling his paper to Hezekiah Niles. His
abolitionist instincts emerged only after he moved to the Shenandoah
Valley in 1810 to become a Presbyterian minister. Bourne, unlike most
of his reforming contemporaries (especially in Virginia), saw the antislavery slaveholder as a contradiction in terms. Despite the common
liberal assumption that widespread emancipation depended on sympathetic masters, Bourne excluded slaveholders from his congregation
and urged the Presbyterian hierarchy in Philadelphia to implement
the same policy nationally. In 1816, he published *The Book and Slavery Irreconcilable*, perhaps the most vehement attack on the religious
credentials of slavery that had ever appeared in the United States.
William Lloyd Garrison would later cite Bourne's book as one of the

inspirations for his own move into radical abolitionism. At the climax of his book, Bourne reproduced the most radical sections of David Rice's Kentucky speech on the evils of slavery. Strikingly, in so doing he took a scalpel to the text and removed Rice's admissions that a free society would involve the blending of the races.[9]

The motivation behind this pointed redaction became clearer in his *Picture of Slavery in the United States of America* (1834), which he published soon after joining Garrison's pioneering American Anti-Slavery Society. Slave plantations, Bourne wrote, were "a scene of promiscuous uncleanness, of the most abhorrent character." For this, he blamed women—specifically, the wives of slaveholders, who "would rather connive at the grossest sensuality in their husbands, sons, fathers, and brothers, than abandon the system which enables them to live in luxury and indolence." His long account of a visit he had made to a mixed-race family on a slave plantation built to a crescendo of revulsion: "That such a system must destroy all feminine purity and domestic confidence is obvious: and that such a perennial fountain of vice long since would have dried up, if the southern women had so determined, is not less undeniable." Bourne recoiled from what he described as the "third race"—the mixed offspring from these unions—whose "numbers would soon preponderate over whites and blacks." The "diabolical perfection" of southern amalgamation would eventually deliver the entire region to this race, unless something was done to break the chokehold of slavery. White southern women ought to turn back the tide, thought Bourne, though "there is no more reasonable prospective of cooperation" from them "than from Satan, the prince of all slave-drivers." Perhaps northern women would "cast off their mischievous prudery," acknowledge the issue directly in their own antislavery writing, and lead their southern counterparts away from their sins.[10]

Here and in his 1837 sequel, *Slavery Illustrated in Its Effects upon Woman*, Bourne mapped the South's descent into sexual depravity in unsettling detail. Young white women in slaveholding families were much too inclined to withdraw from the world, Bourne charged. Isolated in the company of their servants, these women became "the easy prey of the colored girl, their attendant and associate, who ensnares the white female youth into an unhallowed acquaintance with the surrounding iniquity." Race mixing thereafter assumed a terrible, circular logic. A black servant girl would tempt her secluded mistress into sex with slave men as "a fair set-off" for herself having been raped by the white patriarch of the family ("and his sons"). White girls who had been ruined by vengeful slaves would become sirens for innocent husbands, luring a "healthful man from the northern states" with "a good exterior and decorous manners" into "the fetters of hymen." The unfortunate husband, far from the moral certainties of the North, would gradually embrace the horrors of slave driving while his seductress offered "to superintend, direct and provide for the rest of the harem." Only abolition could bring an end to the "amalgamating atrocities" that currently prevailed. If black women could only be placed under the care of their "natural" protectors—black men—"the present system of amalgamation, which is rapidly white-washing the skin and transforming the features of the slaves, would cease."[11]

To understand why Bourne chose to chronicle southern slave households with such visceral prurience, we need to acknowledge the broader context of the antislavery efforts in the late 1820s and 1830s. Bourne, like William Lloyd Garrison, had become critical of the long timelines and slow progress of gradual emancipation. Garrison and his followers had finally accepted the argument of free black activists that slavery should be dismantled immediately. But by dismissing the distancing maneuvers and postponements that had structured the antislavery debate for many decades, the "immediatists" faced a new problem: they were instantly accused, both by slaveholders and antislavery "moderates," of supporting amalgamation.[12]

Abolitionist speeches drew hostile reactions from white crowds in major cities in the 1830s, and the leaders of the immediatist movement faced the threat of injury (or worse) on a daily basis. Churches were regularly attacked if their preacher was suspected of favoring intermarriage. Under this pressure, abolitionists responded by turning the charge against their opponents. The true proponents of interracial sex, insisted the immediate abolitionists, were the grandees of the slave system. But was it possible to excoriate racial mixing in the South without stigmatizing the possibility of interracial marriage in the North? Consider the image used to illustrate George Bourne's *Picture of Slavery* (1834) alongside an 1839 image by the anti-abolitionist lithographer Edward W. Clay of New York. Both depict mixed-race domestic scenes with the cruel eye of the caricaturist: the first has a white couple seated at table with a variety of black and white children, representing "family amalgamation among the Men-stealers"; the second depicts a black husband reclining on a sofa with his white wife and their black child, welcoming another mixed-race couple into their living room. (Even the family dogs are black and white.) Although Bourne's book limited its critique to the "vast harem" of the South, the two images shared a visual language of disgust toward interracial relationships. Abolitionists warned northern audiences that it was southern slaveholders, rather than antislavery immediatists, who threatened to conjure the "third race" of George Bourne's nightmares. In decrying the sexual abuses of slavery, liberal reformers reinforced existing prejudices in the North against any kind of race mixing.[13]

Lydia Maria Child, a novelist and social reformer, became another early member of William Lloyd Garrison's immediatist movement. In a series of antislavery essays and books, she offered readers an intimate picture of slavery's horrors. Black women were portrayed as defenseless, denied even a "sense of shame" amid the constant assaults of masters. White women, on the other hand, became "habituated" to slavery and were "very apt to vindicate the system, upon the ground that it is extremely convenient to have such submissive servants." Child had never visited the South, but her portrait of racial mixing was arrestingly visual: people didn't talk about it, but it was everywhere. She had heard often from people who had visited the South about "seeing a number of mulattoes in attendance where they visited, whose resemblance to the head of the family was too striking not to be immediately observed." Child thought that this open secret could only enrage the slaves, who would find themselves subjected to

(*Top*) From George Bourne's *Picture of Slavery* (1834); (*bottom*) from Edward W. Clay's lithograph series on "Amalgamation" (1839). Bourne's abolitionist tract and Clay's anti-abolitionist image took a similar view of the evils of racial amalgamation. COURTESY OF THE LIBRARY OF CONGRESS (*top*) AND THE AMERICAN ANTIQUARIAN SOCIETY (*bottom*).

the "tyranny or caprice of their own brothers and sisters." Eventually, a sweeping black rebellion would force the federal government to raise an army, "of whose wages the free states must pay their proportion." Child presented race mixing in the South as a threat not only to decency and morality, but to the nation itself.[14]

Intriguingly, in her 1833 attack on slavery, Child proposed the same black migration that Hezekiah Niles had endorsed in 1819. If freed slaves were given the right forms of "moral cultivation," they would be welcome in "families, factories, etc." in the North. Child approached the question of amalgamation with a reassuring disdain. There would always be "distinct classes of society . . . which have only occasional and transient communication with each other." Black people "will form one of these classes." In a century or so, "some negro Rothschild may come from Hayti, with his seventy millions of pounds, and persuade some white woman to *sacrifice* herself to him." Until then, there would be "a sufficient number of well-formed and elegant colored women in the world, to meet the demands of colored patricians." Child found another benefit in this protracted romantic probation: the threat of amalgamation would persuade white legislators to provide education to black men as well as black women, ensuring that the former were "not forced to make war upon their white neighbors for wives." She hoped that prejudices against intermarriage would "melt away" eventually, but thought the prospect irrelevant to the debate about abolition. It was ludicrous to keep blacks in chains on the off-chance that "one of their descendants *may* marry our great-great-great-great grandchild."[15]

While Child presented a plan that deferred racial mixing until the twentieth century, the critics of her book followed the same logic as Thomas Branagan. Proximity would quickly produce racial mixing, they argued, and immediate abolition was a cipher for amalgamation. This argument was made in the harsh language of editorials and pamphlets, but was also taken to the streets in a series of alarming attacks on abolitionist meetings and venues. When Lydia Maria Child returned to the subject in her 1834 book *The Oasis*, which offered a compilation of antislavery essays, she struck a more defensive tone. "On the subject of equality," she wrote, "the principles of abolition-ists have been much misrepresented." She and the other immediatists had "not the slightest wish to do violence to the distinctions of soci-ety, by forcing the rude and illiterate into the presence of the learned and refined." She hoped that black people would have the same educa-tional opportunities and the same civil rights "enjoyed by the lowest and most ignorant white man in America." But the suggestion that she and her associates supported amalgamation was "perfectly ridiculous and unfounded. No abolitionist considers such a thing desirable."[16]

One of Child's key arguments against intermarriage was that black people themselves were opposed to it. There was some truth to this, though the implication that black sentiments mirrored white prejudices was misleading. Free black writing on the subject from the 1820s onward was wearily reactive. Black newspapers rejected the suggestion that African American men were elementally lascivious, reminding readers that it was white men who stalked northern black neighborhoods in search of sex. In 1829, David Walker, the pioneer-ing black abolitionist, declared, "I would not give a *pinch of snuff* to be married to any white person I ever saw in all the days of my life." In 1837, the *Colored American* newspaper dismissed as "moon shine" the idea that blacks and whites could not amalgamate; but if inter-marriage meant that black women would be "cut off from their own people" by marrying white men, "we enter our protest against all such connexions." Meanwhile, the climate of violence that hedged white reformers' views on intermarriage had the same frightening effect upon African Americans. In 1834, the free black minister Peter Wil-liams Jr. watched a mob burn his church in the mistaken belief that he had performed an interracial marriage ceremony there. Forced by a (white) bishop to resign his membership of the American Anti-Slavery Society, Williams insisted that he had never endorsed intermarriage and retreated from the fray.[17]

Having denied any inherent connection between immediate aboli-tion and amalgamation, Lydia Maria Child directed her fire at the slave system. The triumph of abolitionist ideas "would tend to prevent amalgamation, instead of encouraging it," she argued, "for they would place a large defenseless class under the protection of law and public opinion." Taste would prove a better barrier to racial mixing than slavery, which seemed only to have accelerated amalgamation. This quiet confidence that black people could be kept as a "distinct class" without the need for legislation explains the protracted debate over the ban on interracial marriage in Massachusetts, in which the immediate abolitionists became vocal participants during the 1830s. In 1786, a committee of Massachusetts legislators had passed a law to ban marriages between non-whites and whites. The historian David Fowler has suggested that this measure may have been directed at the small-but-significant number of Massachusetts residents with mixed black-Indian ancestry. (The previous 1705 colonial legislation against intermarriage in Massachusetts had prevented black-white unions, but not Indian-white marriage.) Over time, the intermarriage ban became an embarrassment to many Massachusetts reformers. With the exception of Rhode Island, which adopted the Massachusetts law almost verbatim in 1789, no state in New England passed racial restrictions on marriage. Even Philadelphia and New York, with their much larger black populations, kept anti-amalgamation laws from the statute books.[18]

From its earliest issues in January 1831, William Lloyd Garrison's *Liberator* urged state legislators to repeal the ban. In his initial critique, Garrison came closer than any other abolitionist to recapturing the spirit of David Rice on the question of amalgamation. The ban was "wrong in principle" because it flouted "all men are created equal." The only way to restrict marriages between the races would be to insist that "Indians, negroes and mulattoes are not men, and therefore not born free and equal." Assuming that everyone stood "on a perfect equality," intermarriage could be "neither unnatural nor repugnant to nature." In fact, it was "proper and salutary, it being designed to unite people of different tribes and nations." Garrison couldn't resist making fun of the pious defenders of the ban. Would they pass laws preventing the fat from marrying the thin?[19]

A few months later, after gauging the depth of public prejudice, Garrison modified his stance on intermarriage. "I have never advocated nor recommended any such practice," he wrote, "and I am acquainted with no abolitionist who has done so." If the union of the races was "the necessary consequence of restoring that which does not belong to us, and doing justly to our fellow creatures, we cannot help it." As a bill to lift the marriage ban moved through the Massachusetts assembly, the most vocal supporters of repeal maintained that they didn't actually endorse intermarriage. One insisted that "he was averse to the intermarriages of blacks and whites," but felt confident that racial separation could be maintained by "public opinion" rather than statutes. Another denied the charge that, by speaking in favor of repeal, he supported "intermarriages between persons of different colors." An essay in *The Liberator* in the summer of 1831 clarified the matter: "There appears to be a determination among many persons to misunderstand the object of our proposed change in the law, which was not, as is represented, 'to modify the color of our black population,' but to remove from it a disgraceful badge of servitude." Reformers wanted "not to promote the intermarriage of the blacks and whites, but to declare their natural equality as human beings." The idea that one might remove legislative obstacles to racial mixing without actually mixing the races led the proponents of repeal into awkward analogies. Did the repeal of state laws against witchcraft imply support for necromancy and Satanism? If enlightened legislators abolished debtors' prisons, could they be accused of supporting improvident borrowing? The proponents of repeal even invoked the ubiquity of prejudice to clinch their argument. The intermarriage ban did much more harm to the state's image, they argued, than its repeal would do to the social order. Popular prejudices would keep the races apart, and the state could be spared a legal embarrassment that was clumsy and superfluous.[20]

After more than a decade of equivocation, the state assembly finally agreed to repeal the law in 1843. By then the anti-amalgamation reassurances offered by proponents of repeal, along with the growing tide of antislavery feeling in Massachusetts, had reached a tipping point. Many of the most radical opponents of slavery—Arthur Tappan, William Jay, Elijah Lovejoy, and others—had already declared their opposition to intermarriage. In the absence of any positive portrayal of the mixing of blacks and whites, and with the repeal of the Massachusetts ban presented as symbolic rather than practical in its effects, northern antislavery writers were able to present amalgamation as uniquely southern and uniquely depraved. It was against this backdrop that Richard Mentor Johnson rose to national prominence.[21]

IN 1815, WHILE STILL RECUPERATING from the wounds he'd received at the Battle of the Thames, Johnson inherited the slave woman Julia Chinn from his father's estate. They had been intimately acquainted before Johnson's heroics on the battlefield. Chinn bore Johnson's first daughter, Imogene, in 1812; Adaline followed soon after. Over the next quarter century, Johnson became increasingly reliant on Chinn to keep his Kentucky affairs in order during his long absences in Washington, giving her control over his farm and his other slaves. He became a doting father to Imogene and Adaline, insisting that they receive an education and an opportunity to realize their talents. Perhaps the contradiction between his family life and his slaveholding explains Johnson's rambling speech in the House of Representatives during the Missouri crisis of 1819–1820. "No person can more sincerely lament than I do the existence of involuntary servitude in the United States," he began. He dismissed those "philosophers" who had speculated that blacks and whites had been created separately, but also criticized northerners for their hypocrisy. "If your humanity has conquered your prejudice," he asked, "where are your magistrates, your governors, your representatives of the black population? You proclaim them equal, but you are still their lawgivers." For Johnson, the persistence of northern prejudice reinforced the logic of gradualism: slavery would be undone by "slow but certain improvement," rather than by the radical rhetoric of antislavery congressmen on the Missouri question.[22]

Johnson's speech was a strange mixture of antislavery and pro-slavery feints. He insisted on the unity of the human race, but also that "all men are created equal" applied to nations (Britain and the United States, say) rather than individuals. He called for the extension of slavery into Missouri, but produced the Jeffersonian rationale that "diffusion" would spread the slave population more thinly and expedite emancipation. Given its several concessions to slaveholding, this speech was hardly an abolitionist manifesto. And yet the section that was most often recalled later in Johnson's career had a distinct, even zealous, antislavery cast. In the middle of a long appeal for a revived reform movement in the United States ("Encourage Sunday schools, multiply Bible societies"), Johnson seemed to forget his equivocations: "Animate, to deeds of benevolence, abolition societies!" he exclaimed.

In the 1820s, Johnson became a leading proponent of the new democratic politics that would culminate in the election of Andrew Jackson. Like Jackson, he stood up for debtors, bankrupts, and the hardscrabble voters of the "most interior settlements" of the Union. Initially, he kept his mixed-race family at Great Crossings, Kentucky, out of the public eye: after the Missouri crisis, he said little in public about the nation's dilemmas over slavery, and nothing whatever about his private dependencies and entanglements. When a series of failed investments placed him in financial peril in the early 1820s, Johnson devised a novel way to escape from his debts: he would establish an Indian school on his property. Johnson was closely acquainted with the legislators and government officials who were then debating the future of Native Americans in the eastern states. As the intermarriage scandals engulfed the Cornwall Foreign Mission School in 1825, Johnson positioned Great Crossings as the perfect place to educate the next generation of Native leaders. Government officials were beguiled by his proposal, and the Choctaw Indians became the first nation to send students to the new school. The "Choctaw Academy" opened in the final weeks of 1825 with twenty-one students.[23]

Johnson appointed a friend, the Reverend Thomas Henderson, to manage the school. Their long correspondence gives us insight into Johnson's extraordinary world at Great Crossings. While Julia Chinn directed the farm and the household, Henderson oversaw the classrooms and dormitories that would steer the academy's students toward "civilization." Johnson begged Henderson to take charge of the education of Imogene and Adaline as well, and to keep them busy and industrious. But one of the reverend's most important tasks was to preserve what Johnson later called "the order and decorum of black and white and red upon the premises." Johnson encouraged his own family members to play supporting roles in the new enterprise. Julia was a good manager, the colonel told Henderson, and a better doctor than most of the quacks in the county. Imogene and Adaline helped to manage the domestic affairs of the school and also contributed to the teaching. As Native boys arrived at Great Crossings, Henderson gave them new names that would flatter the liberal supporters of the civilization program. By 1826, visitors to the school would encounter George Washington, John Adams, Andrew Jackson, and Henry Clay. A little unsettlingly, one could even see a Richard Mentor Johnson and a Thomas Henderson sitting behind the tight desks of the academy's schoolroom.[24]

The Choctaw Academy prospered, initially at least. Julia cared for the students, while Adaline and Imogene taught them to paint, make maps, and write letters. Johnson took immense pride in relaying the academy's achievements to its political sponsors in Washington. But his commitments in the capital kept him away for long periods, leaving Henderson and Chinn to manage both the farm and the academy's growing roster. Many of the colonel's letters to Henderson were sent from Washington and reflect his anxieties about what might be happening five hundred miles to the west. Johnson urged Henderson not to leave the delicate job of managing his slaves to Julia. "I want your mind impressed with the importance of making my people fear you when complaint is made," he directed in January 1826. ("My people" was Johnson's preferred euphemism for his slaves.) But Henderson proved a reluctant surrogate. His squeamishness about inflicting punishments forced Johnson to hire a local constable to whip his slaves with the requisite intent. While Johnson recognized his dependence on Henderson in the direction of the academy, the train of letters from Washington to Kentucky assumed an air of bullying disappointment.[25]

Even Henderson's authority over the Native students came into question. Some of the Choctaw boys had asked Johnson if they could live in his comfortable house rather than in the Spartan dorms he had built alongside it, but he declined their request. (In his letters to Henderson, he mocked the young Indians for their inflated sense of entitlement.) Others—the children of Native elites, in particular—had been allowed to live in the house, or with white families in the neighborhood. Great Crossings was balanced precariously on racial and class distinctions; the house and the academy would collapse without the careful and frequent application of force. But with Johnson away in Washington, and Henderson overwhelmed by the task he had been assigned, things went awry. Native students who had been quartered in the dormitories managed to sneak into Johnson's house; Indians began to fraternize with Johnson's slaves and steal his whiskey. Eventually, in 1827, two students, Peter King and David Wall, were apprehended inside the Johnson residence in "scandalous" circumstances: evidently they were trying to have sex with the slaves who worked in the house. When word of this incident reached Johnson in Washington, he became furious with the boys and with Henderson. The ferocity of his anger owed something to his role as a father as well as his stewardship of the Choctaw Academy: he told Henderson how much he feared having "my dwelling house invaded, my family degraded and my peace destroyed by a few scoundrels." But although the offenses of Wall and King were serious enough to merit the intervention of the local magistrate, both boys remained at the school.[26]

Their conduct left Johnson with a limited set of options. While he deplored the obvious breakdown of discipline, his fear of racial mixing between slaves and Choctaws was not entirely a projection of his own prejudices. The Choctaws, like many of the other southeastern Indian nations, had adopted a much more hierarchical view of race in the years since the War of 1812. Like the Cherokees and Creeks, the Choctaws had largely discarded their old practice of adopting black people as equal members of their nation, and now viewed interracial sex between Indians and blacks with disdain. Johnson feared that "nonsense will be written to the [Choctaw] nation again about negroes" if news of a scandal at Great Crossings became public, threatening the academy's survival. By the same token, he couldn't easily prescribe the harshest punishments against errant Indians, for fear that news of his cruelty (or of the original infraction) would trickle back to the Choctaw Nation. And so Johnson and Henderson tried to suppress any suggestion that the races were mixing at the Choctaw Academy, despite growing evidence to the contrary.[27]

JOHNSON MANAGED TO KEEP HIS secrets from the public throughout the 1820s. Despite the innuendo of a few Kentucky papers loyal to his political rival Henry Clay, he rose to become one of the stars of the Democratic Party. It was only when he was being spoken of as a possible successor to Andrew Jackson that northern newspapers began to hint that the "father of a colored family" might be an awkward presidential candidate. Johnson was already a polarizing figure in the religious reform movement in the North. He had made powerful enemies during his campaign to keep the postal service running on Sundays, a cause that pitted pious easterners against western settlers. A New York newspaper warned readers in 1831 that one of the congressional champions of Sunday mails was "the father to a coloured family." Without naming Johnson directly, the paper gave enough details to leave little doubt about the politician in question. "Sabbath-breaking is not often a solitary vice," it piously concluded.[28]

What hadn't yet emerged was that, in 1829, Johnson's eldest daughter, Imogene, had married one of his white neighbors. Johnson approved of the marriage and probably played a role in engineering it. Given the incursions of the Choctaw students into his yard, he had a strong motive to move his daughters into married respectability. The union between Imogene and Daniel Pence was, however, as transgressive in its own way as the Indian-slave encounters that had enraged Johnson. Intermarriage in Kentucky was illegal, though Johnson evidently imagined that his light-skinned daughters could find white husbands without attracting undue attention. Johnson gave the couple a substantial tract of land adjoining his house. Imogene would be close enough to Great Crossings to continue her work at the academy, but removed from the nocturnal adventures of its students. Thomas Henderson almost certainly officiated at the ceremony, which was technically a crime. By this point, though, Henderson feared Richard Mentor Johnson far more than the laws of Kentucky.[29]

It was Imogene's sister, Adaline, who finally drew the attention of newspapers across the nation. In July 1831, the *Kentucky Reporter* (a committed supporter of Henry Clay) accused Johnson of bringing Adaline to a Fourth of July barbecue near Great Crossings. As Johnson prepared to give an Independence Day oration, Adaline walked through the pavilion that had been erected for the "ladies and daughters of respectable families" to shelter from the sun. A number of these women "immediately displayed considerable agitation," and they asked the managers of the event to remove Adaline. Johnson "remonstrated, and argued that she was as well educated as any lady there." But the managers insisted that this was not a "debatable matter." While Johnson delivered his speech on the "glories and virtues" of American liberty to the crowd, Adaline sat alone in her father's carriage. Johnson later denied the details of this story in a private letter to a friend, the newspaper editor Preston Blair. Adaline had been invited to the barbecue by "some white females," he insisted, and the incident had been blown out of proportion. But after successfully marrying Imogene into the local white community, Johnson seems to have become complacent about the willingness of his neighbors to accept his family.[30]

Many newspapers amplified the *Kentucky Reporter*'s conclusion that Johnson's actions had been "unfortunate and highly censurable." The story reached as far as Massachusetts, where the response was more measured. The *Journal and Tribune*, a Boston paper, lamented the treatment Adaline had received and hoped for a day when Americans would be "bold and honest enough to expel these prejudices." The *Journal* was more cautious on the question of her sister. "Mixed marriages" of the kind that Imogene Johnson had forged with Daniel Pence were "in bad taste," and "unnatural." William Lloyd Garrison reprinted the entire *Journal* commentary in *The Liberator* along with the original *Kentucky Reporter* article. He praised the Boston paper for its editorial line while offering two dissents. He thought that "Col. Johnson deserves full condemnation, not for being the father of colored children . . . but for his avowed and shameless libertinism." And, while Garrison agreed that, "at the present time, mixed marriages would be in bad taste," he was uncomfortable with the claim that they were "unnatural."[31]

In 1832, Adaline married a white man named Thomas W. Scott. The newspapers that picked up the story—usually under the headline "Marriage Extraordinary!"—argued that both the bride and the groom should be held accountable for their crimes by the Kentucky authorities. Although *The Liberator* had run pieces critical of Johnson's dissolute lifestyle, William Lloyd Garrison came to the defense of Thomas Scott—albeit by comparing his virtuous decision to marry Adaline with the "planters who do not scruple to prostitute their female slaves, and beget as many bastards as possible." (To which group did Richard Mentor Johnson belong? Garrison left this question unanswered.) The most rousing article in support of the Scott-Johnson marriage came from William P. Powell, a free black abolitionist from New Bedford, Massachusetts, who regularly wrote for *The Liberator*. Powell thought Scott's choice sound for two reasons: Adaline was reputed to be "fair and lovely," and her father was one of the most prominent politicians in the United States. There was nothing unnatural about race mixing—Powell himself was married to a Native American woman—and Scott would be "amply rewarded for his degradation" with a pretty wife and a powerful father-in-law. He would need to square his conscience if he held any slaves, of course—and the people of Kentucky would need to be consistent in their views. If they objected to the Scott-Johnson match, how could they choose Richard Mentor Johnson—"the father of the above lady"—to represent them in Washington?[32]

JOHNSON MIGHT EASILY HAVE DEDICATED all his energies to forging his national career, or protecting his mixed-race family at Great Crossings, or making a success of the Choctaw Academy. It proved impossible to do all three simultaneously. The task became immeasurably harder in 1833, when Julia Chinn succumbed to the cholera epidemic that was sweeping the United States. Without her direction and counsel, the academy proved almost ungovernable. Two more Indian students were caught having sex with slaves, and Johnson chided Henderson for appointing these Indians to "watch and keep order inside of the yard." The academy had long maintained a hierarchy among its Native students, with the most privileged granted access to the house and grounds as well as the school, but this had been at the root of many of the academy's disciplinary problems. If these Native monitors were lascivious, it would be like "appointing profligate young men to go into the houses of black people to keep order, which is done by driving away their husbands if they have no pass and then getting into their places." Johnson knew the tricks that allowed white masters to rape slave women, and he bemoaned Henderson's naïveté.[33]

In 1835, when Andrew Jackson began planning his retirement, Johnson became the leading candidate to run alongside Martin Van Buren in the 1836 presidential election. Rumors of his singular lifestyle had been in the public domain for years, but it was in the run-up to the Democratic convention of 1835 that the issue of race mixing became impossible to dodge. When northern and southern newspapers recycled old stories—about Chinn, the barbecue incident, or his daughters' marriages—Democratic officials in Virginia and South Carolina called for Johnson to be dropped from the ticket. Johnson asked his friends to mount a public relations campaign on his behalf.

Poor Thomas Henderson led the way, in a newspaper letter that was printed throughout the United States. Starting with the casual observation that he had once lived near Monticello, and could confirm that the rumors about Jefferson and Sally Hemings were "untrue and unfounded," Henderson walked a narrow path between fact and omission as he addressed what had taken place at Great Crossings. Johnson had never married, so the charge that Julia Chinn had been his wife was baseless. Henderson claimed not to know if Johnson's daughters were "the children of a coloured woman," but he insisted that, even if they were, Johnson was "certainly entitled to more credit in the sight of heaven to have raised them as he did, rather than to have turned them into a negro quarter, or sent them to a cotton farm." There had been made no attempt to "impose" Adaline and Imogene on the company of Johnson's neighbors, though Henderson offered the startling admission that the women were "now married to respectable men, and independently situated." With the help of Henderson and his other friends, Johnson held on to the vice-presidential nomination. But the pressures of his domestic arrangements were already building toward another explosion.[34]

After Julia's death, Johnson had passed control of his household to a slave named Parthene, with whom he probably became involved in a sexual relationship. (She may have been Julia Chinn's niece.) In July 1835, while Johnson was summering at Great Crossings, Parthene and another slave woman announced that they were taking the carriage to pick strawberries. Instead, they collected two students from the Choctaw Academy and rode hard for the Ohio River. The party was eventually apprehended in Columbus, Ohio, although Parthene and the other slave woman managed to escape once again by jumping from the window of a locked hotel room. Parthene was recaptured and sent back to Kentucky. (According to some reports, she was quickly sold to a new owner.) No charges were brought against the Choctaws who had facilitated Parthene's escape, perhaps for the same reason that Henderson had failed to expel the Indian students who had sneaked into Johnson's home in search of sex: the academy couldn't risk alienating the Native nations that sent their young men to Great Crossings. The newspapers reveled in Johnson's discomfort. Parthene had "possessed the Colonel's *confidence*" and shared his bed. Now he had been cuckolded by his own students—"foiled by an Indian—not Tecumseh—at his own game"—and humiliated by his slave.[35]

On the face of it, this story was little different from the embarrassments that had preceded it. But since the furor in 1831 over Adaline's expulsion from the barbecue, the national debate over race and slavery had become even more fraught. William Lloyd Garrison and his allies had galvanized white southerners and northern "moderates" in their opposition to immediate abolition. Southern Democrats had accepted Martin Van Buren's nomination for the presidency, but fretted that he was secretly hostile to slavery. (In 1836 he supported the "gag rule" to keep abolition petitions out of Congress, but he had voted to preserve black suffrage in New York in 1821—albeit with a prohibitive property requirement for black voters.) In this moment of heightened anxiety about slavery and its opponents, Richard Mentor Johnson's black family required urgent explanation.[36]

The *New York Courier*, a Democratic paper, apologized for bringing Johnson's private life into the public realm. But when "a band of fierce and misguided *Fanatics*" was "preaching the immediate abolition of Slavery and the amalgamation of the White and Black," it could hardly keep silent about a man who "habitually and *practically* illustrated their infamous theories." It was Johnson's liberality toward his daughters that most incensed the *Courier*: he had "educated them and endeavored to force them upon society as in all respects equal to those of his free white neighbors." The *Baltimore Chronicle* agreed: "He is indeed the most powerful agent of amalgamation, who, by giving fortunes to half breeds, tempts men greedy of money, but insensible to shame, to mingle the white and African race in a union which merges the fair complexion and the bright intellect of one, in the darkness of color and inferiority of mind which are characteristics of the other." The *Chronicle* approached these events as a question of morality and of national survival. The republics of Latin America, with their "violent feuds" and perpetual instability, had provided a terrible example of the consequences of racial mixing. "With Mr Van Buren's theory of suffrage to aid Col. Johnson's practical amalgamation, what, we ask, is to prevent . . . a similar result in the United States?"[37]

Northern newspapers skeptical of slavery struggled with the association between amalgamation and abolition. The *Connecticut Herald*, no fan of William Lloyd Garrison, accused slaveholders of hypocrisy in their critique of immediate abolition. When an abolitionist "preaches that the negro is a man, and ought to be a free man, and received into his associations with his brother white man, he is denounced as an incendiary from one extremity of the Union to another." But when "R. M. Johnson, the Tecumseh killer, takes his negro slave into his bed and bosom—cherishes her offspring as his children . . . and obtains for them white husbands, thus practicing the most vital tenets of the poor fanatic's preaching, he is to be made Vice President of the United States." Garrison and his supporters had been denounced as proponents of race mixing, and yet Richard Mentor Johnson was "a practical amalgamator." *The Liberator* declared the entire subject "a disagreeable one," noting merely that, by living out of wedlock with Julia Chinn, Johnson had ensured that "the sin of bad taste is merged into the sin of bad morals." When a New Orleans newspaper suggested that Johnson was a "practical abolitionist" as well as a practical amalgamator, and that he would likely win the presidency before long with "the support of the abolitionists," *The Philanthropist*, an antislavery newspaper in Cincinnati, rushed to deny any association: "All this shows us, is how profoundly ignorant are the people of the South of the nature of abolition, and the feelings of abolitionists."[38]

During the campaign of 1836, Johnson became an in-between figure. The tenderness he had shown toward Chinn and his daughters was widely recognized, but virtually no one wanted to identify closely with the practical amalgamator. Defenders of slavery feared a conspiracy in which Johnson would smuggle the radical practices of his private life into the nation's highest councils. Whig newspapers in the North, which were opposed both to slavery and to radical abolitionists, used Johnson either to upbraid slaveholders for their personal immorality or to paint the followers of William Lloyd Garrison as equally misguided. Immediate abolitionists, meanwhile, had been denying since the early 1830s that emancipation would lead to race mixing. Johnson may have followed a different path in his private life than the depraved slaveholders invoked by Lydia Maria Child and George Bourne, but abolitionists saw no gain in defending his domestic arrangements. The sense that Johnson was being crushed by the weight of his personal contradictions was captured in an 1836 lithograph entitled *An Affecting Scene in Kentucky*. The artist has Johnson with his head in his hand, holding a copy of the *New York Courier*, and attended by a free black man and a white abolitionist. His daughters hold a portrait of Julia Chinn. While one Democratic supporter tells him that his old allies will stand by him, another marvels that the "slayer of Tecumseh" should be brought low by "a summer cloud."[39]

In the middle of this ordeal, Johnson received a terrible blow. In 1836, Adaline fell sick and died, prompting one of his most tender letters to Thomas Henderson. "She was a source of inexhaustible happiness and comfort to me," Johnson wrote. "She is gone where sorrow and sighing can never disturb her peaceful and quiet bosom. She is happy, and has left me unhappy." In the depths of his grief, Johnson reached for the comfort of his Bible: "David has given us a memorable example of duty, when he humbled himself before his god and asked the life of his child to be spared." Johnson's analogy was revealing. In the second book of Samuel, King David of Israel had committed adultery by sleeping with Bathsheba, the wife of Uriah the Hittite, a soldier in his army. When Bathsheba became pregnant, David, realizing that his sin would be discovered, arranged for Uriah to be killed. David and Bathsheba were subsequently married, but God punished them by visiting a terrible illness on their son. After a week in which David pleaded with God to show mercy, the boy died. Johnson took heart from David's response. When the "will of heaven was known" and the

A Whig lithograph attacking Richard Mentor Johnson and his mixed-race family ahead of the 1836 election. COURTESY OF THE LIBRARY OF CONGRESS.

child failed to recover, David refused to mourn and instead "endeavored to attend to the duties of life." In his own moment of personal tragedy, Johnson hoped to prove equally resilient.[40]

But even before the 1836 race was over, Johnson would suffer one further loss that haunted him for years to come. On a campaign visit to New York City in July 1836, Johnson's twelve-year-old servant went missing. The boy, Marcellus, was the eldest son of Daniel Chinn, Julia's brother, on whose loyalty Johnson clearly thought he could depend. *The Emancipator*, an abolitionist newspaper, revealed in August that Johnson had placed a runaway slave ad in the local papers soon after Marcellus's disappearance, offering $10 for his safe return. The story became yet another scandal, especially in New England, which Johnson did his best to deny. With the deaths of Julia and Adaline, and the flight of young Marcellus, the domestic idyll that Johnson had imagined for himself at Great Crossings was in ruins. He had been forced to share every phase of its destruction with a national audience.[41]

JOHNSON RETURNED TO NEW YORK in 1838 to look for Marcellus. He and Van Buren had triumphed in the 1836 election, but the acrimony surrounding him during the campaign persuaded observers that his political career was already over. After making inquiries via the free black minister Peter Williams Jr., Johnson met with Lewis Tappan, a New York businessman who was perhaps the most famous abolitionist in the city. In a remarkable meeting at Johnson's hotel, Tappan and Williams handed the vice-president a series of abolition tracts, along with a draft deed of emancipation for Marcellus. If Johnson agreed to sign the deed, Tappan promised, antislavery activists would endeavor to track down Marcellus (who had been seen in Massachusetts). Various accounts of this meeting appeared in the newspapers, though Johnson himself never spoke of it. Abolitionists described Johnson as polite, even sympathetic, when slavery was discussed. "He took pains to express to some of the gentlemen of color his deep interest in the question of their rights and prospects," wrote one witness, "as all he should leave behind him at death (his two daughters) were identified in destiny with them." Johnson also claimed that he would free his slaves in his will. When the abolitionists proposed inserting a reference to the Declaration of Independence in the emancipation deed, however, Johnson had second thoughts. With the advisers in his retinue warning that a written commitment to emancipation would destroy what was left of his political career, Johnson dismissed his visitors and went to the theater. This was the beginning and the end of his abolition experiment.[42]

In the summer of 1839, Postmaster General Amos Kendall—a political fixer who had been one of Johnson's strongest boosters in the early 1830s—forwarded an anonymous letter from a recent visitor to Great Crossings to President Martin Van Buren. The informant claimed to have recently greeted Johnson in the company of "a young Delilah of about the complexion of Shakespeare's swarthy Othello." This was his third wife, or so claimed the visitor; "his second, which he sold for infidelity, having been the sister of the present lady." (Apparently a reference to Parthene's punishment for fleeing to

Ohio with the Choctaw students.) For Kendall, the news confirmed Johnson's effective abdication from the Democratic Party. How could the vice-president "expect for us to countenance and sustain him, when he seems to have lost all self-respect, and openly and shamelessly lives in adultery with a buxom young negro wench? It is too bad, and I could hardly have believed it but from ocular demonstration of the fact." With the Democratic convention of 1840 approaching, Van Buren wrote Andrew Jackson that "the affair of the vice presidency has given our friends a great deal of uneasiness." This proved to be an understatement. For the first and only time in American political history, the Democrats decided not to nominate a vice-presidential candidate. Johnson assumed the incumbent's right to campaign for Van Buren, but his name would not appear on the ticket. His exhausting travels in the summer of 1840 were shaded by the embarrassment of his party's rejection.[43]

Johnson did his best to shut down the slavery issue in 1840, telling Lewis Tappan that the question belonged with the states. Antislavery newspapers reprinted the details of his private life to highlight his hypocrisy, even as many slaveholders concluded that the same facts disqualified him as their champion. The economic crash of 1837, and Van Buren's unpopularity, made the 1840 campaign still more miserable for Johnson than the previous one. At the head of the rival Whig ticket was William Henry Harrison, his old commander at the Battle of the Thames. The two men had never been close, but during the 1830s their parties had fueled a rivalry over their respective roles in history. Harrison blamed Johnson for downplaying his role in the War of 1812; Johnson blamed Harrison for doubting his claim to have killed Tecumseh. Democrats and Whigs held separate events to commemorate the Battle of the Thames, each with a different hero.[44]

It was in September 1840, as the Democratic cause slipped toward defeat, that Johnson's chaotic life reached a moment of singularity. The vice-president brought out thousands of supporters to a rally in Detroit, though he knew that the Whigs were drawing even larger crowds. Detroit, at least, offered the comforts of nostalgia. On the other side of Lake St. Clair was the battleground where he had stared down Tecumseh nearly thirty years earlier. To mark his return, local Democrats had prepared a surprise: they brought out Medard Laba-die, the man who had found Johnson unconscious beside the corpse of his Indian antagonist, and who had carried him into immortality. But while the crowd enjoyed this choreographed reunion, one of John-son's slaves was bidding farewell to the Hero of the Thames. Daniel Chinn, Julia's brother, had been an integral part of Johnson's family and his farm for decades. He had accompanied Johnson on his north-ern travels ever since Marcellus's flight back in 1836. While the crowds recalled Johnson's heroism in Canada, Daniel slipped across the bor-der. Free blacks had been planting communities in Ontario through-out the 1830s, hoping to escape white prejudice by leaving the United States. Daniel, who had been one of the closest witnesses of Johnson's spiraling fortune, chose this moment to join them.[45]

It would be 1845 before American newspapers learned of Daniel Chinn's flight, by which point the political landscape had changed considerably. William Henry Harrison had defeated Van Buren and Johnson in the 1840 election, but had succumbed to pneumonia barely a month after his inauguration. His vice-president, John Tyler, proved so unpopular with the Whig Party that he was dubbed "His Accidency." Johnson harbored dreams of a political comeback, but the Democrats regained the White House in 1844 without the Hero of the Thames. Johnson's struggle to save the Choctaw Academy was no more successful. With a Whig administration in Washington from 1841, Johnson could no longer count on federal officials to keep his secrets. The Native nations that supplied the academy with students lost patience with its mixed results. The War Department forced the firing of Thomas Henderson in 1841; the Choctaws, who had formed the backbone of the school's enrollment, withdrew their pupils the following year. A handful of Chickasaw students who remained at Great Crossings left the school in 1848, and the Choctaw Academy closed its doors forever.[46]

It was amid this cascade of disappointments that the news of Daniel Chinn's escape became public. In the spring of 1845, Chinn bumped into John Aspenwall, a visiting missionary who was touring the free black settlements in Canada. Aspenwall was staggered to encounter "the brother-in-law of Col. Richard M. Johnson, ex-Vice President of the United States, as well as his slave." Chinn sensed an opportunity to set the record straight. Johnson's moral conduct had been far from exemplary, he told Aspenwall, especially since the death of his sister Julia. By 1840, Johnson had fathered children with three different women and was living with his third "wife"—Daniel's own daughter. Aspenwall channeled his outrage in a letter to the *New York Tribune*: "Much credit has been given to the Col. for his generous conduct to this family," he noted. "But his conduct in becoming the father of children by three women . . . and then selling them all, both the women and his own children, to James Peak, to be carried off in slavery, as Mr. Chinn states that he did, may not be quite so highly commended."[47]

Despite his undoubted affection for Adaline and Imogene, Johnson stood accused of selling his other children down the river after Julia's death. Daniel Chinn was better placed than anyone to level this charge, and if we credit Aspenwall's account, the final dissolution of Johnson's mixed-race family assumed the horrific proportions of a George Bourne polemic. But Aspenwall was surely mistaken to suggest that Johnson had received "much credit" for his domestic affairs, which had been the subject of scandal, ridicule, and scorn for more than a decade. Antislavery reformers proved no more willing to identify with Johnson's actions than those proslavery newspapers that sensed an abolitionist conspiracy in his political ascent. Johnson was certainly the most visible proponent of amalgamation during the antebellum years, but his personal and public experiences did little to dent the assumption that the mixing of the races would end in despair.

THAT OTHER PRACTICAL AMALGAMATOR, THOMAS Jefferson, did a better job than Johnson of separating his public persona from his private life. While stories of Jefferson's relationship with Sally Hemings became alarmingly ubiquitous during the presidential election campaign of 1800, Jefferson's friends and neighbors largely succeeded in preventing rumor from becoming fact. Could either man have made a persuasive case for the practical amalgamation that David Rice and others had viewed as the inevitable consequence of black freedom? To do so would have required a genuine commitment to emancipation, rather than a rhetorical disdain for slavery. By practicing amalgamation before abolition, both had upset the sequence of racial integration outlined by radical gradualists like Rice. Regardless of their conscientious scruples or the studied paternalism with which they directed their biracial families, their actions fitted easily into the diabolical versions of racial mixing glimpsed by George Bourne and Lydia Maria Child.

Given the limited evidence he left for historians, the extent of Jefferson's scruples over Sally Hemings and their children remains a matter of speculation. It seems likeliest that he took Johnson's approach to squaring rhetoric, actions, and conscience: both men expressed whatever love they felt for their non-white families by encouraging their children to pass as white. Johnson vigorously promoted this form of racial escapism by facilitating the marriage of Adaline and Imogene to white husbands, despite the laws of Kentucky. The irony of their actions was clear: the only way to scale up this tactic of racial passing, and to realize black equality on a sweeping scale, would be to make interracial sex the cornerstone of social relations in the South. And this prospect would be as alarming to northern reformers as it was embarrassing to southern planters. As with the plans to reverse "degradation" under slavery, the routes to realizing gradual emancipation seemed hopelessly cluttered: by social realities, by prejudice, and by the sheer scale of the problem.

William Short, the Virginia diplomat who had surprised Jefferson in 1798 with his bold advocacy of amalgamation, eventually stopped asking what had happened to the letter Jefferson had filed away in his drawer. After another decade of private and official business in Europe, Short moved back to the United States permanently in 1810 and settled in Philadelphia. It was, in some ways, the best city in the Union in which to test his faith in amalgamation. A large free black population was struggling to establish itself economically and socially against a rising tide of white prejudice. Returned to the miasma of America's racial landscape, Short came to doubt the clarity of his earlier vision. In 1825, seven months before Jefferson's death, Short asked his former mentor to recall the letter he had sent nearly three decades earlier. "At that time I had a very incorrect & imperfect view of the subject," he admitted. Short now realized that "the greatest difficulty only begins where I thought it would end; that is, with these people in their new state of freedom. I am convinced now that this population amongst us is an evil without a remedy." Short didn't explain why he had changed his mind; nor did he state that blacks were permanently inferior to whites. But he asked Jefferson to consider a solution derived from medieval Europe: perhaps state legislatures in the South might "correct their present condition into that of villenage, & attach . . . them to the glebe." In 1798, intermarriage had been Short's solution to slavery. A generation later, serfdom seemed a better prospect.[48]

Was this idea any easier for Jefferson to swallow than Short's previous proposal? There was, after all, something incongruous about asking the author of the Declaration of Independence to endorse feudalism. This time, at least, Jefferson wrote back to his old friend. A transition to serfdom would ease the embarrassments of the slave system, but it would postpone rather than solve the problem of black belonging. Would it not be better, Jefferson suggested, simply to export freed slaves to another country? This was "entirely practicable, and greatly preferable to the mixture of color here." Sally Hemings still lived with him at Monticello when he wrote these words; he had fathered at least half a dozen mixed-race children since beginning his relationship with Hemings in Paris in the 1780s. And yet Jefferson signaled his "great aversion" to amalgamation while endorsing its polar opposite—a permanent and massive form of racial segregation. If Short still wondered about the vast inconsistency that had defined Jefferson's life—perhaps even the life of the republic—he was deterred from further inquiry: "On the subject of emancipation I have ceased to think, because it is not to be a work of my day." It would be left to Short and his contemporaries to implement the vision of racial separation that Jefferson had done so little to uphold.[49]

PART III
COLONIZATION

EIGHT

OF COLOR AND COUNTRY

THE PLANS TO COLONIZE NATIVE Americans and African Americans beyond the United States became popular for a simple reason: they promised to relieve liberal whites from the challenges of integration. American reformers, however, were not the pioneers of non-white colonization. The first colonizing experiments were undertaken by the British and the French, and were not primarily motivated by a fear of racial mixing. Liberal whites in London or Paris did not expect to live alongside the workers of Saint-Domingue or Jamaica after emancipation; their principles would be tested an ocean away from Paris or London. But European proponents of antislavery had to overcome a powerful obstacle to win public support for their cause. European consumers were hooked on the tropical commodities (especially sugar) produced by slave labor. Caribbean slaveholders had transformed the tastes of Europeans in the seventeenth and eighteenth centuries while reassuring consumers of two things: first, that blacks would only work when enslaved; second, that the most lucrative tropical staples could only be produced in the Americas. Colonization, in its earliest forms, was an attempt to challenge the economic logic underpinning the imperial system.

The theory behind the early colonization proposals was simple: Africans would be more productive if they worked for wages rather than in chains. If Europeans could establish agricultural colonies of free blacks, the rationale for the slave trade (and for American slavery more generally) would disappear. The slave plantations of the Americas would be undercut by free labor settlements, and Europe could continue to enjoy its addiction to tropical commodities without moral scruples. This idea had been circulating in Britain since the 1730s, after an unlikely encounter between a dissolute slave trader and an African king. In 1722, Bulfinch Lambe was taken prisoner by Agaja, ruler of the West African kingdom of Dahomey. Lambe worked for Britain's Royal Africa Company, whose raison d'être was to transport enslaved Africans to the horrors of the New World plantations. King Agaja probed his prisoner for details of the American side of this system, wondering why Europeans and Africans didn't produce their staples in West Africa instead. In the crescent that runs from what is now southern Morocco to Nigeria, Africans had cultivated every one of the commodities that underpinned the American slave systems: cotton, indigo, rice, even sugar. Agaja calculated that more money could be made from producing these goods in Africa than from supplying a labor force to American plantations. The King of Dahomey drew up a "Scheme of Trade" for Lambe to deliver to George I in London, and in 1726 the relieved Englishman was given his freedom.[1]

Neither Agaja nor Lambe could be described as a humanitarian. Despite the claims of the antislavery campaigners who later took up this story, Agaja almost certainly expected that the proposed African plantations would be worked by slaves rather than free labor. Lambe, meanwhile, demonstrated his commitment to the Scheme of Trade by avoiding London entirely after his release. Having sold the eighty slaves Agaja had given him as a gift for George I, he took the proceeds to Barbados and then New England, where he became a merchant and investor. Lambe returned to England in 1731, flat broke, and his long absence generated suspicion about the authenticity of the Scheme of Trade. Government officials decided against sending him back to Africa to develop the idea with Agaja—partly because the Royal Africa Company wanted to protect its business in the West Indies.

With the Scheme of Trade dismissed as Lambe's invention, the kingdom of Dahomey continued on its course to becoming a major channel for the transfer of African captives into Atlantic slavery.[2]

When the story of Agaja and Lambe was revived in Britain in the 1780s, it was in the very different context of the emerging international movement against the slave trade. Agaja's antislavery credentials were debated in the British Parliament, and the Scheme of Trade—which argued for the production of tropical goods in Africa rather than America—inspired some of the most prominent British reformers to imagine radical alternatives to the status quo. During the decade following the American Revolution, antislavery activists in Britain and France developed proposals for resettling slaves in free-labor colonies in Africa, crafting a virtuous circle in which humanitarian instincts and economic innovation would reinforce the logic of emancipation. The men who inspired this movement were John Fothergill and Granville Sharp, both of London. Fothergill, a member of the Royal Society, had worked to develop the scientific evidence that would convince governments and investors to support a free-labor plantation system. Sharp became a leading figure in the effort first to ban slavery in Britain, and then to limit the international slave trade itself. Somewhat incongruously, Sharp worked at the Tower of London in the government's Ordnance Office, pushing the paper that coordinated the empire's global networks of slavery and war. He made up for this in his spare time by producing a flurry of antislavery pamphlets, and wearing down his superiors with protests against a series of colonial injustices.[3]

Fothergill and Sharp became friends in the 1770s, and they worked together to produce one of the early triumphs of the nascent antislavery movement in Britain: Chief Justice Lord Mansfield's 1772 decision to grant freedom to James Somerset, the slave of a Boston merchant who had escaped into London's tiny free black community. The Somerset decision was widely interpreted as granting freedom to any slave who made it to the British Isles, an outcome that alarmed

Granville Sharp (1735–1813), central figure, in a mid-nineteenth-century portrait depicting his efforts to rescue Caribbean slaves brought by their masters to London. COURTESY OF THE VICTORIA AND ALBERT MUSEUM.

West Indian planters. This small but significant victory emboldened Sharp, who fought a pamphlet war with the planters' London representatives over their insistence that blacks were permanently inferior to whites. Fothergill, meanwhile, launched expeditions to West Africa and the Caribbean to explore the possibility of a free labor colony. An African site would strike a mortal blow against the slave trade, he reasoned; a Caribbean site might provide a haven for those Africans who had already been enslaved. Fothergill, like Granville Sharp, became interested in the struggles of the American colonists with the British government. Both men befriended Benjamin Franklin, who lived in Britain from 1764 to 1775, and Fothergill acted as a go-between as Franklin became estranged from British officials over the crisis in the American colonies. When the fighting broke out in Massachusetts in

1775, Sharp concluded that his curious double life was no longer viable. He resigned from the Ordnance Office to concentrate exclusively on his reform efforts.[4]

Sharp and Fothergill sympathized with the Patriot side in the American Revolution and believed that "all men are created equal" had universal meaning. Other Britons were less generous in their assessment of the American cause. Samuel Johnson famously complained that "we hear the loudest yelps for liberty among the drivers of negroes." The course of the war suggested that Britain, rather than the new United States, had a keener commitment to liberty across the color line. From 1775, British officials encouraged the slaves of American Patriots to abandon their masters and fight for Britain, promising freedom when the rebellion was subdued. Perhaps 20,000 slaves took up the offer, though many were killed (mostly by smallpox rather than combat) before the king's forces were withdrawn in 1783. To the disdain of Thomas Jefferson and George Washington, who howled about property rights, Britain kept its promise to free these "black loyalists" and resettled them in what was left of the empire. Some traveled to East Florida, which remained under British control. Others went to St. Lucia and Jamaica (as free blacks rather than slaves). Several thousand were resettled in the fledgling colony of Nova Scotia, where they were promised land and political equality with whites. And around half of the evacuees were brought to London.[5]

Virtually all of the members of this unlikely diaspora floundered in the years after the American Revolution, their dreams of an equal stake in the British Empire dashed by prejudice and discrimination. The refugees who ended up in London struggled to find work in the capital. By 1785, their cause had been taken up by Granville Sharp and his network of antislavery reformers. Even the British prime minister was keen to associate with the new Committee for the Relief of the Black Poor, and Sharp sensed opportunity in the midst of charity. Perhaps this was the moment at which he could finally realize the dream of a free-labor colony. John Fothergill had died in 1780, but his former

researcher Henry Smeathman traveled again to Africa to scout locations for a colony. Armed with maps of a place called Sierra Leone,
Smeathman and Sharp persuaded the committee that they should
establish a "Province of Freedom" for the black loyalists. The two men
were relentlessly upbeat about the potential of the scheme, and their
bright visions of a better life resonated with many of the American
refugees. By the winter of 1786–1787, Sharp and his associates had
persuaded hundreds of blacks to join the founding expedition to the
province. Sixty years after King Agaja had drafted his plan, British
reformers were about to create an antislavery colony in the maw of the
African slave trade.[6]

GIVEN THE PROBLEMS FACED BY the black loyalists in London, it's
tempting to see Sierra Leone as an exercise in deportation rather than
colonization. It's certainly the case that the arrival of a large number
of black immigrants in Britain had given Sharp, Smeathman, and the
other promoters of colonization an ideal opportunity to test their theories. But they balked at the suggestion that they were coercing black
people in any way. Nine hundred blacks signed up for the first voyage,
but when lengthy delays before departure—and rumors among the
would-be colonists that they might be sent to Australia instead—led
more than half of the original volunteers to jump ship, the promoters
made no efforts to recover them. The debate over establishing Sierra
Leone was part of a broader conversation about political and moral
reform that had been quickened by Britain's struggles in America.
Smeathman had toyed with founding a white settlement in West Africa
organized on the principles of the Swedish mystic Emmanuel Swe-
denborg. Sharp claimed that he had seen Sierra Leone as a settlement
for "poor people both white and black." (A few dozen white women
who had become romantically involved with black loyalists were part
of the first expedition in 1787.) In the 1780s and early 1790s, some of
the most famous political and religious radicals in Britain—men like

Richard Price and Joseph Priestley—either contemplated emigration or actually moved to the United States. We've already met political and religious radicals like the Countess of Huntingdon or Morgan Rhys, who scoured the American West for locations in which to found their own experimental settlements.[7]

If established societies like Britain were unresponsive to the demands of freedom, Granville Sharp imagined, individuals and communities could remake themselves in new places and refresh the promise of liberty. Sierra Leone, in this sense, was relevant not only to the future of black people, but to everyone. It was for this reason that Sharp made the eccentric decision to govern the colony with the Anglo-Saxon system of "Frankpledge." The system divided a political community into groups of ten households (a "tithing") and one hundred households (a "hundred"). Each tithing would elect a "tithing-man," and the ten elected representatives within each hundred would elect a "hundredor." Public works would be undertaken by all the citizens, with the major decisions carried out by these elected officials. For all its potential problems, Sharp's exhumation of Frankpledge promised a more radical form of governance than the hierarchical political system of Britain. Sharp also recognized its subversive possibilities. Since power would emanate from the bottom of a society through elected representatives at every level, the outward form of that society hardly mattered: "*Colonies*, even *kingdoms* and *monarchies*, may be rendered perfectly free and happy by this glorious patriarchal system of frank-pledge, which is the *only* effectual antidote to unlimited or illegal government of any kind." If society were organized from the bottom up, the pretensions of those at the top would count for little.[8]

Sharp understood the economic potential of Sierra Leone, but he rejected the suggestion that the Province of Freedom would extend the British Empire. Instead, he imagined this as only the first of many test-beds for political radicalism. When he learned from Benjamin Franklin that the Americans had decided to revise their Constitution in the summer of 1787, he told his friend that Frankpledge would be perfectly suited to the new United States. Franklin, polite as always, failed to raise the issue during the Constitutional Convention of 1787; and when Sharp discovered that the new Constitution lacked tithings and hundreds, he sent a wounded letter to Philadelphia. Sharp made the same suggestion to his friends in France a little before the French Revolution, and was again disappointed. In Sharp's mind, at least, Sierra Leone was simply one step in a wider process of political renovation that encompassed whites as well as blacks.[9]

If Frankpledge had radical potential, the founding of Sierra Leone was not its best advertisement. The first expedition reached the African coast in the spring of 1787 after lengthy delays. A combination of bad weather, disease, and strained relations with the indigenous population ensured the collapse of the colony's first settlement, Freetown, before the year was out. The surviving colonists were forced to seek charity (or employment) from the local slave traders, who watched the rise and fall of Sierra Leone with glee. "My attempts to establish a free government by Frankpledge at Sierra Leona have indeed been much frustrated," Sharp confessed to Franklin in January 1788. But he identified "the wickedness and gross intemperance of the settlers themselves, both white and black," as the cause of the colony's swift demise. Sharp's decision to blame the victims was tactical: with many influential observers in Britain ready to write off the West African climate as hopelessly hostile, Sharp and his supporters thought it imperative to hold the colonists, rather than the environment, responsible for these teething troubles. The Sierra Leone effort was reorganized on commercial lines, moving away from Sharp's political utopianism toward the economic logic of the late John Fothergill. Thomas Clarkson, William Wilberforce, and other titans of the British antislavery movement became investors in the new Sierra Leone Company, and the colony was remade in 1792 by the arrival of nearly 1,400 black settlers who had become disgruntled with life in Nova Scotia.[10]

Sierra Leone endured many problems during its first two decades. The colonists chafed against a series of white governors who failed to deliver the promises of land and equality that had drawn black loyalists to West Africa. The commercial potential of the colony was slow to

Sierra Leone, circa 1788. Courtesy of the New York Public Library.

materialize, and the company's officials shuttled between blaming the colonists and reassuring investors that good times were just around the corner. The aftershocks of the era's wars and revolutions regularly threatened the colony's foundations. In 1794, a flotilla of French warships sailed boldly into Freetown's harbor and burned the company's buildings to the ground. And yet the colony not only survived, despite the many colonists who suffered disease, oppression, banishment, or death; it convinced observers in Britain, France, and the United States that black resettlement was a practical prospect.[11]

THE OTHER COLONIZATION EXPERIMENT OF the late eighteenth century came from France, and a figure still more supportive of the American Revolution than Granville Sharp. The Marquis de Lafayette was only twenty years old in 1777 when he crossed the Atlantic to fight for the United States. He was wounded at the Battle of Brandywine in Pennsylvania, fought in numerous battles across the long span of the war, and led the final American effort to kettle the forces of Cornwallis at the 1781 Siege of Yorktown in Virginia. For many Americans,

Lafayette became a potent symbol of the universality of their struggle: they were fighting not for a petty nationalism, but for a world in which peoples would unite against tyranny. But while some American reformers applied this logic to slavery, pointing out the contradiction between "all men are created equal" and the iniquities of unfree labor, there was little before the Yorktown campaign to suggest that Lafayette would embrace the cause of emancipation.[12]

His views were changed by his encounters with two Americans, one white and one black. Lafayette befriended the young South Carolinian officer John Laurens, one of Washington's aides-de-camp in the early phases of the war, who convinced him that slavery was a terrible injustice. Laurens had unsuccessfully petitioned the South Carolina legislature in 1779 to authorize the arming of slaves to fight the British, but he had more luck in opening Lafayette's eyes to the military potential of African Americans. And then there was James Armistead, the Virginia slave who offered his assistance to Lafayette's army in 1781. The marquis sent Armistead across the lines to the British, where he posed as a black loyalist and reported on the details of Lord Cornwallis's camp. Armistead then presented Lafayette with a better idea: he should approach Cornwallis and offer to spy on the Patriots for the British side, thereby becoming a double agent. The ruse worked beautifully. Armistead fed Cornwallis and his staff inflated estimates of US troop numbers while providing a stream of reliable intelligence to the Patriot side. Lafayette showed his appreciation for Armistead's work in a testimonial to the Virginia legislature in 1784, urging them to grant freedom to the former spy in recognition of his services. It would be another two years before the assembly obliged, and more than three decades before an elderly Armistead received a veteran's pension from the state of Virginia. But Armistead had become an indelible part of Lafayette's revolutionary experience. He was immortalized in the most famous portrait of the Frenchman during his American service, standing alongside the general and his horse at Yorktown, and he subsequently changed his name to James Armistead Lafayette.[13]

The Marquis de Lafayette returned to France after Cornwallis's surrender, where he encountered a new generation of antislavery reformers finding its voice. Foremost among this group was Lafayette's friend the Marquis de Condorcet, whose *Reflections on Negro Slavery* (1781) was perhaps the most influential French abolitionist tract to appear before the Revolution of 1789. Condorcet's zealous belief in the immorality of slavery was matched by a caution about emancipation's effects. If slaves were given their freedom "too suddenly," he argued, they would be "reduced to misery." Instead of a plan for immediate abolition, Condorcet proposed a gradual scheme spanning sixty or seventy years, with younger slaves gaining more rights until they attained their freedom. This plan would allow blacks to sample freedom in responsible drafts, thought Condorcet, rather than a dangerous gulp. It would also reassure planters in the French Caribbean that they might adopt free labor without destroying the colonial economy. Like Noah Webster and the many other American proponents of gradual abolition, Condorcet believed that slaveholders could play a crucial role in destroying slavery, if they were given time and space to remake their workforce.[14]

Lafayette proposed two modifications to Condorcet's scheme: the time scale should be accelerated, and the experiment should be undertaken far from the existing plantations of the Caribbean. He then asked George Washington to help him create a black colony in the American interior. "Now that you are going to enjoy some ease and quiet my dear general," wrote Lafayette in February 1783, "let us unite in purchasing a small estate where we may try the experiment to free the Negroes, and use them only as tenants." If they succeeded, their celebrity would do the rest: emancipation would become "general practice" in the United States, and Lafayette would "render the method fashionable in the West Indies." The Frenchman admitted his plans might seem visionary, even deranged; but "I had rather be mad that way, than to be thought wise on the other track." Washington, still preoccupied with the problems of demobilizing the Continental

Army, sent a bland assurance that he would be "happy to join you in so laudable a work." But over the next two years, a concrete commitment from Washington remained elusive. In 1785, Lafayette gave up on the idea of colonizing freed people in North America, instead purchasing land in the French colony of Cayenne, on the coast of what is now French Guiana.[15]

Cayenne was more than 1,500 miles southeast of Saint-Domingue, the center of the Caribbean slave system, but Lafayette thought its isolation a virtue. It supplied him with a laboratory for black improvement away from the eyes of the planters (and the half million or so slaves) of the West Indies. If the experiment worked on a small scale, there was room to bring many more black people to the colony or to export the model. Admittedly, the precedents for a successful settlement there were not reassuring. In 1763, in the aftermath of France's defeat in the Seven Years' War, the French government had promoted Cayenne as a new frontier for white colonization in the Americas. Twelve thousand volunteers sailed from France for America; all but a thousand had been carried off by disease and starvation within two years. Lafayette thought that his black colonists might do better. He bought land and slaves from one of the few remaining plantation owners and, in a show of his ambition and influence, persuaded Louis XVI to do the same.[16]

Lafayette wrote excitedly to Washington in 1786 about "the experiment which you know is my hobby horse." Washington told the marquis that Cayenne offered "generous and noble proof of your humanity," and he praised his friend for realizing that it was better to free slaves gradually than "to set them afloat at once." With this airy benediction, Washington left Lafayette to continue his work. The marquis, who directed the entire enterprise from France, instructed his managers to ban corporal punishment and offer religion, wages, and other incentives that could guide black workers from slavery toward freedom. The plantation began to produce cloves and other spices under the new regime, and Lafayette's managers reported that the black "colonists" were much improved in their manners and character.

And then the French Revolution happened. Initially, the turmoil in France failed to undo Lafayette's work. Even after the marquis was thrown into jail in 1792 for his political views, it seemed that the experiment taking place half the world away might not be disrupted. Lafayette's wife wrote to the Jacobins begging them not to interfere with the work that her husband had undertaken. But the French authorities soon confiscated Lafayette's colony along with his other property. His slaves were transferred to new owners with a more conventional view of plantation order. Most slaves in the French Caribbean enjoyed at least a taste of freedom in the 1790s, either through legislation in Paris or armed struggle, and the blacks of Cayenne were no different: they briefly overthrew the authority of their masters and demanded their share of the French Revolution's egalitarian promises. But in 1802, when French authorities decided to reestablish slavery in the colony, they quickly overcame any black resistance. That same year, Lafayette accepted compensation in lieu of his Cayenne holdings. The marquis's emancipation experiment was over.[17]

In French popular memory, the black colony faded fast. Cayenne became more famous for its terrifyingly remote prison, Devil's Island— which later counted Alfred Dreyfus and Steve McQueen among its inmates—than for its brief role in the antislavery movement. Lafayette, however, never abandoned his view that colonization might solve the conundrum of emancipation. When he emerged from five years in jail, he discovered that the once flourishing French antislavery movement had dissipated. Those activists who had not been subdued by the violence of the Revolution found themselves caught up in Napoleonic nationalism. If French abolitionism had run its course, Lafayette hoped that posterity would look more kindly on the achievements of William Wilberforce, Thomas Clarkson, and Granville Sharp. Sierra Leone, after all, had survived the French Revolution and the European wars that followed. "Let us hope that we may also possess a Sierra Leone," wrote Lafayette, "and that the two governments [Britain and France] will come to an understanding, to place both these philanthropic enterprises beyond the chances of European quarrels." Colonization represented "the only reparation we can offer to the blacks for the crimes of several ages." It was a view that he would retain throughout his life, and that he would bring back to the United States on his final visit three decades later.[18]

EUROPEAN COLONIZATION PLANS WERE INCUBATED almost exclusively by white reformers. In North America, by contrast, the first proposal for relocating African Americans came from a group of black petitioners. In April 1773, four Massachusetts slaves—Peter Bestes, Sambo Freeman, Felix Holbrook, and Chester Joie—asked the colonial assembly to implement a gradual emancipation scheme modeled on the system that had recently been adopted in Spanish America. Even absolutist Spain had given its slaves the opportunity to work one day each week for wages that might eventually fund their emancipation. The Massachusetts petitioners promised that, if a similar system were adopted in New England, they would "transport ourselves to some part of the coast of *Africa*" after purchasing their freedom. Their plea was reprinted in Boston as the appendix to a Patriot oration. The (white) publisher observed that, at a moment when so many white people in America were complaining about being vassals to the British, it would be churlish to suppress the appeal of those Americans who were held in "real slavery."[19]

That same year, the white Rhode Island minister Samuel Hopkins proposed a missionary scheme that would evolve into a plan for colonization. Having consulted with Ezra Stiles, the president of Yale College, Hopkins began looking for volunteers among the black population of New England to spread the gospel on the West African coast. He selected two members of his church, Bristol Yamma and John Quamine, and raised funds for their training. (Both had been born in Africa.) Stiles and Hopkins secured an endorsement for their scheme from Phillis Wheatley, the celebrated black poet from Boston, and persuaded the president of Princeton to oversee the education

of the would-be emigrants. Though the plan fell apart amid the tur-
bulence of the American Revolution, Samuel Hopkins had already
begun to think about a larger plan in which African Americans might
advance the cause of Christianity and escape from the lamentable hostility of their white neighbors. In a 1776 pamphlet attacking slavery,
he lamented the "strong prejudices" that prevented white Americans
from recognizing blacks as "by nature and by right, on a level with our
brethren and children." He outlined three options for a mass emancipation. Slaves could be freed in situ, and granted an equal place in
the new United States; they "could be moved into those places in this
land, where they may have profitable business, and are wanted"; or
"they may be transported to Africa, where they might probably live
better than in any other country." By 1776 Hopkins had reimagined
his missionary enterprise as a beachhead for black colonization.[20]

African Americans became interested in emigration for a variety
of reasons between the American Revolution and the Civil War, and
a desire to escape from white prejudice was paramount among them.
In January 1787, another petition was organized in Boston to request
public support for black colonization. The ringleader on this occasion was Prince Hall, the cofounder of America's first black Masonic
Lodge. Boston's free black population had suffered enough discrimination from whites to "induce us to desire to return to Africa, our
native country," he thought. Hall and the seventy-two other black sig-
natories hoped to "live among our equals" in Africa, "and be more
comfortable and happy than we can be in our present situation." This
petition made no more impact on the legislature than the 1773 appeal
of Peter Bestes et al. had. But the willingness of blacks in both Massachusetts and Rhode Island to consider resettlement in Africa, and the
founding of Sierra Leone that same year, drew the attention of white
reformers who were concerned about slavery's future.[21]

These local and international strands of colonization enthusiasm were brought together in the 1780s by William Thornton, whose
background fitted him superbly for the task. Thornton had been born
in 1759 on the island of Tortola in the Caribbean. His parents were

Quakers but also sugar growers, with a plantation worked by more than a hundred slaves. Thornton studied medicine in Britain and joined the circle of reformers surrounding John Fothergill. During a long stay in Paris in 1784, he befriended Benjamin Franklin, who was finishing up his diplomatic duties in France, and Henry Smeathman, the pioneering explorer of Sierra Leone. Thornton decided that he could no longer square his conscience with his family's plantation, and returned to Tortola to ask his mother and stepfather to release the slaves he would eventually inherit. Quakers on both sides of the Atlantic were in the vanguard of the new antislavery movement, but Thornton's parents were not among their number. He spent months on the island, acquainting himself with the conditions and capacities of the slaves and badgering his parents. Eventually, they told him that, if they were ever to grant his request, they couldn't simply divide the plantation and allow freed people to live alongside slaves. Instead, Thornton would need to get the manumitted slaves off the island.[22]

Already acquainted with the ideas of Fothergill and Smeathman, Thornton now had a personal stake in black colonization. He traveled to Philadelphia in 1786, where he reached out to the members of the new Pennsylvania Abolition Society, and lectured black and white audiences in the major eastern cities on the virtues of an African colony. Thornton proposed that slaves should make their way slowly toward freedom, and should then have the option of being "carried over to Africa to become proprietors of land." A colony would settle the nerves of American planters who were conscious of slavery's immorality but anxious about living alongside their slaves in freedom. It might also offer a sanctuary to blacks who were already freed, but who endured the (unwarranted) prejudices of whites. Thornton didn't forget the rationale that had originally guided the British proponents of colonization: a successful free labor colony would generate profits that could be used to liberate caravans of captured Africans before they were shipped from the West African coast. He was proposing a new form of ethical capitalism in which the middlemen of the slave trade would be bankrupted by enlightened commerce.[23]

To his surprise, Thornton found in the winter of 1786–1787 that the communities of color he had hoped to recruit had their own views about colonization. He lost the argument that a new settlement should be pacifist in its orientation: free blacks in Providence, Newport, and Boston would not move to Africa without the ability to defend themselves from slave traders and European soldiers. They also told Thornton that they would only consider moving to a colony "perfectly independent" of Europe. If they were made in any way "dependent on England," Thornton told his London friend John Lettsom, "none here will engage." Like Granville Sharp, Thornton had no problem accepting this anticolonial proviso. In Boston, he reported that his revised draft for a black settlement ("I hate the word *colony*") had won the approval of Samuel Adams, not to mention "thousands" of blacks. He asked Lettsom to pitch the scheme to government officials in London. Britain had an opportunity to prove that "a man that Nature clothed with a white skin, shall not, merely on that account, have the right of wielding a rod of iron." The alternative was to do nothing, and hope that the slumbering volcano of slavery would never erupt. Thornton's warning against inaction— delivered three years before the outbreak of the Haitian Revolution— was uncannily prescient. "The British, as well as other nations, have, in this respect, everything to gain and everything to lose."[24]

Thornton's plans stalled for two reasons, one personal and one geopolitical. Despite the pushback he'd experienced from free black audiences in New England, Thornton couldn't resist placing himself at the center of his schemes. He would lead the expedition to Africa, he declared, giving up "every pleasure of society, every tie of relationship, for a while, on their account." The vision of a black exodus led by a white Moses sat uneasily even with Samuel Hopkins, who thought Thornton "too flighty and unsteady" for the role of national liberator. Free blacks rolled their eyes. They would prefer to send their own emissary to West Africa to scout for a site, they told him, and were "on our guard against being imposed upon in this very important affair which we have in view." The larger obstacle to Thornton's progress was the dismal failure of the first settlement at Sierra Leone in 1787.

Granville Sharp had heard of Thornton's initiative and realized that the difficulties of the first settlers would make Thornton's task harder. Sharp wrote him (via John Lettsom) in early 1789 with reassurances. The Province of Freedom had been laid low by the foibles of its first settlers rather than by the climate, Sharp insisted. The Englishman remained confident that Sierra Leone could be refloated, though its continuing problems did little to persuade African Americans that they should gamble their lives on colonization.[25]

Thornton was undaunted. He prepared another recruiting pamphlet for Philadelphia's free black community and lobbied legislators in the new federal Congress—including influential southern planters—in support of colonization. But the new Sierra Leone Company was less interested than Sharp had been in recruiting migrants from the United States, partly because Sharp's attack on the character of his first colonists had been so persuasive. (William Wilberforce blamed African Americans for the initial failures in the Province of Freedom—the black loyalists who had fought for Britain in the American Revolution had been "thorough Jacobins" and "the worst possible subjects," he wrote in 1800.) Company officials in Freetown rebuffed requests from white and black reformers to resettle black Americans. Zachary Macaulay, governor of Sierra Leone from 1794 to 1799, offered to accept just twelve US families on the northern fringes of the colony. Thornton complained to Granville Sharp that the Sierra Leone Company could easily morph into the East India Company if its managers weren't more carefully policed. Rebuffed in West Africa, Thornton returned in 1790 to Tortola, where he hoped to convince the island's assembly to support emancipation. To his horror, the planter-dominated legislature made a cynical counterproposal: Thornton might use colonization to remove the small number of manumitted blacks who were already on the island, and so prevent those still enslaved from glimpsing a happier future. Thornton despaired of making progress on either side of the Atlantic.[26]

Eventually he found another outlet for his enthusiasm. The new federal government had launched a competition to design the buildings for the Federal City on the Potomac. Thornton moved back to Philadelphia in 1792, drew up plans for a US Capitol building, and submitted his entry. With the blessing of Washington and Jefferson, Thornton was named the winner. Having spent more than five years imagining that his contribution to American life would be to spirit black people to Africa, Thornton had found a different way to shape the landscape of the new United States. Like Lafayette, though, he wasn't finished with colonization.[27]

DURING THE 1780S AND 1790S, colonization caught the attention not only of northern blacks and white antislavery reformers in New England, but also of southern planters who imagined that slavery's days were numbered. With more slaves than any other state, Virginia became fertile ground for colonization proposals. Between 1785 and 1800, its most famous statesmen—George Washington, Thomas Jefferson, James Madison, and James Monroe—discussed the possibility of settling African Americans beyond the United States. Jefferson was the pioneer; in 1779, while serving as governor, he floated black resettlement as part of a gradual emancipation plan for the state. In his *Notes on the State of Virginia*, written a few years later, he outlined his thinking in more detail. He began by listing the many obstacles to an integrated society after slavery: "Deep rooted prejudices, entertained by the whites; ten thousand recollections, by the blacks, of the injuries they have received; new provocations; the real distinctions which nature has made; and many other circumstances, which divide us into parties, and produce convulsions which will probably never end but in the extermination of the one or the other race." With these terrible complications in view, he insisted that American slavery, unlike its Roman predecessor, would require two emancipations. First, black people would need to be freed from bondage; then, without delay, white people would need to be freed from the company of blacks.[28]

If Jefferson was an innovator on the subject of colonization, Washington and Madison were introduced to the idea by friends and correspondents. After Lafayette's Cayenne overtures, Washington was pressed on the subject by Jacques-Pierre Brissot de Warville, the Parisian journalist who (with Condorcet and Lafayette) had founded France's first antislavery society in 1788. Brissot sailed for the United States that year on a fact-finding mission. He was optimistic about the prospects of reform: Americans, he wrote, "more than any other people, are convinced that all men are born free and equal." He assumed that slavery had survived in the new US Constitution only because South Carolina and Georgia had threatened to leave the Union, and he expected the anachronism to be removed before long. Washington responded to Brissot's entreaties with pallid reassurances. Of course *he* thought that slavery must be abolished, but it was important that a visitor understand planters' anxieties about the social landscape after slavery. Brissot agreed that the promise of racial separation might expedite abolition.[29]

Brissot's enthusiasm for colonization was fired by William Thornton, whom he met in Philadelphia. The Frenchman was delighted to see Thornton executing "a project first imagined by that great apostle of philanthropy, Doctor Fothergill," and carried forward by "the beneficent Granville Sharp." Brissot was not alone in finding Thornton an impressive advocate for colonization. In July 1787, with the Constitutional Convention underway in Philadelphia, Thornton took rooms in a boardinghouse just a block away from the (secret) debates about the nation's future. He quickly befriended many of the delegates, including his fellow boarder James Madison. Thornton shared his colonization plan, and the Virginian was hooked. A "settlement of freed blacks on the coast of Africa," Madison wrote, "might prove a great encouragement to manumission in the southern parts of the U.S., and even afford the best hope yet presented of putting an end to the slavery in which not less than 600,000 unhappy negroes are now involved." Madison, like Washington and Jefferson, feared that "the prejudices of the whites" would make black freedom in America untenable. But an "external receptacle" would help individuals and state governments to follow the dictates of "humanity and policy" to their logical end: the abolition of slavery.[30]

Colonization ideas circulated freely in Virginia in the 1780s and 1790s, especially after the passage of the 1782 law that allowed masters to manumit their slaves without the permission of the legislature. Conservative white Virginians fretted about the increasing free black population in the state, and liberal whites worried that antislavery would stall if slaveholders became skittish. It was at this moment that the celebrated judge St. George Tucker wrote Jeremy Belknap of Massachusetts on the prospects of racial integration after slavery, though other Virginians had already concluded that this was a pipe dream. George Washington's friend and neighbor Ferdinando Fairfax thought integration impractical, and in 1790 he urged Congress to create a black colony on the African coast. In an article for a Philadelphia magazine, he divided white Virginians into two camps: those who, from the spurs of "natural right and justice," supported abolition; and those who knew that slavery was wrong but feared the "inconveniences" of a general emancipation. White prejudice was too strong to allow blacks to remain in Virginia, Fairfax observed: "Where is the man of all those who have liberated their slaves who would marry a son or daughter to one of them?" Passing laws that would guarantee equality would count for little if "these prejudices, sentiments, or whatever they may be called" continued to operate among whites at large. Better, then, to urge blacks who were already free to establish an African colony, to be reinforced by those slaves who "may become liberated by the voluntary consent of their owners."[31]

That Fairfax published his plan in Philadelphia rather than Virginia is significant. With the help of the antislavery printer Mathew Carey, he hoped to influence the new federal government to adopt black resettlement as a national priority. (St. George Tucker may have had the same motive.) In 1793, the Virginia clergyman John Jones Spooner asked Jeremy Belknap to publish his colonization proposal in the Collections of the Massachusetts Historical Society, offering yet another reminder to northerners that "few here" would oppose "a generous plan" for emancipation if the terms were right. Slavery could be dismantled gradually, he thought, through a "liberal system" in which blacks would "colonize some new country." Emancipation without removal was out of the question, Spooner warned: "There will be no happiness here while they remain mixed with the whites." Within Virginia, the magistrate William Craighead urged the state assembly to lobby federal officials for a black colony in the Northwest Territory. Freed slaves from other states might be sent to the colony, whose inhabitants would have a relationship toward the federal government "analogous to that in which the Indians now stand." That the bulk of this territory belonged to Native nations hostile to US expansion seems not to have troubled Craighead unduly.[32]

Craighead was not the only Virginian to propose the American West as a colonizing venue. James Madison thought that the "interior wilderness of America" might work; so did St. George Tucker, when he finally issued his own antislavery plan in 1796. In his letters to Jeremy Belknap the previous year, Tucker had been skeptical about colonization. He agreed that "deep-rooted prejudices in the minds of the whites" worked against a mixed-race society after emancipation, but thought that a black settlement beyond the frontier could provoke a future race war between blacks and whites (or a more imminent one between blacks and Indians). But Tucker recognized that the alternatives were scarcely more appealing. Blacks could be freed with complete equality; freed but denied civil rights; or kept in slavery. The first option was bound to fail. "Either nature or long habit" had degraded blacks in ways that reinforced white prejudices, he told Belknap. Blacks would respond to those prejudices with violence, and a race war would ensue. But giving blacks second-class citizenship would reinforce white prejudices and "stimulate [blacks] to procure by force what you have refused to grant them." Both scenarios would create economic and social chaos. Leaving slavery untouched, meanwhile, offended the "sacred truth" that "all men are by nature equally free and independent."[33]

The poverty of these three scenarios led Tucker back to colonization. Perhaps, he suggested in his *Dissertation on Slavery*, black people could be persuaded to migrate to the "immense unsettled territory on this continent." He couldn't accept "the banishment of the negroes," but thought that Virginia could encourage their departure by limiting their rights after emancipation. Blacks could be freed from slavery over a number of decades, then subjected to "extensive legal debility": barred from holding public office, owning freehold property, bearing arms, becoming attorneys or jurors, and marrying white people. "The restrictions in this place may appear to favor strongly of prejudice," Tucker admitted. But "whoever proposes any plan for the abolition of slavery, will find that he must either encounter, or accommodate himself to prejudice." He chose the latter—"not that I pretend to be wholly exempt from it, but that I might avoid as many obstacles as possible to the completion of so desirable a work as the abolition of slavery." Tucker would ask freed people to choose between two options: second-class citizenship alongside their former masters in Virginia; or the possibility of complete equality beyond the boundaries of the United States.[34]

Tucker presented the *Dissertation on Slavery* plan to the Virginia assembly in 1797 (he had published it in pamphlet form in 1796). The speaker of the Senate was sympathetic, but the planter interests in the lower house dismissed it without debate. Tucker felt that he could do no more. He confessed to Jeremy Belknap that he'd larded his proposal with "every restriction that I supposed timidity or prejudice could insist on," capturing slavery's sunset in such warm colors as to "lull avarice itself to sleep." Perhaps only "actual suffering"—of slaveholders, not slaves—would "open the oppressors' eyes" to the madness of their predicament. But even in St. George Tucker's Virginia, antislavery and colonization were far from moribund. Tucker had stirred up the opposition of the state's most conservative forces, but the arguments of his *Dissertation* would soon gather momentum.[35]

TWO OBSTACLES STOOD IN THE way of a mixed-race society after slavery: the damage done to black people by their experience of bondage, and the reluctance of white people to accept former slaves as fellow citizens. Both were sources of "degradation" that pulled free blacks into a downward spiral. Reformers accepted that the first was reversible, but what of the second? St. George Tucker admitted that he would make concessions to prejudice to achieve the greater goal of black freedom. But if the argument against slavery was based on privileging reason over prejudice, and rejecting the permanent inferiority of blacks, how could one defer to the same prejudice by denying the possibility of black citizenship? This was a question that tugged at the antislavery pioneers Anthony Benezet and Benjamin Rush, who each played a key role in creating Philadelphia's thriving antislavery culture.

Benezet was born into a Huguenot family in France in 1713, but soon fled with his family to Britain, a refuge from religious persecution. He spent his childhood in London, where he began attending Friends meetings, and in 1731 he moved to the Quaker colony of Pennsylvania. Benezet first became a merchant but found the work uninspiring. In 1739 he turned his attention to teaching and discovered his life's passion. After gaining experience at the Quaker school in Philadelphia, he championed the teaching of groups that were marginalized by the existing education system: girls and African Americans, in particular. He began offering evening classes to black Philadelphians in 1750, and he was the driving force behind the Friends' decision to open a black day school in the city in 1770. Absalom Jones, James Forten, and many other leaders of the city's free black community passed through the school as children; their aptitude and hard work persuaded Benezet that there was "as great variety of talents" among black people "as among a like number of whites." The notion that blacks were "inferior in their capacities" was "a vulgar prejudice, founded on the pride or ignorance of their lordly masters."[36]

Benezet quickly grasped the connection between slavery and prejudice and became a tireless opponent of both. He began writing antislavery essays and pamphlets that anchored arguments about black ability to his experience in the classroom. As the international antislavery movement began to take shape in the 1760s and 1770s, Benezet found admirers on both sides of the Atlantic. Granville Sharp and John Fothergill arranged for Benezet's books to be reprinted in Britain, and Benezet produced abridged versions of Sharp's antislavery tracts. (Sharp liked one of these so much that he sent Benezet's version, rather than his own, to Lord Mansfield and the British prime minister, Lord North.) Fothergill made a donation to the African School and asked Benezet in turn to support his plan for an African colony. Benezet was skeptical. "What shall be done with those Negroes already imported, and born in our families?" he asked in his 1771 *Historical Account of Guinea*. "Must they be sent to Africa? That would expose them, in a strange land, to greater difficulties than many of them labor under at present." He didn't discount the challenges of freeing blacks in situ, however. To become "profitable members of society," black people would need to overcome the "evil habits" that had been grafted into them by enslavement. To undertake this process in the cities of the seaboard, alongside prejudiced whites, seemed a daunting prospect.[37]

The solution, he believed, lay in exploiting the American interior. As early as 1763, Benezet suggested in a letter to an English correspondent that the lands on the east side of the Mississippi River might supply "an advantageous opportunity of beneficial employment for the negroes." In his *Historical Account*, Benezet proposed that black families emerging from slavery be given "a small tract of land" to improve. The discipline of farming and pioneer life would soon make them "industrious subjects." In 1773, he told John Fothergill that the vast tract between the Allegheny Mountains and the Mississippi River was the perfect place to settle black people, but insisted that "the thought of settling them in a body, by themselves," was neither desirable nor feasible. Benezet worried that an independent black settlement would be capsized by the "ignorance and passions" of its degraded inhabitants. "The only rational, safe and just expedient," he concluded, would be "that they be mixed amongst the whites, and by giving them

a property amongst us, make them parties and interested in our welfare and security." Benezet's vision for the West contained not a separate black community, along the lines of Tucker's distant colony, but
a new society in which whites and blacks would perfect the alchemy
of integration without the pressures of the heavily settled seaboard.
Here was a forerunner of Samuel Stanhope Smith's eccentric plan to
encourage black-white marriages beyond the frontier.[38]

Benjamin Rush was another Philadelphian personally acquainted
with the grandees of the British antislavery struggle. He completed his
medical degree in Edinburgh in 1768, then lived for several months
in London as a protégé of John Fothergill. Restored to Philadelphia
in the 1770s, he became deeply influenced by Benezet's antislavery
advocacy and was drawn into the city's lively reform movement. Like
virtually every other early abolitionist, he was a supporter of gradual rather than immediate abolition. "I do not urge the emancipation
of the slaves now among you," he wrote a friend in South Carolina
in 1782. "They are rendered unfit by the habits of vice (the offspring
of slavery) for freedom." Rush urged his friend, who had just moved
from Rhode Island with antislavery intentions, to be patient: "Time
may unfold a method of repairing to their posterity the injustice that
has been done to the present generation." In Philadelphia, Rush was
an energetic promoter of black uplift, proudly reporting to his British
friends that the city's free blacks were "in general more industrious
than the lowest class of white people." In the early 1790s, he secured
donations for the African Church from Granville Sharp and helped
to recruit free blacks for the fight against a yellow fever epidemic in
the city. Rush told Sharp that, for a good Christian, "the globe is the
native country, and the whole human race the fellow citizens."[39]

But Rush was not immune to the lure of racial separation. He
would, after all, attempt to deter intermarriages by identifying black
skin as a symptom of leprosy. In 1787, he developed a more ethe-
real segregation scheme in a magazine essay entitled "The Paradise
of Negro Slaves." The essay described a dream he'd had after reading Thomas Clarkson's celebrated *Essay on the Slavery and Commerce*

of the Human Species, the bible of the British antislavery movement. Rush found himself transported to a beautiful country "inhabited only with negroes." Everyone seemed cheerful until catching sight of Rush, whose presence created "general perturbation." A single African American wandered over to Rush, apologized for the "general panic," and explained that he had entered that portion of heaven reserved for black people. Former slaves were "collected together" in paradise to enjoy "an ample compensation" for their miserable lives on earth. Gradually the black saints warmed up to Rush, telling him stories of the cruelty of slavery and the power of forgiveness. Then another white man, much older than Rush, approached the crowd with a face that was "placid and full of benignity." The new arrival provoked an opposite reaction to the one that Rush had drawn. The former slaves broke into applause and mobbed the "venerable figure," the noise of their shouts waking Rush from his slumber just after he'd recognized his old mentor: Anthony Benezet.[40]

If Rush initially experimented with colonization on the plane of allegory, by the early 1790s he was taking concrete steps to explore racial separation. In 1794, he acquired 20,000 acres of land in Bedford County, in sparsely settled south-central Pennsylvania, and drew up a colonization plan for the Pennsylvania Abolition Society. Rush noted that the free blacks of Philadelphia were forced into professions that merely encouraged "such vices as have been contracted in slavery"—he mentioned the high numbers of free blacks who had become servants and sailors, in particular—and lamented that black people found it difficult to acquire land of their own. To remedy this situation, he offered 5,000 acres for an exclusively black settlement that could vindicate the potential of the race. Like Lafayette in Cayenne, Rush hoped that the success of the settlement would encourage similar schemes throughout the southern states, and that the future of black improvement might be stretched across the expanding frontier. The final component of the plan confirmed its benevolent lineage: "The name of the settlement shall be *Benezet*, after [that] late worthy and indefatigable advocate of the freedom of the blacks."[41]

But while Benezet had written in 1773 of the dangers of isolating blacks from whites, even in settlements in the American interior, Rush believed that these improvement schemes would secure a lasting separation of the races. In a 1793 letter to the comptroller of Pennsylvania, John Nicholson—another patron of free black causes in Philadelphia—Rush moved easily from a discussion of the roof-raising at the new African Church to his plans for a black settlement in the western portion of the state. Rush wanted Nicholson's help in organizing the sale of thousands of acres of land "to *Africans only*," with the state providing credit to those who couldn't raise the funds themselves. "The attraction of color and country is such that I think the offer would succeed," Rush wrote. "And thereby a *precedent* be established for colonizing, in time, all the Africans in our country." Rush's embrace of colonization, even as he worked with Philadelphia free blacks to improve their standing in the city, demonstrates how even the most liberal whites could see skin color and nationality as mutually reinforcing. After 1800, free blacks became increasingly vocal about the dangers that colonization posed to their efforts to throw off the stigma of slavery. But Anthony Benezet's warnings about the need to give black people a stake in the American future were crowded out by a liberal enthusiasm for colonization. An international movement to challenge the premises of the slave trade had morphed into something distinctively American. Black colonies might carry the spirit of "all men are created equal" beyond prejudice, degradation, and—crucially—the borders of the United States.[42]

NINE

The Choice

THE IDEA THAT NATIVE AMERICANS might fare better if they were moved away from European settlers predated the founding of Sierra Leone, the American Revolution, and even the voyage of the *Mayflower*. In 1518, the Spanish friar Bartolomé de las Casas persuaded Charles V to establish an Indian colony on the coast of Venezuela. Native people "must be taken out of the hands of the Christians," Las Casas insisted, "because otherwise they will be killed and the country destroyed." A similar logic inspired the Jesuits in Paraguay, who had resettled nearly 150,000 Guaraní Indians in thirty mission towns by the early eighteenth century. A small number of Jesuit friars presided over the missions, but Spanish settlers were strictly forbidden from entering their territory. The missions were hardly a refuge from empire: instead, they allowed Jesuits to Christianize Indians and encourage them to produce goods for the market. The missions broke up in the late eighteenth century, after Spain decided to expel the Jesuits from the Americas and take direct control of the Indians. For nearly two hundred years, however, the Jesuits had argued that separation was the prerequisite for a successful "civilizing" program.[1]

The Paraguay missions found a distant echo in colonial New England. In 1650, the Massachusetts missionary John Eliot established a network of "praying towns" in which Native Americans were gathered under the supervision of Protestant ministers. Eliot hoped that the separation would be temporary and that, before long, Indians and whites would be merged into a single people. ("All one English," as he put it.) But the praying towns were not as isolated as the missions of Paraguay, and their Native residents struggled to survive the region's regular wars and relentless white encroachment. By the middle of the eighteenth century, most of the Christian Indians had either been forced onto smaller tracts of land—forerunners of the reservations system—or had fled westward to build new lives beyond the reach of whites.[2]

These missionary-led experiments had a common theme: Native peoples would be "civilized" in areas from which white settlers had been excluded. In colonial North America, however, the British government usually pursued a different course. Where white settlers were scarce, and the power of Native Americans was considerable—in upstate New York and the Great Lakes, for example—British officials sought commercial and political alliances with indigenous people rather than a "civilizing" agenda. Indians might consent to be called subjects of the king, but this implied neither conquest nor their submission to "civilization." The American Revolution briefly promised a different calculus. The Continental Congress was desperate for Native allies in the strategically vital Ohio country. In the fall of 1778, US commissioners met at Fort Pitt (the site of modern Pittsburgh) with a delegation of Delawares led by White Eyes, whose son would later endure an unhappy education at Princeton. "The paths between us are grown up with bushes," began the commissioners, and "your and our people's bones are scattered through the woods." The Delawares were open to a fresh start. In return for protection against Britain and its Indian allies, White Eyes would offer US troops safe passage through Delaware territory, and might even send warriors to aid the Patriot campaigns. The American negotiators happily agreed to his terms and promised that the United States would now "consider you as their own people."[3]

What would this mean for the Delawares? One of the treaty provisions clarified the connection: "The parties further agree that other tribes friendly to the interests of the United States, may be invited to form a state, whereof the Delaware nation shall be in the heads, and have a representation in Congress." When the British king had treated the inhabitants of his American colonies as "subjects," that word had a meaning that was broad and shallow: it could accommodate Native Americans in the Ohio country, French Catholics in Quebec, or black slaves in Jamaica. Some historians have argued that it was the capacious nature of this subjecthood that helped to foment the American Revolution: white colonists became frustrated by the refusal of British officials to privilege their claims over those of Catholics or non-white people. If the Revolution was partly an attempt to escape from an imperial system that was inclusive but hierarchical, we can easily imagine that "all men are created equal" referred only to *white* men. And yet here on the frontier, in the midst of the American Revolution, was a treaty promising the Delawares representation in the US Congress.[4]

The historian Gregory Evans Dowd, who has written extensively about Native Americans in the Revolutionary era, dismisses this treaty clause without ceremony: "It is inconceivable that such a proposal was accepted in good faith by even the most broad minded of the commissioners," he writes, "but it certainly illustrates the lengths American agents were willing to run and the lies they were willing to spin in order to achieve Delaware neutrality." The fate of the brief alliance gives credence to his skepticism. The Delawares backed away from their offer to fight alongside the Patriots, and the United States broke its promise to send supplies and trading goods to the Delawares. And then there was the problem of frontier whites, who were less inclined than commissioners or congressmen to distinguish between "friendly" and "hostile" Indians. A grim procession of Indian allies was killed by frontier settlers in 1778, culminating in the murder of White Eyes himself in November—barely two months after he'd signed the treaty that promised an Indian state. George Washington and Congress still felt guilty a decade later, when they agreed to treat White Eyes's son as a ward of the United States.[5]

Should we dismiss the idea of an Indian state as a confidence trick by the US commissioners? Given the precedents of British Indian policy, and the eagerness of Congress to shore up its cause in the West, perhaps the possibility of statehood was not so far-fetched. Persuading Native Americans to enter the Union would present an elegant compromise between Indian rights and the geopolitical ambitions of the United States. Before the federal Constitution of 1787, many Americans viewed the individual states as sovereign nations and the United States as a confederacy rather than a unitary state. If the Delawares could be persuaded to join this confederacy, they would be safely aligned with the United States against the continuing lure of British or Spanish influence. One obvious weakness of the proposal was its assumption that White Eyes could control all of the Indians within the proposed state. Another was that Congress could do the same with the white settlers flooding into the West.[6]

The murder of White Eyes in 1778 was only one of a series of episodes that destroyed goodwill between the United States and the Delawares. The most striking of them came in March 1782, when a group of Delawares in Ohio were attacked by a company of Pennsylvania militiamen. At this late stage of the war, some Delawares had joined with the British and their Indian allies, engaging in sporadic but brutal fighting with white settlers on the border of Pennsylvania and the Ohio country. Others, however, were living in the Pennsylvania mission towns of Gnadenhütten and Salem under the care of Moravian missionaries who had been working to convert them to Christianity. When a raiding party of militant Delawares and Wyandots attacked a white family near Fort Pitt, the Christian Indians were placed in an impossible position. The raiders stopped at Gnadenhütten on their way back to the West with their prisoner in tow—a white settler named Robert Wallace, whose wife and children they had killed. The terrified Christian Indians granted their request for food and shelter. The next night, Wallace escaped from his captors, returned to Fort Pitt, and told his neighbors that the Christian Indians had collaborated with the men who had murdered his family.[7]

Wallace gathered around 150 volunteers, returned to Gnadenhüt-ten, and rounded up the inhabitants. The white vigilantes took a vote and resolved to kill everyone. After a long night in which the Christian Indians—who had been informed of the result of the vote—sang hymns to ward off their terror, Wallace and his associates spent nearly two days bludgeoning and knifing an entire village to death. Even Wallace was forced to break away at one point, acknowledging that the killing hadn't lifted his mood or provided "satisfaction" for the loss of his family. But the slaughter continued, hour after hour—slow, messy, methodical, relentless. When everyone was dead, the volunteers traveled to nearby Salem and brought its inhabitants back to the charnel houses they had created in Gnadenhütten. The massacre ended only when the white settlers could find no one else to kill. Having stolen everything they could carry, the vigilantes returned to Fort Pitt, disarmed the US soldiers guarding the prison there, and murdered four more Indians.[8]

The Gnadenhütten massacre was the culmination of a grassroots hatred of Indians that had been gathering pace on the frontier since the 1750s, ominously shadowing the movement for independence from Britain. It was also a bleak illustration of the problem of sovereignty in the new United States. Back in 1763, when a similar massacre had taken place in central Pennsylvania, Benjamin Franklin had strongly criticized the white settlers responsible for the crime. In 1782, when Franklin received appalled letters from Moravians in Britain who had heard about the massacre, he was shabbily evasive. It was George III who deserved blame for what had happened; the king had started this terrible war and recruited Britain's Indian allies. "Even these horrid murders of our poor Moravians may be laid to his charge," Franklin complained. His Moravian friend James Hutton was repulsed by his logic, and by Franklin's cheap recycling of a newspaper rumor that Christian Indians had provoked the militiamen. It was the US government that should be protecting Indians, Hutton insisted; Franklin should remember that a policy grounded in revenge would serve the United States poorly in the years ahead. The United States now owned the problem of how to bring order and justice to the western interior. In this, American officials would find white settlers to be at least as much of an obstacle as the Native Americans who lived beyond the Appalachians.[9]

THE POSSIBILITY IN 1778 OF Indian representation in Congress was an isolated episode, but not a unique one. In 1785, the Confederation Congress had sent Benjamin Hawkins and three other commissioners to negotiate with the Cherokees in South Carolina. The resulting Treaty of Hopewell confirmed the cession of Cherokee land to the new United States. But also, it marked out permanent boundaries of Cherokee sovereignty in the Southeast, promised that renegade white settlers would be removed by the US government, and gave Cherokees "the right to send a deputy of their choice, whenever they think fit, to Congress." The Cherokees placed themselves "under the protection of the United States" and allowed US officials to regulate their trade with the outside world.[10]

At the Treaty of Holston in 1791, another land cession was agreed. American negotiators referred to "the Cherokee nation" as the contracting party: a term that seemed to imply that the Cherokees were fully sovereign, despite the language of the 1785 treaty. Between Hopewell and Holston, the Cherokees had not taken up the right to send a deputy to the US Congress. Instead, their delegations appeared in the nation's capital with the prerogatives of foreign dignitaries. But the adoption of the Northwest Ordinance in 1787 and the ratification of the Constitution in 1788 complicated the question of sovereignty. The United States now had a strong central government and a clear framework for expansion. The Native peoples of the Ohio region might still hold back the march of new states into the West, but Cherokee country, along with much of the territory of the other southeastern Indian nations, was located within the boundaries of existing states. Cherokee leaders were reluctant to accept the logic of white encirclement. In future years they would invoke the Treaty of Hopewell for its border guarantees and its promise of a Cherokee voice in the US Congress. But as settlers crowded toward the Cherokee lands in North Carolina, Georgia, Tennessee, and later, Alabama, the predicament of these Indians—a nation within a nation—became clear.[11]

Even in 1778, it might already have been impossible for Congress to honor its promise of statehood to the Delawares. The determination of white settlers to encroach on Indian land, regardless of the actions of the national government, helps us to see why federal officials in the 1790s became so wedded to the theory that proximity between whites and Indians would produce "one nation only." If the theory was wrong, what was the alternative? George Washington thought that only a "Chinese Wall" would keep white settlers from Indian lands; Henry Knox fretted that the settlers might burden the United States with its own "black legend" for future historians to decry. In the 1790s, federal officials pressed on with the logic of "civilization-by-proximity," despite abundant evidence that the plan would not work. But while Knox and his colleagues struggled to imagine an alternative, thousands of Native Americans forged their own: they headed west, into the interior of the continent.

Westward migration had been an Indian survival strategy since the earliest phase of white settlement in North America. In the 1790s, even as Little Turtle and Blue Jacket attempted to unite the indigenous peoples of the Northwest against the United States, hundreds of Delawares and Shawnees chose to flee the region and create new lives for themselves in the Louisiana country west of the Mississippi River, which was then controlled by Spain. For federal officials, this migration had an upside and a downside. That Indians were willing to relocate meant fewer obstacles to US expansion, but also offered dangerous new allies to the British or Spanish in the distant interior. And it was proof that the "civilizing" plan was not working. Thomas Jefferson, in a letter to William Henry Harrison in February 1803, presented Indian removal in punitive terms: the United States would "crush" Native Americans who chose the hatchet instead of the hoe by "driving them across the Mississippi." This would not only promote white America's "final consolidation" of the eastern half of the continent, but also serve as "an example to others" that the United States meant to civilize the region, with or without its original inhabitants.[12]

When it became clear in the spring of 1803 that the French (the new owners of Louisiana) were willing to sell the entire territory to the United States, Jefferson's view of western resettlement shifted. Writing to the Revolutionary general Horatio Gates just a few days after the Louisiana Purchase treaty arrived in Washington, he presented Indian removal as a policy imperative rather than a last resort. Louisiana under US control would be "the means of tempting all our Indians on the East side of the Mississippi to remove to the West, and of condensing instead of scattering our population." Jefferson knew that New Orleans and the Mississippi were the immediate prize: they would enable farmers west of the Appalachians to get their goods to market. "The rest of the territory will probably be locked up from American settlement, and under the self-government of the native occupants." Jefferson appeared to be offering the interior of the continent to Native Americans in return for the extension of US rule across the entire continent east of the Mississippi River.[13]

The following month, Jefferson tweaked the plan in a letter to his friend John Breckinridge, a US senator from Kentucky who had been tasked with steering the Purchase legislation through the Senate. "The best use we can make of the [Louisiana] country for some time," Jefferson wrote, "will be to give establishments in it to the Indians on the east side of the Mississippi, in exchange for their present country." He even flirted with the idea of swapping the small French and Spanish population in what is now Missouri with eastern Indians, confirming the Mississippi as a clear border between the United States and Native territory. The Purchase would enable the federal government to oversee an orderly expansion: white people would fill up the lands to the east of the Mississippi, and the government would discourage wildcat settlements on the west bank of the river. The dividing line was not to be permanent, however. "When we shall be full on this side," Jefferson told Breckinridge, "we may lay off a range of states on the western bank from the head to the mouth." The president conceded that many decades would elapse, perhaps even a century, before whites and Indians found themselves competing for the prairies, mountains, and deserts beyond the Mississippi. But in this second letter, Jefferson had already sketched a blueprint for continental mastery.[14]

In its first quarter-century of existence, the US government had presented three methods for bringing Native Americans east of the Mississippi under its control. The first was brief and abortive: the offer of statehood or congressional representation that it dangled before the Delawares and Cherokees. The second was the civilization program outlined by Henry Knox and Timothy Pickering, which insisted that Indians and white settlers could become one people within the framework of new western states. The third entailed the relocation of eastern Indians to the lands beyond the Mississippi. This option was initially viewed by Thomas Jefferson as a punishment for Indians' failure to "civilize." After 1803, it evolved in Jefferson's mind into something else. The president began to think that the attractions of Louisiana—boundless land and indefinite relief from white encroachment—would persuade embattled Native Americans to abandon their ancestral homelands willingly, even happily. They wouldn't be coerced into leaving, Jefferson assured himself. Instead, the eastern Indians would be offered a choice.

THE GUINEA PIGS FOR JEFFERSON'S new policy were the Cherokees, arguably the most powerful of the southeastern Indian nations. Under the pressures of white settlement and internal disputes, small numbers of Cherokees had been relocating since the 1780s to what is now Arkansas. More than 5,000 would make the trip before 1820, although the vast majority of the Cherokee population remained in the East. Those who went west found a new set of problems in Arkansas, where the local Osage Indians were far from pleased to see them. In the East, meanwhile, the Cherokee Nation was divided between the Upper Towns, which were interested in accepting elements of the "civilizing" program and staying in the East, and the Lower Towns, which were more committed to their traditional way of life—and curious about resettlement in Arkansas. This geographical division was accompanied by a generational one: younger Cherokees through-out the nation felt that their elders were too ready to cut deals with the US government.[15]

In a message to the Cherokees in January 1806, Jefferson announced that the United States now controlled the entire Louisi-ana region and would be happy to resettle any Cherokees who pre-ferred to live there. Two years later, with the Cherokees more divided than ever about their future, Jefferson was more specific. If the Upper and Lower Towns couldn't resolve their differences, he would approve a territorial division between them. The Lower Cherokees could "choose to continue the hunter's life" and "settle on our lands beyond the Mississippi where some Cherokees are already settled." The Upper Cherokees could remain in the East, "be placed under the government of the U.S., become citizens thereof, and be ruled by our laws." Very soon, they would "be our brothers, instead of our children." Jefferson's munificence was hedged with warnings about the awesome respon-sibilities of U.S. citizenship. Cherokees who chose to remain would have to prove their commitment to agriculture and trade, and per-suade their women to spin cloth rather than plant crops. "All this is necessary," he concluded, "before our laws can suit you or be any use to you." But if the residents of the Upper Towns followed the plan, they would "become truly one people with us."[16]

The irony of the president's promise of citizenship for Indians who remained in the East was that the Cherokees' chief tormentors in Ten-nessee and Georgia formed his political base. Jefferson's Democratic-Republican Party was championed by southern and western voters with little patience for the "civilizing" theories that had been pio-neered by the Federalists in the 1790s. The problem of squaring Jef-ferson's citizenship offer with the political realities of the Southeast fell to Return J. Meigs, the US agent to the Cherokees who would later defend William Crawford's intermarriage plan in 1816. Meigs ran the Cherokee Agency in Tennessee from 1801 until his death in 1823. Like Jefferson, he was sentimental about the achievements of white settlers, and he lacked some of the eastern hauteur of Henry Knox or Timothy Pickering. When he was required to curb squatters and other white trespassers on Indian land—as in 1809, when he summoned federal troops to remove nearly 2,000 illegal settlers from Cherokee country—he did so with a heavy heart. "These people bear the appellation of intruders," he wrote to a friend in Tennessee, "but they are Americans. Our riches and strength are derived from our citizens, [and] in our new country every man is an acquisition." White migration was the bane of Meigs's working life, but he absolved individuals from blame. The "disposition to migrate" was like "the laws of gravitation." Nothing would contain it, "until the shores of the Pacific Ocean make it impossible to go farther."[17]

Initially, Meigs took the same line as Jefferson on the future of Native Americans. "You see now," he told the Cherokees in 1808, "that you have your choice to stay here and become industrious like white people . . . or go over the Mississippi where meat is plenty and where corn may be raised as well as here." But in his conversations with Cherokee chiefs, Meigs began to wonder if this decision should be left to individuals. Wouldn't the entire Cherokee Nation benefit from the new surroundings of Arkansas, "a situation where all may have objects of pursuit agreeable to them"? Cherokees who chose farming and "domestic manufactures" would be able to continue their journey toward civilization in the West; those who preferred traditional pursuits would be able to preserve their old habits unmolested by settlers. For both groups, "protection and the fostering hand of Government will go along with you." Meigs was vague about the exact nature of the federal government's support in the West, though he promised to provide "a rallying point and a common center for cementing and perpetuating our friendship." With so much land on the other side of the Mississippi, Meigs concluded, there was room enough for both visions of the Cherokee future.[18]

Cynics might supply a simple explanation for Meigs's conversion: he recognized the value of the Cherokees' eastern land. Despite his campaigns against squatters, Meigs counted state politicians, businessmen, and land speculators in Georgia and Tennessee among his friends. In the summer of 1808, he told Secretary of War Henry Dearborn that the United States would likely make a fortune from the sale of vacated lands. But Meigs had other motives for recommending migration. He worried that the current Cherokee country in the Southeast was too vast to force the majority of the nation onto the path of "civilization." (He told officials in Washington that, whatever the availability of land west of the Mississippi, the Cherokees should be given only half the area they had held in the East, to deter them from hunting.) And he had a strong—we might say paradoxical—commitment to the idea of the Cherokees as "a distinct people." The "civilizing" policy envisaged Indians discarding their tribal identities and embracing US citizenship. (This was long before the rise of the hyphenated American.) But Meigs had won influence with the Cherokees by telling them that they were more advanced in farming, manufacturing, and even the "knowledge of literature" than "all the red men of America put together." In the debate over westward migration, he tugged at their national pride: "To preserve your nation from being lost," he told the Cherokees in August 1808, "you must not let your people straggle one or two at a time." Small bands of migrants would not do; they would have to "go in large parties" or risk losing their considerable achievements. While federal officials had previously promised to make Indians indistinguishable from whites, Meigs positioned "civilization" as the hallmark of Cherokee identity.[19]

In his new commitment to a western home for the entire Cherokee Nation, Meigs supplied state officials in Tennessee and Georgia with something they had always lacked: a liberal argument for Indian removal. Since the 1780s, federal officials had clashed with the state governments in the Southeast over their inability or unwillingness to police white settlement. Meigs hadn't changed his views on the iniquity of illegal settlers—"intelligent and mischievously cunning people who still keep alive ancient prejudices," as he called them in 1809—but he no longer believed the Cherokees should remain on the lands that those settlers coveted. Two factors checked the momentum of Meigs's resettlement scheme. The Upper and Lower Towns repaired their differences in 1809 at a national council and rejected the government's migration offer. When eight hundred dissident Cherokees agreed to move to Arkansas in 1810, the national council refused to sanction the sale of their land to the United States. Meanwhile, the growth of the pan-Indian movement, led by Tenskwatawa and Tecumseh, made federal officials wary of pushing too hard on the issue of resettlement. By 1811, with the Cherokees united against migration, and open warfare taking place between whites and Indians in the Northwest, the prospect of removal had receded from view.[20]

Meigs continued to pressure his superiors in Washington, grounding the case for Cherokee migration in their innate equality with whites. "I am sensible that there are strong prejudices against them," he wrote Secretary of War William Eustis in 1811, but this was no reason to doubt their potential. "It is my opinion that their bodily and mental powers are by no means inferior to those of the white people." The Cherokees were like an orphaned baby left at the doorstep of a wealthy family. If the United States chose to neglect them, they would surely perish; if it took a proactive approach to helping them—by resettling them in Arkansas, say—they would rise to adulthood and "one day help to defend the house." Meigs conceded that the Cherokees had refused to leave. "They have now some, though erroneous, ideas of their distinct sovereignty and independence," he told Eustis. These would become only more dangerous if the Cherokees became a people not of 15,000 (as Meigs estimated them to be in 1810), but twenty times that number. The southeastern states and the federal government would be haunted by the problem of "a government within a government" if the Cherokees weren't quickly resettled.[21]

Jefferson and other federal officials had originally treated the far West as a place of sanctuary from the reforming zeal of the United States. With this in view, Meigs conceded that "placing the people over the Mississippi would seem to be a dereliction of civilization of the Cherokees." On closer inspection, he had determined that this was not the case. He told Secretary Eustis that he had recently met with one of the western Cherokees, who had reported that even those Indians who had crossed the Mississippi to protect their traditions had succumbed to the logic of "civilization" in the West. Instead of shielding Indians, migration might very well accelerate the "civilizing" process. This left the intractable problem of the Cherokee national council and its refusal to approve removal, even if the plan would "perpetuate or at least lengthen out their national existence." Their obstinacy was a consequence of their geographical situation, thought Meigs. The Cherokees couldn't be expected to make nimble choices about the future while gorging on their vast landholdings in the East. Their consent would, of course, be preferable. But if they failed to agree to an exchange of their eastern land for a new western home, they should not "have the right to put their veto on any measure deliberately determined and decreed by the Government." Was Meigs ready to pursue this logic to its end? "In my opinion it would be charity in the government to compel them to make an exchange if it cannot be effected otherwise," he wrote. Before sending the letter, he read the words over and crossed them out.[22]

JAMES MADISON'S INSISTENCE THAT MEIGS drop the removal issue paid dividends during the War of 1812. Cherokee leaders declined the overtures of Tecumseh, unlike the Red Sticks, their Creek neighbors. At the Battle of Horseshoe Bend in March 1814, which subdued the Creek insurgency against the United States, the Cherokees fought alongside Andrew Jackson, their future tormentor. The defeat of the Creeks in the South, and of the pan-Indian forces of Tecumseh in the Northwest, coincided with Britain's decision to give up its long struggle for influence in the Mississippi Valley. British ambitions in this regard had survived the American Revolution, Jay's Treaty of 1794, and even the Louisiana Purchase; but not the comprehensive defeats of the War of 1812. Britain's departure removed the last European ally of Native peoples hoping to resist the expansion of the United States.[23]

The British peace negotiators who met with American officials in the Belgian city of Ghent in the summer of 1814 knew that Britain's alliance with Native Americans had been a primary cause of the war. Under orders from foreign secretary Lord Castlereagh, however, they were instructed to reach a compromise on the Indians' long-term future. An "adequate arrangement" of Native concerns was a *"sine qua non* of peace" for the British government, and Britain thought that even the United States would benefit from an alternative to the "regular and progressive system of encroachment" by white settlers onto Indian land. At Ghent, the negotiators unveiled their proposal: the United States should withdraw to the boundaries fixed by the Treaty of Greenville in 1795, leaving the territory between that line and Canada—northwestern Ohio, Indiana, Michigan, and Illinois—"as a useful barrier between both states." The US commissioners were so incensed that they walked away from negotiations for three months. The British enjoyed the satisfaction of burning the White House that August, but lost key battles at Baltimore and Lake Champlain. Castlereagh tried and failed to persuade the Duke of Wellington to cross the Atlantic and rescue the war effort; Britain drifted toward defeat. When peace negotiations resumed in December, the buffer-state proposal was dead. The British commissioners inserted weak clauses on Indian land rights in the eventual treaty, which the United States ignored. By 1815, the entire area south of the Great Lakes was under the jurisdiction of the US government.[24]

In the United States, one of the effects of the War of 1812 was to recast the Indian question as a matter of charity rather than statecraft. The strategic isolation of Native people prompted newspapers, reformers, and politicians to reevaluate the nation's responsibilities. "Now that tranquility reigns in our borders," wrote the leading newspaper of Washington, DC, in 1817, "it is not amongst the least pleasing events that are happening, to witness the sympathy which is excited towards the INDIANS of our country." The paper insisted that "the day must at last come, when our Indians will form a portion of our great 'American family of Freemen,' participating in the enjoyment of rights, civil and religious, analogous to ours." But the postwar conversation about Indian policy included a bleaker set of arguments that were grounded in the protracted failure to secure Jefferson's dream of "one people only." One missionary suggested that, since the progress of the gospel had been scant among Native Americans, God might have intended "that they should become extinct, and their places supplied by Christianized inhabitants." A Philadelphia newspaper in 1818 noted that more than twenty years of "civilizing" efforts had proven "abortive." With this in view, how could one not conclude that "extinction is the inevitable fate of this race of man?"[25]

The debate over the future of Native Americans after 1815 shuttled between enthusiasm and despair, between a wild optimism about the civilizational potential of Indians and a maudlin suspicion that genocide was providentially decreed. Largely missing from this debate was an appreciation of the very different struggles facing Native people in different regions of North America. In the Old Northwest, Tecumseh's defeat had destroyed Native hopes of undoing William Henry Harrison's land grab. White settlers rushed into the region at an unprecedented rate, and Native societies were subjected to impossible pressures. In the Southeast, on the other hand, the progress of "civilization" among the Cherokees and the Creeks—and the willingness of the former and a portion of the latter to side with the United States in the War of 1812—had spared Indians the sweeping devastation visited on the Native worlds of the Northwest. For the southeastern Indians, the immediate challenge was to ward off the land hunger of hostile state governments, a predicament that worsened as Mississippi (1817) and Alabama (1819) achieved statehood. The cotton industry drove the incorporation of these areas. Squatters saw an opportunity to obtain a foothold in the cotton business by claiming Indian land. Larger landholders pressured state legislators to obtain sweeping cessions for their lucrative operations.[26]

In the years before the War of 1812, Return Meigs had lost faith in the logic of civilization-through-proximity. He imagined the West as a place in which the "civilizing" process could advance without the interference of state governments. During the controversy over William Crawford's intermarriage proposal in 1816, the secretary of war had more faith than Meigs in the Cherokees' eastern prospects. If the Cherokees remained in Georgia, Tennessee, and Alabama, Crawford told Meigs, they would be "fitted for the honourable character of citizens of the United States." Both men believed that Native Americans might form an integral part of the American nation, though they disagreed on how this might be achieved. Crawford pulled rank, ordering Meigs to police existing treaties and to protect the Cherokees from settler encroachment. Meigs dutifully followed Crawford's directions, sending polite circulars to white "intruders on the Cherokee lands" across four states in the Southeast. (Meigs told them that he hoped they would leave Indian territory "without putting the government to the expense of sending military force.") Meigs followed his orders from Washington, but he wasn't convinced by them. He continued to believe that the federal government lacked the resources to prevent the slow erosion of Indian sovereignty in the East.[27]

Then there was the question of citizenship. Like free blacks, Native Americans in the early United States relied on state governments to determine who counted as a citizen. Given the prevailing attitudes of southern state officials, in particular, this was not a reassuring prospect. The governor of Tennessee, Joseph McMinn, told William Crawford in October 1816 that any Cherokee who remained in his state would be entitled "to all the rights of a free citizen of color of the United States." This would oblige Indians to pay taxes without gaining the right to vote—hardly the equal citizenship that Crawford had mooted. In 1824, the governor of Georgia told John Calhoun, Crawford's successor in the War Department, that eastern Indians should occupy "a middle station between the negro and the white man." Missionaries in the Southeast reported that even white people who had intermarried with Cherokees feared they would "not be admitted to the rights of freemen" if the states extended their sovereignty over Indian country. If Crawford was sincere about citizenship in the East, how could he compel southern state governments to honor his promise?[28]

Given the unappealing nature of the choice before them—abandonment of their homelands or second-class citizenship—the Cherokees devised a third option: they would remain in place, continue to embrace the "civilizing" program, but establish themselves as "a free and distinct nation" within the borders of the existing states. This resolve created apoplexy in Washington and in the state capitals of the Southeast. Return Meigs tried to talk them out of it. Whites were sure to encroach on their land, he warned Indian leaders; better to "save your national existence" by fleeing to the West. Privately, Meigs was furious with his charges. What did they think they were doing with "erroneous ideas of their sovereignty and independence?" To recognize Indian nations within the existing states of the Union would be to create "a monster in our politics." Meigs looked back to the Treaty of Hopewell in search of a solution. In 1785, the Cherokees had purchased protection from the United States at the price of sovereignty. "Their political state in relation to the United States is that of minors," Meigs assured himself. Didn't this give US officials the right to determine what was best for the Indians? John Calhoun reassured Congress that he would never allow "small bodies, with savage customs and character . . . to exist in an independent condition in the midst of civilized society." Meigs told himself that he could best defend the Indians' natural rights by ignoring their wishes. He suppressed the upsetting thought that the Cherokees "refuse to be saved by us."[29]

From 1817 to 1819, Meigs and his superiors in Washington pushed hard for a plan that would force the hand of the Cherokees. US officials asked them to register for individual tracts of land, known as "reserves," which would be theirs to farm when the authority of the southeastern states was extended over Indian areas. Any Cherokees who declined to register were expected to move to the West. While federal negotiators laid the groundwork for the division of Indian land, and the absorption of Cherokee country into the existing states, Calhoun and Tennessee governor McMinn hinted that Indians could best complete the "civilizing" process through removal. Calhoun was critical of the Cherokees' "high tone" in declaring their independence in the East; in the West, however, he promised that "the Cherokee nation will obtain time, before they can be crowded by the whites, to become civilized, and capable of enjoying the advantage of equal laws." Calhoun and McMinn were not subtle in outlining the alternative. If the "protecting arm of the United States" were withdrawn from the Southeast, the Cherokees' existing progress would be drowned in a flood of "fraud and violence."[30]

The eastern Cherokees numbered around 12,000 in 1817, and only a few hundred agreed to take reserves under the government's plan. The rest waited to see if Monroe and Calhoun would substantiate their threats. A confrontation was averted by the economic collapse of 1819. Federal officials had estimated the cost of purchasing the entire Cherokee territory in the Southeast—14 million acres—at around $300,000. This was a steal, in terms of the eventual value of the land, but more than Congress could afford in the midst of a recession. Instead, the Cherokees reluctantly agreed to sell around 4 million acres, extinguishing their claims to land in North Carolina and Tennessee. They had come under huge pressure from Georgia to yield the heartlands of their nation, but held out regardless. Their persistence preserved many of the areas in which Cherokee "civilizing" had been most pronounced, and enraged state officials in Milledgeville who had expected to be permanently rid of the Cherokees.[31]

Nearly 1,000 Cherokees moved from the ceded areas into the main towns in Georgia, bolstering the "civilizing" heartland of the nation. Cherokee leaders lamented the loss of so much land, but they thought their cessions to the southeastern states had produced a final settlement and a permanent border. Within the new bounds of their country, the Cherokees accelerated their "civilizing" program. Over the next decade, they centralized their political structures, drafted a constitution, built churches and meetinghouses, and founded a newspaper. The national council declined to support private land-holding, the acme of the federal "civilizing" program, since its members thought they could best defend their sovereignty collectively. In other ways, the Cherokees built a society that blended the realities of the southern economy and the mores of the northern missionaries who lived among them. Cherokees owned slaves and farmed cotton; they formed temperance groups and supported liberal causes (even black colonization). Against the unpalatable options presented by federal and state officials, the Cherokees were determined to prove that another way was possible.[32]

FROM THOMAS JEFFERSON TO JAMES MONROE, American presidents offered Native peoples a choice about where and how they might ultimately live. The choice initially seemed simple: Indians could embrace "civilization" and stay put, or they could pursue their traditions indefinitely on the western side of the Mississippi. The protracted standoff between southeastern Indians and state governments, and the Indian uprising that underpinned the War of 1812, put an end to this rhetoric. When the Cherokees forged their own version of "civilization," but declined to settle for second-class citizenship, Return Meigs recast the options: Indians could stay in the East and face being overrun by white people, or move west and consolidate their "civilizing" experiment. With newspapers speculating that Native Americans might vanish entirely, this ultimatum had a bleak undertone: Indians would have to choose between survival in the West and extinction in the East.

Meigs continued to pressure the Cherokees to negotiate land cessions with US commissioners. In the final months of 1822, as he approached his eighty-second birthday, he received a definitive answer. Cherokee leaders told him that they were "determinedly opposed to disposing of one foot of land and therefore have determined not to meet any commissioners on the subject." Meigs was appalled. The rebuff was "little short of a declaration of independence," he told John Calhoun. The secretary of war resolved to send negotiators regardless. By the time Calhoun's delegation arrived in Cherokee country, Meigs had contracted pneumonia, after giving up his tent to a visiting Indian chief and sleeping in the winter air. Meigs died in January 1823. He had been with the Cherokees for more than two decades, and had spent most of that time trying to persuade them to acknowledge the choice he had set before them. In making sense of their refusal to do so, he decided that Indians might not be the best judges of their own welfare and potential. If the US government knew better, would it need to secure their consent for its actions? Did the Cherokees have a choice after all? In the years after Meigs's death, these questions were resolved with surprising haste.[33]

TEN

OPENING THE ROAD

BY THE EARLY 1800S, LIBERAL reformers in the North and the Upper South had identified two rationales for black colonization. It would persuade slaveholders to part with their slaves, and it would enable free blacks to fulfill their potential without the deadening effects of white prejudice. The alternative to colonization—an integrated, race-blind society under the rubric of "all men are created equal"—required a societal commitment to black uplift, including a well-resourced effort to undo the damage done to black people by slavery. It might also require the amalgamation of the races. Since even the most ardent opponents of slavery recoiled from amalgamation, the prospect of this integrated society seemed remote. Morality, justice, and the long-term security of the United States demanded that slavery be abolished, yet the mechanisms for establishing equality between freed people and whites were wholly inadequate. Facing the challenge both of educating and supporting black people after slavery, and subverting the supposedly intractable prejudices of poorer whites, liberal reformers saw colonization as the *deus ex machina* of the antislavery cause.

The curious logic of colonization—that racial separation might vindicate racial equality—forced the proponents of black removal into awkward juxtapositions. The Dartmouth College lecturer Moses Fiske, in an oration delivered in 1795, urged his compatriots to heed the contradiction between their founding ideals and the persistence of slavery. Americans were "tyrannical libertymen," he insisted. "We cannot continue to hold them in bondage, without doing violence to our consciences; nor can we free them without extraordinary measures." The solution was to create "a large province of black freemen" in the West, in which former slaves would be "prepared for citizenship" and "formed into a state." Separation would "bring them to an equal standing in point of privileges with whites." The Philadelphia Quaker John Parrish agreed. Black people had the potential to become "as useful members of the community as those of a different complexion," he argued in 1806. As a supporter of the Pennsylvania Abolition Society, Parrish was closely involved in Philadelphia's uplift efforts. But he feared that the "distinction of color" would militate against an integrated society. Better, then, for Congress to "assign a tract within some part of the western wilderness," and for slaveholders to release their slaves "on condition of their so removing" there. Parrish, like Fiske, offered "liberty and the rights of citizenship" in the West. To slaveholders and whites more generally, he promised a form of abolition that would "preserve the distinction of nation and color."[1]

Colonization was the inevitable destination of Thomas Branagan's tortured antislavery journey. Having decided in 1805 that the South was corrupting the North with free blacks, Branagan thought a western colony—at least 2,000 miles from Philadelphia—would reconcile "the rights of man" with his multiplying hang-ups about integration. Removed to the distant interior, blacks would become "free and independent citizens of America, in a separate state of their own." Presenting the new state as a way to realize the good intentions of "benevolent slaveholders," Branagan contrasted the experiences of black people in eastern cities with the boundless opportunities of the West. "The citizens of the new state," he promised, "instead of picking bones in gentlemen's kitchens, would imbibe a noble spirit, learn a habit of managing business . . . and feel an ambition to be versed in politics." The same logic tempted even those reformers who hoped to overcome degradation without separation. Noah Webster, whose preference was

for slaveholders to educate and uplift their slaves, presented colonization as a fallback plan. "The project of exporting all the blacks in the
United States," he observed in 1793, "would, if practicable, be attended
with many desirable effects." But the logistical challenges of sending
black people overseas were enormous, and it would mean the loss of
their labor to the national economy. Webster wondered if they could
be freed and given "a portion of land in the United States" instead.[2]

David Rice, who led the effort to ban slavery from Kentucky in
1791, had been willing to accept even the amalgamation of the races
as the price of securing a general emancipation. Three years later, he
told a friend in Philadelphia that most Kentuckians were in favor of
gradual abolition. The problem was that the richest residents in the
state had the most to gain from expanding slavery, and "the rich make
the laws." Many people who claimed to oppose slavery cited the "difficulties attending the emancipation of slaves" to explain their inaction.
Rice suggested a way to break the impasse: perhaps abolitionists could
lobby Congress "to lay off a state in the western lands for the use of the
blacks, and make provision for their government, protection, instruction, etc." After years of encouraging emancipation in situ, even Rice
concluded that a black colony might supply "something to awaken the
conscience"—the catalyst that would turn liberal sentiments into antislavery actions.

These early proponents of colonization imagined a central role
for the federal government in arranging black removal. John Parrish
and Thomas Branagan, writing after the completion of the Louisiana
Purchase, thought that the new lands west of the Mississippi provided a perfect location. Parrish reminded his readers that the federal
government had recently paid ransoms to Barbary pirates who captured American sailors in North Africa. By the same logic, the government could use public money to create a black colony to the west
of the United States. Both St. George Tucker and Ferdinando Fairfax
published their colonization proposals in Philadelphia rather than
Virginia, to draw the eye of national legislators. Although reformers acknowledged that emancipation would depend on the consent

of slaveholders, they looked to the federal government to supply the resources and leadership that would make colonization a realistic option.[3]

When the federal government moved to its permanent home on the Potomac in 1800, colonization proponents followed southward. Samuel Harrison Smith, a newspaper editor from Philadelphia, moved his paper and printing business to Washington in December 1801. An avid supporter of Jefferson, he was rewarded with a series of federal printing contracts. His *National Intelligencer* became the most important and influential newspaper in the United States. Along with his wife, Margaret Bayard Smith, he was a fixture of the capital's emerging social scene. He was also a firm opponent of slavery. In 1805, he published a series of essays entitled "Thoughts on the True Path to National Glory." Cataloging the nation's strengths and weaknesses, Smith identified slavery as "unquestionably the greatest misfortune by which we are beset." He took heart from the fact that so many slaveholders were keen to "diminish this evil," and suggested that the federal government inaugurate a giant public works program in which slaves built the roads and canals that the new nation desperately needed. These improvements would be so valuable to the nation that the federal government could afford to free the slaves and compensate their owners for the loss. With the public works complete, and the slave owners happily recompensed, the liberated slaves could be "planted in a colony . . . under the immediate protection of the United States."[4]

Smith took the outline of this plan from another Philadelphia resident who followed the government to Washington. William Thornton, the pioneer of black resettlement, moved to the Federal City in 1794 (when it was still a swamp) to oversee the construction of his design for the capitol building. In 1802, in search of another challenge, he took charge of the new US Patent Office—a post he held until his death in 1827. The Thorntons and the Smiths became prominent socialites throughout the Jefferson and Madison administrations. Thornton's interest in colonization was undiminished. In 1802, he tried to persuade Jefferson to buy Puerto Rico from Spain, and to make the island a refuge in which black people "might enjoy the rights and privileges of free men." Napoleon's unexpected offer of Louisiana the following year sent Jefferson in a different direction, but Thornton persisted. In 1804, he outlined the scheme that Smith would rework the following year. "The rights of humanity" demanded the abolition of slavery, but the social consequences of emancipation were hard to predict. White people "might occasionally forget" that they could no longer dictate terms to blacks. "Animosity might ensue, and hatred succeed." Better for everyone that the destiny of freed people be worked out in the far West.[5]

As for the people who already lived in that region, Thornton was typically upbeat. "The Indians are said to have an antipathy to the blacks," but this was entirely circumstantial: Native Americans could never admire a people who seemed so thoroughly subdued by the whites. When blacks were restored to freedom, however, Indians would respect their neighbors and even seek to emulate their example. "The Indians themselves require protection," thought Thornton; perhaps the federal government might undertake multiple experiments in nation building beyond the Mississippi. "What a consoling reflection would it be," he concluded, "that a free and virtuous government, had placed under the wings of the American Eagle nations of white, red and black men—all in peace, all in fraternity, all in happiness." The diverse peoples of North America could come together, thought Thornton, if they would consent to live apart.[6]

WHILE THORNTON AND SMITH FLOATED their proposals for racial separation, the first serious attempt to involve the federal government in colonization was already underway. Even though Gabriel's Rebellion had been thwarted in August 1800, it shattered the nerves of Virginia's slaveholding class. Dozens of black people were arrested and condemned to death. In October, Gabriel himself was hanged along with six supposed ringleaders. But Virginia's governor, James Monroe, thought that executing dozens of black men "less criminal in comparison" to the ringleaders would do nothing to defuse tensions in the state. He knew that the conspirators had styled themselves on Washington and Lafayette, and he was haunted by the thought that he might now be on the wrong side of history. "We have had much trouble with the negroes here," Monroe wrote his friend Thomas Jefferson. Would it now be prudent "to arrest the hand of the executioner?" Jefferson, who was then battling John Adams for the presidency, took the time to consider Monroe's dilemma carefully. Clemency seemed a noble and far-sighted gesture, but Jefferson doubted that pardoning the conspirators would eliminate their restiveness. "Is there no fort and garrison of the state or of the Union where they could be confined?" Jefferson wondered. Or perhaps the Virginia assembly could "pass a law for their exportation?"[7]

Monroe took this idea to the state legislature, which debated various proposals to contain the threat of another uprising. One would repeal the 1782 law that authorized private manumissions. This idea was rejected, suggesting that Virginia's planters weren't quite ready to abandon their antislavery pretensions. The assembly was friendlier to Monroe's proposal that the state sell the condemned conspirators through the Spanish slave markets of New Orleans, ensuring their disappearance from Virginia without the metronomic horror of the hangman's rope. But the assembly wanted more control over the removal process. Monroe was given authority to negotiate directly with the president of the United States to secure a new territory outside Virginia to which "persons obnoxious to the laws or dangerous to the peace of society may be removed."[8]

Why did Virginia's legislators want their own territory, when the Spanish solution seemed to provide indefinite release from rebellious slaves? The answer was revealed when Monroe finally managed to pitch the idea to the recently inaugurated president of the United States—Thomas Jefferson. Monroe noted proudly that "motives of humanity" had inspired the transportation plans; he asked his friend whether territory might be obtained in the West or on "a neighboring island" for resettling black Virginians. But Monroe wasn't only talking about thwarted conspirators. Weren't slaves more generally a threat to Virginia's survival? If statesmen in Richmond and Washington were to consider the issue "beyond the contracted scale of providing a mode of punishment for offenders," he suggested, "vast and interesting objects present themselves to view." Slavery was an "evil" entailed on the state by the British, and Virginians had inherited "the extreme difficulty of remedying it." Colonization might not only remove rebels but encourage a wider emancipation. Could the president supply "a tract of land in the Western territory of the United States for this purpose?"[9]

The arc of the antislavery debate in Virginia bent toward Monroe's thinking. St. George Tucker's 1796 colonization plan had been rejected by the state assembly, but in 1801 the legislature was willing to consider drastic measures. That same year, Tucker's cousin George produced his own proposal for colonization that closely tracked Monroe's ideas. George argued for a black colony on "the western side of the Mississippi" with inducements that would encourage slaveholders to manumit their slaves on condition that they be colonized. (He also expected free blacks to move to the colony "voluntarily," recycling his cousin's idea that "additional taxes and disabilities on them here" might focus their thinking.) But on receiving Monroe's letter, Jefferson fell silent. It was only when the governor reminded the president of the subject in November 1801 that he received a response.[10]

"I have not been unmindful of your letter," Jefferson insisted. In fact, he had been mulling the claims of five areas that might sustain Monroe's black colony. The lands north of the Ohio River were currently being auctioned off by the federal government; Virginia might buy tracts in that region, though it would force the question of whether the colony might eventually become "a part of our union." Canada or Louisiana seemed promising, but neither the British nor the Spanish were likely to sell territory for this purpose. Africa, meanwhile, should be regarded as "a last resort, if all others more desirable should fail us." The remaining possibility was Saint-Domingue, where the slave revolt against France would soon culminate in the independent nation of Haiti. Jefferson wrote admiringly of the leaders of the Haitian Revolution, noting that they had "organized themselves under regular laws and government." Better still, the rebel leader Toussaint L'Ouverture and his associates would have no qualms about welcoming the instigators of a slave revolt. They could hardly fail to see acts "deemed criminal by us" as "meritorious."[11]

Monroe again took Jefferson's ideas to the Virginia legislature—which was still keeping the whole affair under tight secrecy—and received approval for the "vast and interesting objects" he had discussed with the president. There would be two resettlement tracks: one for unruly slaves that led toward the Spanish markets of Louisiana, another for "such negroes or mulattoes as may be emancipated" that led toward a new black colony. The legislature and Monroe looked to Jefferson to take the lead: "The day is not distant when this subject must have a definitive regulation from the councils of the country," wrote the governor in February 1802. The seriousness with which the Virginia legislature had treated his vague proposals seems finally to have nudged the president into action. He raised the issue with Spanish, Dutch, and Portuguese diplomats, in case territory could be found for an African American colony in Louisiana, the Caribbean, or South America. He also asked the US ambassador to Britain, Rufus King, to sound out officials of the Sierra Leone Company about relocating black Virginians in West Africa.[12]

Jefferson's instructions to King were simple: inform the company directors that the United States wished to join forces with Britain in promoting black resettlement, since it would be better to have "one strong rather than two weak colonies." Strangely, though, Jefferson spliced together the two tracks that the Virginia legislature had kept separate. King was to ask the company directors to accept both manumitted slaves and "insurgent negroes." As James Monroe later observed, promising freedom in Sierra Leone to rebellious slaves in Virginia might not be the best way to deter another Gabriel. As for the British, Sierra Leone's "benevolent" sponsors had long blamed the colony's teething troubles on rebellious traits that had rubbed off on the black loyalists during their years in America. Jefferson's incongruous blend of meritorious freedmen and dangerous insurgents seemed like a hard sell. Perhaps the US ambassador saw the funny side of his orders. By the time King asked William Wilberforce for permission to send both groups to Sierra Leone, he had found a silver lining: "The former will include our most meritorious slaves, and the latter will not be the idle and vicious, as these would not possess sufficient influence of their associates to become leaders in schemes of insurrection." Company officials told King and his fellow US diplomats that they had had their fill of unruly Americans, and the plan went no further.[13]

James Monroe retired from the Virginia governor's mansion in the fall of 1802. For the previous two years, he and the state legislature had badgered Jefferson repeatedly to create a black colony. Monroe turned over the governor's chair to John Page, who had been one of Jefferson's best friends since childhood. If the president imagined that a new face in Richmond would mark the end of the state's colonization lobbying, he was soon disappointed. Page was another planter who felt the tug of conscience on the question of slavery. (It was Page who delivered the manuscript of St. George Tucker's *Dissertation on Slavery* to the antislavery printer Mathew Carey in Philadelphia.) He wrote to Jefferson in 1803 to ask for an update on colonization planning, and found his old friend in an upbeat mood. The final success of the Haitian Revolution seemed imminent, which might open one avenue for black resettlement. "The acquisition of Louisiana," Jefferson continued, "may also procure the opportunity desired." Whether west of the Mississippi or in the Caribbean, events "may open to the legislature of Virginia the reserve which their resolution contemplates."[14]

Page excitedly reported Jefferson's suggestions to his colleagues in Richmond, and on 25 January 1804, the assembly passed two resolutions, one public and one secret. The former praised Jefferson for his brilliant handling of the Louisiana negotiations. The secret resolution directed Page to secure a portion of this territory as "the desired asylum for the free negroes and mulattoes and such as may be hereafter emancipated." Page told Jefferson that the legislature would initially try to persuade Virginia's 19,000 free blacks to move to the colony, with state and federal officials inaugurating a fund to pay for "the purchase, removal and education of young slaves" who could follow those free black pioneers into the West. (Page thought that a "moderate" tax on slaves, and donations from "benevolent" northerners, would supply the needed funds.) To avoid any confusion, Page urged that "insurgent negroes" should be sent to Haiti, where their rebelliousness might find an appreciative audience. The western colony would be reserved for black people who had been "educated and trained up in principles and habits which might render them worthy of the freedom conferred on them." Page didn't go as far as northern colonization proponents in suggesting that a black settlement in North America might eventually become a state of the Union. But his careful shepherding of "uncorrupted" freed people into the American interior reflected his hope that colonization would produce a settled, successful, and friendly neighbor to the American republic.[15]

It was at this moment, with Page imagining a colony for free blacks and emancipated slaves to the west of the Mississippi, that Jefferson began to backpedal furiously. In a letter punctuated by staccato qualifications, he denied that he had the power "to propose any specific asylum for the persons who are the subjects of our correspondence." Haiti was still "too unsettled" for any serious overture from the United States. Sierra Leone was closed to black Americans. As for Louisiana, the option that Jefferson himself had proposed to Page a year earlier, the president could do nothing without consulting with the white inhabitants of the region (presumably the residents of New Orleans) and with Congress. Whether these parties would agree to the idea "is not within my competence to say." Page retreated to the Virginia legislature, which concluded that the president might not be the best midwife of its black colony. Lawmakers passed a resolution enjoining Virginia's representatives in the US Congress "to exert their best efforts for the purpose of obtaining from the general government a competent portion of territory in the country of Louisiana to be appropriated to the residence of such people of color as have been or shall be emancipated in Virginia." Jefferson withdrew from the process, and the executive office made no further commitments to black colonization for more than a decade.[16]

There are plenty of reasons why Jefferson might have gone cold on the Louisiana proposal. From the reports of Lewis and Clark, he knew that the trans-Mississippi West was hardly an empty canvas. He might have fretted about an alliance (or a war) between blacks and Indians, or about what might eventually happen when territorial expansion brought the United States face to face with the grandchildren of its black exiles. He may also have judged that the political risks of a federal colonization scheme—or even a public proposal—were too great, given the certain opposition of South Carolina and Georgia. Then there was the question of how a colonization proposal might have been received by the slaves themselves, especially in the shadow of the Haitian Revolution. The resolutions on this subject passed by the Virginia legislature from 1801 to 1805 remained a closely guarded secret within and beyond Virginia for more than a decade. In Virginia alone, there were more than 350,000 slaves in 1802—nearly 40 percent of the state's total population. Most colonization proponents expected resettlement to take place slowly, and deliver only the youngest slaves from bondage. How would older slaves take the news that freedom would be reserved for generations yet unborn? For the president to go public with a colonization scheme would run the same risks that Jefferson memorably captured in his most famous metaphor: white Americans had a wolf by the ears, and could "feel the danger of either holding or letting him loose."[17]

Whatever his reasons, Jefferson's refusal to found a black colony for Virginia encouraged planters in their inaction. Moses Fiske, the New Hampshire abolitionist, had argued for colonization in 1795 precisely because it would resolve the contradiction of antislavery slaveholders. If planters who styled themselves as liberal continued to hold slaves after the creation of a black colony, their moral agonies would be exposed as "specious," and reformers would know them for what they were: "tyrannical libertymen." Once the road toward a black colony had been opened, slaveholders would have no excuse for sustaining the contradiction between the nation's founding ideals and its unequal realities. Jefferson's public and private lives were defined by that contradiction, and he resisted calls throughout the final decades of his life to do more to promote the cause of emancipation. If there was an opportunity in 1804–1805 to launch an experiment in antislavery colonization, with the support of the state that contained more slaves than any other, Jefferson proved remarkably reluctant to grasp it. Perhaps this tells us something not only about the practical and political difficulties that lay in the way of implementing racial separation, but also about Jefferson's reluctance to give up the system that had underpinned his wealth, his social standing, and his most intimate relations.

The coda to this story was brief and bleak. Since Gabriel's Rebellion, conservatives in the Virginia assembly had been trying to revoke the 1782 manumission act and freeze the number of free blacks in the state. Governors Monroe and Page both hoped to defend and expand private manumissions by acquiring territory beyond Virginia: they were colonizationists without a colony, and desperate to acquire one. But with no progress in Washington on the state's repeated requests for territory in Louisiana or elsewhere, the legislators in Richmond finally ran out of patience. A plan to prohibit manumissions failed to pass in 1806, but the compromise bill that was enacted in its place had a similar effect. From now on, slaveholders would be prevented from freeing their slaves unless they could promise that, within a year of manumission, the freed person would leave the state of Virginia forever. Without a colony to satisfy this requirement, private manumissions slowed to a trickle. The result of Virginia's five-year pursuit of colonization was a law that tied emancipation to black resettlement, without the territory that would reveal "benevolent" slaveholders as sincere reformers or dissembling cynics. The slave population continued to grow, slaveholders' vaunted benevolence went untested, and Virginia sank further into the abyss.[18]

AFTER 1805, AS THE FEDERAL government drew closer to war with the northwestern Indians and with Britain, the cause of colonization was championed by private individuals. The most influential of these was a free black sea captain from Massachusetts named Paul Cuffe. Free blacks in New England had debated the merits of emigration from the United States since the early 1770s. In the 1790s, more than seventy black Philadelphians drafted a petition to Congress requesting a program of gradual emancipation and "an asylum . . . similar to the one prepared by the British in Sierra Leone." For Paul Cuffe, the idea of colonization took hold slowly. His father, Kofi, had been born in Ghana in the early eighteenth century and sold to a wealthy New England Quaker named Ebenezer Slocum. In the 1740s, Slocum freed Kofi and hired him to work as a caretaker on the Slocum family farms in the Elizabeth Islands (the small island chain that sits between Martha's Vineyard and Cape Cod). Kofi married a Wampanoag Indian woman called Ruth Moses, and the couple had ten children— including the one who would go by the name of Paul Cuffe. Kofi and Ruth became wealthy enough to buy a large farm back on the mainland in 1766, but the family felt the sting of prejudice from their white neighbors.[19]

Like James Forten in Philadelphia, the young Paul Cuffe took to sea during the American Revolution, running goods across the British blockade to relieve Quaker families on Martha's Vineyard and Nantucket. After 1783, Cuffe spent years in the whaling trade, and eventually he raised enough money to buy his own vessel. By 1796, he was sailing regularly to the heartlands of slavery, clutching his identity papers while keeping a sharp eye on commercial opportunity. Slaves working on the Virginia coast watched in amazement as Cuffe and his black crew slid past them. When his ship docked in Wilmington and Philadelphia, white reformers were just as impressed. At precisely the moment that Thomas Jefferson was turning his back on the prospect of a black colony in Louisiana, Paul Cuffe became acquainted with the reformers of the Pennsylvania Abolition Society and their international antislavery network.[20]

Paul Cuffe (1759–1817), free black sailor and crucial go-between for the emerging British and American colonization movements. Courtesy of the Library of Congress.

Cuffe almost certainly heard about Sierra Leone soon after its foundation in 1787, and he may have attended William Thornton's colonization meetings in the late 1780s. It was during Jefferson's second term in office, however, that Cuffe came to the attention of the men who had created Sierra Leone. In 1807, the colony was transferred to the direct control of the British government. The directors of the Sierra Leone Company founded a new organization, the African Institution, to promote the view that West Africa could satisfy Europe's addiction to tropical commodities without slavery. Pennsylvania Abolition Society president James Pemberton told William Wilberforce, Thomas Clarkson, and Granville Sharp about Cuffe's successful shipping business. This resulted in an invitation for Cuffe to visit Britain and Sierra Leone, with the hope that he might become a key figure in the creation of a successful African trade. While they had declined to accept Jefferson's "insurgent negroes," the institution's directors thought that Cuffe might recruit "some sober families of black people in America to settle among the Africans": in particular, free blacks from New England rather than slaves from Virginia. The arrival of these new colonists would have a salutary effect on indigenous Africans living on the fringes of Sierra Leone, whom the institution hoped to convert to Christianity and "civilization." (This scheme was "as nearly similar . . . to the civilization of the Indians on the borders of these American states as different circumstances admit," Pemberton told Cuffe.) After consulting with free black leaders and white reformers, and confirming the details with the governor of Sierra Leone, Paul Cuffe embarked from Philadelphia in December 1810 for his first visit to the Province of Freedom.[21]

Cuffe spent more than two months in Sierra Leone, long enough to take stock of the colony's many problems. Cuffe convinced himself regardless that at least some black Americans should "find their way to Sierra Leone," and that it was too early to dismiss the experiment of West African colonization. He carried a cargo of tropical goods from Freetown to Liverpool, delighting the members of the African Institution, who thought him providentially chosen for the work. Cuffe then sailed back to Sierra Leone, his head filled with plans to grow silk and other tropical crops there, and returned to America in the spring of 1812. It was Cuffe's misfortune, and the African Institution's, that their plans for a transatlantic revival of Sierra Leone's prospects coincided with a new war between Britain and the United States. Cuffe had been assured by James Monroe, Madison's secretary of state, that the US government would be "always ready to render me their help." But the embargos and disruptions of the war grounded his efforts. Cuffe continued to lobby anyone who might help, including Timothy Pickering, the former secretary of war, who was now a Massachusetts congressman; Dolley Madison, the president's wife; and members of the US Senate, who even passed a bill exempting Cuffe from the ban on trading with the enemy during wartime. The House of Representatives, which had styled itself as the nation's patriotic guardian, would not approve even the slightest deviation from its anti-British course. Though the Senate bill was rejected, several members recognized "the benefits which would result to the United States" from "the emigration of free blacks, a part of our population which we could well spare."[22]

Becalmed by the war, Cuffe built new alliances with black and white reformers. He befriended faculty members at Andover Theological Seminary in Massachusetts, and his spirits were raised by a series of newspaper articles written by one of the seminary's graduates. Under the heading of "Paul Cuffe's Mission to Sierra Leone," the essays argued for colonization not as a means to remove free blacks from the United States, but as a weapon in the battle against slavery. African Americans "belong to the human race," wrote the author, and "possess all the natural and unalienable rights of men." Cuffe also corresponded with Jedidiah Morse, a veteran reformer who had helped to found many of the leading religious institutions in New England: Andover Seminary, the American Bible Society, and the American Board of Commissioners for Foreign Missions. Morse, who knew several members of the African Institution, kept William Wilberforce informed of Cuffe's progress and searched for potential colonists among the free blacks of Boston. When peace returned in 1815, Cuffe reached out to free black leaders across the seaboard. Regarding "the African channel," he wrote James Forten: "When it can be opened, I hope we may not let it be shut." The plan would take time to germinate, but "great good" would follow in "the days of the succeeding generation." After three years, Cuffe's return to Freetown finally gained a fair wind.[23]

CUFFE SET SAIL FOR AFRICA in December 1815, carrying more than three dozen emigrants. "I am endeavoring to have a road opened from England to America to Sierra Leone," he had written his brother from Liverpool in 1811. But even before the war, there were reasons to doubt

Thomas Jefferson's old claim that one strong colony would do better than two weak ones. The African Institution was never more than lukewarm toward American emigration. Congress had worried that African American colonists might give an advantage to British commerce. Officials from Sierra Leone had already traveled to Georgia in search of "the best kind of cotton seeds" to plant in West Africa, alerting southerners to the possibility that the Province of Freedom might become a serious commercial rival. In the summer of 1815, William Wilberforce told a fellow member of the institution that Cuffe should be persuaded to move permanently to Sierra Leone, where he could coordinate trade between Britain and Africa without the distractions of his former life in the United States. Although Cuffe arrived safely in Freetown in February 1816, after a voyage beset by storms, he was not to succeed in his efforts to co-opt Sierra Leone as a destination for African Americans. Instead, he became the inspiration for a renewed effort to establish a black colony under the American flag.[24]

Cuffe's early expeditions had created huge interest among free black and white reformers from Virginia to Massachusetts, but it was the War of 1812 that became the catalyst for a new colonization movement in the United States. In Virginia, slaveholders were relieved to have gotten through the war without a major slave revolt, but they were reminded by those who fled to the British lines that African Americans would remain an internal enemy as long as slavery persisted. Antislavery reformers in the North argued that colonization would spur gradual emancipation in the South. Clergymen positioned black emigrants as the means by which the entire African continent could be brought to Christianity. Religion had always been central to the antislavery effort, and it's not surprising that the chief instigator of what became the American Colonization Society was a clergyman. Robert Finley grew up in Princeton, New Jersey, the son of a Glasgow wool merchant who had come to America to follow his religious mentor, the Scottish-born Princeton president John Witherspoon. After graduating in the Class of 1787, Finley spent a year teaching in Charleston, South Carolina. He hadn't needed this southern sojourn to witness the horrors of slavery: New Jersey passed a gradual emancipation law only in 1804, nearly a quarter century after neighboring Pennsylvania, and Princeton was filled with southern students and their "servants." But Finley's time in Charleston confirmed his aversion to slavery. When he came home in 1792 to study theology, he became especially close to Samuel Stanhope Smith, Princeton's dogged defender of the unity of the races.[25]

Over the next twenty years, Finley served as a Presbyterian minister and schoolteacher in Basking Ridge, New Jersey, while maintaining his ties to Princeton—where he was, at various moments, student, college tutor, and eventually trustee. Finley met slaves and free blacks both in his church and at the college, and he discussed the problems of slavery and black integration with Samuel Stanhope Smith and other liberal whites. Eventually he reached the conclusion that colonization offered the best prospect both of delivering New Jersey's free black population from "degradation" and of expediting the abolition of slavery in the South. In November 1816, he convened a meeting in Princeton to share his thinking with his learned friends. With their help, he drew up a petition to present to the New Jersey legislature. "While the love of liberty" had produced widespread emancipation in the North, and was "gradually effecting" the abolition of slavery in the South, it was terrible to see "the degraded situation in which those who have been freed from slavery remain." Sadly, "from a variety of considerations," free blacks would suffer from degradation "while they continue among the whites." The abolition of slavery in the United States was approaching a critical mass, thought Finley, but liberal Americans had not solved the problem of a growing free black population. His advocacy of colonization was grounded in antislavery convictions, but initially directed at the social consequences of emancipation.[26]

Meanwhile, back in Virginia, the secret debates over colonization during the Jefferson administration were about to spill into the public domain. The agent of this disclosure was Charles Fenton Mercer, son of a wealthy judge and planter, and yet another Princetonian. An opponent of slavery, he hoped that the state might be weaned from its dependence on slaves and guided toward a future of industrialization and free labor. Incredibly, he had been a member of the state assembly for six years before he learned of the abortive colonization projects of the early 1800s. During a particularly heavy drinking session, he heard a tipsy state senator denounce Thomas Jefferson as a hypocrite who had done nothing to advance Virginia's requests. Mercer, so stunned by this claim that he remembered it on the other side of his hangover, sought out the clerk of the Senate the next day and requested the journals of the secret legislative sessions. Amazed by his state's persistent advocacy of colonization, and by the fact that the whole story had remained a secret, Mercer went public. He promised to introduce a new colonization bill in the next session of the legislature, and traveled to Washington to tell his friends what he'd learned. He bumped into two of them in the gallery of the House of Representatives: Francis Scott Key, the Maryland lawyer who had recently written the words to "The Star-Spangled Banner," and Elias B. Caldwell, his old roommate at Princeton, who happened to be both the clerk of the Supreme Court and Robert Finley's brother-in-law. Both pledged to work their contacts in Washington to promote a new drive for black resettlement. Mercer traveled north to share his nascent plans with friends in Baltimore, Philadelphia, and New York. On his return journey in October 1816, he stopped off in Princeton to consult with Samuel Stanhope Smith on how northern states might be persuaded to join a national colonization effort.[27]

It's unclear whether Mercer actually met Robert Finley during his travels through New Jersey, but it seems very likely that the southern and northern tracks of this colonization effort became fused in the fall of 1816. At a meeting in Princeton in November of that year, Finley and his friends drafted a petition to the New Jersey legislature requesting that the federal government create a black colony. The following month, Finley traveled to Washington clutching the handwritten draft of a new and grander colonization scheme. He met with Elias Caldwell and his family on his arrival, then made an unannounced visit to the house of newspaper editor Samuel Harrison Smith and his wife Margaret. Margaret answered the door, still applying her makeup ahead of an evening reception at the White House. "Meaning it quite for a joke," she suggested that Rev. Finley—who was still wearing his heavy boots—might like to accompany her and her husband. To Margaret's horror, Finley agreed. (She at least made him rush out to buy a pair of shoes.) An hour later, the Smiths found themselves introducing the excited minister to Washington's elite. Finley "conversed a good deal" with President Madison, and then with James Monroe, who at that moment was secretary of state and president-elect. Before he had unpacked his bags in Washington, Finley had pitched his colonization scheme to the two most powerful men in the United States.[28]

Samuel Harrison Smith immediately published Finley's colonization pamphlet, and its ideas coursed through Washington in the weeks before Christmas. "Thoughts on the Colonization of Free Blacks" ran to just eight pages, but it represented a considerable advance on Finley's original petition to the New Jersey legislature. He outlined the two rationales for colonization: it would resolve the difficulties experienced by free blacks in the North, and it would unleash the hidden liberality within the hearts of slaveholders in the South. Finley recognized that southerners needed a safe way to make good on their convictions. The "most natural and easy answer" was to establish "a colony or colonies"—perhaps in the distant West, though more likely in Africa. "By this means," Finley wrote, "the evil of slavery will be diminished, and in a way so gradual as to prepare the whites for the happy and progressive change." Better still, the colonists would bring "rays of knowledge" into the "benighted regions" of Africa. In a kind of reverse manifest destiny, Africa would be transformed by American emigrants expanding from west to east. This inspired Finley's most daring suggestion. Perhaps God had "suffered so great an evil to exist as African slavery" to secure the greater good of a civilized and Christian Africa. An African colony could launder American history, turning the nation's deepest shame into its greatest achievement.[29]

Finley's triumphant visit culminated with the founding meeting of the American Colonization Society on 21 December 1816. Drawn by Samuel Harrison Smith's promotional articles in the *National Intelligencer*, and by the capital gossip about Finley's political ascent, twenty of the most powerful men in Washington committed themselves to a black colony. Henry Clay of Kentucky chaired the meeting; Daniel Webster of Massachusetts and John Randolph of Virginia were in attendance, along with the New England missionary Samuel Mills, Elias Caldwell, Francis Scott Key, and one of the founding generation of colonization proponents: Ferdinando Fairfax, the Virginia planter who had published his own plan back in 1790. There was one notable absentee. William Thornton, still running the Patent Office, couldn't get away from his desk. But he told Henry Clay that he was thrilled to find a new generation determined to "blot from the records of Eternity the highest stigma of humanity." The meeting adjourned, and the new members of the American Society for Colonizing the Free People of Color in the United States met again a week later—this time in the Hall of the House of Representatives. For the next half century, colonization remained at the heart of national politics.[30]

TWO PARTS OF THIS STORY have encouraged historians to doubt the American Colonization Society's antislavery ambitions. First, its full name reflected Robert Finley's original emphasis on colonizing "free people" rather than slaves. Second, many of its early supporters were slaveholders. Free blacks and white abolitionists would later present the ACS as a proslavery conspiracy, a mechanism to remove free blacks and thereby to consolidate the slave system. Some historians have swallowed that critique whole; others have seen the society as an unfortunate alliance between naïve northern reformers, duplicitous slaveholders, and racists who wanted free blacks removed from America's cities. As we have seen, however, the founding of the ACS was part of a much larger debate over the social consequences of emancipation. Northern reformers and concerned slaveholders had come to see physical separation as a prerequisite for a successful society after slavery. Colonization promised to supply the "outlet" for free people that opponents of slavery had been seeking for decades.[31]

An initial emphasis on removing free people was, for virtually everyone connected with the society, a tactical maneuver. Free blacks would establish and direct the colony in its early stages; when the colony had proved its viability, slaveholders and state legislatures would embark on wider emancipation schemes that would swell its ranks. Much has been made of the fact that one founding member of the ACS, the Virginia politician John Randolph, lavishly declared at its founding meeting not only that the society would "not in any wise affect the question of Negro slavery," but that it would "materially tend to secure the property of every master in the United States" by insulating slavery from the disruptive influence of free blacks. But even Randolph, a complicated politician who has often been mistaken for a proslavery ideologue, acknowledged in the same speech that there were "hundreds, nay thousands of citizens" who would rush to free their slaves if they were provided with an African outlet. Randolph and other ACS supporters were zealous in their reassurances that neither the society nor the federal government could ever compel slaveholders to give up their property. Such assurances did not alter the widespread conviction that a black colony would make it easier for conscientious slaveholders to free their slaves. During the succeeding decades, as the ACS became a powerful lobbying force nationally and in the states, politicians in Maryland, Virginia, and elsewhere in the South debated whether colonization should be left to individual masters or written into law by state legislatures. Virtually none of the proponents of colonization, however, boasted that it would strengthen the slave system. It was for this reason that the ACS made enduring enemies in South Carolina and Georgia, where antislavery sentiment had never gained traction.[32]

At a moment in which the North and the South seemed to be diverging on the subject of slavery, the society's founders were determined that the ACS should be a national organization. Northern states had experienced plenty of problems in managing the transition from slavery to freedom, but by 1804 they had each adopted a legislative framework for abolition. Complaints about the "degradation" of free blacks or the problems of white prejudice in the North could not alter the basic fact that slavery itself was on the road to extinction north of Delaware. This achievement isolated southern states, which had made no progress toward placing abolition on the statute books. Prejudice and degradation were national problems after that date, but southerners felt increasingly exposed on the question of slavery. Some northern reformers became critical of the South's laggardly course. Others wondered whether northern assaults on southern slavery might entrench the institution. The appeal of colonization lay in its potential to bind together reformers in both sections of the Union. By emphasizing the problems of integrating black people after slavery, it distracted from the glaring difference between North and South—slavery was disappearing in the former and expanding in the latter—and suggested that both sections of the Union had the same interest in black removal.

One of those cautious northern reformers was Pennsylvania Quaker Jesse Kersey, who traveled southward in 1814 to assess the extent of antislavery sentiment among planters in Virginia and Maryland. After visiting dozens of slaveholders, he was relieved to learn that "all are solicitous to promote a termination of slavery." In a fascinating correspondence with St. George Tucker, the Virginia colonization pioneer, Kersey acknowledged that the nerves of slaveholders were frayed. "Slavery must be touched with great delicacy," he wrote. Liberal planters in the Upper South were terrified that any sudden moves would provoke a slave uprising. The trick would be to promote a "progressive and happy termination" of the institution by gradually freeing slaves in an overseas colony. "By a kind of geometrical progression," Kersey promised, "the country would be opened and an asylum furnished for the reception of these people." Before long, southern masters would free their slaves at such speed that the colony would struggle to resettle them all. In turn, the colony's expanding population would carry

Certificate of James Madison's membership of the American Colonization
Society. Madison served as the society's president from 1833 until his death
in 1836. COURTESY OF THE LIBRARY OF CONGRESS.

civilization and Christianity into the African interior. The society's
redeemed colonists would reassemble the shards of their American
experience in a republican mirror across the Atlantic.[33]

Some members of the society were less inhibited than others in
declaring the ACS's antislavery ambitions. Francis Scott Key was
eager to reassure slaveholders that their cooperation would be voluntary, and he proposed that the ACS constitution should disavow any
intention to secure a general abolition in the South. At the society's
1818 meeting, his fellow members declined to support this restriction. Bushrod Washington, grandson of the first president of the
United States, insisted that "the effect of this institution" would be
"the slow, but gradual abolition of slavery." Charles Fenton Mercer
lamented the 1806 Virginia law that deterred masters from manumit-
ting their slaves by insisting on the removal of freed people from the
state. An overseas colony, Mercer declared, would at last allow "many
thousands" of slaveholders to "yield to the suggestions of humanity."
When Mercer promised that the state of Virginia would give "every

facility to emancipation" after the establishment of the colony, Henry Clay rushed to his feet. Ever the politician, Clay denied that *every* slaveholder would be compelled to embrace emancipation. But he acknowledged that a black colony would "remove the impediments to the exercise of benevolence and humanity," allowing southern legislators to resume the course of prudent antislavery that the nation's founding ideals had marked out for them.[34]

Within a year of its establishment, the American Colonization Society had recruited dozens of illustrious members from across the Union. William Crawford, who had recently retired from the Department of War, became a vice-president. So did Richard Rush (son of Benjamin); John Taylor of Caroline, the celebrated Virginia political theorist; and Andrew Jackson. At the 1818 meeting, the society's mission was vividly defined by Robert Goodloe Harper, a former US senator from Maryland. Having spent his entire life in the midst of slavery—he had lived in Virginia and North and South Carolina before moving to Maryland—Harper concluded that blacks and whites could not happily live alongside each other after emancipation. The social and racial mixing that would be a prerequisite for republican equality was "closed for ever, by our habits and our feelings, which perhaps it would be more correct to call our prejudices." Even Paul Cuffe, "respectable, intelligent and wealthy as he is," wrote Harper, "has no expectation of ever being invited to dine with any gentleman in Boston, or marrying his daughter." The sense of exclusion could only fuel the anger and despair felt by black people. Free blacks and slaves had been made to feel like a "distinct nation" with no stake in the prosperity and security of the United States. Against the "inferiority" and "degradation" they had experienced in America, Harper contrasted the life that they would enjoy in Africa. "Transplanted to a colony composed of themselves alone," he promised, "they would enjoy real equality." Before long, black colonists would "become equal to the people of Europe or of European origin, so long their masters and oppressors."[35]

Harper acknowledged that the gradual departure of free blacks from the United States might, as John Randolph had suggested, relieve planters from the immediate pressure of a black uprising. But he insisted that "there is another advantage, infinitely greater in every point of view, to which it may lead the way." A black colony would "rid us gradually and entirely of slaves and slavery." When free blacks and former slaves were gathered together in Africa, "the whites who might visit them, would visit them as equals." There, black colonists could work as schoolteachers, magistrates, clergymen, army officers, judges, and politicians. They would build a society that was recognizably American, but in which black people would "feel the noble emulation to excel in all the various departments of life." Like Robert Finley, Harper took care to present colonization's advantages not only in terms of the relief offered to anxious whites by the end of the black presence in America, but also in terms of the benefits that would accrue to the colonists themselves. It would be black people who would gain the most: they would be released from slavery, and they would have the opportunity to realize and vindicate their equality.[36]

THE ACS COULD HARDLY HAVE wished for a more supportive figure in the White House than James Monroe, who cushioned the society from an increasingly turbulent debate about slavery and government intervention (which would culminate, for Monroe at least, in the Missouri crisis of 1819–1821). Monroe knew that planters from South Carolina and Georgia had identified the ACS as an antislavery organization; he also knew from his own experience in Virginia that, without a colony, the society could achieve very little. Presidential involvement in the creation of a black colony would be highly controversial, given the abdication of the federal government from the slavery debate and the sensitivities of Deep South lawmakers. But Monroe had been committed to colonization since 1800, when he had searched for a response to Gabriel's Rebellion. Now elevated to the highest office in the land, he resolved to secure for the ACS what Thomas Jefferson had failed to supply in 1801.[37]

He did so in close collaboration with a number of ACS supporters in Congress, including Charles Fenton Mercer, who was elected to the US House of Representatives in 1817. Rather than drafting legislation to create a colony, Mercer approached black resettlement through an old argument about slavery and government action. Back in 1807, when Congress had debated the details of its impending ban on the foreign slave trade, northern and southern representatives had clashed over how to dispose of contraband Africans who had been illegally trafficked to America. The eventual compromise left the matter with the states, a solution that seemed especially unfortunate when the illegal slave trade surged after the War of 1812. Increasing numbers of Africans were intercepted off the American coast and turned over to state authorities for processing; most of them ended up in southern ports, where the "rescue" concluded with their sale at auction. The 1807 Slave Trade Act was supposed to stop any new Africans from being enslaved in America. Yet in the South, the act was having the opposite effect. Capitalizing on the revulsion of liberal thinkers in the North and Upper South to this practice, Mercer pledged to stop the problem at its source. Congress should approve funds to police the waters of West Africa, and the president should take charge of resettling rescued slaves.[38]

During the 1807 debate in Congress, the idea that rescued slaves should be placed under the control of the federal government was anathema to Deep South representatives. In 1819, in the midst of a noisy battle over Missouri, the same principle slipped past the House and the Senate with little fuss. Monroe was given responsibility for the "safekeeping, support and removal" of captured slaves, with Congress supplying $100,000 for the purpose. Legislators also granted Monroe the power to send warships to Africa. Ostensibly, this new Slave Trade Act would allow the United States to police the sea lanes in search of illegal slaving vessels. But at the urging of William Crawford, now Monroe's treasury secretary, the president and his cabinet pushed the interpretation of the act to the limits of plausibility. To ensure that the federal government had somewhere to take rescued slaves, the US Navy would work with ACS officials to secure territory in West Africa.

After more than three decades of lobbying from northern and southern colonizationists, the ACS and James Monroe had finally opened the road toward an American "Province of Freedom."[39]

Monroe's attorney general doubted whether this imaginative reading of the Slave Trade Act was legal. Ignoring his advice that the matter be sent back to Congress, Monroe urged ACS officials to make haste. The society had sent a scouting mission to Africa in 1818 to make inquiries in Sierra Leone, and then identified Sherbro Island (about fifty miles south of Freetown) as a promising spot for an American colony. The following year, with a green light from Monroe, ACS officials recruited eighty-six black volunteers—two-thirds of them women and children—and a colonizing expedition set sail from New York. This venture fared no better than the original mission to Sierra Leone in 1787. The emigrants quarreled with ACS officials over how the new settlement would be managed, and they struggled with malaria and other diseases. Barely two months after their arrival at Sherbro Island in March 1820, most of them (including the white agents of the ACS) were either sick or dying. Monroe and the ACS quickly dispatched another expedition, which learned some lessons from the failures of the first. The would-be colonists were landed in Freetown, where they could enjoy the relative safety of Sierra Leone while the ACS agents negotiated with local leaders nearly three hundred miles to the south. The society's agents couldn't persuade the local ruler, King Jack Ben, to abandon his interest in the slave trade, which diluted the antislavery potential of the settlement plan. While ACS representatives did sign a deal with the king, its terms and promises inspired little confidence. The representatives left without making a firm plan to return.

At this point, as patience began to wane in Washington, Monroe ordered a US naval commander, Lieutenant Robert F. Stockton, to take charge of the effort. Stockton was an avowed colonization supporter who had once been a pupil of Robert Finley. He left the United States in the fall of 1821, landing at Cape Mesurado, two hundred miles south of Freetown, in December. (The cape was midway between the sites of the two previous attempts to found an American colony.) ACS officials knew that the cape had a magnificent harbor, and that the indigenous ruler of the region, King Peter, had pledged never to part with it. Stockton imagined that the grandeur of the society's plans would change Peter's mind. After a brief audience, the king told Stockton that he wasn't minded to sell, but that he would discuss the matter again the following day. As historian Eric Burin has noted, Peter (like Jack Ben) may not have been entirely inflexible. If he parted with the land and the colony failed—surely the most probable outcome, given the Americans' failures to date—Peter could keep the money and claw back his territory. In the unlikely event that it succeeded, he could demand commercial privileges from his new neighbors. In the meantime, drawing out the negotiations was an obvious way to secure the best deal. Without informing his guest of his intentions, Peter left Stockton waiting on the coast and retired to his village to await a better offer.[40]

Stockton's lack of patience for diplomatic niceties must have seemed an asset to American officials, who were exasperated by the failure of the two previous attempts to found a colony. When the lieutenant realized that Peter would not be keeping their appointment, he pursued him on foot into the interior. Stockton finally apprehended the king eight miles inland and resumed negotiations. With Stockton's pistol aimed at his head, Peter determined to wrap things up sooner rather than later. On 15 December 1821, the king and five other indigenous leaders signed a treaty ceding Cape Mesurado in perpetuity. The American Colonization Society, five years after its founding, had a colony. The capital of this new settlement, like the capital of the United States, would be named after its chief founder: it was called Monrovia. The colony itself would be called Liberia. That poetic flourish had come from Robert Goodloe Harper, who had more confidence than anyone that the colony's transplanted inhabitants would vindicate the principle of separate-but-equal.[41]

IN 1824, JAMES MONROE INVITED the Marquis de Lafayette to visit the United States. It had been forty years since Lafayette had left the new nation a hero; on this, his first and only return visit to the American republic, he was treated like a deity. During a tour that lasted more than a year, Lafayette covered 6,000 miles and visited all twenty-four states. Honors, accolades, and gifts weighed down the hero of the American Revolution as state assemblies and civil associations struggled to outdo each other in displaying their gratitude. The US Congress granted the marquis more than 20,000 acres of land in Florida Territory. From the free black community of Boston, where Lafayette was fondly remembered for his antislavery convictions, the marquis received a poem instead:

> *As the Whites gained the Freedom for which they contended,*
> *Could you have supposed, when the war had thus ended,*
> *That they would hand over the African race,*
> *To Thraldom unceasing, and endless disgrace—*
> *Inflicting more evils, as thousands to one,*
> *Than the Rulers of Britain on them had e'er done?*

Slavery was rarely far from Lafayette's mind during his tour. He lingered for nearly two weeks at Monticello with Thomas Jefferson, James Madison, and James Monroe. The current president of the United States, along with his two illustrious predecessors, listened to Lafayette's appeal that more should be done to promote abolition. Colonization, they all agreed, was the key to achieving that goal.[42]

Lafayette had chastised Jefferson in 1820 for supporting the extension of slavery to Missouri, and he rejected his friend's arguments about diffusion. Like mainstream American reformers of the 1820s, however, Lafayette became a strong supporter of the American Colonization Society. In February 1825, in the company of the chief justice of the Supreme Court and other federal dignitaries, Lafayette thanked the ACS annual meeting for honoring him with its "perpetual vice-presidency." This accolade was, the marquis acknowledged, an honor "accordant to the principles of all my life." Lafayette followed Liberia's progress closely, but he was interested in other colonization schemes, too. On his American tour, he was accompanied by the young British reformer Frances Wright, whose political radicalism and hatred of slavery had been learned from her family and sharpened by her acquaintance with Lafayette. In 1825, after taking stock of the urgency of the slavery problem in the American South, Wright announced that she would found her own colonization experiment at Nashoba in Tennessee. With encouragement from Madison, Jefferson, Monroe, and even Andrew Jackson, Wright purchased a small farm and ten slaves. Like Lafayette in Cayenne forty years earlier, she hoped to persuade slaveholders that free labor would be more lucrative than slavery. Once underway, her experimental farm would generate profits that would enable her to buy more slaves, who would earn their way to freedom and colonization outside the United States. Here, she imagined, was an engine for turning slaves into free people, and free people into colonists.[43]

Wright was touched by Lafayette's offer of financial support, but she poured her own wealth into the scheme. (Her parents had died young, leaving her a fortune.) Knowing little about farming, however, she found it impossible to break even, let alone make the profits that might set her emancipation machine in perpetual motion. Lafayette, now back in France, followed Wright's progress nervously. His network of American correspondents doubted she could hold out for long; several predicted that Nashoba would end in disaster. Lafayette, though, staked a great deal on her success. His tour had enabled him to see just how extensive and insidious slavery had become in the forty years since he'd tried to recruit Washington to the colonization cause. Was it possible to remove millions of black people from North America? If not, antislavery would surely grind to a halt, with terrible consequences for everyone.[44]

Lafayette toyed with the idea of reprising his Cayenne experiment on the lands Congress had given him in Florida. He told Jefferson to consider Mexico or "those wide republics of South America" as "an additional vent for liberated negroes." From Tennessee, meanwhile, he learned that Frances Wright had had a change of heart. Madison had already warned Lafayette that Wright seemed blasé about the location of the "external asylum" to which her slaves would eventually be transferred. Lafayette informed Madison that Wright now believed "total colonization" was "next to an impossibility." Instead, she planned to convert her farm into a school, to reverse the process of degradation, and to "soften and finally do away [with] prejudices of color." Initially, Lafayette kept an open mind about this. But when Wright announced to a Memphis newspaper that she would also promote the amalgamation of the races at Nashoba, Lafayette's liberal friends in the North and the South reacted with horror. From New York, one of Wright's strongest supporters, Charles Wilkes, broke the bad news to the marquis. Wilkes had always admired Wright's antislavery zeal; now he could only regret the "delusions" that had rendered Wright and her fellow organizers "useless to others and pernicious to themselves." The experiment collapsed. Wright freed her slaves and escorted them to a new life in Haiti—where they settled on land belonging to Jean Pierre Boyer, the Haitian president.[45]

Lafayette's idea of a black colony in Florida proved no more successful than Nashoba. His correspondent there warned him in 1829 that a free-labor experiment could not be inaugurated "without awakening sectional jealousies." The first tobacco and sugar crops in the territory had done well, but a report of commercial advantage might excite unscrupulous planters as well as enlightened reformers. (Lafayette was warned that the prospect of lucrative crops might induce landowners to "rivet" rather than break "the chains of slavery.") With his alternatives receding from view, Lafayette renewed his commitment to the American Colonization Society. The managers thanked him in 1829 for "his enlightened approbation of their benevolent scheme," and Lafayette became an especially close friend of Ralph Gurley, the ACS secretary. Gurley and James Madison—who would soon become the society's president—attempted to cheer Lafayette up, insisting that their cause was moving forward. State legislatures

The American Colonization Society settlement of Monrovia, Liberia, c. 1824. The settlement was named for President James Monroe, who had done so much to facilitate its creation. COURTESY AMERICAN ANTIQUARIAN SOCIETY.

in Virginia, Maryland, and Kentucky were clamoring to debate new colonization proposals, Gurley reported. The ACS made ample use of Lafayette's endorsement, and Gurley arranged for its magazine and annual reports to be sent to his country seat outside of Paris.[46]

At the end of his life, Lafayette retained the beliefs he had forged as a young man. Human beings were essentially equal. Slavery was a violation of natural rights. Colonization was the best mechanism to secure gradual emancipation. He lived long enough to see the development of an international colonization movement that founded two colonies on the western shores of Africa. But he also realized that, despite its illustrious supporters and sweeping rhetoric, the American Colonization Society was inadequate to the task of resettling millions of slaves. Unwilling to endorse the radical conclusion of Frances Wright—that only amalgamation and integration could solve the problem—Lafayette was stuck where he'd always been: juggling hopes and plans for colonization experiments while the problem of slavery increased by orders of magnitude.

In the last year of his life, Lafayette received a letter from the free black reformer James Forten, who wondered how someone who had been "the great advocate of the liberty and happiness of all the human family" could support colonization. Forten and Lafayette were among the last living veterans of the Revolutionary War, and the Philadelphian could not resist plotting the divergence of their long lives. "It may not be amiss here to state that the writer of this," Forten explained, "was one of those who like yourself, participated in the glorious struggle for that liberty which a *portion* of the American people now enjoy." Lafayette and Forten had "bled to obtain" freedom and independence for the United States. And yet while "millions" were now enjoying the benefits of their achievement, African Americans were still "denied a home in that land which gave us birth." With all this in view, might the marquis reconsider his support for the American Colonization Society, and recognize the right of black people to enjoy the "fruits of Liberty" in the United States? Lafayette received Forten's letter, but he never replied. The following year, when the United States mourned the death of its most revered ally, the American Colonization Society led the way in offering tribute to this "illustrious benefactor of the human race."[47]

ELEVEN

In These Deserts

B ETWEEN 1810 AND 1830, MORE than a million white settlers
poured into Ohio, Indiana, Michigan, and Illinois. Across the
same period, whites and their slaves swelled the population of Alabama, Georgia, and Mississippi by more than 650,000. The population
of Georgia doubled. Indiana and Illinois, which achieved statehood
in 1816 and 1818, respectively, saw their populations increase by a factor of thirteen. In 1830 there were thirty times as many people living
in Alabama as there had been before the War of 1812. These stagger-
ing developments rested on a simple fact: from the Great Lakes to the
Gulf of Mexico, Native Americans were losing huge tracts of territory.
Where settlers weren't carving out claims for themselves, the federal
government had an eye on future expansion. In 1819, Secretary of War
John Calhoun told the Michigan territorial governor, Lewis Cass, that
the "rapid and dense settlement" of Michigan's Lower Peninsula would
be "best effected by an entire extinguishment of the Indian title" ("if,"
he added as an afterthought, "it can be effected on fair terms"). Federal officials provided the negotiators, the soldiers, and the finances
that made the settlement rush possible. In public, they described it as
providential.[1]

With so many people heading west, John Calhoun and Congress
looked for new ways to manage the effects of the land-grab on Native
peoples. In March 1819, Congress voted to spend $10,000 annually

on "the civilization of the Indian tribes adjoining the frontier settlements." Calhoun called for a "radical change" in US Indian policy,
promising to unleash civil society to do what the government had
struggled to achieve. Churches, associations, and even individuals were invited to apply for money from the new "civilizing fund."
Richard Mentor Johnson proposed his Choctaw Academy; Calhoun
received numerous applications from the major evangelical organizations in the United States. For the next two decades, missionaries and
government officials became closely involved in the making of Indian
policy, each hoping to profit by the arrangement. Missionary groups
saw the fund as a chance to win souls; politicians saw missionaries as
go-betweens (and sometimes stooges) in the effort to reconcile Native
Americans to territorial expansion. Both sides came to understand
the other's motives and concerns; religious and political goals became
thoroughly entangled.[2]

The most compelling application to the War Department came
from Jedidiah Morse of New Haven, the Congregationalist minister
who had helped recruit black colonists for Paul Cuffe's 1815 expedition to Sierra Leone. Morse was a member of the American Board of
Commissioners for Foreign Missions (ABCFM), which sent US missionaries around the world in search of converts. He was also editor
of the influential religious magazine *The Panoplist*. While some in
the missionary community argued that American evangelists should
focus solely on overseas activities—the vast fields of China and India,
in particular—Morse insisted on retaining missions to Native Americans within the United States. He considered himself well qualified to
advise the government on the prospects of Christianity and "civilization" at the frontier. He had written a series of textbooks on American
geography that were used in schools across the nation. Determining
that he could not grasp the challenge of Indian "civilizing" until he
had seen Native peoples up close, he wrote Calhoun in 1819 to propose
a tour of the entire Indian population east of the Mississippi. His itin-
erary arced westward from New Haven, crossing New England, New
York, and the entire Great Lakes region before sweeping back to the

states of the Southeast. He planned to examine and interrogate Indian communities from New England to Wisconsin to Florida, and then present the government with a plan that would advance its civilizing ambitions.[3]

Calhoun agreed to fund the expedition. Morse left Connecticut in the spring of 1820, traveling through New England to Albany, then across to Buffalo. (In the process he became one of the first Americans to use the Erie Canal.) From Buffalo he made for Detroit, then Mackinaw, and eventually Green Bay. Although Morse had planned to continue throughout the West and South, he felt the strain of traveling more than 1,000 miles in just a few weeks. He left Wisconsin and returned to New Haven without visiting the "civilizing" Indians of the Southeast. Despite this omission, his *Report to the Secretary of War*, published in 1822, offers a fascinating snapshot of liberal thinking about Native Americans. Morse insisted that Indians were "of the same nature and original, and of one blood with ourselves." There was no reason to doubt their potential for civilization, and William Crawford had been right about amalgamation. Morse looked forward to a time when "intermarriage with them become[s] general," when "they would be literally of one blood with us." Before that happy day, Indians had to be brought across the "awful gulf" between civilization and savagery. Morse's first proposal was for a civilizing squadron of white volunteers—missionaries, blacksmiths, farming experts, and teachers—who would establish themselves as a "parental" government in the midst of Indian nations. Morse called them "Education Families," and thought that they might be deployed throughout the West.[4]

He knew enough about the frontier, however, to concede that "unprincipled white persons"—rogue settlers and selfish traders— would stymie the "civilizing" work. During his tour, Morse had heard many Indians complain of "bad white men" who corrupted their morals and stole their land. "It is very difficult to prevent these evils," Morse observed, "while Indians and white people live in the near neighborhood of each other." His solution was to deliver Native people from the clutches of their would-be oppressors: "Their colonization on

some sequestered spot, selected and prepared with judgment and liberality, under the direction and patronage of the Government, would
place them in circumstances for improvement, far more eligible than
those in which they are now placed." Morse had floated the idea with
Native leaders during his tour, claiming an august precedent: Hadn't
Tecumseh himself "conceived a plan of collecting all the Indians of
N. America on some portion of the continent, not inhabited by white
people . . . to live in a state of independence"? Morse told Secretary
Calhoun that the Miami leader, Joseph Richardville, had agreed to
consider colonization. Most Indians he'd met were less sanguine
about the prospect.[5]

In his report, Morse proposed a compromise. The larger nations
and those that were deeply divided over colonization should be
allowed to stay where they were. The "*smaller* tribes, and remnants
of tribes" would be "collected in one body" beyond the rim of white
settlement. The Stockbridge Indians, originally from Massachusetts,
proved that migration might have beneficial effects. They had moved
to upstate New York in the 1780s and, facing renewed pressure on
their lands after the War of 1812, had recently negotiated a treaty with
the Menominee and Ho-Chunk Indians for a new home in Wisconsin. Morse thought this area would make a perfect location for the
resettlement of Indians from across the United States. If the plan took
off, "it will be a large colony, enough perhaps to form a Territory or
even a *State*." Indians would be "collected here, educated together, and
received into the Union, and to the enjoyment of the privileges of citizens." Morse reminded Calhoun of the draft treaty with the Delawares back in 1778, and its tentative provision for Indian statehood.
The United States had been struggling to integrate Native Americans
for decades. The solution had been in plain sight since the American
Revolution.[6]

Morse's proposal proved extremely influential as the government
inched toward Indian removal. His method for implementing it,
though, was less successful. Morse was keenly aware of the American
Colonization Society, and he decided to create a similar organization

in Washington to lobby for Education Families and Indian coloniza-tion. The "American Society for Promoting the Civilization and Gen-eral Improvement of the Indian Tribes Within the United States" may have defied an easy acronym, but its resources and methods were reas-suringly familiar. The "Civilization Society" would be based in Wash-ington and cultivate an elite membership. All former presidents were to be patrons, along with the judges of the Supreme Court and the governors of the states and territories of the United States. Inevitably, perhaps, its membership would overlap with the ACS. Elias B. Cald-well and Francis Scott Key, architects of the American Colonization Society in its earliest years, agreed to serve as secretaries of Morse's new organization. Morse wrote to dozens of the nation's most influen-tial figures to inform them that they were now patrons of his society.[7]

Morse's rush to found a private society was misjudged. Although Calhoun was keen to harness civil society to realize his vision of "benevolent" expansion, he was not inclined to turn over the mak-ing of Indian policy to a group like the ACS. The political contexts of the two resettlement efforts were very different. The managers of the American Colonization Society knew that the federal government found it fiendishly difficult to craft a national policy on slavery. The society worked in the space created by this impasse, hoping to convert state governments and ordinary slaveholders to its vision of benevo-lence. Indian affairs, however, were still firmly under federal jurisdic-tion. Morse's overconfidence manifested itself in his belief that every national figure would be honored to join his new Civilization Society. When Morse informed Thomas Jefferson that he had been appointed a patron, Jefferson declined the position and warned Morse about setting up "this wheel within a wheel"—a private society assuming the government's functions. Jefferson was much harsher in a letter to Madison: "These clubbists of Washington," he wrote, "have under-taken to embody even the government itself into an instrument to be wielded by themselves and for purposes directed by themselves." In his reply, Madison sheepishly confessed that he had already accepted Morse's invitation: the architect of the Constitution hadn't recognized the Civilization Society as a threat to the republic. Madison downplayed his involvement by assuring Jefferson that the society wouldn't amount to much, and in this he was prescient. The Civilization Society was little more than a letterhead, and it quietly folded soon after its first meeting. Morse's ideas about separation were more durable. He secured the approval of the ABCFM for Indian colonization in 1824, and his proposal lingered in the minds of federal officials.[8]

Had Jedidiah Morse reached the Southeast during his grand tour, he would have encountered Native nations that did not fit his colonizing blueprint. The "civilized" Indians of the region, led by the Cherokees, had largely rejected the choice between second-class citizenship in the East and a glorious future across the Mississippi. The refusal of Cherokee leaders in 1823 even to meet with US commissioners astonished federal officials. It also emboldened politicians in Georgia and Alabama to threaten the unilateral extension of state sovereignty over Native areas. The spurned commissioners sent a wounded letter to the Cherokees reminding them that the federal government had spent "upwards of half a million dollars . . . to qualify you for citizenship." If the president determined they were ready to be citizens, "you must become so." In a sign of their desperation, the commissioners even invoked the Treaty of Hopewell to suggest that, if the Cherokees insisted on retaining their collective sovereignty, they could move to the West and become "a Territory of the United States, with the right of representation in Congress." To hold out against both options would be a poor reward for the government's long commitment to "civilization." Worse, it might retard the progress of white expansion. Would the Cherokees now "lay waste a city, that a wigwam might rise upon its ruins?"[9]

The Cherokee national council gracefully dissected the commissioners' cant. Of course the Cherokees didn't propose to replace cities with wigwams: Had anyone in Washington been paying attention to the progress of civilization among the southeastern Indians? The Cherokees' ambition was not to hold up the march of modernity, but to raise "monuments of science . . . on the dust of our progenitors."

Cherokee cities would rise where "the wigwam is tottering into ruins." The only threat to this vision came from the unprincipled whites who stole Indian land and violated solemn treaties. Cleverly, the Cherokees finessed the question of whether their independence from Georgia and Alabama would be permanent. Instead, they portrayed themselves as Americans-in-training, not yet "completely civilized," and therefore, given the acknowledged unscrupulousness of frontier whites, not yet ready for the kind offer of citizenship. The Cherokee council inverted the emerging paradigm of civilization-through-removal while discarding the previous program of civilization-through-proximity. In place of the rival US visions of their future, Cherokees asked merely for time and space to complete their development on their own lands.[10]

It was in this environment that James Monroe revealed his hand. In two messages to Congress, in 1824 and 1825, the president rejected Georgia's claim that the United States should recognize state sovereignty over Indian lands. He also insisted that any effort to impose removal on the Indians would be "unjust." However, "it would promote essentially the security and happiness of the tribes within our limits if they could be prevailed upon to retire west and north of our States and Territories." Monroe had wholeheartedly embraced the logic of Jedidiah Morse's report. In their current location, the president determined, "it will be difficult, if not impossible, to control their degradation." Without removal, "extermination will be inevitable." A new home in the West, however, would encourage "all the arts and usages of civilized life" without harassment from greedy whites. Disparate Indian nations would become a single "civilized people," and the endless conflicts between Native Americans and whites (and different Native nations) would yield to "permanent peace." Despite Morse's caution about resettling larger Indian nations, not to mention his failure to visit the South on his tour of Native Americans, Monroe singled out the southeastern nations as likely beneficiaries of this "well-digested plan." Monroe had become the first American president to argue that every eastern Indian—even those who had made considerable progress toward the acme of "civilized" society—would benefit from western colonization. He gave vital support in his first term to the effort to resettle black people in Africa; at the end of his second, he offered the same solution for Native Americans in the "vast territory" west of the Mississippi.[11]

THE EFFORT TO SECURE MONROE'S vision culminated in Andrew Jackson's removal policy, one of the most controversial episodes in the history of the United States. The two men at the center of this effort were Thomas McKenney, head of the US Bureau of Indian Affairs, and Isaac McCoy, a Baptist missionary. McKenney was a Maryland merchant who, after serving with distinction in the defense of Baltimore during the War of 1812, was rewarded by Madison with the post of superintendent of Indian trade. He was responsible for the factory system through which the federal government supplied finished goods to its frontier outposts in return for furs and pelts from the Indians. McKenney's interest in Native Americans went beyond their economic usefulness, however. He had many friends in the missionary community, and happily agreed in 1818 to intercede on behalf of an ABCFM clergyman who had become unpopular in Washington for opposing Calhoun's efforts to remove the Cherokees. McKenney positioned himself as a critical friend to Calhoun, nudging federal Indian policy toward "benevolent" ends. He lost his job when Congress abolished the factory system in 1819, but Calhoun brought him back to the War Department to head the new Bureau of Indian Affairs during James Monroe's second term. By 1824, McKenney enjoyed considerable influence over the entire sweep of Indian affairs. He would do more than anyone to promote the cause of Indian colonization inside the apparatus of government.[12]

His counterpart in this effort came to Washington by a more circuitous route. Isaac McCoy was born in western Pennsylvania in 1784 and lived his entire life in the West. Inheriting the Baptist faith of his parents, in 1803 he felt a call to preach in Vincennes, Indiana—the headquarters of William Henry Harrison's halting effort at civilization-through-proximity. McCoy began preaching to the town's population of Anglo settlers, French traders, Indians, and blacks while working as a jailer to make ends meet for his family. (McCoy's brood easily outpaced his resources. His wife, Christiana, was more or less constantly pregnant: she would give birth to thirteen children in total.) Initially, McCoy displayed no special interest in Native Americans. During the War of 1812, he preached to the militiamen and soldiers that Harrison threw at Tecumseh, hurrying between sermons with a rifle on his shoulder. It was during a journey he made from Vincennes to St. Louis in 1816, through the human wreckage of the war, that McCoy witnessed the disruption of kinship groups, trading networks, and landholdings at first hand. McCoy informed the Baptist Board of Missions that he would tour the region and determine how best to serve its remaining Indians.[13]

In 1817 and 1818, McCoy traveled nearly 3,000 miles through the Old Northwest, becoming an accidental archaeologist of Native suffering and resistance. He met Indians who had fought alongside Tecumseh and Tenskwatawa. He visited with Miamis, Weas, Potawatomis, and Shawnees who had known Little Turtle and Blue Jacket and fought against Arthur St. Clair and Anthony Wayne. McCoy was received politely by the Delaware leader William Anderson, who had moved from Ohio to Indiana in the 1780s, but found the chief unusually resistant to his overtures. McCoy's assistant would later discover that, as a young man, Anderson had been one of only a handful of survivors of the Gnadenhütten massacre of 1782. (After that, when approached by white people, "no persuasion could overcome his abhorrence.") McCoy knew that US negotiators were combing the Northwest in search of new territorial cessions. In 1818 alone, the Wea were forced to give up lands in Illinois, Indiana, and Ohio in exchange for a small reservation near what is now Terre Haute. The Potawatomi were induced to sell a huge tract in central Indiana. Chief Anderson's Delawares, recently arrived from Ohio, were moved again to a new home west of the Mississippi. McCoy pushed ahead regardless. In 1820, he and Christiana offered to educate Indian children alongside his own growing family at Fort Wayne, more than seventy-five miles from the nearest white town. With eight Indian pupils on his roll, McCoy's Indian mission was underway.[14]

To begin with, life was hard. The Baptist board was slow to provide support. Children and adults struggled through the winter with moccasins instead of boots, and McCoy had to choose between food and warmth. In December 1820, he cursed a French trader who had gotten the school excited about a holiday he would rather have ignored. On Christmas Day, he took his students for carriage rides in the snow; instead of presents, he and Christiana gave every child an apple and a hug. Conditions were so desperate that McCoy was forced to hire an elderly Potawatomi woman to assure parents that the school was doing its best by the children. This tactic seems to have worked, by the measure of McCoy's student rolls. In October 1821, the McCoys were teaching nearly fifty pupils, roughly a third of them girls, drawn from six different Indian nations. The school finally received support from the Baptist board and caught the eye of Lewis Cass, the governor of Michigan Territory. Cass met with McCoy in Detroit and gave the grateful missionary nearly $450 worth of clothes and food for the school. He promised to lend the services of the Fort Wayne blacksmith to the effort, but thought McCoy should seek more substantial assistance from Washington.[15]

Thus began McCoy's long and increasingly involved relationship with the federal government. One of the first people he wrote was Richard Mentor Johnson, a fellow Baptist, who made his own foray into Indian education during the 1820s. When McCoy visited Washington for the first time in January 1822, Johnson introduced him to Thomas McKenney and John Calhoun. The secretary of war mentioned the federal "civilizing" fund, but advised McCoy to relocate his school to take advantage of an education annuity promised to the Potawatomi Indians in a recent treaty. McCoy returned to the school and, at the government's expense, moved his mission from Fort Wayne to Carey Station, on the border of Indiana and Michigan. He had high hopes for the new endeavor, but the winter was harsh. The pages of McCoy's journal filled with terrible stories about Native poverty, alcohol, and hopelessness, and he and Christiana struggled to insulate the children from the collapsing worlds around them. When he learned in the spring of 1823 from a group of Ottawas that the recent Treaty of Chicago—the treaty that now supplied the funding for Carey Station—had ceded their lands without their permission, McCoy despaired. If they were right, and the government was determined to force Native people into the far West, was there any point in continuing with his mission?[16]

Troubled by these Sisyphean reflections, McCoy devised a new plan. Instead of moving his school to chase Native peoples who were ever receding farther west, why not move both the school and the Indians to a place in which the "civilizing" process would not be interrupted? McCoy later presented this idea as a flash of inspiration— something that came to him during one of the interminable horseback rides that structured frontier life. It seems more likely that his embrace of the "colonizing scheme" was filtered through two sources. McCoy had been in Washington the previous January when Jedidiah Morse had published his own colonization report, and he had actually met with Morse on that trip. Then there was McCoy's membership in the Indiana chapter of the American Colonization Society. In a breach of the Baptist board's protocols for Indian missions, McCoy taught an African American boy named Jesse Cox alongside his white and Native students. He hoped eventually to send him to Liberia. McCoy's plan for an Indian colony was very similar to Morse's 1822 proposal, and his rationale for Native resettlement was substantially the same as the ACS's argument for black emigration.[17]

McCoy set down his ideas in the summer of 1823 in a letter to Lewis Cass, Richard Mentor Johnson, and Johnson's brother, Congressman John Johnson. McCoy judged that the public's sympathies were currently aroused in favor of the Indians, but that "there is no established asylum to which civilized Indians may repair" to avoid the "embarrassing and unpleasant effects" of frontier settlers. From his long personal experience, McCoy could confirm that whites at the frontier impeded the "civilizing" process. If the United States could provide "a country somewhere in the extensive regions of the West, no small distance beyond the frontier of white settlements," Indians might enjoy the "privileges of *men*" and, ultimately, be prepared "to be identified as citizens of the U.S." After sending the letter, McCoy worried he had gone too far. Was he guilty of "extravagance in thinking, and vanity in attempting things too high?" He was relieved to hear that his powerful friends loved the proposal. The colonization principle, John Johnson told McCoy, would enable Indians to circumvent "the deep rooted prejudices of the whites" and "associate upon equal terms." McCoy was invited to visit Washington and share his plan with the Monroe administration.[18]

McCoy later told his friends that he had been responsible for James Monroe's endorsement of Indian colonization in 1824 and 1825. In fact, Jedidiah Morse and Thomas McKenney had already made similar arguments. But McCoy had a credibility that other colonization proponents lacked. When he pitched the idea of racial separation to John Calhoun on his trip to the capital in January 1824, he was speaking as a missionary with years of experience: of educating Native children, certainly, but also of the bankruptcy of old ideas about civilization-by-proximity. Calhoun, who had been thinking about Indian colonization for several years, was easily persuaded. The Baptist board resolved to support the plan, and McCoy traveled north to promote colonization in New York and Boston. When McCoy argued for Native resettlement, his examples of Indian "degradation" were drawn from his immediate experience: it was the Potawatomis, Miamis, and Ottawas, northwestern nations that had been sliced to ribbons by American expansion, who seemed the likeliest candidates for removal. The Cherokees and the other southeastern Indians were, by contrast, bright examples of what Native Americans might achieve if they were given time and space to develop. (The proposal to colonize the northwestern Indians, McCoy insisted, "requires no stronger argument in its favor, than a comparison of the flourishing

Cherokees.") McCoy must have noticed, though, that the focus of the national debate over the future of Native people had shifted from the Northwest to the Southeast. It was the Cherokees, Choctaws, Chickasaws, and Creeks—the so-called "civilized tribes"—that were caught in a standoff with the southern states. And yet these were the nations that both McCoy and Jedidiah Morse had exempted from their blueprints for an Indian colony.[19]

WHEN JOHN QUINCY ADAMS ASSUMED the presidency in March 1825, his cabinet debated whether to retain Monroe's resettlement plan. State officials in Georgia had just engineered a fraudulent treaty to obtain a huge cession of Creek land, and the federal government could no longer postpone a decision on the future of southeastern Indians. Henry Clay, Adams's secretary of state, supported the fraudulent treaty and disavowed integration. It was "impossible to civilize the Indians," he told the cabinet, since they were "not an improvable breed." James Barbour, the new secretary of war, was "shocked" at Clay's illiberal views. Barbour's first instinct was to "incorporat[e] the Indians within the States of the Union," but Georgia's intransigence gave him pause. If citizenship placed Native peoples under the sovereignty of their assailants, what could the United States do to help them? He received his answer from Thomas McKenney, who urged him to adopt the colonizing scheme. Barbour had doubts about its efficacy: new conflicts might erupt between rival Indian nations in the West, and the governing mechanisms that would regulate the colony and bind it to Washington were unclear. And what would happen if Indians refused to go? Given the mounting crisis in the Southeast, however, colonization seemed the best option. In February 1826, Barbour proposed a massive Indian Territory from Lake Huron to the Gulf of Mexico. The president would appoint a governor and judges, and an Indian assembly would be organized as quickly as possible. John Quincy Adams thought the plan "full of benevolence and humanity," though he doubted it was practicable. He asked his cabinet for alternative suggestions, "but they had nothing more effective to propose." As Adams confessed to his diary, "I approved it from the same motive."[20]

McCoy had no doubts that the policy was benevolent, and his success in Washington reassured him of its viability. He was back in the capital to lobby his cause in March 1826, soon after the formal adoption of Indian colonization by the Adams administration. Barbour was struggling to find the votes in Congress for the proposal, so McCoy befriended yet more legislators. Back at Carey Station that summer, Michigan governor Lewis Cass urged McCoy to write up his plan for an Indian colony and to promote it in the major cities of the seaboard. McCoy gladly accepted the invitation. His *Remarks on the Practicability of Indian Reform, Embracing Their Colonization* (1827), began with a vociferous rebuttal of the arguments that had been leveled against Native rights. Anyone who believed, after John Locke, that the Indians had forfeited their claim to land by being "too thinly scattered" should note that "precisely the same thing might be urged against us by Chinese invaders." The appearance of Indian inferiority was entirely circumstantial. The "calamities" suffered by Native Americans "originated in their degradation," which was "stamped on them by our first acts towards them." As with the "wretched Africans," popular prejudice fed a terrible cycle in which Indians became ever more degraded in the company of whites. When Native people were given time and space to become civilized, they would puncture this prejudice and vindicate their equality. The colonizing plan, McCoy concluded, "proposes to place the Aborigines on the same footing as ourselves." It would "commence and improve, much after the manner of all new settlements of whites." By leaving the company of their scornful neighbors, Native Americans would eventually persuade eastern whites that they were no different from them.[21]

McCoy gave a copy of his book to every congressman in Washington in December 1827. He met again with James Barbour, Richard Mentor Johnson, and President Adams. Although he felt exhilarated at the progress of his cause, his letters and journals betray the exhaustion and solitude of his new career. McCoy missed his family terribly. His loneliness in Washington may explain the origin of an unusual, even fateful friendship with the Georgia congressman Wilson Lumpkin. A close ally of Andrew Jackson, Lumpkin would do more than any other politician to expel the Cherokees from his state. In 1827, as a freshman in Washington, he kept McCoy company during his long stays in the capital and assured him of Georgia's benevolent intentions. He lamented the "wretched condition" of the Indians and hoped for the success of the "emigration plan." By any estimation, Lumpkin was no ally of Native Americans; he was in the vanguard of his home state's effort to extend its sovereignty over Indian lands. He was particularly scathing about the ABCFM missionaries in Cherokee and Creek country who relayed the plight of the "poor dear Indians" (Lumpkin's phrase) to concerned Christians in the northern states. Later, Lumpkin would dismiss all evidence of Cherokee "civilizing" as smoke and mirrors: only the "half breeds" knew anything about farming or constitutions, he insisted. "Real Indians" remained what they had always been. But Lumpkin recognized McCoy's potential as a lobbyist for Native resettlement, and courted him in the language of benevolence. Before long, the unlikely couple were working to push Congress toward a removal bill.[22]

But which Indians would benefit from colonization in the West? In his *Remarks on Indian Reform*, McCoy had again invoked the Cherokees as a counterexample: their eastern settlements demonstrated what was possible if Indians were given opportunities to embrace civilization. Even here, however, McCoy subtly laid the groundwork for a shift in his views. If the southeastern Indians had achieved so much despite the "pressure of opposing obstacles" in Georgia and Alabama, imagine what they might become in a pristine colony far from white interference. For now, McCoy stopped short of endorsing a general removal scheme. "It does not come within the scope of my design to contrive for the Cherokees," he wrote in a footnote. But in 1828, as the crisis in the Southeast worsened, it seemed that contriving some design for the southeastern Indians was a national imperative. The Cherokees had founded their own newspaper under the direction of Cornwall Foreign Mission School alumnus Elias Boudinot, who urged his compatriots not to leave their villages and farms to "try a system of civilization, uncertain and unprecedented." To quit the harassments of Georgia for the unknowns of a western colony would be "jumping out of the frying pan and into the fire." Missionaries wrote northern churches and newspapers with firsthand accounts of Cherokee resistance, calling for a grassroots movement against removal. Georgia and Alabama threatened unilateral action unless the federal government expelled the Native nations of the Southeast. In the midst of all this, James Barbour asked Congress to approve a scouting mission to the lands beyond Missouri that might sustain an Indian colony. Isaac McCoy spent six weeks in Washington lobbying for the bill's passage, gaining an insight into the trials of the legislative process. He was rewarded with a positive vote and a commission as one of the expedition's leaders.[23]

THOMAS MCKENNEY WAS CONVINCED THAT liberal reformers would embrace the logic of Indian colonization if they would only allow him to explain it properly. He was especially keen to win over Jeremiah Evarts, the secretary of the ABCFM, who had been so unhappy with the board's handling of the Ridge and Boudinot intermarriages at the Cornwall school in 1825. The ABCFM, after all, had supported Jedidiah Morse's colonizing plan in 1822. Evarts and the board were strong supporters of black colonization, and they could hardly doubt the good intentions of Isaac McCoy (whom Evarts got to know in Washington). In 1825, Evarts told McKenney that he would be "delighted" to see Indian colonization succeed, but the obstacles seemed intractable. Beyond his anxieties about the viability of a western colony, Evarts was the defender of a string of ABCFM missions in the Southeast that, in the board's flattering estimation, had brought the Cherokees across Jedidiah Morse's "awful gulf" between savagery and civilization. Evarts was loath to risk this achievement to satisfy a land grab by slaveholders in Georgia and Alabama.[24]

With Evarts immovable on the issue of Native colonization, McKenney thought he might have more luck with the Indians themselves. In the fall of 1827, he accepted James Barbour's invitation to discuss the colonization plan with the Native nations of the Southeast. In October, McKenney met with the Chickasaws and made two promises: colonization would require their consent, and the federal government would not abandon them in the West. McKenney invoked the Treaty of Hopewell to suggest that the United States had always wanted to embrace Native peoples as equals, and promised that the new colony would have the status of a federal territory. The Chickasaw leadership agreed to the principle of a colony and outlined their terms: the establishment of schools in every county of any new territory; instruction on "how to spin and manage household affairs"; military protection and training of a Native militia; a government "in all respects like one of your territories (Michigan, for example)"; and "the right of suffrage to our people." McKenney hurriedly said yes and waited while the Chickasaw leaders put the proposal to their people. He wrote to Washington saying that he was on the verge of a breakthrough. And then, after more than a week of deliberation, the Chickasaws returned. "We are thankful for your advice," they told McKenney, "but more than sorry that we have been unanimous in declining to accept it." The Chickasaw negotiation exposed the hole at the center of McKenney's strategy. He had insisted that colonization should be completely voluntary, and he had warned the Indians that the federal government could not protect them on their current lands "without coming into collision with state sovereignty." Now that the Chickasaws had said no, what happened next? Stalling, McKenney persuaded them to send a delegation on the western tour that Isaac McCoy was planning for the following summer. Perhaps if they saw the paradise that awaited them, they would change their minds.[25]

When McCoy led a party of Potawatomi and Ottawa Indians into the West in 1828, he stopped in St. Louis to await McKenney's

Chickasaw representatives. But the Chickasaws were delayed, and McCoy's northwestern participants seemed intent on proving the theory that white frontiersmen were the principal cause of Indian degradation. After several weeks in which McCoy fretted constantly about the heavy drinking of the Indians in his group, he resolved to push ahead without the Chickasaws. Just beyond the Missouri state line, in what is now Kansas, he made everyone dismount while he said a prayer for his future colony. "O thou father of the fatherless," he began, "grant that in these deserts, where I have been allowed the privilege of bowing the knee and lisping a song, prayers and praises may arise from the thousands of people saved by thee." The group made slow progress, and their entire survey took them only 150 miles west into Kansas. But their encounters with Native people, both indigenous to the region and removed from the East, went well. McCoy even bumped into the man who had once been the most notorious Indian in America: Tenskwatawa, spiritual leader of the pan-Indian confederacy that assembled in the years before the War of 1812. The Prophet had moved to Kansas with members of the Ohio Shawnee Nation the previous year. They had endured a particularly horrific removal experience, but, according to McCoy, at least, Tenskwatawa made no complaints. The Shawnees seemed settled and comfortable, and they were far from the whites who had made their lives untenable in the East.[26]

McCoy took a similarly positive view of the environment. He was impressed by the prairie country, which he judged at least as fertile as the lands on the other side of the Mississippi, and he was delighted by its improving influence on the Indians who had accompanied him from the Northwest. While these Indians had been flighty and occasionally frightening when the party had been waiting on the Chickasaws, the passage into open country had worked a miraculous change on their character. Chandonois, a Potawatomi, was a prime example. Back in St. Louis, he had spent his days in a drunken stupor; McCoy knew it was time to head west when Chandonois returned to their lodgings one night and buried his axe into the head of one of the expedition's horses. And yet here on the prairie, away from grog shops and low life, Chandonois had become friendly and good-humored: a Sancho Panza to McCoy's Quixote. The Potawatomi noted politely that the region was thinly wooded, and McCoy wondered how, if the countryside was as fertile as it seemed, white settlers could be kept away. The party heard news of hostile Indians in the vicinity, even though they were just a few days' ride from Missouri. (They were skirting the eastern edge of Comanchería, the vast Comanche Empire, which was then approaching the peak of its power.) McCoy noted all of this but seemed strangely untroubled.[27]

In what should have been the moment at which McCoy's schemes were tested against practicalities, the idea of colonization had become a kind of escapism: a way for him to exchange the grim history of white-Indian relations for a fantasy of western progress and emulation. McCoy's attachment to colonization had passed the point at which it could be loosened by evidence, and his principal supporters in Washington—Thomas McKenney and James Barbour—seemed to endorse colonization for sincere and benevolent reasons. (Wilson Lumpkin and Andrew Jackson were in the wings.) McCoy blocked out the skepticism of his northwestern Indian companions as they rode back into Missouri. When he repeated the journey with the southeastern Indians, who had by then arrived in St. Louis—Chickasaws, Choctaws, and Creeks—his experience was different. The Potawatomis and Ottawas had been friendly and voluble. The southeastern Indians seemed reluctant and disengaged, as if making the trip under duress. When this second tour was over, McCoy couldn't resist asking if they had been impressed by what they had seen. The Chickasaws took the unusual step of committing their stonewalling to paper: "We are not able to give you any account of the present tour," they wrote. With that, they headed east, and McCoy returned to his family for the first time in six months.[28]

MCCOY WAS BACK IN WASHINGTON in January 1829 for the last months of the Adams administration. The House Committee on Indian Affairs reprinted his report on the Kansas country and supported his colonization plan. Indians who chose to remain where they were should receive "ample reservations," the committee declared, while western colonists would be "elevated into rights and privileges such as we enjoy." But the congressional session ended before the colonization plans could be implemented, and Washington nervously awaited the arrival of the president-elect, Andrew Jackson. For Jeremiah Evarts and the missionaries posted among the southeastern Indians, the election of 1828 was an apocalyptic event. Jackson had been synonymous with hostility toward Native people since the 1790s, and everyone knew he was sympathetic to the states seeking removal. Evarts rushed to Washington and took a room in the same boardinghouse as the president-elect. When Jackson granted Evarts an audience, he told him that the federal government would no longer restrain Georgia from extending its sovereignty over Indians who lived within the state. Jackson intended to appoint John Eaton, another Tennessean with a reputation for hostility toward Indians, as his secretary of war. (Evarts had hoped that Jackson might pick William McLean of Ohio, whom Isaac McCoy had converted to the cause of colonization.) Evarts concluded that any pretense of seeking Indian consent for resettlement had now disappeared. Having abandoned hope of a remedy in Washington, Evarts returned to New England to build a popular insurgency against the Jacksonian vision of removal.[29]

At this point, McKenney and McCoy had been arguing for western resettlement for more than five years. Native colonization had been government policy for most of that period, though the Monroe and Adams administrations had lacked the will or the votes to push a plan through Congress. Inaction was not something to fear from Andrew Jackson, and the advocates of colonization now faced a difficult decision. McCoy admitted that his allies in Washington were mostly "on the Adams side of the political effervescence," but his friendship with Wilson Lumpkin gave him direct access to the incoming president.

He met with Evarts again and was "grieved to discover that, in regard to colonizing the Indians in the West, his views and efforts ran in a channel opposite to mine." Evarts should have been a natural ally of benevolent causes, and had clearly toyed with Native resettlement earlier in the 1820s; but the "civilized" nature of southeastern nations, and his own missionary investment in the region, made him a formidable enemy of Indian colonization. Could McCoy realize his vision of racial separation—with its extensive commitments to a new Indian Territory in the West—with the support of Andrew Jackson? Lumpkin arranged for him to meet the new president and his secretary of war just a few weeks after the inauguration.[30]

McCoy said nothing in his journal about the substance of his discussion with the president. Instead, he wrote that, during the long walk back to his boardinghouse, he became "so deeply impressed with the magnitude of my undertakings and of the many obstacles that opposed [them]" that he "burst into tears, and found myself comparable only to a weeping child." Days later, McCoy still felt the urge to cry constantly. He was pitching his Indian colony to an administration that was ideologically unsuited to his principles and assumptions. The Baptist Board of Missions was on the verge of withdrawing its support for McCoy's scheme, swayed by Evarts and his insistence that removal would effect the "speedy extermination" of the Indians. And it was clear that Jackson would pursue the removal of precisely those Native nations that McCoy had originally exempted from his colonizing plans. But McCoy and McKenney had come too far to abandon their idea. McCoy prepared a second edition of his *Remarks on Indian Reform*. A new section insisted that, although the Cherokees had "come out boldly" against colonization, it would be folly to recognize an independent state inside the "acknowledged boundaries of another independent state." McCoy dismissed the idea that the Cherokees' prosperity in their current location ruled out the possibility of resettlement in the West. Didn't rich people often move from one city to another? And he confirmed that when they were colonized beyond the Mississippi, the Cherokees would find themselves on a path toward citizenship. The southeastern Indians would have to leave the United States now to re-enter it in the future.[31]

Jackson and the new secretary of war, John Eaton, pushed a different line in their messages to the southeastern Indians. Jackson told the Creeks that resettlement in the West would allow them to retain their traditions and their sovereignty. (Jackson accused them of failing to abandon hunting and rejecting agriculture, mirroring the misleading arguments of Wilson Lumpkin and state officials in the Southeast.) Eaton, meeting Cherokee chiefs in April 1829, promised that the federal government would provide "a paternal and superintending care" in the West; he said nothing about territorial government, citizenship, and equality. McCoy was back in Washington in May, meeting with Jackson and Eaton along with his usual friends in Congress. As Jeremiah Evarts built a protest movement against removal in the northern states, McCoy wrote to his friends there in the hope that they could organize pro-colonization petitions. ("Please forward [them]," he wrote, "to Hon. Wilson Lumpkin, Washington City.") Thomas McKenney even resorted to astroturfing. He helped found the New York Board for the Emigration, Preservation and Improvement of the Aborigines of America, along with a few friends in the Dutch Reformed Church, and gave a stirring address at its first (and only) meeting. White people had become "alienated from the Indians" solely by historical accident, McKenney claimed. In an Indian Territory to the west, Native people would obtain "all privileges . . . civil, political and religious" and "attain an elevation to which, in their present relations, they can never aspire." McKenney brandished a promise from Secretary Eaton that "nothing of a compulsory course" would be done to effect removal.[32]

While McCoy and McKenney juggled reassurances about the Jackson administration's intentions, pro-removal politicians used McCoy to vouchsafe their humanitarian bona fides. Lewis Cass, in a long and influential essay in the *North American Review*, cited McCoy's *Remarks on Indian Reform* to justify western resettlement. Wilson Lumpkin read entire pages of the *Remarks* to the House of

Representatives, insisting that the views of "one of our most experienced, pious and persevering missionaries" should silence the administration's critics. McCoy offered removal advocates a crucial link with the Adams and Monroe administrations. Lumpkin noted, accurately, that the previous two presidents had joined the Baptist missionary in advocating a federal colonization program. Why, then, did northern critics insist that Andrew Jackson had invented the policy?[33]

Ahead of the vote on the Indian Removal bill in the spring of 1830, McCoy focused his efforts on securing support from thirty wavering members of the House of Representatives. He came to see his involvement as pivotal to the outcome. The split in the Senate was clear: 28 in favor of removal, 20 opposed. In the House, the result was agonizingly close: 102 in favor, 97 opposed. Many factors might have swung the vote one way or the other, and defeat for the bill in 1830 might only have postponed the passage of similar legislation (or outright war in Georgia). But the influence of McCoy, McKenney, and the other proponents of colonization had a profound effect. Successive administrations had promoted the claim that Native American resettlement was a benevolent measure, but had failed to force the issue in Congress. McCoy and McKenney clung to colonization despite the fact that the removal bill lacked even the barest liberal cladding. It provided for the exchange of Indian land for western territory and promised aid to enable Native Americans to travel to the new Indian country. It said nothing about state-building, education, territorial status, suffrage, or citizenship. It was plainly intended to secure removal, not colonization.[34]

Isaac McCoy kept silent about the bill's deficiencies. Thomas McKenney, on the other hand, began to second-guess himself as the debate raged around him. He knew the members of the ABCFM very well, and had been trying for years to convince Jeremiah Evarts that colonization was inevitable. (He had also told the New York Emigration Board that he shared exactly the same ambitions for the Indians as Evarts and the anti-removal campaigners, and differed only on the methods required to secure the Indians' future.) "I have taken a deep stake in this business of emigration," he told a friend in the Senate, "and stand committed to the Indians and the public for a fulfillment of all that I have promised the one, and assured the other, *would be done.*" In a letter to Cyrus Kingsbury, who had been one of the first ABCFM missionaries in Cherokee country back in 1817, McKenney readied a *mea culpa.* He had originally believed, with Kingsbury, that the southeastern Indians could be preserved in their current location, but he had been compelled by circumstance to abandon that hope as "wholly delusive." What if colonization were no less illusory? McKenney admitted that, if the skeletal removal legislation were not followed by the "suitable benefits" he and McCoy had promised, the Indians would become "wretched, and finally disappear." In that bleak future, "then will the cause of mourning be with those who seek, by this mode, to save them."[35]

McCoy and McKenney had transformed the idea of Indian removal. For Thomas Jefferson, the West would allow Native peoples to preserve their traditions for decades, perhaps centuries, without further interference from the whites. The Louisiana Purchase could offer an escape hatch from the American republic and its ceaseless hunger for economic and social "progress." Colonization proponents hitched the opposite argument to the same outcome: they insisted that Indians were no different from whites, and that their future lay in an embrace of "civilized" values and practices that could only be secured, paradoxically, through separation. As white Americans came to see that the settling of the West would be measured in decades rather than centuries, the notion that Indians could take refuge from "civilization" anywhere on the continent became harder to defend. It was at this moment in the debate, with even liberal voices suggesting that Native Americans were doomed to extinction, that the logic of colonization became suddenly and urgently persuasive—not only to McCoy and McKenney, but to the perplexed administrations of James Monroe and John Quincy Adams.

That Andrew Jackson, John Eaton, Wilson Lumpkin, and the other southeastern removal advocates were not seriously committed to colonization seems painfully self-evident. But it would be wrong to assume that, because McKenney and McCoy opted to work for removal in 1830, their attachment to an Indian colony was phony or fleeting. As both later admitted, they stayed their course even under the alarming direction of Andrew Jackson because of a deeper conviction about the rightness of their cause. Both men imagined that, when the southeastern Indians were physically removed to the "deserts" that McCoy had surveyed in 1827, the argument for fulfilling the colonization promise would become as irresistible as the argument for removal had previously been. In this, their confidence was misplaced.

Epilogue
AN ENTERPRISE FOR THE YOUNG

Edward coles had one thing on his mind. It had been nearly five years since he'd challenged Thomas Jefferson to devise "some plan for the gradual emancipation of slavery." In the meantime, he had seen out his service with James Madison in the White House, but had not yet freed his own slaves. After failing to find suitable land in Ohio, and undertaking a diplomatic mission to Russia for Madison, in the spring of 1819 he was finally ready to make good on his promise. He announced to his eighteen slaves that he had bought land in Edwardsville, the capital of Illinois Territory, and gave them the choice to accompany him or remain in Virginia. Excepting two elderly and infirm women, all chose to make the trip. In deference to his family's wishes, he said nothing about emancipation until he reached Pittsburgh, where he rented a flatboat to carry the party down the Ohio River. "Soon after getting on board the boat," he later wrote his mother, "I called them all together, and told them, not only of my intention to free them, but that they were actually free."[1]

Coles told this story on many occasions during the rest of his long life, but the details remained the same. When he made his announcement, "the effect on them was electrical." His former slaves stared silently, unable to believe what had happened: "As they began to see the truth of what they had heard, and to realize their situation, there came on a kind of hysterical giggling laugh. After a pause of intense and unutterable emotion, bathed in tears, and with tremulous voices,

307

they gave vent to their gratitude, and implored the blessings of God on me." Coles told them they were at liberty to leave him right there. He would, however, prefer to supply each family with 160 acres of land in Illinois, both "as a reward for their past services" and "a stimulant to their future exertions." Coles resolved to cushion the "recoiling effects of so suddenly breaking the bonds of slavery." In turn, his freed slaves would prove that "the black race were not inferior to the white, and were equally qualified to enjoy all the blessings [of] freedom."[2]

Illinois joined the Union as a free state in the year of Coles's arrival. To his surprise, he discovered as many opportunities to argue about slavery as he had had in Virginia—perhaps more, given that conservative settlers wanted to amend the state constitution to permit slaveholding. Coles had taken a job in the land office at Edwardsville, and as he came to realize the illiberal proclivities of at least some of his new neighbors, he entered politics for the first time. He ran for governor in 1822 and, with the conservative vote split between rival candidates, found himself leading the state only three years after his arrival. His tenure in office was dominated by the slavery issue. The proslavery faction called a referendum to force a constitutional convention that would make Illinois a slave state; Coles led the campaign for a no vote. He was incredulous that any Illinoisan would seek out the "curse of our southern brethren." Virginians could at least blame the British for introducing slavery; they allowed it to continue solely because of "the difficulty of removing it." To adopt slavery in Illinois would be to "establish and legalize what we know to be wrong from choice." A sin of omission in the slave South, he wrote, became a sin of commission in the free North. Coles asked his friends on the East Coast—including James Madison and William Crawford—for help.[3]

The Quaker philanthropist Roberts Vaux of Philadelphia agreed to write a pamphlet in support of the antislavery cause, and to ship it with an anonymous title page to St. Louis for collection by the governor. (Coles was anxious to avoid the impression that a Philadelphian was telling Illinoisans what to think.) "Can it be that a people professing to believe that 'all men are free and equal,' is to be found willing even to deliberate upon such a question?" asked Vaux's pamphlet. Coles, who became the proprietor of a local newspaper to ensure that his views would reach the public, made a similar point in a series of articles ahead of the referendum. "Who is he that has so little of the spirit of '76 flowing in his veins, as to be able coolly to sit down to advocate slavery?" Coles grounded his arguments in human brotherhood. He dismissed the claim of "natural distinctions" between the races, warning that slavery would present "a strange contradiction to our principles, and a gross anomaly and incongruity in our political institutions." The proslavery faction, meanwhile, was tireless in its persecution of the governor. Coles's new enemies brought a lawsuit against him for transporting freed slaves into Illinois, a practice that had been outlawed by the legislature a month before his arrival. There was no way that Coles could have known about the new law during his journey from Virginia, a point he made repeatedly to the court. But his opponents tied him up in litigation and drained his morale.[4]

"They have all behaved uniformly well," Coles told Roberts Vaux of his former slaves in 1824, "and are honest, industrious and prosperous." He was convinced he had done nothing wrong by freeing them—"The only complaint against me is that I am a friend to the equal rights of man"—but the lawsuit unsettled him. Coles had a pittance to live on after his legal bills and the costs of the referendum campaign, and he felt terribly alone. It was at this moment that he first expressed support for colonization. "In furnishing a country for the Negroes," he wrote in his newspaper, "the great barrier on our part to their emancipation is removed." Coles later claimed that he had supported the American Colonization Society since its founding in 1816. There is no evidence of this in his correspondence. He helped found an auxiliary of the ACS in 1826, and he attended the annual meeting of the parent society in Washington in 1827. It was the vitriolic struggle over slavery in Illinois that made him a convert.[5]

In August 1824, 60 percent of voters rejected the proposed constitutional convention. Illinois was spared from slavery, though Coles's faith in integration and coexistence had been dealt a fatal blow. Perhaps

Coles endorsed colonization during the referendum campaign for tactical reasons, to reassure voters that keeping slavery out of the state would
not produce an influx of free blacks. But if he picked up the threads of
black removal for political expediency, he had soon woven them into
his broader critique of slavery. After spending two weeks traveling with
Lafayette during the Frenchman's tour of 1825, Coles left the governor's
office in 1826 and told his former slaves to consider emigration to Liberia.
He conceded that they had behaved impeccably since their manumission,
and had given his political enemies no ammunition with which to damage him during the referendum debate. But colonization now seemed
to promise "incalculable" benefits to the United States and Africa "in
ridding the one of a degraded and degrading population, and restoring
to the other her own peculiar people, civilized and christianized." Coles
offered to pay for his former slaves to emigrate. He even volunteered to
lead them to the promised land in person, as William Thornton had done
nearly forty years earlier. But "they are . . . so happy and content where
they are," he wrote, "that they seem reluctant to change their situation."[6]

Coles's journey from emancipation to colonization was neatly
encapsulated in three newspaper articles recording Fourth of July celebrations in his adopted state. In 1819, the first Independence Day after
his arrival in Edwardsville, he raised his glass to "the rights of men,"
which "appertain equally to him, whether his complexion be white,
red, or black." Three years later, at the celebration in nearby Kaskaskia,
he toasted "Principles, not Men." But back in Edwardsville, presiding
over the Independence Day celebrations of 1827, he offered the crowd
"Liberia—Destined to rid America of Negroes, and to give to Africa
civilization and Christianity." Coles knew that his former slaves were
unwilling to leave the United States. "I still hope," he wrote in 1827,
"that they may yet be disposed to emigrate." In the following years,
he made several attempts to persuade state legislators in Virginia to
adopt a colonization plan. Eventually he settled in Philadelphia, where
he found a wife, had a family, and made a fortune—the things he had
hoped to do in Illinois. One of the first things he did there was write
James Madison and implore the former president to free his slaves.[7]

WHEN HE HAD ASKED THOMAS Jefferson to do more for emancipation in 1814, Edward Coles had confronted him with the Declaration of Independence. When William Short had made a similar overture to Jefferson in 1798, he had offered the more incendiary suggestion that planters might marry their slaves. Short, like Coles, lived a fascinating life after his cajoling of Jefferson. He moved back to the United States from Europe during the War of 1812, basing himself (as Coles later would) in Philadelphia rather than Virginia. Initially, he was skeptical of the American Colonization Society. Free blacks "will not consent to go," he told Jefferson, and masters would hesitate to free their slaves (a fair summary of what happened in the coming decades). Short's views on how best to end slavery were not set. He was sure that diffusion was a bad idea, and thought that black people might be amenable to resettlement in Haiti. He proposed serfdom for freed slaves in his 1825 letter to Jefferson, but he was also closely involved in philanthropic work with Philadelphia's free black population.[8]

Through his membership of the Pennsylvania Abolition Society, William Short became a friend of Roberts Vaux, who had worked with Coles to keep slavery out of Illinois. Vaux was also an early skeptic of the ACS, despite being urged by no less than Thomas Clarkson to embrace some version of racial separation as a means of ending slavery. (Clarkson thought that freed people should be given "land in some distant part of the United States" and representation in Congress.) In 1827, Short and Vaux discussed founding a new black school in Philadelphia. Short wondered if they could go further, and establish racially integrated orphanages or poor houses. Piecing together exactly what they discussed is difficult. Going by Vaux's letters, Short seems to have suggested that mixed-race institutions might be an instrument for encouraging intermarriage across the color line. Vaux had to remind Short of the "deep rooted prejudice" of the city's white residents about the "propriety of encouraging marriages." The initiative would surely fail, and perhaps even produce "some act of legislation that would involve the unfortunate people whose welfare thy kindness seeks to advance." Better to segregate one's philanthropy and work around the city's racial mores.[9]

William Short, like Edward Coles, had been radicalized against slavery at the College of William and Mary. When he had left the United States for France in 1784 to serve as Jefferson's personal secretary, he had told his family to treat his only slave, Stephen, as a free man: he was to come and go as he pleased, choose his employer, and work for wages. More than forty years later, in his affluent Philadelphia home, Short was dragged back into the world he had rejected. His younger brother Peyton, who had engaged in land speculation and various risky ventures in Kentucky, had run up considerable debts. When Peyton died in September 1825, William intervened to ensure that eleven of Peyton's slaves were kept from the auction block. William's conscience was assuaged, though he now found himself living a double life. He was a wealthy businessman who moved in Philadelphia's most liberal circles, but he was also an absentee slaveholder looking once more to free himself from slaves. He began to wonder if colonization might resolve the contradiction.[10]

William Short relied heavily on his nephew, Charles Wilkins Short, to oversee the lives and labor of five of Peyton's slaves: Old Charles, Lucy, James, David, and Young Charles. Old Charles, Lucy, and James were elderly, their "constitutions considerably impaired," and stayed with Short's nephew in Lexington; David and Young Charles were hired out to a slaveholder named James Breathitt. Short wrote Breathitt in 1833 to ask for his views of emancipation. "Upon the subject of the negroes or slaves," Breathitt replied, "I have been opposed to slavery and am now an advocate of the Colonization Society." Their rapport established, Breathitt made Short an offer. If Charles and David were not to be sent to Liberia, and Short was keen to withdraw from the world of slaveholding, perhaps "you would not object to selling young Charles to me, inasmuch as I own his brother?" Breathitt was keen not to be misunderstood: "I am opposed to slavery and do not mean to own more than two men," he promised. "I suppose that $350 would be about right for him?" Short's reply does not survive, but from the backpedaling of Breathitt's next letter it seems to have been irate. "I would not on any account have you do violence to your feelings in relation to that unfortunate race of people called slaves. In fact I myself regret that I live in a slave state."[11]

Colonization promised an escape from these tawdry negotiations. For James, Old Charles, and Lucy, Liberia had come too late. For David and Young Charles—one in his thirties, the other just twenty—colonization seemed more promising. The ACS insisted that free blacks and slaves would embrace Liberia when its advantages were calmly explained. Short's nephew knew otherwise, saying: "It is most true, indeed, that all our slave population have a great repugnance to the Colonization scheme, and but few of the free negroes can be induced to embark in it." After he spoke with David and Charles, however, Charles Wilkins Short was happy to inform his uncle that the two younger slaves had an "eager desire" to accept the offer. He and his uncle rushed to make arrangements for the slaves' departure.[12]

Although the American Colonization Society paid for the passage of freed people to Liberia, its ships left American ports infrequently, and slaveholders were responsible for delivering their former slaves to the quay at the appointed time. During the many months in which William Short and his nephew worked out the details of David's and Charles's departure, David—who had parents and a wife in Lexington—wondered if he was making a terrible mistake. When Charles Wilkins Short dismissed his suggestion that his elderly mother might accompany him to Africa, David offered to sell himself to another slaveholder to avoid the journey to Liberia. His skepticism spread to Charles, and in the summer of 1839 both men declared their unwillingness to leave. William Short was exasperated. Didn't they realize that he couldn't free them in Kentucky unless they agreed to leave the state? (Kentucky had adopted a version of Virginia's law insisting that freed people leave within a year.) Charles Wilkins Short promised to talk sternly with the men, and "not fail to hold *in terrorem* over them, your determination to sell them, if they should prove so foolish and stupid as to prefer slavery in Kentucky to freedom in Africa." He could only apologize to his generous uncle. "I shall be really mortified and vexed," he wrote, "if these silly people should frustrate your benevolent intentions towards them."[13]

Even if his slaves were "incorrigibly blind to their best interests," William Short was nervous about threatening David and Charles into leaving the United States. His nephew ought to explain their best interests to the men, Short wrote, but should "certainly not force them into it by threats of any kind." Charles Wilkins Short now apologized for raising the prospect of "compulsory measures," but he urged his uncle to remember the context. It was "debatable" whether those "who are entirely incapable of judging for themselves" should overrule the best intentions of their benefactors. In the end, however, the wishes of his uncle would be honored: "You may rest assured, my dear Uncle . . . that no coercive measures, or alarming threats, shall be made to bear on these poor fellows." David chose to stay in Kentucky, and William Short marked his frustration in a very particular way. From now on, Charles Wilkins Short would be required to withhold the wages David earned from being hired out. These would be forwarded to Charles in Liberia. David, whom William Short bitterly dubbed "the anti-African," would work for colonization even if he refused to be saved by it.[14]

On 15 November 1839, Charles—who now took the name Charles Gist—left Kentucky on the long overland journey for Norfolk, Virginia, and his passage to Liberia. "If I ever do any good in the world," he wrote William Short, "it will be owing to you in making me a free man." From this time forward, Short became ever more invested in Gist's future. After an anxious wait, Short learned from his nephew that Gist had arrived safely on the ACS sailing ship *Saluda* at the end of March 1840. Conditions in Liberia were tougher than he had expected, and Gist's gratitude was punctuated by urgent requests for money. Short contacted his friends in the Colonization Society and asked for their help. "I shall be disposed to make Charles rich," Short told his nephew in 1841, "for a Liberian." Short was approaching his eighty-second birthday, and he found it hard to hold a pen. But, he wrote, "I have so much more interest in Charles than in any other subject, I have employed all my force to write of him."[15]

In the last years of his life, William Short watched Charles Gist with rapt attention. His nephew sent him letters describing Gist's farm at Bexley, sixty miles south of Monrovia, and his plans to cultivate coffee. "I feel as a new man," Gist wrote during his second summer in Africa, "and am trying to improve myself for usefulness in our rising Republic." Then the tone of Charles's letters became bleak. He struggled to make a success of the farm, even with the money he received from the Shorts. He hinted that he would like to return to America. "I have been deterred from writing to him," Charles Wilkins Short confessed to his uncle, "from a want of proper decision in my own mind on this very subject." Short's nephew was opposed to bringing back Charles Gist. "The more I see of negro freedom in this country, the more I am convinced of its useless or even injurious tendency," he wrote his uncle. If the Shorts funded Gist's return, what would happen to him in Kentucky? "He may not be willing to return to a state of nominal slavery," Charles Wilkins Short admitted. Perhaps his uncle would like Charles Gist to call on him in Philadelphia? It would "doubtless afford him great satisfaction to see a benefactor to whom he owes so much." If William Short felt nervous at the prospect of bringing his two lives together, his nephew's other suggestion was far worse: "Perhaps you might choose to take him into your service?"[16]

In the event, Charles Gist stayed in Liberia, and the Shorts tried to keep him afloat. Charles Wilkins Short realized how much his uncle had invested in Gist's success. In addition to Gist's letters from Africa, he sent William a gradual emancipation plan that had been written by Kentucky's ACS auxiliary. The prospects for many more Charles Gists in the state looked promising, he told his uncle, especially if Liberia continued to advance. In Philadelphia, William Short tinkered with the provisions of his will. In 1847, making his final revision, he bequeathed $10,000 to the American Colonization Society. Charles Gist's experiences in Africa—and the positive words he had received from his nephew on antislavery feeling in Kentucky—augured well for the cause.[17]

Then, abruptly, Gist's progress was terminated. In November 1848, the *Liberia Herald* reported "a most atrocious murder at Bexley." A man named William Blain had been shot, "the supposed murderer one Guest." Charles Wilkins Short learned the details early in 1849.

Blain and Gist had left Kentucky on the same wagon train in 1839 for the journey to Liberia. They had ended up as neighbors and friends in Bexley, until Blain had begun sleeping with Gist's wife. The murderer was quickly apprehended and sentenced to hang. Charles Wilkins Short wrote to his brother to discuss the lurid story. Should he tell their uncle, who was now in his ninetieth year? "It may open his eyes to the futility of the scheme of colonization," he thought, "to which he has been a liberal contributor." In the end, he decided against it. Charles Gist died on 1 May 1849 on the scaffold in Monrovia. William Short died peacefully at his home in Philadelphia seven months later. The American Colonization Society received its huge bequest from the Short estate, and in the 1850s it used the money to fund a revival of its fortunes.[18]

AFTER HELPING TO PASS THE Indian Removal Act of 1830, Isaac McCoy awaited his reward: an Indian colony in the West. But he first had to dispel the anti-removal protests that continued to pour into Washington. In a series of articles for a Washington newspaper, he insisted that treaties with the Indians had been "merely matters of convenience to us, and of humanity towards them." If the United States recognized an absolute right of sovereignty in the case of the Cherokees, other Indians would make similar claims that would "threaten the very existence of our government." The essential principle of westward migration was no different for Indians than for whites: "If government were now to make a similar offer . . . to the citizens of the United States, I risk nothing in saying that thousands of families would be located there in less than a year." When precisely this phrase appeared in Andrew Jackson's Annual Message to Congress that December, McCoy congratulated himself for inspiring it.[19]

Beyond the continuing protests of northern removal opponents, the obstacles to founding a colony were considerable. Jackson had already begun to coerce Native Americans to accept tracts of land in

Kansas, but a number of nations adamantly refused to comply. Since the 1830 act insisted that removal would be voluntary, the next steps seemed uncertain. At the same time, McCoy became nervous that the administration's plans for western uplift were less ambitious than his own. In 1830, Jackson told Congress that the West would allow "wandering savages" to "pursue happiness in their own way and under their own rude institutions." The following year, Lewis Cass announced that, once they were removed to the West, Indians should be left "in the enjoyment of their peculiar institutions." McCoy shivered at the thought that Cass was ready to abandon the removed Indians in precisely the place that the work of "civilization" should begin. If this was his intention, he told his journal, "our cause would, humanly speaking, be ruined." Cass had been the recipient of McCoy's original colonization proposal in 1823 and had commissioned his *Remarks on Indian Reform* four years later. Had Cass been humoring him all along? For his part, Cass realized that McCoy's usefulness had not yet expired. He offered conciliating words during their meetings, asked McCoy to meet with the Cherokees in Washington, and sent him to survey the western tracts that would grease the removal treaties.[20]

In 1832, McCoy moved his family permanently to a cabin on the western edge of Missouri. A mile beyond his front door was the unorganized land where McCoy planned a territorial government for Native Americans. During his frequent visits to Washington during the rest of that decade, McCoy's main objective was to lobby for the creation of "Aboriginia," as he called the proposed Indian Territory. The administration's removal treaties did little more than grant a fixed tract of land to each Native nation, along with compensation for their westward passage. McCoy's plans were much more ambitious. He called on the federal government to mark out a vast area encompassing what is now Kansas, as well as parts of Nebraska and northern Texas, and to guarantee it to Native people in perpetuity. Whites would be prohibited from settling there. The president would appoint a (white) governor and encourage disparate Native nations to form a single governing council. Finally, Aboriginia would send an Indian delegate to the US

Congress. McCoy outlined the thinking behind his plan in a series of pamphlets he prepared in his new western home. The Indian Territory would give Native people "the privileges of citizenship within a population exclusively their own." The West would be a place of reinvention rather than tradition: "They go to the country not to remain hunters, but to become a component part of the community of the United States." White "prejudices" had denied Indians a place in the East, but a western colony would "make them a part of ourselves."[21]

In 1834, McCoy's supporters in Congress drafted a bill that contained all of these provisions. It was mauled by a man whom McCoy had once thought an ally: John Quincy Adams, who had now returned to Washington as a member of the House of Representatives. "What does the bill contain?" Adams asked on the floor of Congress. "A project not only for the erection of an Indian Territory, but for an Indian State, to be admitted hereafter as one of the sovereign States of this Union." Adams complained that the Indian Territory bill gave Jackson extraordinary power to appoint the territory's governor and manage its affairs. He also hinted that one "Indian State" might soon become "two or three, or half a dozen." As the three most powerful parties in the debate argued over his proposal, McCoy despaired of the motives and sincerity of politicians. The Cherokees and other eastern nations refused even to negotiate with the Jackson administration; northern reformers opposed anything that might equate removal with benevolence; and southeastern politicians who had embraced McCoy in 1829 found him less compelling now that the Indian Removal Act had become law.[22]

Throughout the 1830s, McCoy's commitment to colonization became increasingly entangled with his material survival. He had been told by Jackson's supporters that, if an Indian Territory were organized, he would be appointed its superintendent. (That word was substituted for "governor" after Adams's assault on the 1834 bill.) He received little remuneration from the Baptist Board of Missions, and he wasn't sure he wanted a missionary post, which would increase his salary but limit his claims to patronage. Life on the extreme edge of the United States was hard. His family was often sick, and his journal marked multiple

bereavements. ("It is exceedingly hard to be deprived of our dear children," he wrote simply of his daughter Sarah's death in 1835.) McCoy
promised his wife and children that preferment and an august title were
just around the corner, and put them to work printing pro-colonization
pamphlets on the rudimentary press that the Baptist board had sent
into Indian country. They ironed and folded pages, stitched binding
and corrected typos. McCoy sent his arguments for Indian colonization
to every congressman and member of Jackson's cabinet—and was dis-
mayed when the Board of Missions billed him for the cost. During the
long periods between legislative sessions, with the family in desperate
straits, he worked as a bookkeeper for a local store and put lodgers in
the bedrooms of his recently deceased children. When McCoy turned
fifty-one in 1835, he reflected that he had traveled tens of thousands of
miles in pursuit of Indian colonization. Had he achieved anything for
his trouble? "All this is lamentable," he told his journal.[23]

Then, suddenly, he found himself back at the center of things. When
McCoy went to Washington in 1836, he discovered a new enthusiasm
for the Indian Territory bill among congressmen. John Tipton, US senator from Indiana, had been avidly reading the pamphlets McCoy sent
from the Kansas border. Quietly, Tipton asked if he would ghostwrite
speeches on Indian matters. Members of the House Indian Affairs
Committee did the same. McCoy wrote excitedly to his wife, Christiana,
that the House committee would soon publish a bill "embracing substantially the fundamental principles of our colonization scheme." As
always, McCoy's popularity in Congress reflected more than the benevolence of his sponsors. In 1835, a Cherokee splinter group had agreed
to a removal plan with the United States. The Treaty of New Echota
was the product of a desperate debate within Cherokee society about
whether the nation should hold out in the East or take the best terms it
could wring from Jackson. The leaders of the "Treaty Party" were John
Ridge and Elias Boudinot, the students who had been the subjects of
such scorn after finding white wives in Connecticut. The remainder of
the Cherokees, ably represented by their leader, John Ross, complained
to Congress (and their supporters in the northern states) that the Treaty

Party did not represent the majority of the nation. McCoy said very little about the Treaty of New Echota in his journal. A missionary colleague urged him to oppose ratification, and McCoy froze. Privately, he acknowledged that the treaty should be renegotiated. He also knew that John Ross and his people would never consent to move westward. Caught between an immediate injustice and his vast plans for western redemption, McCoy declined to intervene. The Treaty of New Echota passed the Senate in the spring of 1836 by a single vote.[24]

With Cherokee removal sanctioned by Congress, McCoy hoped his territorial bill would pass. But the controversy surrounding the fraudulent treaty, along with the outbreak of armed resistance by Seminole and Creek Indians opposing removal, meant the legislative session ended without a vote on the measure. McCoy returned to Washington the following year and received the assurances of Richard Mentor Johnson, vice-president under Martin Van Buren, that he would support his schemes. Johnson told McCoy that he was "possibly hoping for the presidency at a future day." He promised that the colony (and the superintendent's position) would soon be in McCoy's reach. McCoy met with Martin Van Buren and the new secretary of war, Joel Poinsett, and moved into John Tipton's house to coordinate the campaign for an Indian Territory. The 1837 session also passed without a vote. When McCoy returned in 1838, Wilson Lumpkin, now a US senator from Georgia, assured him that this would be his year: Van Buren wanted the bill to pass and would make McCoy superintendent. McCoy met with John Quincy Adams and felt that he'd won his acquiescence, if not his support. He produced more arguments and reports for his friends in Congress, hoping that his moment had finally come. When the debate on the territory began in April, McCoy sat in the Senate gallery listening proudly to speeches he had written. This time, the Senate voted for the creation of the territory by a clear majority. If the House now followed suit, McCoy's fifteen years of lobbying would not have been in vain.[25]

That month, six hundred miles southwest of Washington, the US Army arrived at the Cherokee capital and began to build stockades. Van Buren had sent the military to compel the Cherokees to accept the

Treaty of New Echota. With rifles and bayonets, the army announced its intention to march 10,000 Cherokees along the Trail of Tears to the western future they had consistently rejected. Back in the capital, ahead of a vote on the Indian Territory in the House, the debate had already been colored by early rumblings of sectionalism. Was McCoy's colony a clever ruse to impede the expansion of the South, and to divert white settlers to the free states north of the Missouri Compromise line? (John Calhoun, now a US senator from South Carolina, had voted against the bill for this reason.) McCoy left Washington to visit his family before the end of the session, nursing a renewed anxiety about the fate of his bill. In his absence, House lawmakers failed him once again: the legislative session expired before the plans could be debated. "This is not a little discouraging," wrote McCoy. It would be the last time his colonization plan came close to the statute book.[26]

As US troops rounded up the Cherokees in the summer of 1838, McCoy's leading ally in Congress, Senator John Tipton of Indiana, was summoned by his home state's governor to assist with an emergency. A portion of the Potawatomi Nation—the same Indians that McCoy had begun teaching in 1820—were refusing to leave Indiana in compliance with the treaties they had signed. It transpired that, as with the Cherokee majority and the Treaty of New Echota, these particular Potawatomis had not signed the agreement they were being ordered to honor. The governor knew that Tipton had worked as an Indian agent before his political career and authorized him to raise a band of militia to resolve the standoff. Tipton lured the Potawatomi leaders to a church, which he surrounded at gunpoint. He rounded up eight hundred men, women, and children and forcibly marched them to Kansas. Hundreds fell ill; nearly fifty died on the journey, half of them children. "We are actuated by kind feelings towards them," Tipton had told the Senate back in April, "by a desire to do them good." The author of those words, Isaac McCoy, was waiting in Kansas to point the Potawatomis toward the land they would now occupy.[27]

McCoy labored to correct removal supporters who insisted that Native Americans were locked in a "rude" state of development, but he was alarmed by the way in which "benevolent" removal opponents insisted that resettling Indians in the West would ensure their extinction. In 1838, as Congress debated the Indian Territory, he went to see an exhibition by George Catlin, an artist who had spent years capturing the lives of "traditional" Indians. Catlin had become a sensation in the cities of the East, but McCoy loathed the message of his art. "While he expressed admiration of many noble traits in Indian character," McCoy wrote, "he held out the ruinous idea which so widely prevails that the Aborigines of our continent are doomed to extinction. No idea could have a more paralyzing tendency in all our efforts for the improvement of the Indians, and no doctrine could be more unphilosophical and absurd." For McCoy, Catlin embodied the romantic resignation about Native people that had consumed the northern reform movement. McCoy had failed to win over those reformers in 1830, but had at least carried the day in Congress. With the Indians now in position to receive the remedy he had prescribed, he found himself fighting against a southern view that Native peoples could never shake off their savage traits, and a northern view that removal was the death knell of their race. "Only suppose Indians to be like all other human beings," McCoy insisted, "and all becomes plain and easy."[28]

After driving the Potawatomis to Kansas, John Tipton announced his retirement from the Senate. The Indian Territory bill did not return to Congress, and McCoy was left alone in his quest for Native unity and congressional representation. On the other side of the Trail of Tears, the enemies of the Treaty Party sought out John Ridge and Elias Boudinot, the Native alumni of the Cornwall Foreign Mission School who had signed away the Cherokees' eastern homeland. The debate over whether the southeastern Indians should remain in the East or relocate to the West had raged within Native nations for more than four decades. Its resolution in 1839 was horrific. Harriett Gold had died three years earlier, and didn't have to watch her husband being hacked to death by his assailants. Sarah Northrop was not so fortunate.[29]

In 1841, Secretary of War John Bell, McCoy's old ally in the congressional removal struggle, appointed him a "special agent" to mediate disputes in the Indian country and report on the illicit trade in liquor. A quarter century after he started his mission to the Indians, in the western idyll that he had done so much to create, McCoy watched history repeat itself. White settlers flooded onto Indian lands, and white traders peddled alcohol to Native people. McCoy died in June 1846, already anxious that the tide of white settlement would break once more on Indians who had been granted a "permanent" refuge just a decade earlier. Within a few years of McCoy's death, the congressmen who had declined to support his Indian colony would turn its heartland into the Kansas Territory—a place where white people would fight about slavery, and from which many Native people would once again be removed. When the nation's attention turned to Kansas thereafter, it was not to admire McCoy's colony, but to argue over what had supplanted it.[30]

IN 1814, THOMAS JEFFERSON PASSED the baton of antislavery to Edward Coles: "This enterprise is for the young," the former president told the junior abolitionist. Jefferson may not have intended the Declaration of Independence to leach into debates over Native people and African Americans, but "all men are created equal" proved hard to contain. The Revolutionary generation rejected the idea that blacks or Indians were permanently inferior to whites. Reformers argued for education and uplift: bringing people of color into the orbit of whites would reveal their common humanity and potential. But the mechanisms for securing this outcome were vague and inconsistent. Were slaveholders responsible for educating their slaves before freeing them? Should states take the lead in supporting free blacks, or was this a job for civil society? Could whites overcome their prejudices to embrace intermarriage? One consistent feature of liberal reform was its assumption that poorer whites would do the heavy lifting of integration, whether in the eastern cities or on the frontier. When those poorer whites failed to play the role they had been assigned, reformers could wring their hands and lament the force of other people's prejudices—another source of "degradation" holding back the progress of blacks and Indians.

For the generation to which Jefferson bequeathed these dilemmas, colonization offered a way out. Proponents of racial separation insisted on the improvability of blacks and Indians, displayed lavish concern for their struggles, and promised that colonization would vindicate human brotherhood. In North America, a black or Indian colony might become a state, or part of a new political federation in which the races were happily partitioned. In Africa, a black colony would mirror the achievements of the United States, taking American values and influence into the heart of the continent. Liberal reformers recalled the most notorious episodes of forced migration—the Spanish expulsion of the Moors in 1492, or the French expulsion of the Huguenots a century later—and assured themselves that American colonization would be different. Blacks and Indians would consent to their own removal, if they were given enough time to appreciate what they might achieve elsewhere. Propelled by these assumptions, parallel programs of racial separation had won considerable support by the 1820s.

Given the sensitivities of South Carolina and Georgia, black colonization could not become the official policy of the US government (that is, until those states left the Union, when Abraham Lincoln's administration embraced colonization without delay). But James Monroe was a warm friend to the American Colonization Society during his presidency. Without his elastic interpretation of the 1819 Slave Trade Act, the ACS could not have founded Liberia, the beachhead for its renovation of Africa. Monroe's embrace of Indian resettlement in 1824 rested upon exactly the same logic, bringing the two separation schemes into brief alignment.

By the end of the 1820s, the logic of colonization came under sustained attack. Isaac McCoy and Thomas McKenney agreed that the transfer of the eastern Indians to the West was worth any price—even the opprobrium of northern churches and the benevolent societies that had been happy to endorse Liberia. Every frustrated colonizationist faced the temptation that he or she knew best: that it might be necessary to impose a solution on blacks and Indians who couldn't recognize their true interest. It was Andrew Jackson who dispensed with the principle of consent, destroying McCoy's chances of winning liberal supporters for his colonization plan. The idea of settling and "civilizing" Native people away from whites returned to the national debate in the 1850s and 1860s, and the question that had shaped federal Indian policy in the early nineteenth century was still being asked a century later: Should Native Americans be brought to "civilization" apart from white people, or among them? But the 1830 Indian Removal Act had two transformative effects: it enabled the most concerted program of ethnic cleansing in American history to take place, and it allowed northern reformers to embrace the trope of the "vanishing Indian." McCoy was a fierce critic of the latter. He spent his final years lamenting those who, "professedly mourning over the calamities of the Indians," predicted that they would now disappear. He was unable to see how his support for removal had fed the romantic nihilism of his opponents.

William Lloyd Garrison was in jail in April 1830, unable to pay a fine he had incurred for slandering a slaveholder in Baltimore. From his cell, he followed the removal debate in the newspapers. He was especially taken with the principled stand of Theodore Frelinghuysen, a senator from New Jersey. Garrison had been a lukewarm supporter of black colonization, but the publication of David Walker's *Appeal to the Colored Citizens* in 1829 shook his faith in its benevolence. After meeting with free black writers and activists across the eastern seaboard and poring over the American Colonization Society's reports, he accused the society of demonizing free blacks and consolidating slavery's hold on the nation. Black people, Garrison declared, are "as unanimously opposed to a removal to Africa, as the Cherokees from the council-fires and graves of their fathers." In 1831, a free black meeting in New York noted the curious fact that the most prominent defenders of the Cherokees in the removal debate had been enthusiastic supporters of the ACS: "We hope that those who have so eloquently pleaded the cause of the Indian will at least endeavor to preserve consistency in their conduct." But although the society lost several prominent supporters to Garrison's movement for immediate abolition, it continued to offer the most "respectable" avenue for antislavery sentiment throughout the antebellum period. Politicians like Frelinghuysen, along with the Massachusetts senators (and secretaries of state) Edward Everett and Daniel Webster, remained in the ranks of the society. Henry Clay became its president after James Madison's death in 1836, and the ACS held its coalition together between the North and the Upper South until secession.[31]

Black colonization also assumed a life beyond the operations of the ACS. The overwhelming majority of free blacks expressed skepticism or outright hostility toward the society from its earliest days, but their complaints were sometimes qualified by a willingness to consider other options for resettlement. In January 1817, just a few weeks after the society's founding, free blacks in Washington declined its invitation to "return" to Africa, but called for "the colonizing of the free people of color on the waters of the Missouri River, under the government of the United States." James Forten, along with the Quaker reformer Roberts Vaux, debated Thomas Clarkson's suggestion that free blacks emigrate to Haiti. (Around 5,000 did so in the early 1820s, though many returned to the United States.) Even Garrison's close allies were willing to consider some form of colonizing plan, provided it was purged of the involvement of slaveholders. In the mid-1830s, Garrison's old mentor Benjamin Lundy, whose antislavery newspaper had inspired *The Liberator*, entered talks with Mexican officials to create a black colony in Texas. His plans were halted by the triumph of Sam Houston and the proslavery American settlers who wrested the province from Mexico, but Lundy had won support from a number of abolitionists for his black settlement—including Lydia Maria Child, one of Garrison's strongest supporters.[32]

After 1830, colonization was taken up by state legislatures in the Upper South and by new auxiliary organizations. Maryland appropriated state funds for colonization from 1831. The Virginia assembly

ANTI-SLAVERY ALMANAC. 33

COLONIZATION ADDRESSING ITS BELOVED VICTIMS.

A radical abolitionist attack on colonization, 1843. COURTESY OF THE NEW YORK PUBLIC LIBRARY.

came agonizingly close to following suit in 1832. The Pennsylvania Colonization Society drew many of Philadelphia's most prominent residents into its orbit. (William Short and Edward Coles appear side by side in its members' register.) The Whig Party, which emerged in the mid-1830s under the influence of Henry Clay and Daniel Webster, was closely linked to colonization and dismissive of Garrison and immediate abolition. If we measure colonization's influence by the number of migrants resettled in Liberia—barely 10,000 in the four decades before the Civil War—it seems marginal to the building crisis over slavery. But if we look instead at how antislavery "moderates" during this period imagined the aftermath of emancipation, we can see that colonization was never far from their thoughts. When the Whigs dissolved in the early 1850s under sectional pressure, the new Republican Party made colonization the cornerstone of its plans for the nation. Republican congressmen offered sweeping visions of the continental realignment that would follow the abolition of slavery. White settlers would fill up the American West with farms and free labor; freed slaves would forge tropical homesteads in Mexico or Central America. The regions south of the United States would become, in the words of one prominent Republican, "our India—under happier auspices."[33]

It's easy to imagine the antislavery struggle as the process by which the ideas of William Lloyd Garrison or Frederick Douglass attained critical mass in the northern states. In fact, "moderate" antislavery reformers held out against radical abolitionists throughout the antebellum period: not because they favored slavery, but because they feared the social consequences of abolition. Even if we assume that Abraham Lincoln and the Republicans hoped to destroy slavery from the outset of the Civil War, it is a profound mistake to imagine that, in doing so, they embraced the visions of Douglass or Garrison. When war finally came in 1861, only a tiny minority of northerners had accepted the logic of radical abolition. For the vast majority, from Lincoln outward, only colonization made emancipation seem viable.

The alternative—emancipation and an integrated society after slavery—posed challenges even to radical abolitionists. To antislavery moderates, it was an outcome to be denied or avoided. During Lincoln's famous debates in 1858 with Stephen Douglas, his rival in the US Senate race in Illinois, the future president insisted that to deny black people a "humble share in the Declaration of Independence" would be to "muzzle the cannon that thunders its annual joyous return." To Douglas, this sounded like an endorsement of a race-blind society. "If you Black Republicans think that the negro ought to be on a social equality with your wives and daughters," Douglas told the crowd, "you have a perfect right to do so." But in Lincoln's argument, which rested upon more than half a century of liberal thinking, to invoke the Declaration of Independence was hardly to support social equality. Slavery should be ended by "systems of gradual emancipation," Lincoln conceded, but separation, not integration, would follow. His preference would be to "free all the slaves, and send them to Liberia." In the midst of this argument, it was Lincoln, rather than Douglas, who invoked the prospect

From an 1864 tract promoting black colonization after the Emancipation Proclamation. Colonization (in Africa or elsewhere) remained among the most popular solutions to "the negro problem" through the Civil War years into Reconstruction. FRONTISPIECE TO HOLLIS READ, THE NEGRO PROBLEM SOLVED, COURTESY OF THE NEW YORK PUBLIC LIBRARY.

of amalgamation. "I will add that I have never seen, to my knowledge, a man, woman or child, that was in favor of producing a perfect equality, socially and politically, between the negro and white people," Lincoln said. He could think of only one exception: "That is the case of my friend Douglas' old friend, Colonel Richard M. Johnson." Like the abolitionists of the 1830s, Lincoln invoked the Practical Amalgamator not to legitimize racial mixing but to tether it to slavery. As the crowd roared with laughter, Lincoln announced that he didn't need a law to resist the temptation of marrying black women. He would be happy to support one if it helped Douglas show the same discipline.[34]

When we restore racial separation to its rightful place—as the principal means of imagining slavery's demise in the early republic—we can begin to see its insidious influence on American history. Colonization enabled reformers to break the link between emancipation and integration: it allowed slavery's opponents to acknowledge "all men are created equal" without having to imagine a race-blind society on the other side of abolition. Colonization was not just a diversion, but a rewiring of white thinking about race. The abolition of slavery in the northern states might have produced a template for a broader process of emancipation in the South. Instead, colonization targeted free blacks as well as slaves, and allowed its proponents to affirm black potential while insisting that black people should be settled elsewhere. And when a war over slavery finally arrived, the foundations of black belonging in the northern states were hopelessly shallow. During the war, northerners sought reassurance that slaves would remain in the South after emancipation. In 1865, the Republican governor of Ohio proposed to give freed people a colony stretching from South Carolina to Florida, to be settled using the same methods that St. George Tucker had favored in 1796: a squeeze on civil and political rights for black people outside the colony, and complete equality for those who chose to settle within it. When it became apparent that freed people would remain mostly where they were, the future of the South assumed a different aspect in the North. Reconstruction collapsed in 1877, and a new version of "separate but equal" succeeded its liberal predecessor.[35]

In 1834, the abolitionist James Birney condemned colonization as "an opiate to the conscience." I wonder, though, if its advocates were entirely desensitized to its moral contradictions. Virtually every colonization supporter confronted the problem of consent. "They refuse to be saved by us," Return Meigs had written despairingly of the Cherokees in 1817. When Isaac McCoy pushed for his Indian Territory bill two decades later, he knew that the southeastern Indians could only be colonized at the point of a gun. William Short was tormented by his slave David's decision to reject his benevolent offer of freedom in Liberia, and could only think of him thereafter as "the anti-African."

And Edward Coles became a staunch supporter of colonization not only in defiance of his decision to free his slaves in Illinois, but in the knowledge that the people he had freed were determined to forge their lives in America.[36]

Coles kept an eye on his former slaves throughout his life. He was especially close to Robert and Kate Crawford, who managed his farm in Illinois after he left for Philadelphia in 1831. "I take pleasure in speaking so highly in your praise," he wrote them in 1837, "not only because worth is deserving of praise, but because there is a prejudice in narrow minds against you." While Coles attended meetings of the Pennsylvania Colonization Society, he insisted to Robert and Kate that they had "confirm[ed] my opinions of the unity and equality of man." In his 1844 autobiography, which was never published, Coles qualified his enthusiasm. "Although they have succeeded well, enjoyed their freedom, and led happy lives, I still believe it would have been best for them and their posterity if they had removed to a country occupied by people of their own color." Coles had concluded that physical differences would ensure that "the white and black man, even as the white and red man, will never till man changes his nature, associate as equals, and live in harmony and social intercourse." Prejudices were too strong, especially when multiplied by the stigma of slavery. Coles had told all this to Robert Crawford, and he had even offered him money to move to Liberia. "But he has not yet acceded to my proposition," Coles noted, "being, as he says, so fully engrossed and happily occupied in attending to his family, his farm and his congregation."[37]

In the 1850s, Coles made both his sons life members of the American Colonization Society on their fourteenth birthdays. He donated another $1,000 to the society and was appointed one of its vice-presidents. Despite his many ties to Virginia, Edward Coles remained a Union man as the nation crumbled. In 1861, when Abraham Lincoln made his way from Illinois to Washington to assume the presidency, he met with Coles—who was then seventy-five years old—in Philadelphia. The president-elect told the former governor that he was "held in universal reverence in Illinois," and Coles filled with pride. A year later, Coles was mortified to learn that his youngest son had been killed at the battle of Roanoke Island—fighting for the Confederacy. In December 1862, Coles wrote the last letter that survives in his hand. The Crawfords, his former slaves, had been cheated in a land deal, and had turned to their patron for help. Coles condemned them for doing business without seeking his advice, and reminded them that he had offered generous incentives to leave for Liberia. The Crawfords should have taken up his offer, Coles told them, before they became too old to make the trip. In the summer of 1865, as the states were ratifying the Thirteenth Amendment, Coles made the final revisions to his will. When he died three years later, the American Colonization Society received $6,000. The grateful managers of the ACS used the bequest to fund a new recruitment drive in the southern states. After his own death, and the demise of the slave system he had hated, Edward Coles was still doing the work of colonization.[38]

In the South Hall of the Illinois state capitol building, a mural commemorates Edward Coles. The image, painted in the 1880s, captures the moment in 1819 when Coles freed his slaves on the Ohio River. Coles stands near the center of the painting, his hat in one hand. Most of his slaves have their arms raised to heaven; those closest to him are bowing at his feet. The mural tells you nothing about what happened to them, or about Coles's subsequent journey into the shoals of colonization. Instead, it fixes the former governor in the state's pantheon of antislavery crusaders. Lincoln is close by, captured in 1831 crossing into Illinois to make the state his home. Ulysses Grant is just down the hall, assuming command of his army at the start of the Civil War. Illinois, like most other states in the Northwest, tried hard throughout the antebellum period to keep its black population to a minimum. The Coles image suggests the reverse: that the West had become the place in which, under the direction of a benevolent master, black people might find freedom.

Coles's commitment to antislavery was unstinting, but the journey he plotted for black people led in the other direction. Given the refusal of his former slaves to accept his offer of a new life in Liberia,

Governor Coles Freeing His Slaves on the Ohio River Below Pittsburgh (1886). This mural in the Illinois state capitol building recalls Coles's celebrated act of manumission in 1819 on the Ohio River, rather than his eventual advocacy of the American Colonization Society. COURTESY OF MARK W. SORENSEN.

perhaps he realized that his new solution to the problem of emancipation represented a retreat from the radicalism of his youth. When he had worked in the White House for James Madison during the War of 1812, Coles had visited the congressional library as often as he could to make notes on the iniquities of slavery. Using the scraps of paper that came across the president's desk—invoices, invitations, calling cards—he copied passages about Roman emancipation, Russian serfdom, and the universality of the human race. Amid the fragments that document his awakening as a liberal reformer, only one passage appears twice. Coles was fascinated by a couplet from Ovid's *Metamorphoses*, which seemed to capture the dilemma of the antislavery slaveholder. It might serve equally as an epitaph for colonization:

> *I see the right, approve it too;*
> *Condemn the wrong, and yet the wrong pursue.*[39]

Acknowledgments

O NE EASY WAY TO DETERMINE that you've spent forever on a project is to get started just after your first child is born. As I finish this book, my (now) nine-year-old is rolling her eyes and calling me a noob. I can't blame anyone but myself for taking so long, not least because so many people have been so generous and helpful in steering me toward the finishing line.

The book began as a loose end in my doctoral dissertation, and I should start by thanking my adviser, Daniel T. Rodgers, for his guidance and inspiration. I've tried to spare Dan the cascading drafts of this new book, but I hope that whatever's worthwhile here bears the mark of his teaching. I'm still in the debt of many of the other people I met during my time in grad school: Alec Dun, Drew Isenberg, Kevin Kruse, Paul Miles, Ken Mills, and Peter Silver, in particular.

My argument that Native American removal and African colonization shared a common framework of liberal "benevolence" was first developed in an article for the *Journal of American History*. I'm extremely grateful to the outside readers for supporting and sharpening my thesis, and to Ed Linenthal for publishing it. I've been fortunate to wander into the history of black colonization at a moment when that topic has been transformed by a group of terrific scholars: thanks, in particular, to Bronwen Everill, Matthew Hetrick, Samantha Seeley, Marie Stango, and Bev Tomek.

I was the very grateful recipient of two year-long research fellowships while working on this project. The first was from the Stanford

Humanities Center, and it was during my happy time in Palo Alto that I figured out how I was going to tell the story. Aron Rodrigue, then the director of the Humanities Center, was a terrific host. I learned a ton from Jim Campbell, Caroline Winterer, and Richard White, all Stanford regulars; and from my fellow Fellows, especially Mark Feldman, Greg Mann, and Cabeiri Robinson. I was always bothering the sterling administrative staff, especially the wonderful Bob Barrick; and it was at Stanford that I bumped into Pekka Hämäläinen, who has been a fast friend ever since.

My other research leave came courtesy of a British Academy fellowship: many thanks to Richard Carwardine for supporting my application, and to Helen Langan at the BA for her help in administering the fellowship. I was lucky enough to spend this leave year as a visiting researcher at the Rothermere American Institute at the University of Oxford. The RAI introduced me to a terrific group of American historians, including Mara Keire, Peter Thompson, Stephen Tuck, Steve Tufnell, David Turley, and, during his tenure as Harmsworth professor, Richard Blackett (one of the three or four most famous American historians who are also Stoke City fans). The then-director of the RAI, Nigel Bowles, was extremely welcoming and supportive; the same goes for Huw David and Jane Rawson. Nigel's successor as director, Jay Sexton, was an early and enthusiastic supporter of this project, and I owe him more beers than either of us can keep track of. Oxford also introduced me to Sebastian Page, a dogged and fearless historian of colonization. I thank Seb for all the help he's given me in recent years, and look forward very much to his forthcoming book on "race adjustment" in the mid-nineteenth century.

My archival work on the book has been supported by a number of institutions. I was fortunate to spend time at the Library Company of Philadelphia and the Historical Society of Pennsylvania, where I became especially indebted to Jim Green and Krystal Appiah. At the American Antiquarian Society, I was warmly looked after by Paul Erickson and his staff and by countless kind and helpful librarians. (A shout-out here to Jackie Penny, "the fixer," who rushed to my rescue as

I chased down illustrations during the book's manic production stage.) In Worcester, I also got to know Mary Kelley, which was a huge thrill, along with Marina Moskowitz and Simon Newman (who were kind enough to invite me to Glasgow to talk about Jefferson and colonization). At the Robert H. Smith International Center for Jefferson Studies at Monticello, meanwhile, I was treated way too well by Kate Macdonald, Tasha Stanton, and Andrew Jackson O'Shaughnessy. Monticello was the perfect place for the final phase of editing on the book, not least because the intellectual community in Charlottesville (not to mention the restaurant formerly known as Pizza Bella) takes some beating.

One racks up huge debts to librarians on a project like this. I want to say a special thank you to Jim Holmberg at the Filson in Louisville, who put me in touch with the incredibly generous Deborah Skaggs Speth; Deborah shared her detailed notes and research on the Short family and set me straight on a number of issues relating to William Short's vexed relationship with the slaves he owned in Kentucky. I'm also grateful to Laurent Ferri, the keeper of the Lafayette collection at Cornell, who helped me track down some crucial letters that had somehow slipped out of the catalog. I was especially confident about finding these letters because of the wonderful work of Anne C. Loveland, who was kind enough to reply to my email about Lafayette sources—more than forty years after she'd been through the same files in researching her terrific book *Emblem of Liberty*. In a similar vein, I owe a very big thank you to Nicholas Gordon, whose fascinating and deeply researched biography of Edward Coles is online at Nick's website (www.poemsforfree.com/edwardcoles.html). Nick is one of the few people alive to have peered into a trunk of papers held closely by surviving members of the Coles family, and I'm indebted to him for his recollection of what he found there many moons ago.

Researching the book led me not only to physical archives but to the growing collection of online material that, with a fair wind, will help to expand and democratize access to history writing in the future. To everyone who's worked so hard to place historical material on the Internet without a paywall, I'm extremely grateful.

I began this book as a member of the History Department at the University of York: many thanks to Sarah Burton, Stuart Carroll, Simon Ditchfield, Alex Goodall, Hannah Greig, Chris Renwick, and David Wootton for their help and advice during my time at York. During the final phase of this project, I've been a member of the history faculty at the University of Cambridge. I'm grateful to my new colleagues—to Gary Gerstle, Julia Guarneri, Joel Isaac, Lawrence Klein, Sarah Pearsall, and Andrew Preston, in particular—for the very warm welcome I've received at Cambridge; and, in Trinity Hall, to Clare Jackson, Jeremy Morris, and the other Fellows and staff. I'm also indebted to the late Michael O'Brien, who died with appalling abruptness during my first year in the new job and who leaves an enormous hole that stretches far beyond Cambridge.

It will be clear by this point that I've been on a lucky streak throughout the project. I really hit the jackpot, though, when Lara Heimert of Basic Books acquired my book. Many thanks to Jill Marsal, my agent, for making that happen, and for all her work on the book proposal. I owe Jill and Lara my apologies for taking so long to get the book done—though one of Lara's many talents is knowing precisely when to badger a daydreaming author into delivering what's been promised. I'm extremely grateful to her for championing the book, giving me so much time to write it, and offering unerring suggestions on how to make the drafts better.

The editorial and production folks at Basic have been fantastic: a huge thank you to Alia Massoud, Shena Redmond, Brian Shotwell, Leah Stecher, and everyone else in production and marketing who worked on the book. Thanks also to Kathy Streckfus for her brilliant copyedit.

Some of my biggest debts are to the poor souls who read the manuscript in its various incarnations. First up, the team of hardy pioneers who traversed the mountainous first draft: Lara Heimert, of course, but also Jane Dinwoodie, Karen Ferguson, and Ari Kelman. Jane offered extremely helpful suggestions about the Native American sections in particular; Karen reminded me that "separate but equal" has a liberal history that stretches into the twentieth century as well as back into the eighteenth; and Ari offered his usual mix of fulsome praise ("There aren't a lot of important things wrong with this book") and trenchant criticism ("You need to cut about 200 pages, and those cuts need to come from every single chapter"). The second draft was better—or, at least, shorter—but benefited hugely from the careful input and expertise of Luke Clossey, Eric Burin, Terry Meyers, Steve Kantrowitz, Christina Snyder, and Yael Sternhell. Luke is an old friend, and the best reader of anything and everything. Eric is the dean of the new history of African colonization, and all of us working in the field have benefited hugely from his work and friendship over the years. Yael made some incredibly helpful suggestions, especially on the style and pacing of the book. I bumped into Terry in Williamsburg, and he gave me terrific insights into the fate of antislavery at William and Mary College (not to mention a priceless line edit). Steve and Christina I basically cold-called. I'm not even sure if you're allowed to do that, but both of them saved me from many errors of fact and interpretation. Since Christina was finishing up her own book about Richard Mentor Johnson at the time, her advice was especially generous and very much appreciated.

A final trio of readers deserves a special mention. Peter Onuf has been a fantastic mentor and friend across the lifetime of this project, and it was a huge pleasure and privilege to have his views on the manuscript. He also introduced me to Christa Dierksheide, who did more than anyone to get the revised draft of the book over the goal line. Christa manages to sustain superhuman levels of generosity and affableness, while also leaving you in no doubt about what she actually thinks of an idea or argument. I got more done in a month at Monticello than I could have in a year back in the United Kingdom, thanks mostly to Christa. And then there's Andy Graybill, who has been a warm friend to this project from the very beginning. Although I like to indulge Andy's vision of himself as Ari Gold, his terrific work on intermarriage and racial amalgamation has been just as useful to me as his matchless talent for introducing like-minded people and talking up research. The fact that I was a really bad host when Andy finally brought his family to England for a once-in-a-lifetime visit—I was submerged in the production process on the book—was terrible recompense for his ceaseless generosity. But I figure that, now that I've mentioned it here, he won't hold a grudge. Right?

For favors big and small, I'd also like to thank Margaret Abruzzo, Sari Altschuler, Asli Bali, David Blight, Max Edelson, Theresa Strouth Gaul, Arika Easley Houser, Wyn James, Peter Jaros, Walter Johnson, Mary Kelley, Linda Kerber, Johann Neem, Paul Polgar, Zachary Sell, Mark W. Sorensen, Alan Taylor, Christopher Wilkins, Nicholas Wood, Karin Wulf, and Joseph Yannielli. Jane Dinwoodie and John Bowes kindly corrected the original drafts of the maps at the front of this book; thanks to them and to the long-suffering Brian Shotwell, who actually produced the maps. Thanks also to Matthew Cotton and the anonymous readers at Oxford University Press for their very helpful suggestions and corrections. Inevitably I will have omitted several people who have been incredibly generous; I can only promise that this will haunt me more than it will bother them.

My parents and the rest of my family in Bristol remain an amazing source of love and encouragement. So, too, my daughters and my wife. Talking about how much they mean to me in a venue like this would only get me into trouble, so I'll just say that this book, for what it's worth, is for you. And that, now that my desk is clear, I can start working on the *Minecraft* novel we talked about.

Notes

ABBREVIATIONS

ASPIA   *American State Papers: Indian Affairs,* 2 vols. (Washington, DC: Gales and Seaton, 1832–1834)

BFP   Papers of Benjamin Franklin, digital edition (http://franklinpapers .org/franklin)

CFP   Coles Family Papers, Historical Society of Pennsylvania, Philadelphia

CWS   Papers of Charles Wilkins Short, Filson Historical Society, Lexington, Kentucky

ECP   Edward Coles Papers, Princeton University Library

ECHSP   Coles Family Papers, Historical Society of Pennsylvania

GSL   Letterbook of Granville Sharp, York Minster Library Archive, York, United Kingdom

GWP   Papers of George Washington, digital edition (http://founders .archives.gov/about/Washington)

IMP   Papers of Isaac McCoy, Kansas State Historical Society, Topeka, Kansas

JAH   *Journal of American History*

JER   *Journal of the Early Republic*

LP   Arthur H. and Mary Marden Dean Lafayette Collection, Cornell University Library

MHS   Collections of the Massachusetts Historical Society, Boston

NSV   Thomas Jefferson, *Notes on the State of Virginia* (Paris: n.p., 1782 [1785])

RCIA   Records of the Cherokee Indian Agency in Tennessee, 1801–1835, Correspondence and Miscellaneous Records, M-208, National Archives

RVP   Vaux Family Papers, Series 1, Roberts Vaux, Historical Society of Pennsylvania, Philadelphia

THP   Thomas J. Henderson Papers, Filson Historical Society, Lexington, Kentucky

TJLC   Thomas Jefferson Papers, General Correspondence, 1651–1827, Library of Congress

TJP   Papers of Thomas Jefferson, digital edition (http://founders.archives.gov/about/Jefferson)

TP   *Territorial Papers of the United States*, ed. Clarence Edwin Carter et al., 28 vols. (Washington, DC: Government Printing Office, 1934–1975)

WHH   Logan Esarey, ed., *Messages and Letters of William Henry Harrison*, 2 vols. (Indianapolis: Indiana Historical Commission, 1922)

WMQ   *William and Mary Quarterly*

WSP   Papers of William Short, Library of Congress

WTP   *Papers of William Thornton, 1781–1802*, ed. C. M. Harris (Charlottesville: University Press of Virginia, 1995)

INTRODUCTION: THE PREHISTORY OF "SEPARATE BUT EQUAL"

1. Edward Coles to Thomas Jefferson, 31 July 1814, TJP.

2. Edward Coles, "Autobiography" (1844), ECHSP; Suzanne Cooper Guasco, *Confronting Slavery: Edward Coles and the Rise of Antislavery Politics in Nineteenth-Century America* (DeKalb: Northern Illinois University Press, 2013).

3. Coles to Jefferson, 31 July 1814; Coles, "Autobiography"; Annette Gordon-Reed, *The Hemingses of Monticello: An American Family* (New York: Norton, 2008).

4. Jefferson to Coles, 25 August 1814, TJP.

5. Coles to Jefferson, 26 September 1814, TJP.

6. Abraham Lincoln, "Address on Colonization to a Deputation of Negroes," in Abraham Lincoln, *Collected Works of Abraham Lincoln*, Roy P. Basler, ed., 8 vols. (New Brunswick, NJ: Rutgers University Press, 1953), 5:370–375; Kate Masur, "The African American Delegation to Abraham Lincoln: A Reappraisal," *Civil War History* 56, no. 2 (2010): 117–144.

7. David Walker, *Walker's Appeal . . . to the Colored Citizens of the World* (Boston: Printed for the Author, 1829), 55.

8. Winthrop D. Jordan, *White over Black: American Attitudes Toward the Negro, 1550–1812* (Chapel Hill: University of North Carolina Press, 1968), 566; J. M. Opal, "The Labors of Liberality: Christian Benevolence and National Prejudice in the American Founding," *JAH* 94, no. 4 (2008): 1082–1107.

9. Rachel N. Klein, *Unification of a Slave State: The Rise of the Planter Class in the South Carolinian Backcountry, 1750–1808* (Chapel Hill: University of North Carolina Press, 1992), 150–151.

10. St. George Tucker, *A Dissertation on Slavery, With a Proposal for the Gradual Abolition of It* (Philadelphia: Mathew Carey, 1796), 29–30.

CHAPTER 1: BECOMING GOOD CITIZENS

1. St. George Tucker to Jeremy Belknap, 24 January 1795, in "Queries Regarding the Slavery and Emancipation of Negroes," MHS (1795), 191–193. On Tucker, see Phillip Hamilton, "Revolutionary Principles and Family Loyalties: Slavery's Transformation in the St. George Tucker Household of Early National Virginia," *WMQ* 55, no. 4 (1988): 531–556.

2. Belknap to Benjamin Rush, 7 April and 10 August 1788, 18 July 1792, in Benjamin Rush Papers, Library Company of Philadelphia, series 1, vol. 30, folders 3, 5, 22.

3. Belknap to Samuel Hazard, 7 May 1790, in ibid., 219–222.

4. "Queries Relating to Slavery in Massachusetts," MHS, 5th series, vol. 3 (1877): 375–431, 382; "Queries Regarding Slavery," 210.

5. "Queries Regarding Slavery," 206–209; Tucker to Belknap, 29 June 1795, in "Queries Relating to Slavery," 409.

6. Ibid., 408–409.

7. John Adams to Belknap, 22 October 1795, in ibid., 416; James Sullivan to Belknap, 30 July 1795, in ibid., 412–416.

8. James Roger, *Buffon: A Life in Natural History* (Ithaca, NY: Cornell University Press, 1997); Lee Alan Dugatkin, *Mr. Jefferson and the Giant Moose: Natural History in Early America* (Chicago: University of Chicago Press, 2009), 10–24.

9. Buffon, *Natural History*, trans. William Smellie (London: A. Strahan and T. Cadell, 1791), 3:3, 3:57–207, 7:395.

10. Ibid., 9:396–309, 3:152–153.

11. Winthrop Jordan, *White over Black: American Attitudes Towards the Negro, 1550–1812* (Chapel Hill: University of North Carolina Press, 1968), 218–223; Ashley Montagu, *Man's Most Dangerous Myth: The Fallacy of Race*, 6th ed. (Lanham, MD: Rowman and Littlefield, 1997), 62–63; Michael O'Brien, *Conjectures of Order: Intellectual Life and the American South, 1810–1860*, 2 vols. (Chapel Hill: University of North Carolina Press, 2004), 1:221–230; Roxann Wheeler, *The Complexion of Race: Categories of Difference in Eighteenth-Century British Culture* (Philadelphia: University of Pennsylvania Press, 2000).

12. Buffon, *Natural History*, 5:95–152; Gilbert Chinard, "Eighteenth Century Theories on America as a Human Habitat," *Proceedings of the American*

Philosophical Society 91 (February 1947): 27–57; William Carmichael to Thomas Jefferson, 15 October 1787, TJP, 12:238–242; Jefferson to Robert Walsh Jr., 4 December 1818, TJLC; Antonello Gerbi, *The Dispute of the New World*, trans. Jeremy Moyle (Pittsburgh: University of Pittsburgh Press, 1973), 242–243.

13. Dugatkin, *Jefferson and the Giant Moose*, x–xii; *NSV*, 69–103, 109–110; "Nature Degenerates in America," *Richmond Enquirer*, 24 October 1806, 4; "The Inimitable Hog," *Spirit of the Press* (Philadelphia), 8 November 1806, 2.

14. *NSV*, 263–264.

15. David Ramsay to Jefferson, 3 May 1786, in Robert L. Brunhouse, "David Ramsay, 1749–1815: Selections from His Writings," *Transactions of the American Philosophical Society*, vol. 5, part 4 (Philadelphia, 1965), 1–250, 101; Gilbert Imlay, *A Description of the Western Territory of North America* (Dublin: William Jones, 1793), 184–185; Colin Kidd, *The Forging of Races: Race and Scripture in the Protestant Atlantic World, 1600–2000* (Cambridge, UK: Cambridge University Press, 2006), 109–110.

16. De Witt Clinton, *A Vindication of Thomas Jefferson* (New York: David Denniston, 1800), 15. In fact, Clinton twisted Jefferson's quotation to suit his purposes: rather than declaring himself "convinced" by the equal potential of both races, Jefferson actually told Banneker that "nobody wishes more than I do to see such proofs as you exhibit, that nature has given to our black brethren talents equal to those of other men." The quiet implication of Jefferson's original letter was that these proofs had not yet been supplied. Jefferson to Benjamin Banneker, 30 August 1791, TJP.

17. Kidd, *Forging of Races*, 24–25, 79–121; O'Brien, *Conjectures of Order*, 1:247, 249.

18. Michel Delon, "Prejudice," in Delon, ed., *Encyclopedia of the Enlightenment* (Abingdon, UK: Routledge, 2013), 1086–1088; J. M. Opal, "The Labors of Liberality: Christian Benevolence and National Prejudice in the American Founding," *JAH* 94, no. 4 (2008): 1082–1107.

19. Thomas Paine, *Letter Addressed to the Abbé Raynal* (Philadelphia: Melchior Steiner, 1782), 44–45.

20. Ibid., 416.

21. *NSV*, 261–265; Henrik Mouritsen, *The Freedman in the Roman World* (Cambridge, UK: Cambridge University Press, 2011), 10–35.

22. Kathy Stuart, *Defiled Trades and Social Outcasts: Honor and Ritual Pollution in Early Modern Germany* (Cambridge, UK: Cambridge University Press, 1999), 9, 113–114, 131, 223. I'm grateful to Mark Jenner for this reference.

23. *The Laws of Harvard College* (Boston: John and Thomas Fleet, 1798), 5; Stephen Farley, *An Oration, Pronounced at Hanover, N.H., July 4, 1804* (Hanover, NH: Moses Davis, 1804), 3; Noah Webster, *A Compendious Dictionary of the*

English Language (Hartford, CT: Sidney's Press, 1806), 80; Noah Webster, *An Oration at Amherst, July 4, 1814* (Northampton, MA: William Butler, 1814), 5.

24. Edward Gibbon, *The History of the Decline and Fall of the Roman Empire*, 6 vols. (Dublin: Luke White, 1788–1789), 3:3, 39; Abbé Raynal, *A Philosophical and Political History of the Settlements and Trade of the Europeans in the East and West Indies*, 3rd ed., trans. J. O. Justmond, 8 vols. (London: W. Strahan and T. Cadell, 1783), 1:10, 1:91, 3:126, 5:298, 6:380, 6:395, 7:417; Abbé Raynal, *Philosophical and Political History*, 1st ed., trans. J. O. Justmond, 4 vols. (London: T. Cadell, 1776), 3:166.

25. Mary Wollstonecraft, *A Vindication of the Rights of Men*, 2nd ed. (London: J. Johnson, 1790), 92, 128–130; Mary Wollstonecraft, *A Vindication of the Rights of Women*, 3rd ed. (London: J. Johnson, 1796), 2, 34, 38, x.

26. Timothy J. Coates, *Convicts and Orphans: Forced and State-Sponsored Colonizers in the Portuguese Empire, 1550–1755* (Stanford, CA: Stanford University Press, 2001), esp. xv–xx, 29–41; G. Paterson, *The History of New South Wales* (Newcastle, UK: Mackenzie and Dent, 1811), 506.

27. [Samuel Hopkins], *A Dialogue Concerning the Slavery of the Africans* (Norwich, CT: Judah P. Spooner, 1776), iii, 45, 44, 49.

28. Noah Webster, *Effects of Slavery, on Morals and Industry* (Hartford, CT: Hudson and Goodwin, 1793), 6.

29. Ibid., 8–10.

30. Ibid., 13, 18, 21, 32, 13.

31. David Rice, *Slavery Inconsistent with Justice and Good Policy* (Philadelphia: Parry Hall, 1792), 4, 6, 16, 35; *NSV*, 299; Robert H. Bishop, *An Outline of the History of the Church in the State of Kentucky* (Lexington: Thomas T. Skillman, 1824), 57, 95–96; Asa Martin, "The Antislavery Movement in Kentucky Prior to 1850," PhD dissertation, Cornell University, 1918, 12–25; Lacy K. Ford, *Deliver Us from Evil: The Slavery Question in the Old South* (New York: Oxford University Press, 2009), 39.

32. Rice, *Slavery*, 22–23, 17, 15, 25.

33. Ibid., 34, 32.

34. John E. Kleber, ed., *The Kentucky Encyclopedia* (Lexington: University of Kentucky Press, 1992), xx; Stephen Aron, *How the West Was Lost: The Transformation of Kentucky from Daniel Boone to Henry Clay* (Baltimore: Johns Hopkins University Press, 1999), 89–91.

35. Henry Clay, *The Papers of Henry Clay*, James F. Hopkins et al., eds., 10 vols. (Lexington: University Press of Kentucky, 1959–1992), 1:3–8.

36. *Minutes of the Proceedings of a Convention of Delegates* (Philadelphia: Zachariah Poulson Jr., 1794), 8, 24; *Minutes of the Proceedings of the Second Convention of Delegates* (Philadelphia: Zachariah Poulson Jr., 1795), 30;

Minutes of the Proceedings of the Sixth Convention of Delegates (Philadelphia: Zachariah Poulson Jr., 1800), 21.

CHAPTER 2: A FEW BAD MEN

1. Elias Boudinot, *A Star in the West* (Trenton, NJ: D. Fenton et al., 1816), 87, 160, 193; Anthony F.C. Wallace, *Jefferson and the Indians: The Tragic Fate of the First Americans* (Cambridge, MA: Harvard University Press, 1999), 130–160; Ronald Meek, *Social Science and the Ignoble Savage* (Cambridge, UK: Cambridge University Press, 1976); J. G. A. Pocock, *Barbarism and Religion*, vol. 4, *Barbarians, Savages and Empires* (Cambridge, UK: Cambridge University Press, 2005), 157–180.

2. Noah Webster, *A Collection of Essays and Fugitive Writings* (Boston: I. Thomas and E. T. Andrews, 1790), 233; Stuart Banner, *How the Indians Lost Their Land: Law and Power on the Frontier* (Cambridge, MA: Harvard University Press, 2005), 85–111; Daniel K. Richter, *Facing East from Indian Country: A Native History of Early America* (Cambridge, MA: Harvard University Press, 2001), 189–216; Bernard W. Sheehan, "The Indian Problem in the Northwest: From Conquest to Philanthropy," in Ronald Hoffman and Peter J. Albert, eds., *Launching the "Extended Republic": The Federalist Era* (Charlottesville: University Press of Virginia, 1996), 190–222.

3. Benjamin Franklin to William Johnson, 12 September 1766, and Samuel Wharton to Franklin, 2 December 1768, BFP; Nicholas Guyatt, "Benjamin Franklin and the Problem of Racial Diversity," in David Waldstreicher, ed., *The Blackwell Companion to Benjamin Franklin* (Oxford: Blackwell, 2010), 183–210.

4. John Sugden, *Blue Jacket: Warrior of the Shawnees* (Lincoln: University of Nebraska Press, 2000), 36–64.

5. "Instructions to the Governor of the Territory of the United States Northwest of the River Ohio," 26 October 1787, ASPIA, 1:9; Sugden, *Blue Jacket*, 65–69; Banner, *How the Indians Lost Their Land*, 121–129.

6. Henry Knox, "Report to Congress," 10 July 1787, TP, 2:33, 35; Mark Puls, *Henry Knox: Visionary General of the American Revolution* (New York: Palgrave Macmillan, 2008); Banner, *How the Indians Lost Their Land*, 129–140.

7. Henry Knox to George Washington, 7 July 1789, ASPIA, 1:53; Knox to Washington, 27 December 1790 and 26 December 1791, GWP.

8. Knox to Washington, 27 December 1790, GWP; Wallace, *Jefferson and the Indians*, 165–170.

9. Alfred Bush, "Princeton University," in Frederick E. Hoxie, *Encyclopedia of North American Indians* (Boston: Houghton Mifflin, 1996), 173; Colin G. Calloway, *The American Revolution in Indian Country: Crisis and Diversity in*

Native American Communities (Cambridge, UK: Cambridge University Press, 1992), 37.

10. Knox to Washington, 4 January 1790, *ASPIA*, 1:59–64; Knox to Washington, 7 July 1789, GWP.

11. Gerard H. Clarfield, *Timothy Pickering and the American Republic* (Pittsburgh: University of Pittsburgh Press, 1980).

12. Timothy Pickering to Washington, 31 December 1790 and 8 January 1791, in Octavius Pickering, *The Life of Timothy Pickering*, 4 vols. (Boston: Little, Brown, 1867), 2:468, 470; George Morgan White Eyes to Washington, 2 June, 8 July, and 8 August 1789, GWP; Elizabeth Thompson to Washington, 18 August 1789, GWP; Washington to Pickering, 20 January 1791, in Pickering, *Life of Pickering*, 2:474; Peter Silver, *Our Savage Neighbors: How Indian War Transformed Early America* (New York: Knopf, 2008), 116–117.

13. Pickering to Washington, 8 January 1791, and Washington to Pickering, 20 January 1791, in Pickering, *Life of Pickering*, 2:471–472, 474.

14. Arthur St. Clair to Alexander Hamilton, 9 August 1793, Papers of Alexander Hamilton, digital edition, http://founders.archives.gov/about/Hamilton; George Morgan to Board of Treasury, 25 September 1788, GWP; *An Oration, Delivered at Marietta, July 4, 1788* (Newport, RI: Peter Edes, 1788), 10.

15. John May, *Journal and Letters of Col. John May* (Cincinnati: Robert Clarke, 1873), 41, 59, 48–49, 103; Francis Paul Prucha, *The Sword of the Republic* (Lincoln: University of Nebraska Press, 1969), 17–19.

16. Knox to Washington, 15 June 1789, *ASPIA*, 1:13; Arthur St. Clair to John Jay, 13 December 1788, *TP*, 2:166–170, 168; Rufus Putnam to Washington, 28 February 1791, *TP*, 2: 337–339; St. Clair to Washington, 1 May 1790, *TP*, 2:245.

17. Knox to Washington, 22 January 1791, David Humphreys to Washington, 7 July 1790, Knox to Washington, 7 July 1789, and Knox to Washington, 4 January 1790, GWP; "Report of the Secretary of War to Congress," 10 July 1787, *TP*, 2:31.

18. *TP*, 2:33; Prucha, *Sword of the Republic*, 20–21; Colin Calloway, *The Victory with No Name: The Native American Defeat of the First American Army* (New York: Oxford University Press, 2014), 63–68.

19. Knox to Washington, 10 December 1790, *TP*, 2:313; Harvey Lewis Carter, *The Life and Times of Little Turtle: First Sagamore of the Wabash* (Urbana-Champaign: University of Illinois Press, 1987), 88–97; Seneca Chiefs to Washington, 1 December 1790, Knox to Washington, 27 December 1790, Washington to the Seneca Chiefs, 29 December 1790, Seneca Chiefs to Washington, 10 January 1791, GWP; Message to Congress, 8 December 1790, *ASPIA*, 1:83; Washington to Knox, 26 December 1791, GWP.

20. Knox to Washington, 22 February 1791, GWP; Knox to Pickering, 25 February 1791, Pickering to Knox, 28 February 1791, Pickering to Samuel Hodgdon, 28 February 1791, in Pickering, *Life of Pickering*, 2:482–485.

21. Sugden, *Blue Jacket*, 117–127; Carter, *Little Turtle*, 100–110; Prucha, *Sword of the Republic*, 22–27; Calloway, *Victory with No Name*, 76–128.

22. Belknap to Benjamin Rush, 7 June 1792, in Benjamin Rush Papers, series 1, vol. 30, folder 21, Library Company of Philadelphia; Benjamin Hawkins to Washington, 20 February 1792, William Stoy to Washington, 19 February 1792, GWP; Calloway, *Victory with No Name*, 129–139.

23. "Address to the Senate and House of Representatives," 6 November 1792; Knox to Washington, 12 March 1793, GWP; Prucha, *Sword of the Republic*, 27–29; "Cabinet Opinion on a Proposed Treaty at Lower Sandusky," 25 February 1793, GWP; Sugden, *Blue Jacket*, 132–138; Calloway, *Victory with No Name*, 139–146.

24. Journal of Timothy Pickering, 12 August 1793, in Pickering, *Life of Pickering*, 3:52; Benjamin Lincoln, "Journal of a Treaty Held in 1793," MHS, 3rd series, vol. 5 (1836): 165–166.

25. Prucha, *Sword of the Republic*, 28–35; Stuart Rafert, *The Miami Indians of Indiana: A Persistent People* (Bloomington: Indiana Historical Society, 1996), 52–53; Paul David Nelson, *Anthony Wayne: Soldier of the Early Republic* (Bloomington: Indiana Historical Society, 1985).

26. Knox to Anthony Wayne, 5 January 1793, in Richard C. Knopf, ed., *Anthony Wayne, a Name in Arms: Soldier, Diplomat, Defender of Expansion Westward of a Nation* (Pittsburgh: University of Pittsburgh Press, 1960), 165; Prucha, *Sword of the Republic*, 35–38; Carter, *Little Turtle*, 128–136; Sugden, *Blue Jacket*, 159–180.

27. "A Treaty Between the United States of America and the Tribes of Indians Called the Six Nations," *ASPIA*, 1:545; Gerard H. Clarfeld, *Timothy Pickering and the American Republic* (Pittsburgh: University of Pittsburgh Press, 1980), 148–152; Carter, *Little Turtle*, 136–137; Timothy D. Willig, *Restoring the Chain of Friendship: British Policy and the Indians of the Great Lakes, 1783–1815* (Lincoln: University of Nebraska Press, 2008), 23–24; Helen Hornbeck Tanner, "The Glaize in 1792: A Composite Indian Community," in Peter C. Mancall and James H. Merrell, eds., *American Encounters: Natives and Newcomers from European Contact to Indian Removal, 1500–1850* (New York: Routledge, 2000), 404–425.

28. Henry Knox, "General View, Communicated to Congress, December 30, 1794," *ASPIA*, 1:543–544.

29. Sugden, *Blue Jacket*, 200–207; Carter, *Little Turtle*, 145–153.

30. Washington to Pickering, 1 July 1796, GWP; Meeting of US Commissioners and Creek Chiefs, 23 June 1797, *ASPIA*, 1:601.

31. "Pantheon and Rickett's Amphitheatre" (advertisement), *Gazette of the United States*, 26 November 1796, 2; Sugden, *Blue Jacket*, 213–217.

32. George Washington, "To the Chiefs and Warriors, Representatives," 29 November 1796, GWP; Timothy Pickering, "To the Brothers, Sachems, Chiefs, and Warriors of the Seneca Nation," 4 September 1790, in Pickering, *Life of Pickering*, 2:456–457.

CHAPTER 3: CORRECTING ILL HABITS

1. Samuel Stanhope Smith, *An Essay on the Causes of the Variety of Complexion and Figure in the Human Species* (Edinburgh: C. Elliot, 1788), 94–98; ibid., 2nd ed. (New Brunswick, NJ: J. Simpson, 1818), 92–95; Samuel Stanhope Smith, "On the Relation of Master and Servant," in Smith, *Lectures . . . on Subjects of Moral and Political Philosophy*, 2 vols. (Trenton, NJ: Daniel Fenton, 1812), 2:159–179; Jennifer Epstein, "Slaves and Slavery at Princeton," BA thesis, 2008, Princeton University.

2. Charles White, *An Account of the Regular Gradation in Man and in Different Animals and Vegetables; and from the Former to the Latter* (London: C. Dilly, 1799), 137–138; Smith, *Essay*, 2nd ed., 249, 268–269; *NSV*, 256.

3. *NSV*, 269–270; Smith, "Relation of Master and Servant," 177, 172.

4. Ibid., 174–176; George Bourne, *The Book and Slavery Irreconcilable: With Animadversions upon Dr. Smith's Philosophy* (Philadelphia: J. M. Sanderson, 1816), 144.

5. Noah Webster, *Effects of Slavery, on Morals and Industry* (Hartford, CT: Hudson and Goodwin, 1793), 37–38.

6. Ibid., 38–40.

7. Jerzy Lukowski, *Disorderly Liberty: The Political Culture of the Polish-Lithuanian Commonwealth in the Eighteenth Century* (London: Continuum, 2010), 99–120. On the question of slaves as property, see James Oakes, "Conflict vs. Racial Consensus in the History of Antislavery Politics," in John Craig Hammond and Matthew Mason, eds., *Contesting Slavery: The Politics of Bondage and Freedom in the New American Nation* (Charlottesville: University of Virginia Press, 2011), 291–303, 292–293.

8. "Address from the New York Manumission Society," *Minutes of the Proceedings of the Sixth Convention of Delegates from the Abolition Societies* (Philadelphia: Zachariah Poulson Jr., 1800), 13–17; Hilary J. Moss, *Schooling Citizens: The Struggle for African American Education in Antebellum America* (Chicago: University of Chicago Press, 2009); Paul J. Polgar, "'To Raise Them

to an Equal Participation': Early National Abolitionism, Gradual Emancipation, and the Promise of African American Citizenship," *JER* 31, no. 2 (2011): 229–258. See also Stephen Kantrowitz, *More Than Freedom: Fighting for Black Citizenship in a White Republic, 1829–1889* (New York: Penguin, 2012).

9. "Petition of Absalom Jones and Others," in John Parrish, *Remarks on the Slavery of the Black People, Addressed to the Citizens of the United States* (Philadelphia: Kimber, Conrad, 1806), 50; Sidney Kaplan, *The Black Presence in the Era of the American Revolution, 1770–1800* (Greenwich, CT: New York Graphic Society, 1973), 81–94; Gary B. Nash, *Forging Freedom: The Formation of Philadelphia's Black Community, 1720–1840* (Cambridge, MA: Harvard University Press, 1988), 100–133.

10. *Minutes of the Proceedings of the Eleventh American Convention for Promoting the Abolition of Slavery* (Philadelphia: Kimber, Conrad, 1806), 35–38; Richard Newman, "The Pennsylvania Abolition Society and the Struggle for Racial Justice," in Richard Newman and James Mueller, eds., *Antislavery and Abolition in Philadelphia: Emancipation and the Long Struggle for Racial Justice in the City of Brotherly Love* (Baton Rouge: Louisiana State University Press, 2011), 118–146, 136–137; Julie Winch, *A Gentleman of Color: The Life of James Forten* (New York: Oxford University Press, 2002), 156. On Peter Williams Jr., see John H. Hewitt, *Protest and Progress: New York's First Black Episcopal Church Fights Racism* (New York: Garland, 2000), 13–39.

11. Winch, *A Gentleman of Color*, 55–106.

12. David Nathaniel Gellman, *Emancipating New York: The Politics of Slavery and Freedom, 1777–1827* (Baton Rouge: Louisiana State University Press, 2006), 48–51.

13. Leon F. Litwack, *North of Slavery: The Negro in the Free States, 1790–1860* (Chicago: University of Chicago Press, 1961), 30–63; Alexander Keyssar, *The Right to Vote: The Contested History of Democracy in the United States*, rev. ed. (New York: Basic Books, 2009), 43–49, 315–320; Winch, *A Gentleman of Color*, 293–295; Phyllis F. Field, *The Politics of Race in New York: The Struggle for Black Suffrage in the Civil War Era* (Ithaca, NY: Cornell University Press, 2009), 34–38.

14. Craig Robertson, *The Passport in America: The History of a Document* (New York: Oxford University Press, 2010), 131; Nathan Perl-Rosenthal, *Citizen Sailors: Becoming American in the Age of Revolution* (Cambridge, MA: Harvard University Press, 2015).

15. Litwack, *North of Slavery*, 30–40; Rogers M. Smith, *Civic Ideals: Conflicting Visions of Citizenship in U.S. History* (New Haven, CT: Yale University Press, 1997), 174–181.

16. *Annals of Congress*, 16th Cong., 2nd sess., 13 February 1821, 1134, and 12 February 1821, 1095–1096; Robert Pierce Forbes, *The Missouri Compromise and Its Aftermath: Slavery and the Meaning of America* (Chapel Hill: University of North Carolina Press, 2007), 110–111; Smith, *Civic Ideals*, 175–177.

17. Matthew E. Mason, "Slavery Overshadowed: Congress Debates Prohibiting the Atlantic Slave Trade to the United States, 1806–1807," *JER* 20, no. 1 (2000): 59–81; Bruce Bendler, "James Sloan: Renegade or True Republican?" *New Jersey History* 125, no. 1 (2010): 1–19; Padraig Riley, "Slavery and the Problem of Democracy in Jeffersonian America," in Hammond and Mason, *Contesting Slavery*, 227–246.

18. *Annals of Congress*, 9th Cong., 2nd sess., 16, 18, 29 December 1806, 172, 175, 183, 185, 224, and 20 February 1807, 477.

19. Samuel Hodgdon to Timothy Pickering, 10 July 1800, in *Naval Documents Related to the Quasi-War Between the United States and France* (Washington, DC: US Government Printing Office, 1938), 6:133–34; "Domestic," *Independent Gazetteer*, 2 September 1800, 3; Nash, *Forging Freedom*, 139–140; Winch, *A Gentleman of Color*, 126; Mark E. Dixon, *The Hidden History of the Main Line: From Philadelphia to Malvern* (Charleston, SC: History Press, 2010), 22–24.

20. *Annals of Congress*, 9th Cong., 2nd sess., 29 December 1806, 224–226.

21. Ibid., 7 and 8 January 1807, 266–267, 270, 10 February 1807, 477–478. It's worth noting that this northern willingness to absorb freed slaves was a world removed from the similar debate during the Civil War, when northern legislators sought reassurances that emancipation would keep former slaves in the South.

22. Mason, "Slavery Overshadowed," 67–71.

23. *Annals of Congress*, 9th Cong., 2nd sess., 31 December 1806, 238–239; Gary B. Nash, *The Forgotten Fifth: African Americans in the Age of Revolution* (Cambridge, MA: Harvard University Press, 2006), 75–86.

24. Eva Shepard Wolf, *Race and Liberty in the New Nation: Emancipation in Virginia from the Revolution to Nat Turner's Rebellion* (Baton Rouge: Louisiana State University Press, 2006), 1–84.

25. Douglas Egerton, *Gabriel's Rebellion: The Virginia Slave Conspiracies of 1800 and 1802* (Chapel Hill: University of North Carolina Press, 1993); Wolf, *Race and Liberty*, 118–129; James Sidbury, *Ploughshares into Swords: Race, Rebellion, and Identity in Gabriel's Virginia, 1730–1810* (Cambridge, UK: Cambridge University Press, 1997); Lacy K. Ford, *Deliver Us from Evil*, 49–67.

26. Egerton, *Gabriel's Rebellion*, 18–33.

27. Ibid., 34–49; Sidbury, *Ploughshares into Swords*; and Michael L. Nicholls, *Whispers of Rebellion: Narrating Gabriel's Conspiracy* (Charlottesville: University of Virginia Press, 2012).

28. *Proceedings of the Sixth Convention,* 9; *Minutes of the Proceedings of the Seventh Convention of Delegates from the Abolition Societies Established in Different Parts of the United States* (Philadelphia: Zachariah Poulson Jr., 1801), 22, 30–33, 38, 39.

29. *Minutes of the Proceedings of the Tenth American Convention for Promotion the Abolition of Slavery* (Philadelphia: Kimber, Conrad, 1805), 22–23; Wolf, *Race and Liberty,* 123–126.

30. *Minutes of the Proceedings of the Eleventh American Convention for Promoting the Abolition of Slavery* (Philadelphia: Kimber, Conrad, 1806), 13; *Minutes of the Proceedings of the Twelfth American Convention* (Philadelphia: J. Bouvier, 1809), 14–17; Lewis Leary, "Thomas Branagan: Republican Rhetoric and Romanticism in America," *Pennsylvania Magazine of History and Biography* 77, no. 3 (1953): 332–352; Beverly Tomek, "'From Motives of Generosity, as Well as Self-Preservation': Thomas Branagan, Colonization, and the Gradual Emancipation Movement," *American Nineteenth Century History* 6, no. 2 (2005): 121–147.

31. Thomas Branagan, *A Preliminary Essay, on the Oppression of the Exiled Sons of Africa* (Philadelphia: John W. Scott, 1804), 93–116.

32. Ibid., 232–233; Thomas Branagan, *Serious Remonstrances, Addressed to the Citizens of the Northern States* (Philadelphia: Thomas T. Stiles, 1805), 38–39, 33–34, 17.

33. Tomek, "'From Motives of Generosity,'" 131–132; "Massacre of All the Whites at St Domingo," *Aurora,* 5 June 1804, 2; Thomas Branagan to Thomas Jefferson, 17 November 1805 and 27 April 1806, TJLC; Branagan, *Remonstrances,* 72; Nash, *Forging Freedom,* 173–183, 205, 208; Ashli White, *Encountering Revolution: Haiti and the Making of the Early Republic* (Baltimore: Johns Hopkins University Press, 2010).

34. Branagan, *Remonstrances,* 69, 33, 57.

35. Ibid., 119–124; *NSV,* 251–265.

36. "Queries Regarding Slavery," 414, 402, 406.

37. James Forten, *Letters from a Man of Colour* (Philadelphia: n.p., 1813), 8, 9–10, 5, 2; Winch, *A Gentleman of Color,* 168–174.

38. *Minutes of the Adjourned Session of the Twentieth Biennial American Convention* (Philadelphia: Samuel Parker, 1828), 36–37, 39. All emphasis is in the original unless otherwise noted.

CHAPTER 4: ONE NATION ONLY

1. Morgan John Rhys, "Diary of a Horseback Journey Through the United States, 1794–95," in John T. Griffith, *Rev. Morgan John Rhys: The Welsh Baptist Hero of Civil and Religious Liberty of the Eighteenth Century* (Carmarthen, UK: W. M. Evans and Son, 1910), 134–135; Gwyn A. Williams, *The Search for*

Beulah Land: The Welsh and the Atlantic Revolution (London: Croom Helm, 1980), 74–106.

2. John Morgan Rhys, *Altar of Peace: Being the Substance of a Discourse Delivered in the Council House at Greenville, July 4th, 1795* (Philadelphia: Ephraim Conrad, 1798), 9, 11.

3. Anthony Wayne to Timothy Pickering, 17 May and 28 June 1795, in Richard C. Knopf, ed., *Anthony Wayne, A Name in Arms: Soldier, Diplomat, Defender of Expansion Westward of a Nation* (Pittsburgh: University of Pittsburgh Press, 1960), 417, 430–434.

4. Rhys, *Altar of Peace*, 12; Charles Crawford, *An Essay upon the Propagation of the Gospel* (Philadelphia: J. Gales, 1799), 48–49.

5. [Silas Wood], *Thoughts on the State of the American Indians* (New York: T. and J. Swords, 1794), 9–11, 17–22, 35; "Silas Wood," in Ruth L. Woodward and Wesley Frank Craven, *Princetonians, 1784–1790: A Biographical Dictionary* (Princeton, NJ: Princeton University Press, 1991), 455–462.

6. Merritt B. Pound, *Benjamin Hawkins: Indian Agent* (Athens: University of Georgia Press, 1951); Robbie Franklyn Ethridge, *Creek Country: The Creek Indians and Their World, 1796–1816* (Chapel Hill: University of North Carolina Press, 2003); Benjamin Hawkins, *Letters, Journals and Writings of Benjamin Hawkins*, C. L. Grant, ed., 2 vols. (Savannah, GA: Beehive Press, 1980), 1:ix–xxvii.

7. "Instructions to Leonard Shaw," 17 February 1792, *ASPIA*, 1:247; James Seagrove to Edward Telfair, 17 September 1793, *ASPIA*, 1:409–410; Alexander Hamilton to George Matthews, 25 September 1794, *ASPIA*, 503–504; "Information by Richard Finnelson," *ASPIA*, 290–291; Gregory Evans Dowd, *A Spirited Resistance: The North American Indian Struggle for Unity, 1745–1815* (Baltimore: Johns Hopkins University Press, 1992), 109–110.

8. Interview of William Blount and Plamingo, 9 August 1792, in *ASPIA*, 1:287; Dowd, *A Spirited Resistance*, 112–113; Michael D. Green, *The Politics of Indian Removal: Creek Government and Society in Crisis* (Lincoln: University of Nebraska Press, 1982), 33–36.

9. James Wilkinson and Benjamin Hawkins to Henry Dearborn, 15 July 1802, in *ASPIA*, 1:670; Ethridge, *Creek Country*.

10. Gideon Blackburn, "Mission to the Cherokee Indians," *Panoplist*, June 1807 and February 1808, 39–40, 416–418.

11. Hawkins to Dearborn, 6 September 1801, in Benjamin Hawkins, *The Collected Works of Benjamin Hawkins*, Thomas Foster, ed. (Tuscaloosa: University of Alabama Press, 2003), 385; Thomas Jefferson to Hawkins, 18 February 1803, TJP; Anthony F.C. Wallace, *Jefferson and the Indians: The Tragic Fate of the First Americans* (Cambridge, MA: Harvard University Press, 1999), 206–240.

12. Ethridge, *Creek Country*, 19–21; Dowd, *A Spirited Resistance*, 149–157; Green, *The Politics of Indian Removal*, 36–43.

13. Robert M. Owens, *Mr. Jefferson's Hammer: William Henry Harrison and the Origins of American Indian Policy* (Norman: University of Oklahoma Press, 2007), 3–66; Adam Jortner, *The Gods of Prophetstown: The Battle of Tippecanoe and the Holy War for the American Frontier* (New York: Oxford University Press, 2012), 61–62; Jefferson to Henry Harrison, 27 February 1803, *WHH*, 1:70–73.

14. Stuart Banner, *How the Indians Lost Their Land: Law and Power on the Frontier* (Cambridge, MA: Harvard University Press, 2005), 143; Wallace, *Jefferson and the Indians*, 220–224.

15. Harrison to Dearborn, 15 July 1801, *WHH*, 1:25–30; Peter C. Mancall, *Deadly Medicine: Indians and Alcohol in Early America* (Ithaca, NY: Cornell University Press, 1995); William E. Unrau, *White Man's Wicked Water: The Alcohol Trade and Prohibition in Indian Country, 1802–1892* (Lawrence: University of Kansas Press, 1996); Jortner, *Gods of Prophetstown*, 63–64, 70–71; Wallace, *Jefferson and the Indians*, 295–297.

16. "Speech of the Little Turtle," 27 December 1801, in *Memorial of . . . a Committee Appointed for Indian Affairs* (Washington, DC: [n.p.], 1802), 5–7; Dowd, *A Spirited Resistance*, 134–136; Jortner, *Gods of Prophetstown*, 88–91; Harvey Lewis Carter, *The Life and Times of Little Turtle: First Sagamore of the Wabash* (Urbana-Champaign: University of Illinois Press, 1987), 156–163; Harrison to Dearborn, 15 July 1801, *WHH*, 1:29, 154–155; Unrau, *White Man's Wicked Water*, 10–11.

17. Harrison to the General Assembly, 29 July 1805, *WHH*, 1:154–155; Unrau, *White Man's Wicked Water*, 17–18.

18. Carter, *Little Turtle*, 156–183; John Sugden, *Blue Jacket: Warrior of the Shawnees* (Lincoln: University of Nebraska Press, 2000), 208–253.

19. R. David Edmunds, *The Shawnee Prophet* (Lincoln: University of Nebraska Press, 1983); Dowd, *A Spirited Resistance*, 123–147, 28–41; Jefferson to Dearborn, 28 August 1807, TJP; Dowd, *A Spirited Resistance*, 33–40, 123–131; Jortner, *Gods of Prophetstown*, 97–107.

20. Dowd, *A Spirited Resistance*, 108; "Talk by the Indian Chief La Maiquois," 24 May 1807, in *ASPIA*, 1:798; Jortner, *Gods of Prophetstown*, 136–137; William Wells to Harrison, 20 August 1807, *WHH*, 1:239; Tenskwatawa to Harrison, 1 August 1808, *WHH*, 1:299–300.

21. Harrison to Dearborn, 1 September 1808, *WHH*, 1:302; Harrison to William Eustis, 14 July 1809, *WHH*, 1:355–356; Owens, *Mr. Jefferson's Hammer*, 153–154, 199; Jortner, *Gods of Prophetstown*, 151–153.

22. Robert M. Owens, "Jeffersonian Benevolence on the Ground: The Indian Land Cession Treaties of William Henry Harrison," *JER* 22, no. 3 (2002): 405–435; Jortner, *Gods of Prophetstown*, 156–165.

23. Jefferson to Harrison, 22 December 1808, *WHH*, 1:323; Owens, "Jeffersonian Benevolence," 413, 426–430.

24. Wells to Dearborn, 31 December 1807, in C. E. Carter, ed., *TP*, 7:510–511; Paul A. Hutton, "William Wells: Frontier Scout and Indian Agent," *Indiana Magazine of History* 74, no. 3 (1978): 183–222; Donald H. Gaff, "Three Men from Three Rivers: Navigating Between Native and American Identity in the Old Northwest Territory," in Daniel P. Barr, ed., *The Boundaries Between Us: Natives and Newcomers Along the Frontiers of the Old Northwest Territory, 1750–1850* (Kent, OH: Kent State University Press, 2006), 143–160.

25. Harrison to Eustis, 18 July 1810, and Harrison to Tenskwatawa, 19 July 1810, *WHH*, 1:446, 447–448; Harrison to Eustis, 22 August 1810, *WHH*, 1:459–469; Dowd, *A Spirited Resistance*, 140–141; Edmunds, *Shawnee Prophet*, 90–92; Jortner, *Gods of Prophetstown*, 171–176.

26. Harrison to Eustis, 6 August 1811, *WHH*, 1:542–544; Harrison to Eustis, 22 August 1810, *WHH*, 1:467.

27. Harrison to Eustis, 28 August 1810, *WHH*, 1:470; Harrison's Annual Message to the Indiana House of Representatives, 12 November 1810, in *WHH*, 1:487–493; Harrison to Eustis, 6 and 7 August 1811, 17 September 1811, 29 October 1811, in *WHH*, 1:542–546, 548–550, 570–572, 605.

28. Harrison to Eustis, *WHH*, 1:618–631; Jortner, *Gods of Prophetstown*, 187–200; Owens, *Mr. Jefferson's Hammer*, 213–222.

29. "Speech of Tecumseh," 18 September 1813, *WHH*, 2:542; Owens, *Mr. Jefferson's Hammer*, 222–239; Jortner, *Gods of Prophetstown*, 201–218.

30. Andrew Jackson to Harrison, 28 November 1811, *WHH*, 1:665; John Adams to Jefferson, 10 February 1812 and 12 June 1812, TJP; Jefferson to Adams, 20 April 1812 and 28 June 1812, TJP.

31. Jefferson to Baron von Humboldt, 6 December 1813, TJP.

32. DeWitt Clinton, *Discourse Delivered Before the New-York Historical Society, 6th December 1811* (New York: James Eastburn, 1812), 47–50.

33. Diedrich Knickerbocker [Washington Irving], *A History of New York, from the Beginning of the World to the End of the Dutch Dynasty*, 2 vols. (New York: Inskeep and Bradford, 1809), 1:50, 52, 54, 58–64. I am grateful to Peter Jaros for sharing this reference.

34. "Traits of Indian Character," *Analectic Magazine* 3, no. 2 (1814), 145–156; Washington Irving, "Traits of Indian Character," in *The Sketch Book of Geoffrey Crayon, Gent.*, 2 vols. (London: John Murray, 1820), 2:215–216.

35. Elias Boudinot, *A Star in the West* (Trenton, NJ: D. Fenton et al., 1816), iv; Nathaniel Scudder Prime, *A Plan for the More Successful Management of Domestic Missions* (Albany, NY: Henry C. Southwick, 1816), 14.

CHAPTER 5: TO THE MIDDLE GROUND

1. George Green Shackelford, *Jefferson's Adoptive Son: The Life of William Short, 1759–1848* (Lexington: University Press of Kentucky, 1993); Annette Gordon-Reed, *The Hemingses of Monticello: An American Family* (New York: Norton, 2008), 536–539.

2. William Short to Thomas Jefferson, 27 February 1798, TJP.

3. According to his correspondence journal, Jefferson received Short's letter on 24 June 1798, less than a week before his departure for Monticello. "Epistolary Record or Summary Journal of Letters, 1783–1826," TJLC; Gordon-Reed, *Hemingses of Monticello*, 535–536.

4. Pedro Carasco, "Indian-Spanish Marriages in the First Century of the Colony," in Susan Schroeder et al., *Indian Women of Early Mexico* (Norman: University of Oklahoma Press, 1997), 87–103; Martha Menchaca, *Recovering History, Constructing Race: The Indian, Black, and White Roots of Mexican Americans* (Austin: University of Texas Press, 2001), 53–57; J. H. Elliott, *Empires of the Atlantic World: Britain and Spain in America, 1492–1830* (New Haven, CT: Yale University Press, 2006), 79–83; Filipa Ribeiro da Silva, *Dutch and Portuguese in Western Africa: Empires, Merchants and the Atlantic System, 1580–1674* (Leiden: Brill, 2011), 195–196; Olive Patricia Dickason, *Canada's First Nations: A History of Founding Peoples from Earliest Times* (Norman: University of Oklahoma Press, 1992), 167–173; Saliha Belmessous, *Assimilation and Empire: Uniformity in French and British Colonies, 1541–1954* (Oxford: Oxford University Press, 2013), 35–42, 112–114; Ronald Hyam, *Empire and Sexuality: The British Experience* (Manchester: Manchester University Press, 1990), 115–117; Damon Ieremia Salesa, *Racial Crossings: Race, Intermarriage, and the Victorian British Empire* (Oxford: Oxford University Press, 2011).

5. Abbé Raynal, *A Philosophical and Political History . . . of the Europeans in the East and West Indies*, trans. J. O. Justamond, 8 vols. (London: W. Strahan and T. Cadell, 1783), 2:231–235; William Roberts, *An Account of the First Discovery, and Natural History of Florida* (London: T. Jefferys, 1763), v–vi.

6. William Robertson, *The History of America*, Books IX and X (London: A. Strahan, 1796), 94–95.

7. Christopher Leslie Brown, *Moral Capital: Foundations of British Abolitionism* (Chapel Hill: University of North Carolina Press, 2006), 91–101; Pierre H. Boule, "Racial Purity or Legal Clarity? The Status of Black Residents in Eighteenth-Century France," *Journal of the Historical Society* 6, no. 1 (2006): 19–29.

8. Gary B. Nash, "The Hidden History of Mestizo America," *JAH* 82, no. 3 (1995): 941–962; Alfred N. Hunt, *Haiti's Influence on Antebellum America: Slumbering Volcano in the Caribbean* (Baton Rouge: Louisiana State University Press, 1988); Ashli White, *Encountering Revolution: Haiti and the Making of the Early Republic* (Baltimore: Johns Hopkins University Press, 2010).

9. David H. Fowler, *Northern Attitudes Towards Interracial Marriage: Legislation and Public Opinion in the Middle Atlantic and the States of the Old Northwest* (New York: Garland, 1987); Joel Williamson, *New People: Miscegenation and Mulattoes in the United States* (Baton Rouge: Louisiana State University Press, 1995).

10. Patrick Henry to George Rogers Clark, 1 January 1779, in William Wirt Henry, *Patrick Henry: Life, Correspondence and Speeches*, 3 vols. (New York: Charles Scribner's Sons, 1891), 3:219; William Wirt, *Life of Patrick Henry* (New York: McElrath and Bangs, 1831), 255–260; Theda Purdue, *"Mixed Blood" Indians: Racial Construction in the Early South* (Athens: University of Georgia Press, 2003), 1–32.

11. Countess of Huntingdon to Henry, 8 April 1784, in Henry, *Patrick Henry*, 3:253.

12. Henry to Joseph Martin, 4 February 1785, in Wirt, *Life*, 3:272; George Washington to James Jay, 25 January 1785, Washington to Selina, Countess of Huntingdon, 27 February 1785, Washington to Richard Henry Lee, 8 February 1795, Lee to Washington, 27 February 1785, GWP.

13. Morgan John Rhys, *The Altar of Peace, Being the Substance of a Discourse Delivered in the Council House, at Greenville, July 4th, 1795* (Philadelphia: Ephraim Conrad, 1798), 12.

14. Henry Knox to Washington, 29 December 1794, in *ASPIA*, 1:543–544; George William Van Cleve, *A Slaveholders' Union: Slavery, Politics and the Constitution in the Early American Republic* (Chicago: University of Chicago Press, 2010), 187–203.

15. Benjamin Rush to Nathaniel Greene, 16 September 1782, in Benjamin Rush, *The Letters of Benjamin Rush*, L. H. Butterfield, ed., 2 vols. (Princeton, NJ: Princeton University Press, 1951), 1:285–286; Rush to Granville Sharp, August 1791, in ibid., 1:608–609; Donald J. D'Elia, "Dr. Benjamin Rush and the Negro," *Journal of the History of Ideas* 30, no. 3 (1969): 413–422; Gary B. Nash, *Forging Freedom: The Formation of Philadelphia's Black Community, 1720–1840* (Cambridge, MA: Harvard University Press, 1988), 104–105.

16. Pennsylvania Abolition Society circular, 14 January 1795, in Rush, *Letters of Benjamin Rush*, 1:756–59; Benjamin Rush, "Observations . . . That the Black Color . . . of the Negroes Is Derived from the Leprosy," *Transactions of the American Philosophical Society* 4 (1799): 289–297; Rush to Jefferson, 4 February 1797, in Rush, *Letters of Benjamin Rush*, 1:785–786.

17. Abigail Adams to William Stephens Smith, 18 September 1785, in Richard Alan Ryerson, ed., *The Adams Papers, Family Correspondence*, vol. 6 (Cambridge, MA: Harvard University Press, 1993), 365–369.

18. David Rice, *Slavery Inconsistent with Justice and Good Policy* (Philadelphia: Parry Hall, 1792), 16, 26–27.

19. *NSV*, 258; Gilbert Imlay, *A Topographical Description of the Western Territory of North America* (London: J. Debrett, 1792), 185–201.

20. Marquis de Chastellux, *Travels in North America, in the Years 1780, 1781, and 1782*, 2 vols. (London: G. G. J. and J. Robinson, 1787), 2:44, 199–200.

21. Chastellux to Jefferson, 2 June 1785, Jefferson to Chastellux, 7 June 1785, Jefferson to Chastellux, 2 September 1785, TJP; "The State of Slavery in Virginia," *Columbian Magazine*, June 1787, 479–480.

22. Samuel Stanhope Smith, *Lectures . . . on Subjects of Moral and Political Philosophy*, 2 vols. (Trenton, NJ: Daniel Fenton, 1812), 2:174, 176.

23. Ibid., 2:176–179.

CHAPTER 6: WE SHALL ALL BE AMERICANS

1. Theda Purdue, "Race and Culture: Writing the Ethnohistory of the Early South," *Ethnohistory* 51, no. 4 (2004): 701–723; Andrew Frank, *Creeks and Southerners: Biculturalism on the Early American Frontier* (Lincoln: University of Nebraska Press, 2005); Jennifer Brown and Theresa Schenck, "Métis, Mestizo, and Mixed Blood," in Philip J. Deloria and Neal Salisbury, *A Companion to American Indian History* (Oxford: Blackwell, 2002), 321–338; Kathleen DuVal, "Indian Intermarriage and Métissage in Colonial Louisiana," *WMQ* 65, no. 2 (2008): 267–304; Andrew R. Graybill, *The Red and the White: A Family Saga of the American West* (New York: Norton, 2013).

2. Tiya Miles, *Ties That Bind: The Story of an Afro-Cherokee Family in Slavery and Freedom* (Berkeley: University of California Press, 2005); Ann Marie Plane, *Colonial Intimacies: Indian Marriage in Early New England* (Ithaca, NY: Cornell University Press, 2000); James F. Brooks, ed., *Confounding the Color Line: The Indian-Black Experience in North America* (Lincoln: University of Nebraska Press, 2005); Claudio Saunt, *Black, White and Indian: Race and the Unmaking of an American Family* (New York: Oxford University Press, 2005); Fay Yarborough, *Race and the Cherokee Nation: Sovereignty in the Nineteenth Century* (Philadelphia: University of Pennsylvania Press, 2008); Christina Snyder, *Slavery in Indian Country: The Changing Face of Captivity in Early America* (Cambridge, MA: Harvard University Press, 2010); Barbara Krauthammer, *Black Slaves, Indian Masters: Slavery, Emancipation, and Citizenship in the Native American South* (Chapel Hill: University of North Carolina Press, 2013).

3. Ninian Edwards to William Crawford, November 1815, in William Crawford, *Letter to the Secretary of War . . . Embracing the General and Particular Views of the Indian Trade* (Washington, DC: William A. Davis, 1816), 77–86; Henry Knox to George Washington, 6 July 1789, GWP; Michael D. Green, "Alexander McGillivray," in R. David Edmunds, *American Indian Leaders* (Lincoln: University of Nebraska Press, 1980), 41–63; John Walton Caughey,

McGillivray of the Creeks (Columbia: University of South Carolina Press, 2007); Alexandra Harmon, *Rich Indians: Native People and the Problem of Wealth in American History* (Chapel Hill: University of North Carolina Press, 2010), 83–91; Thomas N. Ingersoll, *To Intermix with Our White Brothers: Indian Mixed Bloods in the United States from Earliest Times to the Indian Removals* (Albuquerque: University of New Mexico Press, 2005).

4. "Instructions to Leonard Shaw," 17 February 1792, in *ASPIA*, 1:247–248; "On Monday Evening," *Dunlap's American Daily Advertiser*, 24 March 1792, 2; "Journal of the Grand Cherokee National Council," *ASPIA*, 1:271–272; Knox to William Blount, 31 January 1792 and 16 February 1792, *TP*, 4:116–117, 119; Henry T. Malone, *Cherokees of the Old South: A People in Transition* (Athens: University of Georgia Press, 1956), 35–38; William G. McLoughlin, *Cherokee Renascence in the New Republic* (Princeton, NJ: Princeton University Press, 1986), 39–42; Ruth L. Woodward and Wesley Frank Craven, *Princetonians, 1784–1790: A Biographical Dictionary* (Princeton, NJ: Princeton University Press, 1991), 51–53.

5. John P. Brown, *Old Frontiers: The Story of the Cherokee Indians from Earliest Times to the Date of Their Removal to the West, 1838* (Kingsport, TN: Southern Publishers, 1938), 344–348; John R. Finger, *Tennessee Frontiers: Three Regions in Transition* (Bloomington: Indiana University Press, 2001), 99–103, 106–110; McLoughlin, *Cherokee Renascence*, 23–24; Cynthia Cumfer, *Separate Peoples, One Land: The Minds of Cherokees, Blacks, and Whites on the Tennessee Frontier* (Chapel Hill: University of North Carolina Press, 2007), 57–75.

6. "Report of James Carey to Governor Blount," 19 March 1793, *ASPIA*, 1:437; Brown, *Old Frontiers*, 368–369. On the Blount conspiracy, see Andrew R. L. Cayton, "'When Shall We Cease to Have Judases?' The Blount Conspiracy and the Limits of the 'Extended Republic,'" in Ronald Hoffman and Peter J. Albert, eds., *Launching the "Extended Republic": The Federalist Era* (Charlottesville: University Press of Virginia, 1996), 156–189; Jeffrey Allen Zemler, *James Madison, the South, and the Trans-Appalachian West, 1783–1803* (Lanham, MD: Lexington Books, 2014), 165–167; Woodward and Craven, *Princetonians*, 53.

7. Harvey L. Carter, *The Life and Times of Little Turtle: First Sagamore of the Wabash* (Urbana-Champaign: University of Illinois Press, 1987); Paul A. Hutton, "William Wells: Frontier Scout and Indian Agent," *Indiana Magazine of History* 74, no. 3 (1978): 183–122.

8. William Henry Harrison to William Eustis, 7 November 1810, *WHH*, 1:508; Hutton, "William Wells," 199–218.

9. Ann Durkin Keating, *Rising Up from Indian Country: The Battle of Fort Dearborn and the Birth of Chicago* (Chicago: University of Chicago Press, 2012), 132–147.

10. Benjamin Hawkins to Washington, 10 February 1792, GWP; Robbie Ethridge, *Creek Country: The Creek Indians and Their World* (Chapel Hill: University of North Carolina Press, 2003); Merritt Bloodworth Pound, *Benjamin Hawkins: Indian Agent* (Athens: University of Georgia Press, 1951); Hawkins to Alexander McGillivray, 8 January 1786, in Caughey, *McGillivray of the Creeks*, 101–102.

11. Hawkins to Elizabeth Trist, 4 March 1797, in Benjamin Hawkins, *Letters, Journals and Writings of Benjamin Hawkins*, C. L. Grant, ed., 2 vols. (Savannah, GA: Beehive Press, 1980), 1:87–89.

12. Hawkins to Trist, 25 November 1797, in ibid., 1:162–165.

13. Purdue, *"Mixed Blood" Indians*, 16–32, 36–41.

14. Hawkins to Henry Gaither, 15–16 February 1797, in Benjamin Hawkins, *The Collected Works of Benjamin Hawkins, 1796–1810*, Thomas Foster, ed. (Tuscaloosa: University of Alabama Press, 2003), 83–84.

15. Hawkins to Mathew Hopkins, 17 March 1799, in Hawkins, *Writings of Benjamin Hawkins*, 1:243; Purdue, *"Mixed Blood" Indians*, 76.

16. Jefferson to Hawkins, 18 February 1803, Hawkins to Jefferson, 11 July 1803, TJLC; Cumfer, *Separate Peoples, One Land*, 73–75; Hawkins to Henry Dearborn, 1 February 1802, in Hawkins, *Writings of Benjamin Hawkins*, 2:433–434; Undated notebook entry (1803?), in Hawkins, *Collected Works*, 429–430.

17. Jefferson to Hendrick Aupamut, 21 December 1808, TJLC; Crawford, *Letter from the Secretary of War*, 4, 7–8.

18. Chase C. Mooney, *William H. Crawford, 1772–1834* (Louisville: University Press of Kentucky, 1974), 73–92; McLoughlin, *Cherokee Renascence*, 198–203.

19. *The Colonial Policy of Great Britain* (London: Baldwin, Craddock and Joy, 1816), 60, 62–63; Joseph Eaton, *The Anglo-American Paper War: Debates About the New Republic, 1800–1825* (Houndmills, UK: Palgrave Macmillan, 2012), 82–83; "Mr Crawford," *Virginia Argus*, 18 May 1816, 3; Dumas Malone, *The Public Life of Thomas Cooper, 1783–1839* (New Haven, CT: Yale University Press, 1926); Michael Durey, *Transatlantic Radicals and the Early American Republic* (Lawrence: University Press of Kansas, 1997), 24–25; "To James Madison," *Democratic Press*, 16 April 1816, 2.

20. "Notions Worthy of a Kickapoo, or Yahoo," *New York Columbian*, 20 April 1816, 2; "To the Honorable the Secretary at War," *Alexandria Herald*, 20 May 1816, 2; McLoughlin, *Cherokee Renascence*, 47–54, 198–201; "Civilization of the Cherokee Indians," *New York Columbian*, 21 June 1816, 2.

21. "Mr. Crawford," *New York Courier*, 10 July 1816, 2; "Mr. Crawford," *Virginia Argus*, 18 May 1816, 3; "Indian Affairs," *Washington City Weekly Gazette*, 8 June 1816, 230; "The Democratic Papers," *Albany Advertiser*, 5 August 1816, 2.

22. Crawford, *Letter from the Secretary of War*, 7; "Indian Civilization," *National Gazette*, 3 June 1820, 3.

23. William Crawford to Charles Jared Ingersoll, 4 July 1822, in Charles Jared Ingersoll Papers, Historical Society of Pennsylvania, Philadelphia, Box 1, folder 8; Thomas Cooper, *Strictures Addressed to James Madison* (Philadelphia: Jespar Harding, 1824); Sean Wilentz, *The Rise of American Democracy: Jefferson to Lincoln* (New York: Norton, 2005), 240–251.

24. John Demos, *The Heathen School: A Story of Hope and Betrayal in the Age of the Early Republic* (New York: Knopf, 2014); Karen Woods Weierman, *One Nation, One Blood: Interracial Marriage in American Fiction, Scandal, and Law, 1820–1870* (Amherst: University of Massachusetts Press, 2005), 11–33; Theresa Strouth Gaul, ed., *To Marry an Indian: The Marriage of Harriett Gold & Elias Boudinot in Letters, 1823–1839* (Chapel Hill: University of North Carolina Press, 2005), 1–76.

25. Demos, *Heathen School*, 114–115, 117; Thurman Wilkins, *Cherokee Tragedy: The Ridge Family and the Decimation of a People* (Norman: University of Oklahoma Press, 1986).

26. "Intermarriages," *Connecticut Herald*, 10 February 1824, 3; "Married at Cornwall," *Hartford Times*, 10 February 1824, 3; "A New Way to Evangelize," *Gospel Herald*, 21 February 1824, 327; "Intermarriages," *Haverhill Gazette & Patriot*, 21 February 1824, 2; "An Indian Chief," *Washington Whig*, 8 May 1824, 3; "Intermarriage with the Indians," *Connecticut Herald*, 2 March 1824, 3; "Mission School at Cornwall," *Connecticut Herald*, 18 May 1824, 1.

27. "Mission School at Cornwall," *Connecticut Herald*, 18 May 1824, 1; "From the Connecticut Courant," *Religious Miscellany*, 9 April 1824, 187; Theda Purdue, ed., *Cherokee Editor: The Writings of Elias Boudinot* (Athens: University of Georgia Press, 1983), 3–38; Gaul, *To Marry an Indian*, 6.

28. Gaul, *To Marry an Indian*, 13–14, 19–23, 1; Harriett Gold to Herman and Flora Gold Vaill and Catherine Gold, 25 June 1825, in ibid., 83–88.

29. Ibid., 87; Herman Vaill to Harriett Gold, 29 June 1825, in ibid., 90–103.

30. Herman Vaill to Mary Gold Brinsmade, 2 August 1825, in ibid., 116–122; Benjamin Gold to Herman Vaill, 1 September 1825, in ibid., 128–129; Herman Vaill to Benjamin Gold, 5 September 1825, in ibid., 129–132.

31. *The Semi-Annual Report of the Foreign Mission School, Cornwall, Connecticut*, no. 19 (n.p., n.d. [1825]), 5–6; "Missionary Spirit," *Village Register*, 4 August 1825, 2; "Middletown, Conn.," *Niles' Weekly Register*, 9 July 1825, 7; "A Marriage," *Haverhill Gazette and Patriot*, 29 July 1825, 2.

32. E. C. Tracy, *Memoir of the Life of Jeremiah Evarts* (Boston: Crocker and Brewster, 1845), 110–125; "Letter from the Treasurer of the American Board," *Panoplist*, July 1818, 338–346; Jeremiah Evarts to Calvin Chapin, 5 July 1825, in Tracy, *Life of Jeremiah Evarts*, 222–223; Jeremiah Evarts, *Through the South and West with Jeremiah Evarts in 1826*, ed. J. Orin Oliphant (Lewisburg, PA: Bucknell University Press, 1956), 37–41; "To the Editor of the Western Recorder,"

Western Recorder, 9 August 1825, 128. I am indebted to Theresa Gaul for the suggestion that "Crawford" may have been Jeremiah Evarts.

33. "To the Editor of the Western Recorder," *Western Recorder,* 9 August 1825, 128.

34. "Mixed Marriages," *Western Recorder,* 30 August 1825, 140; "Mixed Marriages," *Western Recorder,* 27 September 1825, 155.

35. "Mixed Marriages," *Western Recorder,* 4 October 1825, 159; McLoughlin, *Cherokee Renascence,* 367–368.

36. "Much Ado," *Natchez Ariel,* 5 September 1825, 53; Demos, *Heathen School,* 219–237.

37. Evarts, *Through the South and West,* 114–115, 41–43; Elias Boudinot, *An Address to the Whites, Delivered in the First Presbyterian Church, on the 26th of May, 1825* (Philadelphia: William F. Geddes, 1826), 8, 14.

CHAPTER 7: THE PRACTICAL AMALGAMATOR

1. *Authentic Biography of Colonel Richard M. Johnson of Kentucky* (New York: Henry Mason, 1833), 33–39; John Sugden, *Tecumseh's Last Stand* (Norman: University of Oklahoma Press, 1985), 136–181; David Curtis Skaggs, *William Henry Harrison and the Conquest of the Ohio Country: Frontier Fighting in the War of 1812* (Baltimore: Johns Hopkins University Press, 2014), 281.

2. Annette Gordon-Reed, *The Hemingses of Monticello: An American Family* (New York: Norton, 2008), 41–47; Richard Godbeer, *Sexual Revolution in Early America* (Baltimore: Johns Hopkins University Press, 2002), 190–224; Joshua D. Rothman, *Notorious in the Neighborhood: Sex and Families Across the Color Line in Virginia, 1787–1861* (Chapel Hill: University of North Carolina Press, 2003).

3. David Rice, *Slavery Inconsistent with Justice and Good Policy* (Philadelphia: Parry Hall, 1792), 26–27; Gordon-Reed, *Hemingses of Monticello,* 554–561.

4. Hezekiah Niles, "Mitigation of Slavery—No. 3," *Niles' Weekly Register,* 22 May 1819, 211. Niles's series on "The Mitigation of Slavery" ran across eight issues from 8 May to 21 August 1819.

5. "Mitigation of Slavery—No. 7," *Niles' Weekly Register,* 14 August 1819, 401; "Mitigation of Slavery—No. 6," ibid., 17 July 1819, 343; "Mitigation of Slavery—No. 8," ibid., 21 August 1819, 420.

6. Thomas Branagan, *Serious Remonstrances, Addressed to the Citizens of the Northern States* (Philadelphia: Thomas T. Stiles, 1805), 66–67.

7. "Colonization," *Genius of Liberty,* 7 September 1819, 3.

8. *Debates and Proceedings in the Congress of the United States,* 16th Cong., 1st sess., 17 February 1820, 1391–1392; Robert Pierce Forbes, *The Missouri Compromise and Its Aftermath: Slavery and the Meaning of America* (Chapel Hill: University of North Carolina Press, 2007), 103–106; William F. Freehling, *The*

Road to Disunion: Secessionists at Bay, 1776–1854 (New York: Oxford University Press, 1990), 150–152; Christa Dierksheide, *Amelioration and Empire: Progress and Slavery in the Plantation Americas* (Charlottesville: University of Virginia Press, 2014), 44–47; Thomas Jefferson to Marie Joseph Lafayette, 26 December 1820, and Lafayette to Jefferson, 1 July 1821, in Thomas Jefferson and Marie Joseph Lafayette, with an Introduction by Gilbert Chinard, *The Letters of Lafayette and Jefferson* (Baltimore: Johns Hopkins University Press, 1929), 402, 407; Gordon-Reed, *Hemingses of Monticello*, 285, 601. Eston, Jefferson's youngest son, would also pass as white soon after Jefferson's death.

9. George Bourne, *The Book and Slavery Irreconcilable: With Animadversions upon Dr. Smith's Philosophy* (Philadelphia: J. M. Sanderson, 1816), 118–119, 144; David Brion Davis, *The Problem of Slavery in the Age of Revolution, 1770–1823* (New York: Oxford University Press, 1999), 200–201.

10. George Bourne, *Picture of Slavery in the United States of America* (Middletown, CT: Edwin Hunt, 1834), 87–98.

11. George Bourne, *Slavery Illustrated in Its Effects upon Woman and Domestic Society* (Boston: Isaac Knapp, 1837), 75, 86–87, 95–97.

12. Richard S. Newman, *The Transformation of American Abolitionism: Fighting Slavery in the Early Republic* (Chapel Hill: University of North Carolina Press, 2002).

13. On Clay's lithographs, see Elise Lemire, *"Miscegenation": Making Race in America* (Philadelphia: University of Pennsylvania Press, 2002), 62–65.

14. Lydia Maria Child, *An Appeal in Favor of That Class of Americans Called Africans* (Boston: Allen and Ticknor, 1833), 25, 90.

15. Ibid., 134, 139–140.

16. Lydia Maria Child, ed., *The Oasis* (Boston: Benjamin C. Bacon, 1834), ix, xi.

17. Child, *Appeal*, 139; David Walker, *Walker's Appeal, in Four Articles, Together with a Preamble to the Colored Citizens of the World* (Boston: Printed for the Author, 1829), 11; "Can't Amalgamate," *Colored American*, 29 July 1837, 2. On Williams, see Leslie M. Harris, *In the Shadow of Slavery: African Americans in New York City, 1626–1863* (Chicago: University of Chicago Press, 2003), 197–200.

18. Child, *Oasis*, 200, 65–105; David H. Fowler, *Northern Attitudes Towards Interracial Marriage: Legislation and Public Opinion in the Middle Atlantic and the States of the Old Northwest* (New York: Garland, 1987), 106–108.

19. "An Unjust Law," *The Liberator*, 29 January 1831, 18; "The Marriage Law," *The Liberator*, 21 May 1831, 83.

20. "The Marriage Question," *The Liberator*, 17 November 1832, 183; "Marriage Bill," *The Liberator*, 19 March 1831, 47; "The Marriage Law," *The Liberator*, 30 April 1831, 72; "The Marriage Bill," *The Liberator*, 11 June 1831, 94.

21. Amber D. Moulton, "Closing the 'Floodgate of Impurity': Moral Reform, Antislavery, and Interracial Marriage in Antebellum Massachusetts," *Journal of the Civil War Era* 3, no. 1 (2013): 2–34; Louis Ruchames, "Race, Marriage and Abolition in Massachusetts," *Journal of Negro History* 40, no. 3 (1955): 250–273; Chris Dixon, *Perfecting the Family: Antislavery Marriages in Nineteenth-Century America* (Amherst: University of Massachusetts Press, 1995), 42–44; Harris, *In the Shadow of Slavery*, 198; William Jay, *Slavery in America* (London: F. Westley and A. H. Davis, 1835), 138; "Anti-Slavery Principles of Elijah P. Lovejoy," *The Liberator*, 22 December 1837, 205; "Amalgamation," *The Liberator*, 30 March 1838, 52.

22. Adele Logan Alexander, *Parallel Worlds: The Remarkable Gibbs-Hunts and the Enduring (In)Significance of Melanin* (Charlottesville: University of Virginia Press, 2010), 19–24; Wilma King, "Within the Professional Household: Slave Children in the Antebellum South," *The Historian* 59, no. 3 (1997): 523–540; Leland Winfield Meyer, "The Life and Times of Colonel Richard M. Johnson of Kentucky," PhD dissertation, Columbia University, 1932; *Debates and Proceedings in the Congress of the United States*, 16th Cong., 1st sess., Senate, 345–359. I'm indebted to Christina Snyder for sharing insights from her forthcoming book *Great Crossings: Indians, Settlers, and Slaves in the Age of Jackson* (New York: Oxford University Press), to be released in 2016.

23. Jonathan Milnor Jones, "The Making of a Vice President: The National Political Career of Richard M. Johnson of Kentucky," PhD dissertation, University of Memphis, 1998; Miles Smith, "The Kentucky Colonel: Richard M. Johnson and the Rise of Western Democracy, 1780–1850," PhD dissertation, Texas Christian University, 2013; Ella Wells Drake, "Choctaw Academy: Richard M. Johnson and the Business of Indian Education," *Register of the Kentucky Historical Society* 91, no. 3 (1993): 260–297.

24. Richard Mentor Johnson to Thomas Henderson, 7 December 1835, THP, folder 10; Johnson to Henderson, 9 December 1825, in ibid., folder 1; Carolyn Thomas Foreman, "The Choctaw Academy," *Chronicles of Oklahoma* 6, no. 4 (1928): 453–480.

25. Johnson to Henderson, 13 January 1826, THP, folder 2. See also Johnson to Henderson, 31 December 1826, in ibid., folder 1.

26. Johnson to Henderson, 27 and 28 December 1827, THP, folder 3; Johnson to Henderson, 24 March 1830, in ibid., folder 6; Drake, "The Business of Indian Education," 280–281.

27. Johnson to Henderson, 16 January and 7 March 1828, THP, folder 4.

28. "Great Prospects of the Coloured People," *Western Recorder*, 26 April 1831, 68; Jones, "Making of a Vice President," 221.

29. Beth L. Savage, ed., *African American Historic Places* (New York: John Wiley and Sons, 1994), 249; *Kentucky Marriages, 1797–1865* (Baltimore: Genealogical Publishing Company, 1966), 72.

30. "Novel Incident," *Baltimore Patriot*, 27 July 1831, 1.

31. Johnson to Preston Blair, 16 June 1835, in Blair-Lee Papers, Princeton University, Box 14, folder 3; "A Noble Commentary," *The Liberator*, 13 August 1831, 129.

32. "Marriage Extraordinary," *The Liberator*, 8 December 1832, 194; "The Kentucky Marriage," *The Liberator*, 22 December 1832, 202; Philip S. Foner, "William P. Powell: Militant Champion of Black Seamen," in Foner, *Essays in Afro-American History* (Philadelphia: Temple University Press, 1978), 8–111.

33. Johnson to Henderson, 4 May and 27 May 1834, THP, folder 9.

34. "Col. Johnson," *Hartford Times*, 13 July 1835, 2; "Col. R.M. Johnson," *Portsmouth Journal*, 25 July 1835, 1; Thomas Brown, "The Miscegenation of Richard Mentor Johnson as an Issue in the National Election Campaign of 1835–36," *Civil War History* 39, no. 1 (1993): 5–30; Jones, "Making of a Vice President," 271–318; Smith, "Kentucky Colonel," 224–251.

35. "Fruits of Slavery," *The Liberator*, 25 July 1835, 120; "Fruits of Slavery," *The Liberator*, 1 August 1835, 124; "Robbery of Col. Johnson," *New Hampshire Sentinel*, 23 July 1835, 2; "Correspondence of the Cincinnati Gazette," *Painesville* (Ohio) *Telegraph*, 24 July 1835, 2.

36. Ted Widmer, *Martin Van Buren* (New York: Times Books, 2005), 113.

37. "The Nomination of Richard M. Johnson," *Hagerstown Torch Light*, 11 June 1835, 2; "The Second-Hand Argument," *Kentucky Whig*, 26 August 1836, 2.

38. "Richard M. Johnson," *Connecticut Herald*, 29 September 1835, 1; "Colonel Johnson," *The Liberator*, 4 July 1835, 108; "Southern Action," *Philanthropist*, 14 April 1837, 3.

39. *Hagerstown Torch Light*, 8 September 1836, 2; *Vermont Gazette*, 20 December 1836, 2; "The Vice President of the United States," *Albany Evening Journal*, 1 September 1837, 2; *New York Spectator*, 4 September 1837, 1; Marcus Wood, *Black Milk: Imagining Slavery in the Visual Cultures of Brazil and America* (New York: Oxford University Press, 2013), 83–86.

40. Johnson to Henderson, 26 February 1836, THP, folder 11.

41. *The Emancipator*, 11 August 1836, 59; "Col. R. M. Johnson," *Salem Gazette*, 30 August 1836, 2; "Col. R. M. Johnson," *Connecticut Herald*, 13 September 1836, 4.

42. "Col. R. M. Johnson," *The Liberator*, 8 June 1838, 92; "Interview with the Vice President," *The Liberator*, 22 June 1838, 98; "Scenic and Characteristic Outlines of Congress," *National Magazine and Republican Review*, January 1839, 81–83.

43. Amos Kendall to Martin Van Buren, 22 August 1839 (plus anonymous enclosure dated Georgetown, Kentucky, 12 August 1839), in Martin Van Buren Papers, Library of Congress, microfilm edition, reel 21; Jones, "Making of a Vice President," 342; Donald B. Cole, *A Jackson Man: Amos Kendall and the*

Rise of American Democracy (Baton Rouge: Louisiana State University Press, 2004), 50–53, 211, 227.

44. "Abolition Petitions," *Arkansas Star*, 14 May 1840, 1; "Correspondence with the Vice President," *The Emancipator*, 29 May 1840, 17; William Henry Harrison to John O'Fallon, 21 October 1833, Mss A 031, Filson Historical Society, and O'Fallon to Harrison, 21 April 1834, in ibid.

45. "A Van Buren Convention," *Philadelphia North American*, 7 October 1840, 2.

46. "Boston Notions," *Brother Jonathan*, 28 October 1843, 241; Johnson to J. G. Spencer, 28 November 1841, in THP, folder 16. See also Drake, "Business of Indian Education," 293–294. On Johnson's sadly resilient belief in his own political prospects, see "Letter from Col. Johnson Himself," *Niles' National Register*, 3 February 1844, 356.

47. "The Workings of Slavery," *New-York Daily Tribune*, 1 July 1845, 1; "Developments of the 'Peculiar Institution,'" *Green Mountain Freeman*, 20 June 1845, 1.

48. William Short to Jefferson, 14 December 1825, Jefferson to Short, 18 January 1826, TJLC; George Green Shackelford, *Jefferson's Adoptive Son: The Life of William Short, 1759–1848* (Lexington: University Press of Kentucky, 1993), 176.

49. Jefferson to Short, 18 January 1826, TJLC.

CHAPTER 8: OF COLOR AND COUNTRY

1. Robert Harms, *The Diligent: A Voyage Through the Worlds of the Slave Trade* (New York: Basic Books, 2002), 165–194; Marion Johnson, "Bulfinch Lambe and the Emperor of Pawpaw: A Footnote to Agaja and the Slave Trade," *History in Africa* 5 (1978): 345–350; Robin Law, "Further Light on Bulfinch Lambe and the Emperor of Pawpaw," *History in Africa* 17 (1990): 211–226.

2. Law, "Further Light," 193–194; John Atkins, *A Voyage to Guinea, Brasil, and the West Indies* (London: Caesar Ward and Richard Chandler, 1735), 121–122.

3. Law, "Further Light," 216–220; Christopher Leslie Brown, *Moral Capital: Foundations of British Abolitionism* (Chapel Hill: University of North Carolina Press, 2006), 259–261; Granville Sharp, *Memoirs of Granville Sharp*, Prince Hoare, ed., 2 vols. (London: Henry Colburn, 1828), 48–77; Peter Fryer, *Staying Power: The History of Black People in Britain* (London: Pluto Press, 1984), 115–125; Adam Hochschild, *Bury the Chains: Prophets and Rebels in the Fight to Free an Empire's Slaves* (Boston: Houghton Mifflin, 2005), 41–48.

4. John Fothergill to Granville Sharp, 2 February 1772, in Betsy C. Corner and Christopher C. Booth, eds., *Chain of Friendship: Selected Letters of Dr. John Fothergill of London, 1735–1780* (Cambridge, MA: Harvard University Press, 1971), 374–375; Sharp, *Memoirs*, 1:123–127; John Fothergill,

"Considerations Relative to the North American Colonies," in John Coakley Lettsom, ed., *The Works of John Fothergill, M.D.* (London: Charles Dilly, 1783), 2:383–416, 410–411; Henry Smeathman to John Coakley Lettsom, 19 October 1782, in ibid., 3:183–96.

5. Sharp to General Boyd, 13 March 1773, GSL; Cassandra Pybus, *Epic Journeys of Freedom: Runaway Slaves of the American Revolution and Their Global Quest for Liberty* (Boston: Beacon Press, 2006); Sylvia Frey, *Water from the Rock: Black Resistance in a Revolutionary Age* (Princeton, NJ: Princeton University Press, 1991); Maya Jasanoff, *Liberty's Exiles: American Loyalists in the Revolutionary World* (New York: Knopf, 2011); Cassandra Pybus, "Jefferson's Faulty Math: The Question of Slave Defections in the American Revolution," *WMQ* 62, no. 2 (2005): 243–264.

6. Pybus, *Epic Journeys*, 75–87, 103–119; Stephen Braidwood, *Black Poor and White Philanthropists: London's Blacks and the Foundation of the Sierra Leone Settlement, 1786–1791* (Liverpool: Liverpool University Press, 1994), 22–33, 63–107; Sharp, *Memoirs*, 259–260; Hochschild, *Bury the Chains*, 143–151.

7. Sharp to Lettsom, 13 October 1788, *WTP*; Sharp, *Memoirs*, 1:270; Braidwood, *Black Poor*, 129–161; Richard Brown, *Church and State in Modern Britain, 1700–1850* (London: Routledge, 1991), 341–342; Jenny Graham, "Revolutionary in Exile: The Emigration of Joseph Priestley to America, 1794–1804," *Transactions of the American Philosophical Society*, new series 85, no. 2 (1995): 1–213.

8. Sharp to Lettsom, 13 October 1788, *WTP*, 95.

9. Nicholas Guyatt, "The Complexion of My Country: Benjamin Franklin and the Problem of Racial Diversity," in David Waldstreicher, ed., *A Companion to Benjamin Franklin* (Chichester, UK: Wiley-Blackwell, 2011), 183–210, 203–204; Braidwood, *Black Poor*, 16–17, 44n.

10. Braidwood, *Black Poor*, 181–268; Hochschild, *Bury the Chains*, 174–180, 199–212; Pybus, *Epic Journeys*, 118–119, 139–155.

11. Pybus, *Epic Journeys*, 169–202; James Sidbury, *Becoming African in America: Race and Nation in the Early Black Atlantic* (New York: Oxford University Press, 2007), 92–129; Nicholas Guyatt, "Humdrum Selfishness," *London Review of Books*, 6 April 2006, 31–33.

12. On Lafayette's American journey toward antislavery, see Fritz Hirschfeld, *George Washington and Slavery: A Documentary Portrayal* (Columbia: University of Missouri Press, 1997), 118–128. See also Lloyd Kramer, *Lafayette in Two Worlds: Public Cultures and Personal Identities in an Age of Revolutions* (Chapel Hill: University of North Carolina Press, 1996).

13. On Lafayette and Laurens, see David A. Clary, *Adopted Son: Washington, Lafayette, and the Friendship That Saved the Revolution* (New York: Random House, 2007), 104–105; Hirschfeld, *George Washington and Slavery*, 17–18;

Sidney Kaplan, *The Black Presence in the Era of the American Revolution, 1770–1800* (New York: New York Graphic Society for Smithsonian Institution Press, 1973), 36–38.

14. Laurent Dubois, *A Colony of Citizens: Revolution and Slave Emancipation in the French Caribbean, 1787–1804* (Chapel Hill: University of North Carolina Press, 2004), 177–184; Louis Sal-Molins, *Dark Side of the Light: Slavery and the French Enlightenment*, trans. John Conteh-Morgan (Minneapolis: University of Minnesota Press, 2006), 11–53; Louis Gottschalk, *Lafayette Between the American and the French Revolution, 1783–1789* (Chicago: University of Chicago Press, 1950); David Brion Davis, *The Problem of Slavery in the Age of Revolution, 1770–1823* (New York: Oxford University Press, 1999), 94–96.

15. Marie Joseph Lafayette to George Washington, 5 February 1783, Washington to Lafayette, 5 April 1783, in Founders Online, National Archives, http://founders.archives.gov; Liliana Willens, "Lafayette's Emancipation Experiment in French Guiana, 1786–1792," in *Studies on Voltaire and the Eighteenth Century* 242 (1986): 345–362. Willens notes that contemporaries interchangeably described the colony as "Cayenne" or "Guyane."

16. On the white settlement effort after 1763, see Christopher Hodson, *The Acadian Diaspora: An Eighteenth-Century History* (New York: Oxford University Press, 2012), 79–116. See also Willens, "Lafayette's Emancipation Experiment," 349–353.

17. Lafayette to Washington, 8 February 1786, Washington to Lafayette, 10 May 1786, in Lafayette, *Memoirs, Correspondence and Manuscripts of General Lafayette*, 3 vols. (London: Saunders and Otley, 1837), 2:128, 140; Willens, "Lafayette's Emancipation Experiment," 354–362; Gottschalk, *Lafayette Between the American and the French Revolution*, 244; Dubois, *A Colony of Citizens*, 324–327, 343.

18. Lafayette offered these reflections "some years after" his 1791 vote in the French National Assembly on the need to bestow civil rights on free blacks in the French Caribbean. Lafayette, *Memoirs*, 3:68–70.

19. Kaplan, *Black Presence*, 11–12; James T. Campbell, *Middle Passages: African American Journeys to Africa, 1787–2005* (New York: Penguin, 2006), 16–17.

20. Samuel Hopkins to Philip Quaque, 10 December 1773, in Vincent Carretta and Ty M. Reese, eds., *The Life and Letters of Philip Quaque, the First African Anglican Missionary* (Athens: University of Georgia Press, 2010), 114–115; Campbell, *Middle Passages*, 17–22; Sidbury, *Becoming African in America*, 77–80; Edward E. Andrews, *Native Apostles: Black and Indian Missionaries in the British Atlantic World* (Cambridge, MA: Harvard University Press, 2013), 187–221; Samuel Hopkins, *A Dialogue Concerning the Slavery of the Africans* (Norwich: Judah P. Spooner, 1776), 34, 47–48; Ruth L. Woodward and Wesley

Frank Craven, *Princetonians, 1784–1790: A Biographical Dictionary* (Princeton, NJ: Princeton University Press, 1991), l–li.

21. Kaplan, *Black Presence*, 181–192; Sidbury, *Becoming African in America*, 73–77. See also W. Bryan Rommel-Ruiz, "Colonizing the Black Atlantic: The African Colonization Movements in Postwar Rhode Island and Nova Scotia," *Slavery and Abolition* 27, no. 3 (2006): 349–365.

22. *WTP*, xxxi–xliii; Deirdre Coleman, *Romantic Colonization and British Anti-Slavery* (Cambridge: Cambridge University Press, 2005), 131.

23. William Thornton to Lettsom, 15 February 1787, *WTP*, 43–47; "General Outlines of a Settlement on the Tooth or Ivory Coast of Africa," *WTP*, 38–41; Gary B. Nash, *Forging Freedom: The Formation of Philadelphia's Black Community, 1720–1840* (Cambridge, MA: Harvard University Press, 1988), 101–104; Gaillard Hunt, *William Thornton and Negro Colonization* (Worcester, MA: American Antiquarian Society, 1921).

24. Thornton to Lettsom, 15 February 1787, Thornton to the Elders and Members of the Union Society, Newport, R.I., 6 March 1787, Thornton to Lettsom, 20 May 1787, Thornton to Lettsom, 26 July 1788, *WTP*, 43–53, 56, 71.

25. Thornton to Lettsom, 26 July 1788, Thornton to Lettsom, 15 November 1788, Sharp to Lettsom, 13 October 1788, enclosed in Lettsom to Thornton, 29 January 1789, *WTP*, 58n, 86–97; Samuel Hopkins, "Memoir," in Samuel Hopkins, *The Works of Samuel Hopkins*, 3 vols. (Boston: Doctrinal Tract and Book Society, 1852), 1:139.

26. Hopkins to Sharp, 15 January 1789, Zachary Macaulay to Hopkins, 19 March 1795 and 20 October 1796, in Hopkins, "Memoir," 1:140–142, 150–153; Hunt, *William Thornton*, 18–19; Pybus, *Epic Journeys*, 202; Sidbury, *Becoming African in America*, 121–122; Thornton to the President and Members of the Council of the Virgin Islands," 22 February 1791, and Jabez Doty to Thornton, 25 February 1791, *WTP*, 130–132; William Thornton, *Political Economy, Founded in Justice and Humanity* (Washington, DC: Samuel Harrison Smith, 1804), 3, 6.

27. *WTP*, xlvi–xlvii.

28. Eva Sheppard Wolf, *Race and Liberty in the New Nation: Emancipation in Virginia from the Revolution to Nat Turner's Rebellion* (Baton Rouge: Louisiana State University Press, 2006); Lacy K. Ford, *Deliver Us from Evil: The Slavery Question in the Old South* (New York: Oxford University Press, 2009), 19–24; *NSV*, 251–252, 264–265; Thomas Jefferson, "Autobiography" (1821), *TJP*; Peter S. Onuf, *Jefferson's Empire: The Language of American Nationhood* (Charlottesville: University Press of Virginia, 2000), 147–188; Onuf, "'Every Generation Is an Independent Nation': Colonization, Miscegenation and the Fate of Jefferson's Children," *WMQ* 57, no. 1 (2000): 153–170; Christa

Dierksheide, *Amelioration and Empire: Progress and Slavery in the Plantation Americas* (Charlottesville: University of Virginia Press, 2014), 25–56; Ford, *Deliver Us from Evil*, 35–38.

29. J. P. Brissot de Warville, *New Travels in the United States of America, Performed in 1788* (New York: T. & J. Swords, 1792), 149, 157, 160; Marie-Jeanne Rossignol, "Jacques-Pierre Brissot and the Fate of Atlantic Antislavery During the Age of Revolutionary Wars," in Richard Bessel et al., eds., *War, Empire and Slavery, 1770–1830* (Houndmills, UK: Palgrave, 2010), 139–156.

30. Brissot, *New Travels*, 169–170; Thornton to Jacques-Pierre Brissot, 29 November 1788, Brissot to Thornton, 17 June 1789, Thornton to Etienne Clavière, 7 November 1789, *WTP*, 80–85, 100–101, 103–107.

31. Ford, *Deliver Us from Evil*, 37–38; Wolf, *Race and Liberty*, 39–62; Ferdinando Fairfax, "Plan for Liberating the Negroes Within the United States," *American Museum*, December 1790, 285–287; Gary B. Nash, *Race and Revolution* (Lanham, MD: Rowman and Littlefield, 2001), 146.

32. John Jones Spooner, "A Topographical Description of the County of Prince George in Virginia," in *Collections of the Massachusetts Historical Society for the Year 1794*, vol. 3 (Boston: Joseph Belknap, 1794), 92; Archibald Alexander, *A History of Colonization on the Western Coast of Africa* (Philadelphia: William S. Martien, 1846), 61–62; Beverly C. Tomek, *Colonization and Its Discontents: Emancipation, Emigration and Antislavery in Antebellum Pennsylvania* (New York: New York University Press, 2011), 63–92.

33. Thornton to Clavière, 7 November 1789, St. George Tucker to Jeremy Belknap, 29 June 1795, in "Queries Relating to Slavery in Massachusetts," MHS, 3 (1877), 375–431, 407–409; St. George Tucker, *A Dissertation on Slavery, with a Proposal for the Gradual Abolition of It, in the State of Virginia* (Philadelphia: Mathew Carey, 1796), 10, 29–30, 51.

34. Tucker, *Dissertation on Slavery*, 66, 94–98.

35. Tucker to Belknap, 13 August 1797, in "Queries Relating to Slavery," 427–428; Ford, *Deliver Us from Evil*, 47–48.

36. Maurice Jackson, *Let This Voice Be Heard: Anthony Benezet, Father of Atlantic Abolitionism* (Philadelphia: University of Pennsylvania Press, 2009), 119; Roberts Vaux, *Memoirs of the Life of Anthony Benezet* (Philadelphia: W. Alexander, 1817), 30.

37. Sharp to Anthony Benezet, 21 August 1772, GSL; Jackson, *Let This Voice Be Heard*, 119; Anthony Benezet, *Some Historical Account of Guinea* (London: J. Phillips, 1788), 116–117.

38. Benezet to Joseph Phipps, 28 May 1763, in Anthony Benezet Papers, Collection 852, Haverford College Library; Benezet to Selina, Countess of Huntingdon, 20 May 1774, in ibid.; Benezet, *Historical Account*, 117; Benezet to Fothergill, 27 April 1773, in Benezet Papers, Haverford.

39. Sharp to Benjamin Rush, Rush Family Papers, Series 1, Benjamin Rush Papers, Library Company of Philadelphia; David Freeman Hawke, *Benjamin Rush: Revolutionary Gadfly* (Indianapolis: Bobbs-Merrill, 1971), 64–70; Jackson, *Let This Voice Be Heard*, x, 117–126; Nash, *Forging Freedom*, 104–106; Rush to Nathaniel Greene, 16 September 1782, in Benjamin Rush, *Letters of Benjamin Rush*, L. H. Butterfield, ed., 2 vols. (Princeton, NJ: Princeton University Press, for the American Philosophical Society, 1951), 1:285–286; Rush to Richard Price, 15 October 1785, in ibid., 1:371; Rush to Sharp, August 1791, in ibid., 1:608–609; Absalom Jones et al. to Sharp, 23 November 1793, GSL.

40. Benjamin Rush, "The Paradise of Negro Slaves—A Dream," *Columbian Magazine*, January 1787, 235–238; Jackson, *Let This Voice Be Heard*, x.

41. Rush to the President of the Pennsylvania Abolition Society, undated [1794?], in Rush, *Letters*, 2:754–756. The land deeds are in the Rush Family Papers, Series 1, Box 3, folder 34. (Rush called the land "Safe Retreat.")

42. Rush to John Nicholson, 12 August 1793, in Rush, *Letters*, 2:636–637.

Chapter 9: The Choice

1. Lawrence A. Clayton, *Bartolomé de las Casas: A Biography* (Cambridge, UK: Cambridge University Press, 2012), 154–187; Henry Raup Wagner, *The Life and Writings of Bartolomé de las Casas* (Albuquerque: University of New Mexico Press, 1967), 46–69; Julia Sarreal, *The Guaraní and Their Missions: A Socioeconomic History* (Stanford, CA: Stanford University Press, 2014); Barbara Ganson, *The Guaraní Under Spanish Rule in the Río de la Plata* (Stanford, CA: Stanford University Press, 2003); James Schofield Saeger, "Warfare, Reorganization, and Readaptation at the Margins of Spanish Rule—the Chico and Paraguay (1573–1882)," in Frank Salomon and Stuart B. Schwartz, eds., *The Cambridge History of the Native Peoples of the Americas*, vol. 3, *South America*, Part 2 (Cambridge, UK: Cambridge University Press, 1999), 274–281; David J. Weber, *Bárbaros: Spaniards and Their Savages in the Age of Enlightenment* (New Haven, CT: Yale University Press, 2005), 109–116.

2. J. H. Elliott, *Empires of the Atlantic World: Britain and Spain in America, 1492–1830* (New Haven, CT: Yale University Press, 2006), 74; Richard W. Cogley, *John Eliot's Mission to the Indians Before King Philip's War* (Cambridge, MA: Harvard University Press, 1999); Harold W. Van Lonkhuyzen, "A Reappraisal of the Praying Indians: Acculturation, Conversion, and Identity at Natick, Massachusetts, 1646–1730," *New England Quarterly* 63, no. 3 (1990): 396–428; Julius H. Rubin, *Tears of Repentance: Christian Indian Identity and Community in Colonial Southern New England* (Lincoln: University of Nebraska Press, 2013), 19–38.

3. "Treaty at Fort Pitt," *Collections of the Wisconsin State Historical Society* 23 (1916): 140, 143; Colin G. Calloway, *Pen and Ink Witchcraft: Treaties and*

Treaty Making in American Indian History (New York: Oxford University Press, 2013), 96–97; Richard White, *The Middle Ground: Indians, Empires, and Republics in the Great Lakes Region, 1650–1815* (Cambridge, UK: Cambridge University Press, 1991), 366–412; Gregory Evans Dowd, *A Spirited Resistance: The North American Indian Struggle for Unity, 1745–1815* (Baltimore: Johns Hopkins University Press, 1992), 47–89; Colin G. Calloway, *The American Revolution in Indian Country: Crisis and Diversity in Native American Communities* (Cambridge, UK: Cambridge University Press, 1995); Jane T. Merritt, "Native Peoples in the Revolutionary War," in Edward G. Gray and Jane Kamensky, eds., *The Oxford Handbook of the American Revolution* (New York: Oxford University Press, 2013), 234–249.

4. Calloway, *American Revolution*, 36–37; P. J. Marshall, "A Nation Defined by Empire, 1755–1776," in Alexander Grant and Keith J. Stringer, eds., *Uniting the Kingdom?* (London: Routledge, 1995), 208–222; Hannah Weiss Muller, "Bonds of Belonging: Subjecthood and the British Empire," *Journal of British Studies* 53, no. 1 (2014): 29–58.

5. Dowd, *Spirited Resistance*, 72–78; Calloway, *American Revolution*, 37–39; White, *Middle Ground*, 382–383.

6. David C. Hendrickson, *Peace Pact: The Lost World of the American Founding* (Lawrence: University Press of Kansas, 2003); Mahmood Mamdani, "Settlers and Natives in North America," in Ian Shapiro et al., eds., *Political Representation* (Cambridge, UK: Cambridge University Press, 2009), 159–208; Annie H. Abel, "Proposals for an Indian State, 1778–1878," in *Annual Report of the American Historical Association for the Year 1907*, 2 vols. (Washington, DC: US Government Printing Office, 1908), 1:89–104.

7. Peter Silver, *Our Savage Neighbors: How Indian War Transformed Early America* (New York: Norton, 2008), 266–276.

8. Ibid.

9. Nicholas Guyatt, "The Complexion of My Country: Benjamin Franklin and the Problem of Racial Diversity," in David Waldstreicher, ed., *A Companion to Benjamin Franklin* (Chichester, UK: Wiley-Blackwell, 2011), 198–200.

10. Treaty of Hopewell with the Cherokees, 28 November 1785, in Francis Paul Prucha, ed., *Documents of United States Indian Policy*, 3rd ed. (Lincoln: University of Nebraska Press, 2000), 6–8; Merrit B. Pound, *Benjamin Hawkins, Indian Agent* (Athens: University of Georgia Press, 1951), 45–52; William G. McLoughlin, *Cherokee Renascence in the New Republic* (Princeton, NJ: Princeton University Press, 1986), 21–23.

11. Francis Paul Prucha, *American Indian Treaties: The History of a Political Anomaly* (Berkeley: University of California Press, 1994).

12. John P. Bowes, *Exiles and Pioneers: Eastern Indians in the Trans-Mississippi West* (Cambridge, UK: Cambridge University Press, 2007), 19–35; John

Mack Faragher, "'More Motley than Mackinaw': From Ethnic Mixing to Ethnic Cleansing on the Frontier of the Lower Missouri, 1783–1833," in Andrew R.L. Clayton and Frederika J. Teute, *Contact Points: American Frontiers from the Mohawk Valley to the Mississippi* (Chapel Hill: University of North Carolina Press, 1998), 304–326, 305–307; Thomas Jefferson to William Henry Harrison, 27 February 1803, TJLC.

13. Jefferson to Horatio Gates, 11 July 1803, TJLC; S. Charles Bolton, "Jeffersonian Indian Removal and the Emergence of Arkansas Territory," in Patrick G. Williams et al., eds., *A Whole Country in Commotion: The Louisiana Purchase and the American Southwest* (Little Rock: University of Arkansas Press, 2005), 77–90; Anthony F.C. Wallace, *Jefferson and the Indians: The Tragic Fate of the First Americans* (Cambridge, MA: Harvard University Press, 1999), 241–275; James P. Ronda, "'We Have a Country': Race, Geography, and the Invention of Indian Territory," *JER* 19, no. 4 (1999): 739–755.

14. Jefferson to John Breckinridge, 12 August 1803, TJLC; Wallace, *Jefferson and the Indians*, 251–260.

15. Kathleen DuVal, *The Native Ground: Indians and Colonists in the Heart of the Continent* (Philadelphia: University of Pennsylvania Press, 2006), 164–195; Cynthia Cumfer, *Separate Peoples, One Land: The Minds of Cherokees, Blacks, and Whites on the Tennessee Frontier* (Chapel Hill: University of North Carolina Press, 2007), 112–123; McLoughlin, *Cherokee Renascence*, 97–127.

16. Jefferson to the Cherokee Nation, 10 January 1806 and 4 May 1808, TJLC.

17. McLoughlin, *Cherokee Renascence*, 154–155.

18. Return J. Meigs to the Cherokee Nation at Broomstown, 29 August 1808, Meigs to Henry Dearborn, 3 June 1808, RCIA.

19. Meigs to James Barbour, 3 June 1808; Meigs to the Cherokee Nation at Broomstown, 29 August 1808, RCIA.

20. McLoughlin, *Cherokee Renascence*, 156–167.

21. Meigs to William Eustis, 5 and 6 April 1811, RCIA; Russell Thornton, "The Demography of the Trail of Tears: A New Estimate of Cherokee Population Losses," in William L. Anderson, ed., *Cherokee Removal: Before and After* (Athens: University of Georgia Press, 1991), 75–95.

22. Meigs to Eustis, 30 May 1811, RCIA.

23. Kathryn E. Holland Braund, *Tohopeka: Rethinking the Creek War and the War of 1812* (Tuscaloosa: University of Alabama Press, 2012).

24. Paul A. Gilje, *Free Trade and Sailors' Rights in the War of 1812* (Cambridge, UK: Cambridge University Press, 2013), 257–258; Francis M. Carroll, *A Good and Wise Measure: The Search for the Canadian-American Boundary, 1783–1842* (Toronto: University of Toronto Press, 2001), 23–30; Annie H. Abel, "Proposals for an Indian State, 1778-1878," in *Annual Report of the American Historical Association for the Year 1907*, 2 vols. (Washington, DC: US

Government Printing Office, 1908), 1:270–275; Lord Castlereagh to the British Commissioners at Ghent, 28 July 1814, in *Correspondence . . . of Viscount Castlereagh, Third Series*, 4 vols. (London: John Murray, 1853), 2:70.

25. *National Intelligencer*, 25 October 1817, 3; "Creek Indians," *Franklin Gazette*, 3 September 1818, 2; *A Plan for the More Successful Management of Domestic Missions* (Albany, NY: Henry C. Southwick, 1816), 13–14.

26. Adam Rothman, *Slave Country: American Expansion and the Origins of the Deep South* (Cambridge, MA: Harvard University Press, 2005), 165–216; Calvin Schermerhorn, *The Business of Slavery and the Rise of American Capitalism, 1815–1860* (New Haven, CT: Yale University Press, 2015), 18–21.

27. William Crawford to Meigs, 18 September 1816, RCIA, Correspondence and Miscellaneous Records; McLoughlin, *Cherokee Renascence*, 212–213; Meigs to the Intruders on Cherokee Lands on the Frontier of North Carolina, 17 June 1816, RCIA.

28. Joseph McMinn to Crawford, 26 October 1816, George M. Troup to John Calhoun, 28 February 1824, *ASPIA*, 2:115, 734–735; "Journal of the Mission at Brainerd," *Panoplist*, January 1819, 46; McLoughlin, *Cherokee Renascence*, 212–214; Deborah A. Rosen, *American Indians and State Law: Sovereignty, Race, and Citizenship, 1790–1880* (Lincoln: University of Nebraska Press, 2007). Although the Fourteenth Amendment established the principle that the US government could bestow citizenship directly, Native Americans were excluded from the amendment's provisions unless they had been naturalized by treaty. They only obtained full citizenship as a birthright in 1924.

29. Meigs to Path Killer, 9 August 1817, Meigs to George Graham, 30 October 1817, RCIA; Calhoun to the House of Representatives, 5 December 1818, *ASPIA*, 2:183.

30. McMinn to the King and Chiefs of the Cherokee Nation, 23 November 1818, John Calhoun to McMinn, 29 July 1818 (two letters), *ASPIA*, 2:488, 479–480; McLoughlin, *Cherokee Renascence*, 228–259.

31. McLoughlin, *Cherokee Renascence*, 247–248, 256.

32. Ibid., 277–365; "A Scene in Africa," *Cherokee Phoenix*, 6 March 1828, 3; "The African Colony," *Cherokee Phoenix*, 8 October 1828, 3.

33. "Resolution," 23 October 1822, Meigs to Calhoun, 22 November 1822, RCIA; Henry Thompson Malone, *Cherokees of the Old South: A People in Transition* (Athens: University of Georgia Press, 1956), 73.

CHAPTER 10: OPENING THE ROAD

1. Moses Fiske, *Tyrannical Libertymen: A Discourse upon Negro-Slavery in the United States* (Hanover, NH: Eagle Office, 1795), 4, 8–11; John Farmer, "Alumni of Dartmouth College," *American Quarterly Register* 12, no. 4 (1840):

382; John Parrish, *Remarks on the Slavery of the Black People* (Philadelphia: Kimber, Conrad, 1806), 6; "Sketches of Friends," *Friends Intelligencer* 27, no. 9 (1870): 130–132. See also David Kazanjian, *The Colonizing Trick: National Culture and Imperial Citizenship in Early America* (Minneapolis: University of Minnesota Press, 2003), 89–138.

2. Thomas Branagan, *Serious Remonstrances, Addressed to the Citizens of the Northern States* (Philadelphia: Thomas T. Stiles, 1805), 24–25, 112–113, 37, 93; Noah Webster, *Effects of Slavery on Morals and Industry* (Hartford, CT: Hudson and Goodwin, 1793), 36.

3. Parrish, *Remarks*, 39, 43; John Page to St. George Tucker, 28 February 1796, in Tucker-Coleman Papers, Box 19, Swem Library, College of William and Mary, Williamsburg, Virginia.

4. "Thoughts on the True Path to National Glory," *National Intelligencer*, 25 April 1805, 1; Fredrika J. Teute, "The Uses of Writing in Margaret Bayard Smith's New Nation," in Dale M. Bauer and Philip Gould, eds., *The Cambridge Companion to Nineteenth-Century American Women's Writing* (Cambridge, UK: Cambridge University Press, 2001), 203–220; Teute, "In 'The Gloom of Evening': Margaret Bayard Smith's View in Black and White of Early Washington Society," *Proceedings of the American Antiquarian Society* 106, Part 1 (April 1996): 37–58; Margaret Bayard Smith and Gaillard Hunt, *The First Forty Years of Washington Society* (New York: Charles Scribner's Sons, 1906).

5. *WTP*, xlvii–liii; Catherine Allgor, *Parlor Politics: In Which the Ladies of Washington Help Build a City and a Government* (Charlottesville: University of Virginia Press, 2000), 4–10; Gaillard Hunt, *William Thornton and Negro Colonization* (Worcester, MA: American Antiquarian Society, 1921), 24–26; William Thornton, *Political Economy, Founded in Justice and Humanity* (Washington, DC: Samuel Harrison Smith, 1804), 8.

6. Ibid., 22–24.

7. Douglas R. Egerton, *Gabriel's Rebellion: The Virginia Slave Conspiracies of 1800 & 1802* (Chapel Hill: University of North Carolina Press, 1993); Alan Taylor, *The Internal Enemy: Slavery and War in Virginia, 1772–1832* (New York: Norton, 2013), 94–97; Lacy K. Ford, *Deliver Us from Evil: The Slavery Question in the Old South* (New York: Oxford University Press, 2009), 49–54; Eva Sheppard Wolf, *Race and Liberty in the New Nation: Emancipation in Virginia from the Revolution to Nat Turner's Rebellion* (Baton Rouge: Louisiana State University Press, 2006), 112, 118–121; James Monroe to Thomas Jefferson, 15 September 1800, Jefferson to Monroe, 20 September 1800, TJP.

8. Egerton, *Gabriel's Rebellion*, 147–154; Philip J. Schwarz, *Slave Laws in Virginia* (Athens: University of Georgia Press, 1996), 103–108.

9. Monroe to Jefferson, 15 June 1801, TJP.

10. George Tucker, *Letter . . . on the Subject of the Late Conspiracy of the Slaves, with a Proposal for Their Colonization* (Baltimore: Bonsal and Niles, 1801), 18–19; Ford, *Deliver Us from Evil*, 54–61.

11. Jefferson to Monroe, 24 November 1801, TJP.

12. Monroe to Jefferson, 8 December 1801, Monroe to Jefferson, 13 February 1802, Jefferson to Monroe, 31 March 1802, Monroe to Jefferson, 17 May 1802, TJP.

13. Jefferson to Rufus King, 13 July 1802, Christopher Gore to Jefferson, 10 October 1802, King to William Wilberforce, 8 January 1803, TJP; Ford, *Deliver Us from Evil*, 62.

14. Page to Jefferson, 16 November 1803, Jefferson to Page, 23 December 1803, TJLC; Page to St. George Tucker, 3 January 1796, in Tucker-Coleman Papers, Series 1, Box 19, Swem Library, College of William and Mary.

15. Samuel Shepherd, *The Statutes at Large of Virginia, from October Session 1792 to December Session 1806*, 3 vols. (Richmond, VA: Samuel Shepherd, 1836), 3:111; Page to Jefferson, 29 October 1804, TJLC.

16. Jefferson to Page, 27 December 1804, Page to Jefferson, 2 February 1805, TJLC .

17. Ford, *Deliver Us from Evil*, 63; Jefferson to Lydia Howard Huntley Sigourney, 18 July 1824, TJP.

18. Ford, *Deliver Us from Evil*, 64–65; Wolf, *Race and Liberty*, 121–129.

19. John Coburn to Jefferson, 22 February 1802, John Lynch to Jefferson, 23 December 1810, TJP; Richard S. Newman et al., "Philadelphia Emigrationist Petition circa 1792," *WMQ* 64, no. 1 (2007): 161–166; Richard S. Newman, *Freedom's Prophet: Bishop Richard Allen, the AME Church, and the Black Founding Fathers* (New York: New York University Press, 2008), 146–151; James Sidbury, *Becoming African in America: Race and Nation in the Early Black Atlantic* (New York: Oxford University Press, 2007), 145–168; James T. Campbell, *Middle Passages: African American Journeys to Africa, 1787–2005* (New York: Penguin, 2006), 30–40; Lamont D. Thomas, *Rise to Be a People: A Biography of Paul Cuffe* (Urbana: University of Illinois Press, 1986).

20. Paul Cuffe, *Captain Paul Cuffe's Logs and Letters, 1807–1817: A Black Quaker's "Voice from Within the Veil,"* Rosalind Cobb Wiggins, ed. (Washington, DC: Howard University Press, 1996), 48–54.

21. Cuffe, *Cuffe's Logs*, 56–57; Thomas, *Rise to Be a People*, 36; *Rules and Regulations of the African Institution, Formed on the 14th April, 1807* (London: William Phillips, 1807), 17–18, 29–33; James Pemberton to Paul Cuffe, 8 June 1808, Cuffe to Pemberton, 14 September 1808, Pemberton to Cuffe, 29 September 1808, Cuffe to John James and Alexander Wilson, 6 October 1809, in Cuffe, *Cuffe's Logs*, 77–81; *Life of William Allen, with Selections from His Correspondence*, 2 vols. (Philadelphia; Henry Longstreth, 1847), 1:85–86.

22. Cuffe to William Allen, 22 April 1811, in Cuffe, *Cuffe's Logs*, 119; *Life of William Allen*, 1:99, 103, 107; Cuffe, *Cuffe's Logs*, 212–213, 266–267; Cuffe to Hannah Little, 18 February 1813, in ibid., 237–238; "Paul Cuffe," *New Bedford Mercury*, 27 January 1814, 4; "Sierra Leone," *American State Papers, Commerce and Navigation*, vol. 1, 13th Cong., 1st sess., no. 188, *Historical Register of the United States, Part 1* (Philadelphia: G. Palmer, 1814), 100–103.

23. Cuffe to Peter Williams Jr., 13 March 1815, Cuffe to James Forten, 27 March 1815, Cuffe to Richard Allen, 27 March 1815, Cuffe to Jedidiah Morse, 19 April 1815, Nathan Lord to Cuffe, 12 April 1815, Morse to Cuffe, 14 April 1815, in Cuffe, *Cuffe's Logs*, 321–322, 330–331, 344, 349–350, 351; Richard J. Moss, *The Life of Jedidiah Morse: A Station of Peculiar Exposure* (Knoxville: University of Tennessee Press, 1995), 94. A series of seven articles, entitled "Paul Cuffe's Mission to Sierra Leone," began in the *Boston Weekly Messenger* on 1 July 1814 and concluded on 2 September.

24. Paul Cuffe to John Cuffe, 12 August 1811, in Cuffe, *Cuffe's Logs*, 144–145; *Second Report of the African Institution* (London: W. Phillips, 1808), 7–9; *Life of William Allen*, 1:180–181.

25. Cuffe, *Cuffe's Logs*, 399–400; Taylor, *Internal Enemy*, 300–301; Isaac V. Brown, *Memoirs of the Rev. Robert Finley, D.D.* (New Brunswick, NJ: Terhune and Letson, 1819); Ruth L. Woodward and Wesley Frank Craven, *Princetonians, 1784–1790: A Biographical Dictionary* (Princeton, NJ: Princeton University Press, 1991), 183–187; P. J. Staudenraus, *The African Colonization Movement, 1816–1865* (New York: Columbia University Press, 1961), 15–17.

26. Brown, *Memoirs*, 75–80; "Colony of Free Blacks," *National Intelligencer*, 14 December 1816, 2.

27. Charles Fenton Mercer, *An Address to the American Colonization Society at their 36th Annual Meeting* (Geneva: Monroe, English Bookseller, 1854), 2–3; Douglas R. Egerton, "'Its Origin Is Not a Little Curious': A New Look at the American Colonization Society," *JER* 5, no. 4 (1985): 463–480.

28. "Colony of Free Blacks," 2; Margaret Bayard Smith to Jane Bayard Kirkpatrick, 5 December 1816, in Smith and Hunt, *First Forty Years of Washington Society*, 130–132.

29. Robert Finley, *Thoughts on the Colonization of Free Blacks* (Washington, DC: n.p. [Samuel Harrison Smith], 1816), 5, 7–8; Isaac V. Brown, *Memoirs of the Rev. Robert Finley, D.D.* (New Brunswick, NJ: Terhune and Letson, 1819), 80–81; Nicholas Guyatt, *Providence and the Invention of the United States, 1607–1876* (Cambridge, UK: Cambridge University Press, 2007), 183–194.

30. Staudenraus, *African Colonization Movement*, 23–28; "On Free Black Colonization," *National Intelligencer*, 17 December 1816, 2 (Staudenraus, 257n, suspects that William Thornton was the author); William Thornton to Henry Clay, c. 25 December 1816, in Henry Clay, *The Papers of Henry Clay*, vol. 2,

The Rising Statesman, 1815–1820, James F. Hopkins, ed. (Lexington: University Press of Kentucky, 1961), 264–268.

31. Sidbury, *Becoming African in America*, 168; Wolf, *Race and Liberty*, 167, 170; Charles F. Irons, *The Origins of Proslavery Christianity: White and Black Evangelicals in Colonial and Antebellum Virginia* (Chapel Hill: University of North Carolina Press, 2008), 102; Paul Goodman, *Of One Blood: Abolitionism and the Origins of Racial Equality* (Berkeley: University of California Press, 1998), 14, 16, 130; Gary B. Nash, *Forging Freedom: The Formation of Philadelphia's Black Community, 1720–1840* (Cambridge, MA: Harvard University Press, 1988), 234–235; Joanne Pope Melish, *Disowning Slavery: Gradual Emancipation and "Race" in New England, 1780–1860* (Ithaca, NY: Cornell University Press, 1998), 192; Walter Johnson, "The Racial Origins of American Sovereignty," *Raritan* 31, no. 3 (2012): 50–59, 55; Winthrop D. Jordan, *White over Black: American Attitudes Toward the Negro, 1550–1812* (Chapel Hill: University of North Carolina Press, 1968), 566. The best account of the ACS's contorted benevolence remains George M. Fredrickson, *The Black Image in the White Mind: The Debate on Afro-American Character and Destiny, 1817–1914* (New York: Harper and Row, 1971), 1–42, esp. 7–12.

32. "The Meeting on the Colonization of the Free Blacks," *National Intelligencer*, 24 December 1816, 2; Nicholas Wood, "John Randolph of Roanoke and the Politics of Slavery in the Early Republic," *Virginia Magazine of History and Biography* 120, no. 2 (2012): 107–143. Although Douglas Egerton has established that Charles Fenton Mercer played a key role in the founding of the ACS, his account is misleading in two respects. First, he claims ("Origin," 465) that no one credited Robert Finley as the founder of the ACS until the 1840s, and that the attribution only appeared in the second edition of Isaac Brown's biography of Finley, published in 1857 (Isaac V. Brown, *Biography of the Rev. Robert Finley*, 2nd ed. [Philadelphia: John W. Moore, 1857]), rather than in the original 1819 edition (*Memoirs of the Rev. Robert Finley*). In fact, Brown argues in his first edition for Finley's central role in the creation of the ACS; he even reprints an 1818 letter from an anonymous Washington correspondent declaring Finley to be "the sole mover and promoter" of the ACS. (*Memoirs*, 82.) Second, Egerton depicts Mercer as having "antislavery ideas" but "no vaguely abolitionist notions" ("Origin," 470–471). This awkward construction precedes the claim that Mercer had no confidence in the emancipation potential of colonization, and that he was only interested in removing the free blacks who slowed the industrial development of Virginia's cities. Mercer adamantly believed that slaves could not be freed in situ without doing terrible damage to the social fabric of the South; but in the same 1853 address that Egerton cites on the origins of the ACS, he explained that he'd spent "more than four years

of my life" working to promote colonization after 1816 because he hoped to "furnish, for the benefit of all classes of our southern population, facilities for emancipation, without enduring a greater evil than slavery itself."

33. Mercer, *Address*, 3; *A Narrative of the Early Life, Travels, and Gospel Labors of Jesse Kersey, Late of Chester County, Pennsylvania* (Philadelphia: T. Ellwood Chapman, 1851), 72–82. I'm indebted to Nicholas Wood for alerting me to Kersey's activities. See Wood, "Considerations of Humanity and Expediency: The Slave Trades and African Colonization in the Early National Antislavery Movement," PhD dissertation, Corcoran Department of History, University of Virginia, 2013, 294–295. Jesse Kersey to St. George Tucker, 5 July 1814 and 1 August 1814 (wrongly filed as 1824), in Tucker-Coleman Papers, Swem Library, College of William and Mary, Box 33.

34. *First Annual Report of the American Society for Colonizing the Free People of Color of the United States* (Washington, DC: D. Rapine, 1818), 5–8, 15–18; Ford, *Deliver Us from Evil*, 71–73; Eric Burin, *Slavery and the Peculiar Solution: A History of the American Colonization Society* (Gainesville: University Press of Florida, 2005), 34–45.

35. *First Annual Report*, 29–30, 33, 38. On Harper, see Woodward and Craven, *Princetonians*, 67–83; and Eric Robert Papenfuse, *The Evils of Necessity: Robert Goodloe Harper and the Moral Dilemma of Slavery* (Philadelphia: American Philosophical Society, 1997).

36. Papenfuse, *The Evils of Necessity*, 33, 38.

37. Wood, "Considerations of Humanity," 319–356; Eric Burin, "The Slave Trade Act of 1819: A New Look at Colonization and the Politics of Slavery," *American Nineteenth-Century History* 13, no. 1 (2012): 1–14.

38. Burin, "Slave Trade Act," 7–8.

39. *Proceedings and Debates of the House of Representatives of the United States*, 14th Cong., 2nd sess., 939–941; Staudenraus, *African Colonization Movement*, 34–51; Burin, "Slave Trade Act," 6–10; Wood, "Considerations of Humanity," 322–327.

40. Staudenraus, *African Colonization Movement*, 51–63; Sidbury, *Becoming African in America*, 170–184; Samuel John Bayard, *A Sketch of the Life of Commodore Robert F. Stockton* (New York: Derby and Jackson, 1856), 11–13, 39–47. I'm indebted to Eric Burin for setting me straight on the chronology here. See his essay "The Cape Mesurado Contract: A Reconsideration," in Beverly Tomek and Matthew Hetrick, eds., *Reconsiderations and Redirections in the Study of African Colonization* (Gainesville: University Press of Florida, forthcoming).

41. Staudenraus, *African Colonization Movement*, 63–65; Lamin Sanneh, *Abolitionists Abroad: American Blacks and the Making of Modern West Africa* (Cambridge, MA: Harvard University Press, 1999), 203–205.

42. "Address to General Lafayette," *Columbian Centinel*, 20 October 1824, 4; "Lafayette's Visit to Monticello (1824)," Monticello website, www.monticello. org/site/research-and-collections/lafayettes-visit-monticello-1824, accessed 8 April 2015; A. Levasseur, *Lafayette in America, in 1824 and 1825*, 2 vols. (New York: White, Gallaher and White, 1829), 1:217–219; Marie Joseph Lafayette to Thomas Jefferson, 9 December 1824, in Thomas Jefferson and Marie Joseph Lafayette, with an Introduction by Gilbert Chinard, *The Letters of Lafayette and Jefferson* (Baltimore: Johns Hopkins University Press, 1929), 426; Anne C. Loveland, *Emblem of Liberty: The Image of Lafayette in the American Mind* (Baton Rouge: Louisiana State University Press, 1971), 35–60.

43. "Annual Meeting of the Colonization Society," *African Repository*, March 1825, 15–17; Gail Bederman, "Revisiting Nashoba: Slavery, Utopia, and Frances Wright in America, 1818–1826," *American Literary History* 17, no. 3 (2005): 438–459; Frances Wright to Dolley Madison, 26 July 1825, Papers of James Madison, Library of Congress, microfilm edition, reel 21; Jefferson to Wright, 7 August 1825, TJP.

44. Bederman, "Revisiting Nashoba"; Cadwallader Colden to Lafayette, 19 August 1826, LP, 50:1; Charles Wilkes to Lafayette, 30 September 1826, LP, 91:11; Lafayette to Jefferson, 25 February 1826, in Jefferson and Lafayette, *Letters*, 436.

45. G. W. P. Custis to Lafayette, 25 May 1826, LP, 51:39; Lafayette to James Madison, 27 October 1827, in James Madison Papers Online; http://founders. archives.gov/about/Madison; "Nashoba," *Genius of Universal Emancipation*, 1 March 1827, 52; *Genius of Universal Emancipation*, 8 March 1827, 61; Wilkes to Lafayette, 27 February 1828, LP, 92:8.

46. Bederman, "Revisiting Nashoba"; Moses Levy to Lafayette, 28 April 1829, LP, 92:11; Ralph Gurley to Lafayette, 24 April 1829, LP; James Madison to Lafayette, 1 January 1830, Madison Papers Online; Gurley to Lafayette, 4 September 1832, LP, 60:19c.

47. Forten to Lafayette, 31 July 1833, LP, 3:1b; "Lafayette," *African Repository*, August 1834, 190–191.

CHAPTER 11: IN THESE DESERTS

1. "Exchange of Lands with the Indians," 9 January 1817, *ASPIA*, 2:123; John Calhoun to Lewis Cass, 27 March 1829, in J. Franklin Jameson, ed., *Annual Report of the American Historical Association for the Year 1899*, vol. 2, *Calhoun Correspondence* (Washington, DC: US Government Printing Office, 1900), 158.

2. "Civilization Fund Act," 3 March 1829, in Francis Paul Prucha, ed., *Documents of United States Indian Policy*, 3rd ed. (Lincoln: University of Nebraska Press, 2000), 33; Calhoun to the House of Representatives, 17 January 1820,

ASPIA, 2:200–201; John A. Andrew III, *From Revivals to Removal: Jeremiah Evarts, the Cherokee Nation, and the Search for the Soul of America* (Athens: University of Georgia Press, 1992), 95–97; Herman J. Viola, *Thomas L. McKenney, Architect of America's Early Indian Policy: 1816–1830* (Chicago: Sage Books, 1974), 36–46.

3. Richard J. Moss, *The Life of Jedidiah Morse: A Station of Peculiar Exposure* (Knoxville: University of Tennessee Press, 1995); Calhoun to Jedidiah Morse, 7 February 1820, in Jedidiah Morse, *A Report to the Secretary of War of the United States on Indian Affairs* (New Haven, CT: S. Converse, 1822), 11–13.

4. Moss, *Life of Jedidiah Morse*, 134–138; Morse, *Report*, 13–18, 82, 73–75, 66, 60–64.

5. Morse, *Report*, 85, 78 (appendix), 24–25, 18, 27, 67.

6. Ibid., 83, 24–25, 312–316 (appendix). On the Stockbridge Indians, see David Silverman, *Red Brethren: The Brothertown and Stockbridge Indians and the Problem of Race in Early America* (Ithaca, NY: Cornell University Press, 2010).

7. *The First Annual Report of the American Society for Promoting the Civilization and General Improvement of the Indian Tribes in the United States* (New Haven, CT: S. Converse, 1824).

8. Thomas Jefferson to Morse, 6 March 1822, James Madison to Morse, 28 February 1822, in *First Annual Report*, 20–23; Jefferson to Madison, 25 February 1822, Madison to Jefferson, 5 March 1822, Madison Papers Online, http://founders.archives.gov/about/Madison; *Report of the Annual Board of Commissioners for Foreign Missions* (Boston: Crocker and Brewster, 1823), 14; "Application of the Board of Commissioners for Foreign Missions for Pecuniary Aid in Civilizing the Indians," 3 March 1824, *ASPIA*, 2:446–248. Jeremiah Evarts, the ABCFM secretary, was appointed to the committee to draft the petition to Congress in September 1823, but his name was missing from the text submitted the following March. Given Evarts's leadership of the anti-removal campaign in 1829–1830, his absence may indicate that he disapproved of the petition's references to colonization. However, he had agreed to serve in 1822 as a correspondent for Morse's Civilization Society, suggesting that he was at least familiar with Morse's proposal for an Indian colony. Andrew, *Revivals to Removal*, 118.

9. Duncan G. Campbell and James Meriwether to the Cherokee Council, 21 October 1823, *ASPIA*, 2:469–470.

10. Cherokee Council to the US Commissioners, 24 October 1823, *ASPIA*, 2:470–471.

11. James Monroe to the Senate of the United States, 30 March 1824, *ASPIA*, 2:460; James Monroe, "Eighth Annual Message," 7 December 1824, in James D. Richardson, ed., *A Compilation of the Messages and Papers of the*

Presidents, vol. 2, part 1 (Washington, DC: US Government Printing Office, 1897), 261; "Message of President Monroe on Indian Removal," 27 January 1825, in Prucha, *Documents*, 39–40.

12. Herman J. Viola, *Thomas L. McKenney, Architect of America's Early Indian Policy: 1816–1830* (Chicago: Sage Books, 1974), 47–95; Richard Drinnon, *Facing West: The Metaphysics of Indian Hating and Empire Building* (New York: Schocken Books, 1990), 170–174.

13. George A. Schultz, *An Indian Canaan: Isaac McCoy and the Vision of an Indian State* (Norman: University of Oklahoma Press, 1972), 3–14; Randolph Orville Yeager, "Indian Enterprises of Isaac McCoy, 1817–1846," PhD dissertation, University of Oklahoma, 1954, 9–73.

14. Isaac McCoy, *History of Baptist Indian Missions* (Washington, DC: William M. Morrison, 1840), 43–54, 69; Yeager, "Indian Enterprises," 74–97, 109–134; Schultz, *Indian Canaan*, 30–31; R. David Edmunds, *The Potawatomis: Keepers of the Fires* (Norman: University of Oklahoma Press, 1978), 219–220; Arthur J. Leighton, "'Eyes on the Wabash': A History of Indiana's Indian People from Pre-Contact through Removal," PhD dissertation, Purdue University, 2007, 319–323.

15. McCoy, *History*, 71–91, 111; Yeager, "Indian Enterprises," 135–175.

16. Yeager, "Indian Enterprises," 177–187, 229–245; Ella Wells Drake, "Choctaw Academy: Richard M. Johnson and the Business of Indian Education," *Register of the Kentucky Historical Society* 91, no. 3 (1993): 260–297; McCoy, *History*, 112, 123–125, 131–132, 141, 144; Schultz, *Indian Canaan*, 45, 49.

17. McCoy, *History*, 75, 196–197, 200–201; Yeager, "Indian Enterprises," 250–251; Schultz, *Indian Canaan*, 33, 61–62; William Miles, "'Enamoured with Colonization': Isaac McCoy's Plan of Indian Reform," *Kansas Historical Quarterly* 38, no. 3 (1972): 268–286.

18. Isaac McCoy to Lewis Cass, John T. Johnson, and Richard M. Johnson, 23 June 1823, McCoy to Luther Rice, 10 July 1823, John T. Johnson to McCoy, 7 August 1823, McCoy to Rice, 30 August 1823, IMP.

19. McCoy to Rice, 15 January 1825, McCoy to Richard Mentor Johnson, 16 January 1825, McCoy to Jotham Meeker, 7 March 1825, McCoy to Francis Wayland, 30 November 1825, IMP; McCoy, *History*, 217–218, 256–257; Yeager, "Indian Enterprises," 270–277, 289–291, 297–299; "Carey Station," *American Baptist Magazine* 5, no. 9 (1825): 283; "Carey Station," *American Baptist Magazine* 6, no. 3 (1826): 92.

20. John Quincy Adams, *Memoirs of John Quincy Adams*, Charles Francis Adams, ed., vol. 7 (Philadelphia: J. B. Lippincott, 1875), 56–57, 78–79, 89–90, 113; Charles D. Lowery, *James Barbour: A Jeffersonian Republican* (Tuscaloosa: University of Alabama Press, 1984), 156–167.

21. McCoy, *History*, 274, 279, 319, 321–322; Yeager, "Indian Enterprises," 134–135; Isaac McCoy, *Remarks on the Practicability of Indian Reform, Embracing Their Colonization* (Boston: Lincoln and Edmands, 1827), 7, 10, 29–31.

22. Andrew, *Revivals to Removal*, 158–159; McCoy, *History*, 323–325; Wilson Lumpkin, *The Removal of the Cherokee Indians from Georgia, 1827–1841*, 2 vols. (New York: Dodd, Mead, 1907), 1:46–47; Wilson Lumpkin to Johnston Lykins (for Isaac McCoy), 5 January 1829, IMP.

23. McCoy, *Remarks*, 28–31, 34; McCoy, *History*, 324; Yeager, "Indian Enterprises," 266–270, 358–362; "Indian Emigration," *Cherokee Phoenix*, 21 April 1828, 3; "Report of the House Committee on Indian Affairs on Indians Removing Westward," 7 January 1828, *Register of Debates*, 20th Cong., 1st sess., 18–20 February 1828, 1533–1592.

24. Jeremiah Evarts to Thomas L. McKenney, 14 February 1825, in E. C. Tracy, *Memoir of the Life of Jeremiah Evarts* (Boston: Crocker and Brewster, 1845), 215–216; Andrew, *Revivals to Removal*, 150–155.

25. McKenney to James Barbour, 29 September 1827, cited in Viola, *Thomas L. McKenney*, 208; McKenney to Barbour, 10 October 1827, in *Reports and Proceedings of Col. McKenney on the Subject of His Recent Tour Among the Southern Indians* (Washington, DC: Gales and Seaton, 1828), 5–15, 24; Thomas L. McKenney, *Memoirs, Official and Personal*, 2 vols. (New York: Paine and Burgess, 1846), 1:160, 318–330, 338.

26. McKenney, *Memoirs*, 1:161–162; McCoy to Peter Buell Porter, 29 January 1829, in "Report of the House Committee on Indian Affairs on Removing Indians Westward," 18 February 1829, 20th Cong., 2nd sess., 6–24; McCoy, *History*, 337–339; Schultz, *Indian Canaan*, 106–110; Journal of Isaac McCoy, 1828–1838 typescript, IMP, 6–49; Yeager, "Indian Enterprises," 364–380; R. David Edmunds, *The Shawnee Prophet* (Lincoln: University of Nebraska Press, 1983), 169–185.

27. McCoy, *History*, 341; Schultz, *Indian Canaan*, 107; Yeager, "Indian Enterprises," 379–380; Pekka Hämäläinen, *The Comanche Empire* (New Haven, CT: Yale University Press, 2008).

28. Schultz, *Indian Canaan*, 110; McCoy to Porter, 29 January 1829, 16; Yeager, "Indian Enterprises," 391–392.

29. "Report on Moving Indians Westward," 2–3; Andrew, *Revivals to Removal*, 179–180; Lynn Hudson Parsons, *The Birth of Modern Politics: Andrew Jackson, John Quincy Adams and the Election of 1828* (New York: Oxford University Press, 2009), 155–158; Andrew, *Revivals to Removal*, 199–258.

30. Yeager, "Indian Enterprises," 398.

31. McCoy Journal, 62–63; Yeager, "Indian Enterprises," 399–404; [Jeremiah Evarts], *Essays on the Present Crisis in the Condition of the American Indians*

(Boston: Perkins and Marvin, 1829), 52; Isaac McCoy, *Remarks on the Practicability of Indian Reform, Embracing Their Colonization*, 2nd ed. (New York: Gray and Bunce, 1829), 39–40.

32. Andrew Jackson to the Creek Indians, 23 March 1829, John Eaton to a Delegation of Cherokees, 18 April 1829, in *Documents and Proceedings Relating to the Formation and Progress of a Board in the City of New York for the Emigration, Preservation, and Improvement of the Aborigines of America* (New York: Vanderpool and Cole, 1829), 3–11, 18, 28–32, 41; Yeager, "Indian Enterprises," 405; McCoy to Elon Galusha, 3 February 1830, IMP; Francis Paul Prucha, "Thomas L. McKenney and the New York Indian Board," *Mississippi Valley Historical Review* 48, no. 4 (1962): 635–655; Viola, *Thomas L. McKenney*, 200–222; Susan M. Ryan, *The Grammar of Good Intentions: Race and the Antebellum Culture of Benevolence* (Ithaca, NY: Cornell University Press, 2003), 28–32.

33. *Register of Debates*, 21st Cong., 1st sess., House of Representatives, 17 May 1830, 1018–1019; "Documents and Proceedings," *North American Review* 30, no. 66 (1830): 115; Yeager, "Indian Enterprises," 412–419.

34. The details of removal were worked out in the separate treaties reached with individual Native nations under the Indian Removal Act. Of the four major treaties that secured the removal of southeastern Indians in the 1830s, the Creeks (1832) and Chickasaws (1832) were offered no representation in Congress after removal. The Choctaws asked for representation in their 1830 treaty negotiations, but the request was denied; they continued to ask throughout the middle decades of the century, and they retained an agent in Washington to lobby Congress on their behalf. Only the controversial Cherokee removal treaty (1835) established an entitlement to "a delegate in the House of Representatives," though this person would participate only in debates relating to Native Americans. None of these treaties made any reference to a federal territory or an eventual Indian state. I'm grateful to Christina Snyder for her help with this question.

35. McKenney to Hugh Lawson White, 26 February 1830, in "Records Relating to Indian Removal, 1817–86," Records of the Bureau of Indian Affairs, National Archives; McKenney to Cyrus Kingsbury, 8 March 1830, in Viola, *Thomas L. McKenney*, 222; McKenney to Evarts, 1 May 1829, in *Documents and Proceedings*, 11–19, 37.

EPILOGUE: AN ENTERPRISE FOR THE YOUNG

1. Edward Coles to Rebecca Tucker Coles, 24 April 1819, CFP, 2:22; Kurt E. Leichtle and Bruce G. Carveth, *Crusade Against Slavery: Edward Coles, Pioneer of Freedom* (Carbondale: Southern Illinois University Press, 2011), 50–71;

Suzanne Cooper Guasco, *Confronting Slavery: Edward Coles and the Rise of Antislavery Politics in Nineteenth-Century America* (DeKalb: Northern Illinois University Press, 2013), 67–74; Leichtle and Carveth note that Coles bought one additional slave specifically to keep a family together, so the total number that made the journey west was seventeen. *Crusade Against Slavery*, 58–59.

2. "A Sketch of the Principal Circumstances Connected with the Emancipation of the Slaves of Edward Coles," October 1827, CFP, 3:21; Edward Coles, "Autobiography" (1844), CFP, 2:11; Edward Coles to Rebecca Tucker Coles, 24 April 1819, CFP.

3. "To the Citizens of Illinois," *Illinois Intelligencer*, 4 June 1824, 3.

4. Edward Coles to Roberts Vaux, 27 June 1823, 11 December 1823, 21 January 1824, RVP, 2:13, 15. [Roberts Vaux], *An Impartial Appeal to the Reason, Interest and Patriotism of the People of Illinois* ([Philadelphia]: n.p., 1824), 2; "To the Citizens of Illinois," *Illinois Intelligencer*, 21 May 1824, 3.

5. Coles to Vaux, 21 January 1824; Edward Coles, "Sketch"; *Illinois Intelligencer*, 4 June 1824, 3; Guasco, *Confronting Slavery*, 136.

6. Guasco, *Confronting Slavery*, 129–137; Coles, "Sketch."

7. "By Edward Coles," *Edwardsville Spectator*, 10 July 1819, 2; "Anniversary of American Independence," *Illinois Intelligencer*, 6 July 1822, 2; "Fourth of July at Edwardsville," *Illinois Intelligencer*, 28 July 1827, 1; Coles to James Madison, 8 January 1832, ECP, 1:30; Guasco, *Confronting Slavery*, 137–164.

8. William Short to Thomas Jefferson, 4 July 1817, Coolidge Collection, MHS.

9. Vaux to Short, 26 April 1826, 13, 15, 16, 18, and 21 May 1827, WSP.

10. George Green Shackelford, *Jefferson's Adoptive Son: The Life of William Short, 1759–1848* (Lexington: University Press of Kentucky, 1993), 139–141; Terry L. Meyers, "Thinking About Slavery at the College of William and Mary," *William and Mary Bill of Rights Journal* 21, no. 7 (2013); Deborah Skaggs, "Charles Wilkins Short: Kentucky Botanist and Physician, 1794–1863," master's thesis, University of Louisville, 1982, 55–56; William Short to Charles Wilkins Short, 12 December 1837, CWS, folder 7. I'm extremely grateful to Terry Meyers and Deborah Skaggs for sharing their expertise on William Short and his family.

11. James W. Ewing to William Short, 4 November 1833, WSP; James Breathitt to William Short, 26 November 1833, 8 June 1834, 3 July 1834, 12 September 1836, WSP.

12. Charles Wilkins Short to William Short, 15 November 1837, 3 June 1838, CWS, folders 20 and 21.

13. Charles Wilkins Short to William Short, 3 July, 27 August, 5, 11, 28, 30 October, 18 November 1838, 12 January, 10 March, 3 July 1839, CWS, folders 21 and 22; William Short to Charles Wilkins Short, 28 May 1839, CWS, folder 9;

William Short to Charles Wilkins Short, 12 June 1838, Ralph Gurley to William Short, 3 August 1838, WSP.

14. Charles Wilkins Short to William Short, 3 July 1839, William Short to Charles Wilkins Short, 23 September 1839, 19 January 1840, 25 February 1840, Charles Wilkins Short to William Short, 6 October 1839, CWS, folders 9, 10, 22.

15. Charles Gist to William Short, 21 December 1839, WSP; William Short to Charles Wilkins Short, 16 March 1841, CWS, folder 11.

16. Charles Wilkins Short to William Short, 12 July 1841, 28 September 1842, 30 July 1843, 15 October 1843, 30 December 1843, CWS, folders 24–27.

17. Charles Wilkins Short to William Short, 30 January 1847, CWS, folder 31; William Short, "Will and Testament" (1847), WSP.

18. "More murder!" *Liberia Herald*, November 1848, 3; "Murder of William Blain," *Commercial Advertiser*, 24 January 1849, 2; "For Account and Benefit of Emigrants," *African Repository* 16, no. 1 (1840): 16; Charles Wilkins Short to John Cleeves Short, 18 August 1849, Short-Harrison-Symmes Families Papers, Library of Congress. (I'm indebted to Deborah Skaggs for this reference.)

19. "Indian Reform—No. II," *United States Telegraph*, 19 August 1830, 2; "Indian Reform—No. 5," *United States Telegraph*, 2 September 1830, 2; Andrew Jackson, "Message to Both Houses of Congress," 7 December 1830, *Appendix to the Register of Debates*, 21st Cong., 2nd sess., x; Isaac McCoy, Journal typescript, 16 February 1831, IMP, 137.

20. Jackson, "Message"; Lewis Cass, "Report of the Secretary of War," 21 November 1831, House Document No. 485, 22nd Cong., 1st sess., 713–714; McCoy, Journal, 17 January 1832, 28 March 1832, 15 April 1832, 211, 222, 226.

21. [Isaac McCoy], *Address to Philanthropists in the United States* ([New York]: n.p., n.d. [1832]); Isaac McCoy, "Report to Commissioners on the Indian Territory," 15 October 1832, McCoy correspondence, IMP; Isaac McCoy, "Remarks," *Annual Register of Indian Affairs Within the Indian (or Western) Territory* 1 (1835): 43–45.

22. HR 490, John Quincy Adams, 25 June 1834, *Register of Debates*, 22nd Cong., 1st sess., House of Representatives, 4768–4772.

23. McCoy, Journal, 25 January, 10 March, 13 June, 2 July 1835, 350, 356, 367, 368; George A. Schultz, *An Indian Canaan: Isaac McCoy and the Vision of an Indian State* (Norman: University of Oklahoma Press, 1972), 161–181.

24. Colin G. Calloway, *Pen and Ink Witchcraft: Treaties and Treaty Making in American Indian History* (New York: Oxford University Press, 2013), 121–163; Isaac McCoy to Christiana McCoy, 6 March 1836, IMP; McCoy, Journal, 17–19 May 1836, 408–410; Schultz, *Indian Canaan*, 179.

25. McCoy, Journal, 16 March, 9 January 1837, 16 May, 12 April, 21 April 1838, 431, 423, 491–492, 482, 484.

26. Schultz, *Indian Canaan*, 190–191; McCoy, Journal, 31 July 1838, 505.

27. John P. Bowes, *Exiles and Pioneers: Eastern Indians in the Trans-Mississippi West* (Cambridge, UK: Cambridge University Press, 2007), 72–81; *Appendix to the Congressional Globe*, 25th Cong., 2nd sess., Senate, 18 April 1838, 269.

28. McCoy, "Error of Supposing That Indians Possess Peculiar Propensities," *Annual Register of Indian Affairs* 2 (1836): 78–79; McCoy, Journal, 15 April 1838, 482–483; McCoy, "Plea for the Aborigines," *Annual Register* 2:93.

29. Theda Perdue, *Cherokee Editor: The Writings of Elias Boudinot* (Athens: University of Georgia Press, 1983), 28–32; Theresa Strouth Gaul, ed., *To Marry an Indian: The Marriage of Harriett Gold & Elias Boudinot in Letters, 1823–1839* (Chapel Hill: University of North Carolina Press, 2005), 60–66.

30. Schultz, *Indian Canaan*, 195–203.

31. William Lloyd Garrison, *Thoughts on African Colonization*, 2 vols. (Boston: Garrison and Knapp, 1832), 2:5, 14–17; Mary Hershberger, "Mobilizing Women, Anticipating Abolition: The Struggle Against Indian Removal in the 1830s," *JAH* 86, no. 1 (1999): 15–40.

32. Gary B. Nash, *Forging Freedom: The Formation of Philadelphia's Black Community, 1720–1840* (Cambridge, MA: Harvard University Press, 1988), 235–242; Richard S. Newman, *Freedom's Prophet: Bishop Richard Allen, the AME Church, and the Black Founding Fathers* (New York: New York University Press, 2008), 183–209; Beverly C. Tomek, *Colonization and Its Discontents: Emancipation, Emigration, and Antislavery in Antebellum Pennsylvania* (New York: New York University Press, 2011), 132–150; "At a Meeting of Free People of Colour," *Poulson's Daily Advertiser*, 10 January 1817, 3; Chris Dixon, *African America and Haiti: Emigration and Black Nationalism in the Nineteenth Century* (Westport, CT: Greenwood Press, 2000), 24–52; Ousmane K. Power-Greene, *Against Wind and Tide: The African American Struggle Against the Colonization Movement* (New York: New York University Press, 2014), 17–45; Thomas Clarkson to Vaux, 31 January 1820, RVP, 2:4; Julie Winch, *A Gentleman of Color: The Life of James Forten* (New York: Oxford University Press, 2002), 207–220; Nicholas Guyatt, "'The Future Empire of Our Freedmen': Republican Colonization Schemes in Texas and Mexico, 1861–1865," in Adam Arenson and Andrew R. Graybill, eds., *Civil War Wests: Testing the Limits of the United States* (Berkeley: University of California Press, 2015), 95–117, 97.

33. Ibid., 98–99; Eric Foner, *The Fiery Trial: Abraham Lincoln and American Slavery* (New York: Norton, 2010), 123–131.

34. Harold Holzer, ed., *The Lincoln-Douglas Debates* (New York: Fordham University Press, 2004), 265, 110, 61–62, 189–190.

35. Nicholas Guyatt, "'An Impossible Idea?': The Curious Career of Internal Colonization," *Journal of the Civil War Era* 4, no. 2 (2014): 234–263.

36. James G. Birney, *Letter on Colonization* (New York: Office of the Anti-Slavery Reporter, 1834), 20.

37. Coles to Robert and Kate Crawford, 7 February 1837, ECP, 2:3; Coles, "Autobiography"; Leichtle and Carveth, *Crusade Against Slavery*, 143–144, 183–190.

38. *Alexandria Gazette*, 10 November 1855, 2; Guasco, *Confronting Slavery*, 225–237; "Receipts," *African Repository*, January 1851, 30; "Receipts," ibid., December 1852, 382; "The Late Hon. Edward Coles," ibid., August 1868, 248–249; Coles to Robert Crawford, 22 December 1862, Roberts Coles Collection. This letter remains in the private collection of the Coles family in Virginia. The family has been reluctant to allow researchers to consult these materials. I'm extremely grateful to Dr. Nicholas Gordon, who made detailed notes on this and other Coles letters nearly forty years ago, for sharing his findings.

39. Edward Coles, "Notes on Slavery," ECP, 1:5.

Index

VIC LEUNG

Nicholas Guyatt is a university lecturer in American history and fellow of Trinity Hall, University of Cambridge. He is a regular contributor to *The Nation*, *The London Review of Books*, and *The Guardian*. Guyatt lives in Cambridge, England.